Deep Family

Ben, in his younger days, holding Nick.

The "deep families" in this book go all the way back to pre-Revolutionary times. In addition to the three Southern families chronicled in this book are some who were not blood kin. They were much-loved caretakers who were either slaves or descended from slaves. Old Ben Miller, who had been with our family for sixty years, was such a one. When my mother, Jean Craik Read, who collected the letters that made this book possible, died at the age of ninety-two, he presided over the intimate dinner that followed the funeral and said, "All de Deep family be here." He included himself, of course, and stood at the head of the table, but did not sit down to eat.

— N. C. R.

DEEP FAMILY

*Four Centuries of American
Originals and Southern Eccentrics*

BY NICHOLAS CABELL READ
AND DALLAS READ

*With Material Drawn from
Thousands of Notes and Letters and Documents
Collected During the Lifetime of Jean Craik Read*

NewSouth Books

MONTGOMERY LOUISVILLE

NewSouth Books
P.O. Box 1588
Montgomery, AL 36102

Library of Congress Cataloging-in-Publication Data

Read, Nicholas Cabell, b. 1916.
Deep family / by Nicholas Cabell Read and Dallas Read ; with material drawn from thousands of notes and letters and documents collected during the lifetime of Jean Craik Read.
p. cm.
ISBN 1-58838-178-1 (alk. paper)
1. Read, Nicholas Cabell, b. 1916--Family. 2. Reed family. 3. Craik family.
4. Baldwin family. 5. Alabama--Biography. 6. Virginia--Biography. I. Read,
Dallas. II. Read, Jean Craik, 1881-1972. III. Title.
CT275.R3215A3 2005
929'.0973--dc22
2005004864

*T*HIS BOOK IS DEDICATED TO MY LATE HUSBAND, NICHOLAS CABELL READ, WHO STARTED IT BUT DID NOT LIVE TO SEE IT FINISHED. WE WORKED TOGETHER UNTIL HE BECAME VERY ILL. FROM THAT POINT ON I WAS INCREASINGLY ON MY OWN AND DREW MUCH OF THE MATERIAL FROM HIS LETTERS AND NOTES AND FINISHED IT AFTER HIS DEATH IN 1998.

I HOPE I HAVE DONE WHAT HE WOULD HAVE WANTED. HE WAS A VERY THOUGHTFUL AND LOVING HUSBAND AS WELL AS A FINE CRAFTSMAN AND A MAN OF INTEGRITY. I WAS FORTUNATE TO HAVE HIM FOR THE NEARLY FIFTY YEARS WE WERE TOGETHER.

IN LOVING MEMORY,

DALLAS READ

Contents

Foreword

MARY ANN NEELEY

OBVIOUSLY A LABOR OF LOVE, *DEEP FAMILY* FOLLOWS MEMBERS OF THE Baldwin family through much of the nineteenth and most of the twentieth century, an amazing journey that takes the reader from the Civil War to World War I, communism, and World War II. Nick's and Dallas's "Introduction" gives the details of the background of this family opus, but I, an outsider, have read the material many times during the past ten years or so, and talked and pled with Dallas, urging her to include "this" and exclude "that." Of course it was to no avail, for it is Dallas's and Nick's work—as it should be.

All families have several heroines in their ranks, and the Baldwin clan is no exception. Above all, however, shines Jean Craik Read, a Baldwin granddaughter and Nick's mother, who shares the limelight with Hazel Hedge—a house, a garden, a neighborhood, a world within itself, a magical enclave, a Montgomery legend in its time. These two, Jean and Hazel Hedge, are the voices we readers hear that create the images of the "singing, the apple tree and the gold," to quote Thomas Wolfe, who was not a Hazel Hedge visitor but who would have been had he ventured to Montgomery. A creative and imaginative hostess, Jean entertained many, including John Dos Passos, Tallulah Bankhead, and scores of the known and the unknown ranging from the conservative right to the ultra-left. She welcomed all with humor, graciously plied them with food and drink in an atmosphere of good cheer, and along with Ben, her long-time right-hand man, expressed great delight at their presence.

Nick, beloved son and only child of Jean, Nash, and Hazel Hedge, relates his sheltered growing-up nurtured by grandmother Jennie Craik, aunts, cousins, and a number of African-American friends, all of whom were as much a part of Hazel Hedge as the great elm tree in the yard. As a young man, Nick left Montgomery, but his ties to family and heritage were ever strong. The Southern belief that relatives are still part of who we are, no matter how distant, bound him to the hearthstone of home.

Enough—read this saga, remembering that the letters and expressions were within the family, never meant to be seen by others than those who would understand its innuendoes, personalities and situations. While a few historical facts may take place out of sequence and with local flavor and interpretation, the story portrays people and their parts in the significant and insignificant events that touched their lives.

I was honored to be among a small invited group to attend the interment of Nick's ashes in the old Baldwin plot in Oakwood Cemetery. After the last prayer and a bit of refreshments, everyone began to sing favorite songs from the Hazel Hedge days. The last was a joyously nostalgic rendering of "Black Jack Davy," sung with the full knowledge that those times would never be again, but with the relish of knowing *they had been.*

Mary Ann Neeley, for many years the director of the Landmarks Foundation, is Montgomery's leading historian.

Acknowledgments

DALLAS READ

T
HE BOOK COULD NOT HAVE BEEN DONE WITHOUT THE GUIDANCE
of the historian Dr. Edwin Bridges, of Alabama's Department of Archives
and History, and of Mary Ann Neeley, who directed the Landmarks
Foundation of Montgomery. Nor could it have been done without a great deal of
input from Gayle Stanton-Vitale, the computer editor, who assisted with all aspects
of the book from inception to final production.

Numerous contributors, including Maxine Kiefer and journalists Harold and
Judy Graves, read first drafts of the manuscript with care and assisted with editorial
suggestions. Coworkers Eileen Lavine, Bea Newell, and Shirley Purdy also left their
marks. As the book progressed, the family and others provided background information that clarified and amplified the letters that were the main resource for the
book. Also, a special thanks to Donal McLaughlin for his many contributions.

In Alabama, Baldwin Sanders Smith, William Baldwin, John Yung, and Betty
Baldwin were on call for information about the Baldwins, as in New York were Dr.
Peyton Rous and his sister Marion about the Reads and the Rouses. In Montgomery,
Dodgie Shaffer, Virginia Durr, Eddie Pattillo, Dr. Jane Day, and Bobby Arrington
were very helpful. So was Judge Mark Anderson, who wrote to ask a question and
became part of the project.

There were also those, in addition to the Reads, who lived from time to time at
"Hazel Hedge" in the big old house or one of its cottages out on Carter Hill Road.
They had fond memories and shared them with us. In fact, the first to suggest that

a book should be written was Joyce Hobbs, who came to one of the cottages as a bride with her husband, Truman, long before he was a judge. Another was Shearon Elebash who stayed off and on in the big house at Hazel Hedge for several years. Cottage residents Dot Moore and her son, Russell Moore, were helpful.

Nobody could forget Hazel Hedge. Gould and Mary Beech and a friend, George Stoney, rented a cottage for a few years and had numerous stories to tell us. In Birmingham we found J. Mason Davis, a prominent attorney who is a descendant of the freed slave Jim Hale, who managed the original Baldwin plantation until after the Civil War. Mason collected family records and shared them with us. The list goes on. We are grateful for everyone's help. Our long distance telephone bills reflect the wide assortment of people throughout the states, many of whom we did not know, but who generously answered requests for information.

A call to Don Hale of Cullman, Alabama, alerted us to the existence of a book that described the trouble between the small farmers in the northern hill country of Alabama and the big plantation owners in the central and southern parts that split the state for and against secession. He sent us his own copy of an out-of-print book, *Tories of the Hills,* that described the "War Within the War" that raged inside Alabama for all four years of "The War Between The States," or the Civil War.

Letters came from Frank Ward, Winston Smith, and Captain Carlson in Demopolis who answered our request printed in the *Demopolis Times* to find out how the nearby "Rooster" Bridge across the Tombigbee River got its name—the money was raised in 1919 by an auction of game roosters to build a bridge to carry a transcontinental highway across the river to open the way for trade between the southeast and the west.

A telephone call to Nicholas Cobbs in Hale County introduced us to William Burns Paterson, a teacher from Tullibody, Scotland, who emigrated to the United States to escape the elitist British public school system. He settled in Alabama after the Civil War when there were no schools for more than half the population. He started informally instructing illiterate Negroes where they gathered in wagons and under trees. He was soon asked by a local white planter, Fabius Hill, to set up a school on his plantation for his own children by Negro slaves. From this humble beginning and with support from the county seat of Greensboro, he built the Tullibody Academy, the first public school for Negroes in the state. His story and that of the Paterson family, in advancing public education for Negroes throughout the state and the South, was told by a descendant, Judith Hillman Paterson, in a 1996 article "To Teach the Negro" in *Alabama Heritage* magazine.

Historians collecting the "Papers of Washington" at the University of Virginia found numerous reports prepared for Washington by Dr. James Craik, the Surgeon General of the Revolutionary Army, and made them available to us.

We are also indebted to Mary Anna McNabb, director of the Craik-Patton House in Charleston, West Virginia. She provided information about Dr. Craik, who was awarded land there for wartime service, and his grandson and namesake, the Reverend James Craik, who built what is now known as the Craik-Patton House. The Patton name came from Colonel George S. Patton who bought the property and made it the family home. George S. Patton of World War II fame was his relation.

We also want to thank Stuart Hibben and Georgiella Hefty, both retired from the Library of Congress, writer Simpson Lawson, and Nick's old friend Ledford Carter for their assistance. Also, a word of appreciation to the younger generation of the Reads—our son Nash Read, our daughter "Beka" Medrano, and their families for their patience and support during the writing of *Deep Family*.

Introduction

NICHOLAS CABELL READ

S OME OF THE GREAT STORYTELLERS ARE FROM THE SOUTH, AND THIS goes for many who didn't write their stories down. They just told them within their circle of friends. In Montgomery, Alabama, Jean Craik Read was such a one. Every day things happened, and the busy signals in the early morning on the telephones were a sign that what had happened was being passed on. A dramatist at heart, Jeanie was famous for her stories.

Before Jeanie died, Dr. Edwin Bridges, director of the Alabama Department of Archives and History, heard me repeat one of her stories, and urged me as Jean's son to record it and any others I could remember. As a filmmaker I was uncomfortable recording on tape, so I hunted and pecked my way through thirty stories on a portable typewriter, and gave what I had done to my wife Dallas, who is an editor, to put them together.

This was only the beginning of our work. The manuscript kept getting longer as she discovered thousands of letters and documents that had been collected by Jean. Many of them date back to colonial times and were stashed away in one of the "four sister" houses on South Perry Street in Montgomery (houses built in the 1870s by my great-grandfather, Dr. William O. Baldwin, for his four daughters).

Dallas became an interlocutor—reading, checking, clarifying and interpreting, as she uncovered one letter after another of significance. The letters chronicled the lives and times of three families that arrived in this country from England and Scotland in the sixteen and seventeen hundreds—the *Baldwins,* the *Craiks* and the

Reads. They did not know each other, but separately made their way south and west as their families expanded, to get new lands for the younger generations.

They had several things in common. Wherever they went they were pioneers—taking part in what was happening, seeing and doing new things. They reported on their experiences in letters to other members of the family and saved clippings and reports on events of the times.

They kept everything, and dated almost nothing. Sometimes the letters recorded the days of the month, but almost never the year. Some noted the day of the week and weather conditions—"A Sunny Sunday" or "A Rainy Tuesday." Many were hard to read, and some were made almost illegible because the correspondent wrote horizontally until space ran out, then turned the letter on its side and wrote across what had already been written.*

My mother, Jean Craik, had grown up in one of the "four sister houses," and that is where we found the first letters in a wooden chest carved with dogwood blossoms and inscribed "J. C. R. 1913." The chest had been a wedding present to her from the family wood carver, her Aunt Cecilia—to keep precious things.

The letter on top was dated 1843 and addressed to my great-grandfather, Dr. William O. Baldwin, by a young friend, William Lowndes Yancey, much later known as the "Firebrand of the Confederacy," whose oratory was credited with persuading Alabama and other Southern states to secede from the Union. As a young man, Yancey wrote his regrets that he could not attend Dr. Baldwin's wedding to the "lovely Mary Martin—since I live in Wetumpka, which is too far away to make the trip in one day." Fourteen miles took a long time coming and going on horseback.

However, the letter had another purpose—to give his friend the benefit of his own experience as a newly married man, and urging him "to cross the lintel of my house so that I might exhibit such lessons in domestic intercourse as example may yield. In married life you will find more crosses and vexations than you have ever dreamed. I have observed your faults and I do not find many. You have a quick temper and sometimes use language you should never use in the presence of a lady. You must never swear in front of the lovely Mary Martin."

We felt the letter was worthy of a place among the stories I was doing for the Archives, and it proved a harbinger of things to come. As Dallas dug deeper into the chest there were others, and a year later she came upon a second even larger leather-covered box, also filled with letters and documents.

One of these told us that there had been correspondence between my great-

*This "crossed letter" form of correspondence apparently originated during the period when postage costs for sending letters across the oceans were calculated by the page and were very expensive. Presumably the same factors were at work during the Civil War or there was a shortage of writing paper, or both. A "crossed letter" sounds as if it would be impossible to write and read, but with practice it could be done.

great-grandfather on the other side of the family, Dr. James Craik, and George Washington. Dr. Craik served under Washington in the French and Indian wars and later as Surgeon General of the Revolutionary War. We knew they had remained friends throughout their lifetimes, and must have exchanged letters, but we had found none.

Then we came upon a long memoir from Dr. Craik's grandson, the Reverend James Craik, of Louisville, Kentucky, who reported that when his grandfather left Alexandria for the west on horseback he had taken the George Washington letters with him in two boxes for safekeeping. They had become too cumbersome for the horse to carry over the Alleghenies, so he had left them in a barn on a family farm in western Virginia on the way. Before he could get back, the barn burned down, and the letters were lost.

Since it takes two to make a correspondence, Dallas began looking for the letters that Dr. Craik must have written to Washington during their forty years of friendship, and found the "Papers of Washington" collection at the University of Virginia in Charlottesville. When she telephoned to ask whether they had any letters from Dr. Craik, a friend of Washington, the voice at the other end corrected her, "His *best* friend."

One of the letters from Dr. Craik warned General Washington of the Conway Cabal, a conspiracy among certain officials in the Board of War and Congress and some Army generals to remove Washington as the Commander-in-Chief. Dr. Craik had uncovered the conspiracy on a trip from Washington's headquarters at Valley Forge in Pennsylvania, when he stayed at various army camps on his way home to Maryland, where his wife was very ill.

He wrote Washington, getting his letter past the army censors to the General by asking Mrs. Washington to enclose it with one of her own "where I expect it will be most Safe and Expeditious as her Letters Seldom Miscarry." The letter got there. The conspiracy failed.

We had scarcely reviewed and absorbed the contents of the carved chest and the leather box, when Dallas opened a little-used cupboard in the old house to look for a hammer and found thirteen additional boxes, including many of the speckled black and white variety that are used by accountants to store bills. There were no bills. Only more letters and documents, which spilled over into several large cardboard boxes from the A & P grocery store, where Jeanie had tossed a flotsam and jetsam of correspondence, reminiscences, documents and newspaper clippings.

Putting the letters in order was a formidable task. Information in a letter found in the carved chest in 1992 was clarified in a speckled box opened in 1996. There were speculations about a Baldwin murder in 1874 in letters as late as 1900. A secret love affair stretched through six boxes and sixty years.

Finding this cornucopia of correspondence would have been astonishing in any era, but in this age of instant communication by phone, fax and e-mail, this trove staggered the imagination. It spanned nearly two centuries.

Jean seemed to have saved every letter she had ever received, and kept first drafts of many she sent, and included some that she had neither written nor sent—but gotten from other people. A story with picaresque overtones came in a letter from a cousin, Marion Rous, describing the travail of the grandfather for whom I was named, Nicholas Cabell Read, who at the end of the "War Between the States" had left Lee's army in Virginia vowing never to live under the Union flag.

He went to Mexico where he bought a coffee plantation. Things went well until 1867, when the Mexicans revolted against Emperor Maximilian, who had been put there with their approval by Napoleon III, nephew of Napoleon Bonaparte. Unfortunately, Maximilian lost favor with the Mexicans and was executed. Marion wrote, "No foreigner was safe, so Nicholas beat it for the States, with his parrot on his shoulder and some gold pieces in his pocket." He made his way from Mexico by way of Louisiana, and continued on to Corsicana, Texas, where an old friend, Francis Peyton Wood, had settled after being enticed by a cigar box full of the land's good rich soil.

In 1865, Wood's family had moved from the old tobacco plantation in Virginia to join him in Texas. His wife Pauline, her brother Beverly Scott, and eight children, as well as four freed slaves, made the month-long journey with as many of their household and personal belongings as they could carry. The eldest daughter of sixteen, Ellen, would become the wife of Nicholas Read, my grandfather.

It was a gigantic jigsaw puzzle, with pieces scattered through decades. Taken together these letters and documents trace the personal history of these families back to the beginnings of this country and their emigration south and west in search of new lands. Many of the documents take us back to the Revolution as they relate the experience of three Southern families who lived and died in those times. Others show real insight into the lives of their descendants well into the twentieth century.

Introducing the Family

THIS SECTION INTRODUCES INDIVIDUALS FROM THE THREE FAMILIES that appear in this book—the *Baldwins*, the *Craiks*, and the *Reads*, all of whom got their start in this country before the Revolutionary War.

The Baldwins traced their name back to a "Bold One" (Bold-un) of the First Crusade, a ferocious fighter who went from Flanders to Jerusalem where he led crusaders to victory, and where for a time he and several of his descendants headed the "Christian Kingdom" in Jerusalem.

By the seventeenth century they were in England, preparing to make their way to the New World. In 1639, two *Baldwin* brothers arrived in Connecticut and went on to settle in Virginia. From there, their progeny headed south to find new lands for farms of their own. In North Carolina, one married a Miss Owen, a name they took with them to Alabama where my great-grandfather, William Owen Baldwin was born.

General Washington's future friend Dr. James *Craik* arrived in this country in 1750, when he came from Scotland by way of the West Indies to Virginia, where he practiced as a physician.

The first *Read* arrived in Virginia in 1684. The family stayed there through the Revolutionary War, and was prominent in the House of Burgesses. There are still Reads living in Prince Edward County. However, after the Civil War, the descendants of our family went to Texas.

The *Baldwins*, who got to Virginia at about the same time, headed south through the Carolinas to Georgia and from there to Alabama, which was still a territory, in 1815 or 1816. In those years William Baldwin and his bride, Celia Fitzpatrick, settled on land left behind by the Indians, who had been forced off for their "long march" west. On the plantation, he raised cotton and corn, and had a family of seven children. William Owen Baldwin became a physician and a banker. His brothers were Marion Augustus, a lawyer; Benjamin, a physician; and Phillips, a planter.

In 1843, William Owen Baldwin married Mary Jane Martin and they had seven children. He didn't approve of the Civil War, largely because he didn't think the South with its limited resources could win. However, his sixteen-year-old son and namesake "Willie" ran away from school in Tuscaloosa and enlisted early in the Alabama volunteers. He was a captain in the Confederate Army when he was killed at age nineteen. This left the two older sons, Augustus and Abram, and Dr. Baldwin's daughters, Jennie, Mary, Cecile, and Alma, who figure prominently in this story.

The "Deep Family" in the South meant immediate relatives plus a few close to the family, but not related. In addition to Ben Miller, this included three former Baldwin slaves—"Mammy" Sallie and her daughter Anne, and Jim Hale, who had been freed before the Civil War.

It was not until 1875 that the *Craiks* came to Alabama in the person of George William Craik from Kentucky who married Jennie Baldwin in Montgomery. "Will" was the son of the Reverend James Craik of Louisville, a leader in the fight to keep Kentucky from seceding, and the grandson of the Revolutionary War surgeon general. Will and Jennie had four daughters—Mary Martin ("Darlie"), Juliet ("Judy"), Cecile ("Sheila"), and Jean ("Jeanie").

Darlie married Buckner Speed of Louisville, whose father had been a friend of Lincoln's. They had two children, William and Jane. Darlie and Jane became active Communists in Alabama during the Great Depression. Judy married Charles Pollard, the handsome young physician son of an old Montgomery family, and had one daughter, Jean. Sheila became a writer and married a journalist, Paxton Hibben, and they had one daughter, Jill, in New York.

The *Reads* did not get to Montgomery until 1913, when Jean Craik married Nash Read from Corsicana, Texas. Thus, three families with colonial roots in Virginia, but who had never met, were joined. When I was born in 1916, Jean and Nash named me Nicholas Cabell Read, after his father. The "Cabell" came from a Virginia relative, James Branch Cabell, who authored *Jurgen,* a highly regarded novel that decried ambition, making the point that "a man's hands are soiled in climbing."

You will meet them all in this book.

Deep Family

Jennie Baldwin Craik

1

What's in a Name?

To Southerners there can be a lot in a name. How well I recall my grandmother, Jennie Baldwin Craik, speaking to my mother of some newcomer to Montgomery. "What's his name, daughter? Who are his people?" Perhaps Southerners in particular thought names important because after the "War Between the States," a good name was about all many had left.

Maybe this is why the practice of using family names as first names took hold. No one in the know had to ask Baldwin Sanders Smith who her people were, and it was pretty obvious that Elmore Bellingrath Inscoe came from long-time residents of Elmore County. Gould Beech was a Gould, Winter Thorington a Winter.

Perhaps it was some vestige of the Old South that influenced my wife, Dallas, whose family stayed briefly in the South on its way to California by covered wagon in 1850, to substitute her last name, "Dallas," for her given name, "Helen," when she was old enough to make a choice.

Some people go through life using only initials. There are C. T. Fitzpatrick and J. B. Marshall, for example. And B. T. Johnson, whose initials, it was said, stood for "Bath Tub," since he was the first plumber to put in bathtubs.

Everyone knew where Mildred "Minnie" Reynolds Saffold came from. She was the daughter of a plantation overseer, not very high up on the Old South's social ladder, but she was beautiful and married well. Three of her four daughters wed rich or important men.

"Sir" George Waller was made an Honorary Citizen of Luxembourg, after serving as U.S. minister to that tiny country on the border between France and Germany. He stayed behind until the Germans took over in World War I—"I have met the Hun and smelled their carrion breath." For his courage, he was made an Honorary

Citizen by the Grand Duchess of Luxembourg, and from then on he used the title of "Sir George," as did the rest of Montgomery.

Boys in the South were often called "Buddie," which stood for "Brother," and girls were called "Titta" or "Sister." The Baldwin family had three sons called Buddie Willie, Buddie Martin, and Buddie Gus, and one daughter, Sister Mary (S'Mary for short). One family had four sons known simply as "Big Bud, Little Bud, Bud and Budsy."

Pet names given babies by their Negro (genteely pronounced "nigra") nurses often lasted a lifetime. Old friends still call Algie Hill "Teenie Weenie," and the youngest Clifford Durr daughter Tilla hasn't been able to shake "Baby Sister." Then there is "Lady Bird" Johnson, the wife of President Lyndon Johnson of Texas. Baldwin Smith's sister Etheldra Scoggins, who lives in New Orleans and is now in her seventies, is still called "Baby." On one occasion "Baby" made a telephone call to her friend "Tiny" and was told "Tiny's not here, she's at Squatsie's."

In the old days, families had special names for house servants, since children were not allowed to call them by their first names. "Mammy" was always the senior female servant. Others were "Uncle" and "Auntie," which were acceptable all around.

However, grown black men deeply resented being called "boy," and while the blacks were resigned to "nigras" for "Negroes" or "colored people;" only "poor whites" called them "darkies," "niggers," and "coons." Children became accustomed to "pickaninny," hated "jigaboo," but didn't seem to mind having their heads rubbed by whites for good luck.

At age ten, I had a beloved dog called "Booger," who we took with us when my father drove us to Maine on a summer vacation. It took us five days to get there in his Stutz Bearcat. In Maine we met Mrs. Rhude, a social lady with a New England abolitionist background who admired my dog when I told her it had been named for a famous colored gentleman, Booger T. Washington. She pronounced it "Booker," and it earned me not only a ride in her Cadillac, but one on a motorcycle driven by her chauffeur.

Long before vacations in Maine, my mother Jean would spend the summer at "Kintry," a plantation belonging to her Uncle Ben Baldwin near Verbena, Alabama. Cousin Ben kept fox hounds. His wife, Cousin Kate (I called her Cousin "Tea Cake" because she was a grand cook and made the best tea cakes I ever tasted) took a fancy to a hound puppy and named it *Sí Petita*.

She herself was often called *Tía* Kate, having lived as a child in a Spanish-speaking country. When *Sí Petita* grew up, the man who farmed the place told Cousin Ben, "You've got some good dogs, Doctor, but that dog 'Sweet Potato' is about the best hound I ever seed."

Figaro was a poodle my Aunt Sheila brought us from France. Mammy Ellen, our cook, learned to say *Fait le beau* to make him sit up. After Figaro's demise there was some talk about getting me a French governess so I could learn French. Mammy Ellen was quite put out. "I ain't spoke no French since Fig died," she grumbled, "but I reckon I could bresh up." I never got the governess.

Mother ordered a stone for Figaro's grave with the inscription "*Çi-gît Figaro,*" old French for "Here lies Figaro." Mr. Corbitt, the stone cutter, changed the "*gît*" to "get." He said, "I knew that's what Miz Read meant."

There was even a political dog. Gould Beech, an active Democrat, discovered that a dog could be made to understand how its master felt about a person by his tone of voice when pronouncing a name. Gould had a succession of golden retrievers named "Trumpet," who, if offered a dog biscuit from Nixon or Reagan or Bush, would turn their heads aside, but if offered a morsel from Roosevelt or Truman or Carter would take it at a gulp in tail-wagging ecstasy.

When Air Cadet Charles Chipman came from New Jersey to Maxwell Field in Montgomery for officer training during World War II, his mother admonished, "Now don't go falling in love with any little southern girl named Magnolia." Chip complied. He fell in love with my cousin Petunia whose real name, Mary Gayle, was known to few outside the family. When his mother said, "I hope her name isn't Magnolia," Chip had a hard time answering, "No, it's Petunia." "Tunie's" younger sister Melissa was called "Wisteria."

Their mother was Willey Gayle Martin, a prominent portrait painter. Their uncle was William A. Gayle, the controversial mayor at the time of the Montgomery bus boycott in the 1950s, who put Rosa Parks, a seamstress, in jail when she refused to give up her seat in the front of the bus to a white man. The mayor's nickname was "Tacky." I never learned why. Perhaps his mother, Cousin Mary Gayle, had something to do with it.

Mary Gayle was a formidable old lady. I remember being taken to visit her when she was sick in bed. She was sitting up and there was a very old and sparsely feathered young Plymouth Rock rooster tied by a string to the bed post. She leveled a long bony finger at me and in a surprisingly strong voice commanded: "Kiss Prunus." I looked quickly for a feathered spot and complied.

"Wisteria," like her mother, had artistic talents, and as a young girl went to Florida to take art lessons in Sarasota, which was also the winter headquarters of Ringling Brothers & Barnum and Bailey Circus. She joined the circus. We first saw her in Washington, D.C., where, clad in a replica of the White House, she led the opening parade around the ring. When we met her after the performance, our children wanted to see the "freaks." "Wissie" said she could not accompany us: "The freaks are people, and they are my friends."

She also made friends with the animal trainer, who gave her a lion cub that had been rejected by its mother. "Wissie" fed it from a baby bottle, and eventually gave it to her Uncle "Tacky," who called it Melissa and kept it at home until it began to tear up the furniture. He had a cage built for it at the zoo in Oak Park.

As a full-grown lioness, renamed Molasses, she was prone to letting out loud roars that disturbed the neighbors, especially at night. Since Oak Park was in a predominantly "colored" section, those disturbed were Negroes, who ironically were not allowed to visit the zoo because the park was segregated. Only colored nurses could go if accompanied by their white charges.

Most Negroes got their surnames from the white families who had owned them as slaves. When my great-grandfather married in the 1840s and purchased Sallie and her little daughter Anne they both became "Baldwins." Anne lived with the family until she married. Sallie lived with them most of her adult life, which was a very long one. She died in 1901 at ninety-two, and as part of the "deep family" is buried near the Baldwin plot in Oakwood Cemetery.

There were major exceptions to the practice of white plantation owners bestowing names on their slaves. It was presumed that this was the case with Yancy Martin, a prominent young black politician who was active in the 1972 presidential campaign of George McGovern in Atlanta, as well as raising money to help elect Negroes in the South. Many thought he got his first name from the family of William Lowndes Yancey, the "Firebrand of the Confederacy," who in 1846 resigned his seat in the Congress to lead the fight for secession in Southern states.

Although the irony is appreciated, the conjecture is incorrect. Yancy's name (spelled without the "e") came from his mother, Helen Alice Yancy, a teacher who was the daughter of a half-Cherokee, half-Negro woman and a light-skinned Negro Presbyterian minister. Although miscegenation was against the law in the South, it often occurred, as is evidenced in the light skins, freckles, and even blue eyes of many so-called blacks. Some "passed over," living as "white" and others, like the

Presbyterian minister, stayed in the Negro community.

In Montgomery, as elsewhere in the South, names took on social status, with rank depending on how long the family had been there and how they were related. When Watkins Johnston was dating pretty Mary Goldthwaite, her aunt, Miz Olivia Arrington, who was just about as wide as she was tall, "put on her corset and went over to Tuskegee to tell those Johnstons just who the Goldthwaites and the Arringtons were." Arrington is an important name, and there are several white as well as black Arringtons still in the vicinity—a black mayor of Birmingham, to name one.

The Baldwins and the Craiks were the big names in our Alabama family, and my father, Nash Read, got a little tired of hearing my mother, Jean Craik Read, talk about them. On a trip to Scotland he astonished her by buying six pipes, although he smoked cigars. "Why on earth did you get those?" she asked. "Look at the inscription," he countered, "Craik the Tobacconist —just tradespeople, Jeanie."

2

Dr. Craik and George Washington

D R. JAMES CRAIK ARRIVED HERE FROM SCOTLAND IN 1750. BORN ON the Barony of Arbigland near Dumfries, at the headlands of the North Sea in 1730, he was the illegitimate son of the baron, Sir William Craik, who raised him as his own. He was educated to be a doctor at the University of Edinburgh, which was then the outstanding center for the training of physicians.

Just why he left Scotland for the American colonies is not known. It could have been because his illegitimacy prevented his inheriting either title or lands. He was only twenty when he emigrated, first to the West Indies and then to Virginia.

A few years before Dr. Craik left Scotland, John Paul Jones, the naval hero of the Revolution, was beginning his life at Arbigland as John Paul, the son of a gardener on the Craik estate. He went to sea at twelve as an apprentice, and at seventeen was third mate on the *King George*, a "blackbirder" (slave-trade ship) bound for the West Indies. At some time along the way he added "Jones" to his original name.

He continued on to Virginia, but there is no record that he ever met or knew Dr. Craik there, even though they were both born and grew up on the same estate in Scotland.

Dr. Craik was twenty-four and 6 feet 3½ inches tall when he joined the Virginia Provincial Regiment as its surgeon, and served under Washington, who was twenty-two, through the French and Indian wars. They became fast friends, and remained so for the rest of their lives. When Dr. Craik married Mariamne Ewell, a cousin of Washington's in Virginia, it became a family relationship. Dr. Craik took his new bride across the Potomac to his plantation, "La Grange," in Port Tobacco, Charles County, Maryland, where he practiced medicine and grew crops. There he built for her a fine new mansion with double chimneys and a beautiful walnut stairway with wide treads, delicate spindles, and carved step ends.

In 1770, Craik and Washington ventured into the wilds of western Virginia to examine lands they had been awarded for their military service in the French and Indian wars. The expedition was strenuous and involved adventuring, mingled with the practical purposes in which Washington delighted. The trip was made in winter with two guides, through regions still insecure from the hostility of "savages." They rode horseback to Pittsburgh, and then canoed down the Ohio River as far as the Big Kanawha River, where Craik's lands were located.

In 1774 Dr. Craik asked Washington to be godfather to a son to be named George Washington Craik. Since Washington's marriage had not been blessed with children, his namesake became a surrogate son whom he helped bring up and educate. Dr. Craik had been an active patriot since his arrival in Maryland, so it was not surprising that when Washington was named commander of all the Colonial forces that he asked Dr. Craik to place his medico-military experience at the disposal of his country.

Dr. Craik said that although he was "honored that Washington thought him capable of discharging that office," he could not accept if immediate attendance at camp was necessary, since he was obligated first to inoculate nearby families and their Negroes against smallpox. Washington gave him the choice of becoming senior physician and surgeon of the hospital, with pay of four dollars and six rations per day and forage for one horse, or assistant director general, with pay of three dollars and six rations per day and two horses and traveling expenses. He chose the latter, but it would be awhile before he could give full time to the assignment.

Dr. Craik was with General Washington in Pennsylvania at Valley Forge when he was called home to care for his ailing wife in Port Tobacco. Before he left he learned that there was a plot to replace Washington as Commander-in-Chief, and on his way to Maryland got detailed information on the widespread nature of the conspiracy from officers in various army camps he passed through.

On January 6, 1778, he put what he had learned about the "Conway Cabal," as it was called, in a letter to George Washington. He gave it to Martha Washington to enclose in one of her own to her husband at Valley Forge, knowing that hers would not be opened by military censors. The letter, which is reproduced here, was one of those found in the "Papers of Washington" collection at the University of Virginia in Charlottesville. It reads:

Dr James Craik

Paul Jones

*Silhouettes of Dr.
James Craik and
John Paul Jones,
restored by Donal
McLaughlin.*

Notwithstanding your unwearied diligence and the unparalleled Sacrifice of Domestic happiness and ease of mind which you have made for the good of your Country, yet you are not wanting in Secret Enemies. Base and Villainous men thro' Chagrin, Envy, or Ambition, are endeavoring to lessen you in the minds of the people and taking underhanded methods to traduce your Character.

I was informed by a Gentleman whom I believe to be a true Friend of yours, that a Strong Faction was forming Against you in the New Board of War and in the Congress, and I have investigated it in the camps. In Bethlehem I was told of it, and at Lancaster was assured of it, and I believe it is pretty general over the Country.

It was said Some of the Eastern & Southern members were at the bottom of it, particularly R.H.L and G—l M—n in the New Board of War. The method they are Taking is by holding up General G—s to the people and making them believe that you have had three or four times the number of the Enemy and have done nothing. That Philadelphia was given up by your Mismanagement and that you have missed many opportunities of defeating the Enemy, and many other things ungenerous and unjust.

It is said that they dare not appear as your Enemy, but the New Board of War is Composed of men who could throw Such obstacles and difficulties in your way as to force you to Resign. Had I not been assured of those things from Such Authority as I cannot Doubt, I should not have Troubled you. My Attachment to your Person is such, my Friendship is so Sincere that every Hint which has a tendency to hurt your Honour wounds me.

I write this that you may be apprized and have an eye toward those men and particularly that man G—l M—n. He is plausible, Sensible, Popular and Ambitious, takes great pains to draw over every Officer he meets to his own way of Thinking and is very Engaging. The Above I Can with Sincerity Say I have wrote from pure motives of Friendship and have no Enmity to any of those men, any farther than they are Enemies to you. If they are your Enemies every honest man must naturally conclude they are Enemies to the Country and our Glorious Cause, and will strenuously exert every Nerve to disappoint their Villainous intentions . . .

On my arrival I found Mrs. Craik in a very low & poor State of Health . . . which I am afraid will put it out of my power To rejoin the Army so soon as I could wish. . . . I got the favor of Mrs. Washington To Send this under Cover to you as I expect it will be the most Safe and Expeditious Conveyor as her Letters Seldom Miscarry. May God in his infinite mercy protect you from all your Enemies and Continue your health to finish the Glorious undertaking, is the Sincere Prayer of Your Most Devoted & obliged humble Servant.

James Craik

The "Conway Cabal" was ultimately defeated, and Dr. Craik was now free to take on the momentous task of providing medical care for the ill and wounded soldiers of the Revolutionary War. He was named surgeon general. It was an almost impossible task, covering as it did thirteen colonies stretched thousands of miles down the Atlantic Coast, with few hospitals, and limited facilities and communication. He reported regularly by letter to his immediate superior, George Washington, in the field. Here are excerpts:

From Providence, Rhode Island, where he was looking for space to put patients, Dr. Craik wrote:

I found a place that would put up about 600 sick, but the town council made it impossible to comply with your instructions, saying it would bring contagious diseases. They sent me to look at barns and old barracks with only room for 300—places by no means fit to put well people, being the most dirty vile huts I ever saw.

From Head of Elk, Maryland, on medical personnel:

In answer to the questions put by your excellency, There will not be enough doctors and surgeons, even including those serving under you, and two in Virginia who have been recommended for promotion.

From a camp near Yorktown, Virginia:

The Department is entirely destitute of money. There has not been a single copper to pay a nurse, or an orderly, or to purchase milk and vegetables. In a short time medicines will be wanting.

In Hanover Town there are 200 sick and wounded in storehouses without fire places. In Williamsburg there are 400, some so nasty and naked that it is almost impossible to prevent contagion. We have a number in small pox. They are entirely without blankets. (I need 600). All the hospitals are destitute also of shirts, overalls and clothing. We have sugar and coffee, but need rice and wine. The putrid diseases that now prevail require wine as it is the best cordial that can be given.

These dire appraisals typically concluded with a deferential statement, such as "I have the honor to be, with the greatest respect, Your Excellency's most Obt. humble Servt. James Craik."

It was not until 1783, when the fighting was over, that Dr. Craik wrote his old friend Washington about his own financial concerns. "I gave up an extensive practice to enter the Service, which my age and infirmities will never permit me to regain, and unless I receive more reasonable compensation than the half pay of a captain on my discharge, it will be severely felt by myself and family in years to come."

We do not know how this request was answered, but we do know that during the war and afterwards Washington himself was short of money and asked Dr. Craik to look into the sale of some of his own land. This was before he was chosen as president of the United States and took office in New York City in 1789. When the government moved to Philadelphia for his second term he brought his godson, George Washington Craik, to serve as one of his secretaries. Since accommodations in Philadelphia were limited, Washington and his staff lived in one big house and had their meals together.

It was at Washington's suggestion and with his guidance that his godson began to purchase the books that were to form the nucleus of a personal library. George Washington loved the theater, and among the books bought in 1777 were two volumes of *The Beauties of the English Drama*. These, along with others, were passed down through the Craiks, and were in my mother's library in Montgomery, Alabama. Eventually, I gave them to the museum at Mt. Vernon, Washington's home on the Potomac River.

At the close of the war Dr. Craik returned to Port Tobacco, but shortly afterwards

at the solicitation of Washington moved to Alexandria, Virginia, only a few miles
from Mt. Vernon. He lived at 210 Duke Street, a house that still stands around the
corner from the Presbyterian Church which he attended and where he is buried.
While he was in Alexandria and in nearby Vancluse, Virginia, he and Washington
saw much of each other.

Washington often asked him to handle certain requests. One came from a Mr.
Bowie, a writer or historian, asking for access to Washington's files to get information on his participation in the wars. Washington wrote: "My dear Doctor, any
memoirs of my life, distinct and unconnected with the general history of the war,
would rather hurt my feelings than tickle my pride whilst I lived. I had rather glide
gently down the stream of life, than by an act of mine to have vanity or ostentation
imputed to me. . . . I do not think vanity is a trait of my character."

In 1784, Dr. Craik and Washington made their second long trip west, seven
hundred miles over the Appalachian mountains and down the Ohio to the Monon-
gahela, which they ascended and then struck southward through the pathless forest
until they emerged near Staunton in the Shenandoah Valley. They were accompanied
by Dr. Craik's son William, and General Washington's nephew, Bushrod.

In 1798, when war with France was a probability and Washington was again
asked to lead the Army, he made the appointment of Dr. Craik as head of the
medical department one of the conditions of his own acceptance. However, that
war was never fought.

Their final parting was at Washington's deathbed at Mt. Vernon. Dr. Craik was
called from his nearby home when Washington was taken seriously ill with an acute
sore throat and high fever. Not one to complain, Washington had not reported
early symptoms. What he probably had was acute epiglottides, a virulent bacterial
inflammation of the flap at the back of the throat that closed the windpipe when
swallowing, cutting off the ability to either breathe or swallow. Today with antibiot-
ics it would never reach that stage.

When first advised to take something for his throat, Washington, who believed
that most minor illnesses cured themselves, dismissed his affliction, saying, "Let it
go as it came." By very early the next morning a high fever, extremely sore throat,
and labored breathing were evidence that this was no minor thing, and doctors
including Dr. Craik were summoned at dawn.

Even before they arrived, Washington ordered his overseer to bleed him. Dr.
Craik stepped up this treatment and applied a skin-irritating "blister" of ground

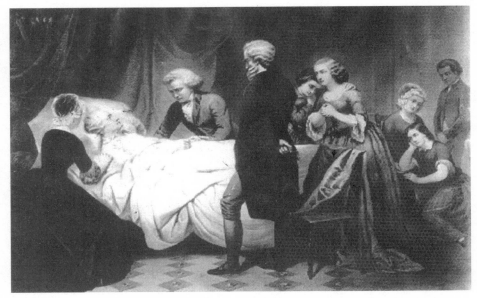

Artist's rendering of George Washington on his deathbed, courtesy Virginia Herald.

Spanish fly to the throat and attempted to feed him a mixture of molasses, vinegar and butter, which brought on a bout of nearly fatal choking. After more bleeding (he lost two and a half quarts of blood in a twelve-hour period) he was given sage tea with vinegar to gargle and nearly suffocated.

Shortly afterwards he rose and dressed and walked around the room, then retired again and in the late afternoon had his wife fetch two wills from his desk. He chose one and had her burn the other. The one he chose specified that at his wife's death the slaves he owned at Mt. Vernon were to be freed. Soon after George's death, Martha chose to free them all.

His physicians continued to apply more blisters and poultices, until he implored them to "let me go off quietly." His last words to his old friend Dr. Craik were, "Doctor, I die hard, but I am not afraid to go." At 10 p.m. he whispered burial instructions, and fearing that he might be buried alive, asked that he not be entombed for at least two days. Twenty minutes later he was dead.

He left his bureau and his circular chair "to my companion and intimate friend, Dr. Craik," who wrote, "When I saw this great man die, it seemed as if the bonds of my nature were rent asunder, and that the pillar of my country's happiness had fallen to the ground."

3

The Growing Years

M Y GREAT-GRANDFATHER, WILLIAM OWEN BALDWIN, WAS BORN IN 1818 on the family plantation on the outskirts of Alabama Town, Alabama. This was about four miles north of where Montgomery came into being about a year later when two nearby settlements, East Alabama and New Philadelphia, joined together to form a county, soon to include Alabama Town. Originally, all three were encampments of the Alibamu Indians who had cleared the thickets on the red bluffs above the river, known collectively as the Chunnanugge Charte.

To the Indians, *Alabama* meant "a fortified camp." The white settlers translated it as "Here We Rest," and as such it became the official motto and went on the state seal when Alabama was admitted to the Union in 1819. The Baldwin plantation was located near one of the remaining Indian settlements, and when he was older, Dr. Baldwin reminisced about the "war-whoops of the savages that frequently broke the stillness of the night."

William Owen was nine years old when his father died in 1828, leaving seven children. He went to school at a nearby academy taught by Addison H. Semple, a highly regarded linguist and scholar.

The mother struggled to educate her oldest son, Marion Augustus, to become a lawyer. The next three boys studied medicine, at a time when one could become a doctor at little cost largely by apprenticeship.

Marion Augustus practiced law and was attorney general of Alabama from 1847 through the "War Between the States." William Owen was a full-time doctor for forty-nine years, as a practitioner of medicine and surgery, specializing as

*Dr. Baldwin,
courtesy American
Medical
Association.*

an obstetrician. His brother Benjamin practiced medicine but spent much of his time on his plantation at nearby Verbena. Phillips, the third brother, spent full time on his plantation near Union Springs.

At age sixteen, William Owen was studying in the office of Dr. J. R. McLeod in Montgomery. After a year, he went to Transylvania University in Lexington, Kentucky, for two years. According to Emmett B. Carmichael in the *Annals of Medical History, 1942*, Baldwin wrote his dissertation on "Puerperal Fever," a forty-one page paper, "with writing that is clear and pleasing." He had wanted to study the classics at the University of Virginia, but that wasn't possible. At nineteen he was back in Dr. McLeod's office treating patients. But all his life he was a great reader of the classics.

Montgomery was then a small agricultural center, strategically located on the Alabama River, where steamboats were beginning to carry people and goods all the way down to Mobile and the Gulf. Most travelers went by stagecoach, and there was a northbound "Horse Express" mail service that carried letters and packages to New York City in only five days.

In a few years, Dr. Baldwin became Dr. McLeod's partner. Then Dr. McLeod shot and killed a juggler, or sleight-of-hand performer, for attempting to abduct his wife, and had to stand trial. He was acquitted, but died within a year, leaving his practice to young Baldwin.

Tall, handsome and successful, William Owen was much sought-after socially, and he wooed and won Mary Jane Martin, the beautiful young daughter of Judge Abram Martin, who was descended from a signer of the Declaration of Independence. Abram Martin had come to Montgomery from South Carolina. He married and was widowed by Jane Patton, who left several small children, including Mary Jane, to be cared for by an aunt, Mary Martin. There is a silver octagonal pitcher engraved to Mary Martin in gratitude for her care of the children, which she gave to Mary Jane when she married Dr. Baldwin, December 7, 1843. It is still in our family. The first panel is engraved:

Presented by
William Patton
to
Miss Mary Martin
in remembrance of her
kind care of his deceased
sister Jane's children
1833

The second panel:

Mary Martin
Daughter of Jane Patton Martin
from her
Aunt Mary Martin
at her marriage to
Dr. William Owen Baldwin
Dec. 7, 1843

The wedding in Montgomery took place without the attendance of one of Dr. Baldwin's friends, recently married W. Lowndes Yancey. Yancey wrote explaining that since he lived in Wetumpka, fourteen miles away, he wouldn't be able to get there and back on horseback in a day. However, since he had been married almost two years, he had some advice to give his friend:

Since "we were first acquaint," as Burns hath it, I have observed you closely, and now upon the eve of uniting your fortunes to a beautiful girl, and more beautiful in soul than in form of feature, I can tell it to you without flattery, because it may benefit you. I am now looking for your faults.

I do not see many, but I remember one brought to mind by only one incident of our last meeting. In a little irritation, too suddenly indulged in, you swore hard. A perfectly bred man should never swear.

You are entering upon a new sphere—a holier and happier one. Restrain your
hasty temperament. If you can restrain it as I have advised, you will find it easier
in your marriage.

Whether or not Doctor Baldwin restrained his hasty temperament, Yancey did
not. In a temper, he shot an uncle by marriage and spent a year in jail for it. Baldwin, on the other hand, lived a serene married life, and seven healthy children were
born to him and Mary Martin. When they married, Dr. Baldwin went to the slave
market to buy a woman to be a house maid. He found a mulatto woman, Sallie,
with a young daughter, and bought them both.

Sallie had other children who had been separated from her and sold to a planter
in Texas. She wept as she told of her misery at losing them. Dr. Baldwin wrote to
get information about the children and found that they would be coming through
Montgomery the next summer and could stop to see her on the way. They did.

The Baldwin household with its seven children was a busy one, and kept Mary
Martin, as well as "Mammy" Sallie and her daughter Anne fully occupied. A freed-
man, "Uncle" Jim Hale, trained as a carpenter, also lived on the place, and became
the special companion of the oldest boy, William Owen Baldwin Jr. ("Buddie
Willie"). The others had nicknames too—Marion Augustus ("Buddie Gus"), Mary
("S'Mary" or "Mamie"), Jean ("Jennie"), Cecilia ("Cecile"), Abram Martin ("Buddie
Martin") and Almira Ann ("Alma").

In 1846 Montgomery became the state capital, replacing Tuscaloosa, and a high
point of land known as Goat Hill was donated for the erection of a statehouse.
Architect Stephen Decatur Button designed the capitol building in Greek Revival
style—to symbolize democracy. It was built with the guidance of a pattern book of
design and embellishment, *Beauties of Modern Architecture* by Minarad Le Fevor.
The six beautiful Corinthian columns were much admired. The capitol was paid for
by the city of Montgomery, backed by business interests. Charles Pollard, a railroad
entrepreneur, was chairman of the building committee.

Not long afterwards, the building caught fire. Many reports state that the building
burned completely to the ground, with nothing left of the exterior. A story regarding Chalres Pollard, however, suggests that only the inside of the building burned,
leaving the outside standing. The state treasurer said that the state did not have
money to repair it and proposed that the state capital be moved back to Tuscaloosa
and housed in its old buildings; Pollard was not about to let this happen. Con-

vinced the fire-gutted building could be restored, he consulted a noted New York architect who agreed. "You did right not to tear it down," the consultant concluded. "Outside of its historical association, it has its special and peculiar value because of the fidelity in which the architect followed the Grecian lines. Preserve it by all means." Charles Pollard told the treasurer that if the building was abandoned the state would have to repay the people of Montgomery the eighty thousand dollars they had spent on it, since it was given to the state in splendid condition with the understanding that henceforth the seat of government was to be Montgomery. So the capital and its capitol should stay there.

Colonel Pollard, who regarded himself a connoisseur of Greek architecture, had built for his own family the most handsome columned house in Montgomery. It stood downtown on Jefferson Street until 1938, when it was torn down to make room for a warehouse. This happened to many other fine antebellum homes, including the old Baldwin house. It didn't happen to the Knox house, built on South Perry Street in 1848, because in 1967, James Loeb, a prominent cotton merchant, founded the Landmarks Foundation to save that residence and other beautiful old homes still standing.

Burning of the Capitol, Montgomery, Alabama, courtesy Fouts.

The Knox house required extensive renovation. It had been turned into a board-inghouse and enlarged by hanging a false floor between the fine Florentine columns in front and partitioning off rooms with plywood. The last Knox to live there in the 1890s, Anne Octavia Lewis, is still remembered by a story reminiscent of the Old South in which the only means of resistance by servants was to "slow down" or "not do." After overseeing the planting of tulip bulbs by a colored man, Mrs. Lewis told him she would pay him "when they come up," and turned away. When she looked again, she found the bulbs uprooted. "They just come up, ma'am," he said.

The Greek influence on Montgomery continued even after the building of the fine old pillared houses ceased. A nearby community was called Mitylene after the birthplace of the Greek poetess Sappho on the island of Lesbos. Many households had replicas of Greek statues in their gardens. We had a statue that I had always thought was a Greek maiden bearing an urn, but which turned out to be a Biblical character, "Rebecca of the Well," placed there by my religious grandmother.

As late as 1927, Jasmine Hill Gardens were developed in nearby Elmore County. They contained fountains and a dazzling array of Greek statuary, brought from Europe by Benjamin Fitzpatrick, the brother of Celia Fitzpatrick, my great-great-grandmother, who had come to Alabama with her husband, William Baldwin, in the early 1800s.

Also, Greek influence came to Montgomery in the form of Greek immigrants who excelled in the restaurant trade. One restaurateur was Speridon Cassimus, who brought fig trees, jujube trees, and Sparta bushes to the city. He presided over the best restaurant, Cassimus, a favorite of my mother and her sisters. In later years, another Greek, Pete Xides and then his son, Edward Xides, operated the Elite (pronounced "Ee-light"), then regarded as the best restaurant in Montgomery. It was noted for its crab gumbo.

There are many other columned houses still standing, among them the Murphy House, built in 1851 by John H. Murphy, a cotton broker, and used as headquarters for the Union Army at the end of the war. It was in falling-down condition when it was restored to become headquarters for the Montgomery Water Works and Sanitary Sewer Board in 1970. Present-day Montgomerians pass under its fluted Greek columns to pay their water bills. The interior is furnished handsomely with antiques, including a pier mirror that reaches almost to the ceiling. When the Wa-

ter Commission meets there on Mondays, they sit on horsehair chairs at a round antique poker table.

It is suitable that such a handsome old house would become headquarters for the Water Works. Water was a big problem in Montgomery. Except for runoff from roofs when it rained, most of the city was supplied primarily from two artesian wells downtown. One was the "Big Basin" in Court Square, since 1885 adorned by a statue of Hebe, the Greek goddess of youth. The "Little Basin" was a few blocks away at Bibb and Commerce. Drinking water from these wells was delivered to residents in bottles.

Over the years the city enacted a spate of ordinances to protect the water supply. Montgomery was a town of flammable buildings. Negro shacks, referred to as "buzzard roosts," lined both sides of Commerce Street near the river. Until 1847,

The Murphy House, courtesy Fouts.

bucket brigades were the only means of fighting fires. A mule-drawn wagon was finally put into service, and an ordinance passed requiring that in order to be licensed, any dray or wagon must carry a barrel of water to fight fires. Anyone washing a buggy, carriage, or animal within fifty feet of the artesian wells, or throwing trash, or bathing in the basin was fined five dollars, unless the offender was a slave, who would receive thirty-nine stripes unless the owner paid the fine.

Other ordinances were enacted specifically targeting Negroes. Slaves from other states could not stay longer than twenty days in Montgomery. The fine for flying kites within city limits was five dollars, but for a slave the punishment was twenty lashes. Although this form of discriminatory punishment was sanctioned by law and regional mores, acts of cruelty to animals were prohibited.

In the 1850s Montgomery had theater and opera, with performances staged by troupes from New York, and P. T. Barnum's circus from New Orleans visited the city. By 1854 the city was lighted by gas. There were cock fights in a vacant lot at Commerce and Tallapoosa—and even an attempt at a bull fight, but the long-horned Texas steers nibbled the grass instead of charging the matadors. The first square of Dexter Avenue was lined with houses of prostitution.

At the same time, the city began to develop men of consequence such as Dr. William Owen Baldwin. As an obstetrician he was unrivaled, and was interested in all aspects of medicine. In 1847, he contributed a scientific paper titled "Observations on the Poisonous Properties of the Sulphate of Quinine" to the *American Journal of the Medical Sciences*. His paper established the fact that in overdoses, quinine could cause death. Since quinine had become a widely used "cure-all" for many ailments in addition to malaria, the article created attention both in the United States and abroad.

Just a few years later when the yellow fever epidemic of 1854 struck Montgomery, killing many residents and prompting downtown stores to close and display signs reading, "closed 'til frost," his prescribed remedy was limited to ten grains of quinine daily. Dr. Baldwin's patients may have died, but never from an overdose of quinine. His practice continued to expand until he was making around fifteen thousand dollars a year, and he was president or chairman of half a dozen medical associations.

In 1849, he attacked quacks and charlatans of all kinds in an address to the Alabama State Medical Association on the subject of "Physic and Physicians." He also criticized medical colleges that "guard their sordid interests instead of protecting the honor and dignity of science" and "individuals who receive diplomas from such institutions . . ."

However, he warned against censuring the doctors indiscriminately because they "constitute the brightest ornaments of our profession. There may be some decaying fruit upon the tree, but why reject the ripe growth of summer warmth and autumn fullness?" This paper met with such favor that seventy dollars was allocated at the next annual meeting of the Association for printing and distributing it to the public. By 1851 he was president of the Alabama State Medical Association.

He worked on many committees and causes, including one to urge the construction of a hospital for the insane, inspired by Dorothea Dix, a pioneer in the movement to provide specialized treatment for the insane. He took his causes seriously, but not himself. He named his high-spirited horse, who had demolished several buggies, Job, after a physician friend of his, Dr. Job Weatherby. He later gave Job, the horse, to Job the physician "since they matched each other in temperament."

Just before the war, Dr. Baldwin completed construction of a new home for his family at Adams and Perry streets. It was described in the *Montgomery Daily Mail* as "the most splendid residence constructed in this city for several years," with dozens of rooms connected by speaking tubes, and doors with knobs and hinges of silver plate. In appearance it was Italianate, with short metal columns in front. The three-story house had an attic and an observatory. The bedrooms had closets and marble wash stands. There was an indoor bathroom

Baldwin House, ultimately torn down.

with hot water piped through tubes connected with a "circulating" boiler in the kitchen. There were cisterns both on the roof and underground, containing nearly one thousand barrels of water. The house cost more than thirty thousand dollars, and the furnishings were elegant. A pier mirror twelve feet tall was brought from England in one of the last ships to run the Civil War blockade.

It was in these surroundings that the children grew up, in a family that was quite wealthy by Montgomery standards, but they were kept busy by their industrious mother, Mary Martin. The boys ran errands and cared for the animals. The girls learned to sew, cook, and serve. One day while serving guests, they got their fingers in the soup. Their father joked, "It will make it taste better."

According to an old friend, "At home with his family, Doctor Baldwin was wont to abandon himself without reserve to jollity and fun, and on such occasions would sing 'Dem Golden Slippers,' 'Rise and Shine,' and 'Get on to Glory' with gusto and action."

He brought up his children, including the four girls, to be independent and to take care of themselves. He educated and helped his three boys go into business. The girls were schooled at Chegaray Institute in Philadelphia, and when they were older, were given allowances to travel. Alma and Cecile went to Sweden. Mary was presented at the Court of St. James. Jennie married before she had time to go traveling.

In the mid-1870s their father bought enough land further up Perry Street to build four houses for the girls, which are still on South Perry and known as the "four sister houses." He put the houses in the girls' names, so that they would always own something of their own. He admitted later that he really had no use for sons-in-law.

4

The War Within the War

ALABAMA PRODUCED MORE COTTON THAN ANY OTHER STATE AND used large numbers of slaves to grow and harvest it. The cotton came into Montgomery from all over the state. Some came raw in wagons from nearby plantations, and from further away by trains and barges. And some was already ginned and baled for reshipment to Mobile by steamship or even directly overseas to England.

Business was booming in Montgomery. The elegant Exchange Hotel became headquarters for cotton traders and brokers from all over the South and offered on its menu "oysters of rare quality, turkeys, lobster salad, and champagne of the best brands."

The chief topic of conversation among the sumptuously fed diners was secession. They were aroused by mass mailings of abolitionist literature from New England and by the disregard in the North for the Fugitive Slave Act, which required the return of runaway slaves to their owners.

A few owners tracked their runaway slaves north. Others used various methods to keep slaves from running away. In Mt. Meigs, a prosperous planter community outside Montgomery, slaves were burned alive on two occasions, in 1854 and 1856, while the citizens of the community gathered to watch.*

By the time Lincoln was elected in November of 1860 he had already made his position clear: "The perfect liberty they sigh for is the liberty of making slaves of other people." This was not the first time that a state or section of the country had contemplated secession. New England considered doing so during the war of 1812, and in the 1830s South Carolina threatened to secede over a federal tax on

* J. Mills Thornton, *Power and Politics in a Slave Society* (Baton Rouge: Louisiana State University Press, 1978), 319.

whiskey. Other states including New Jersey, California, and Oregon had all flirted with secession.

It was the Southern senators in Congress, including Jefferson Davis of Mississippi, who first voted for secession in a secret session held in Washington. It was ironic that earlier Senator Davis had objected to a plan to place a plumed cap on the statue of Freedom on the U.S. Capitol dome, because the cap was a symbol of freed slaves in ancient Greece. Davis protested on the grounds that "its history renders it inappropriate, since our people were born free and would not be enslaved." He was speaking of whites, of course.

Another member of Congress, William Lowndes Yancey, became famous—or infamous as the case may be—when he resigned his seat in Congress in 1846, taking the position that slavery should be permitted in the newly chartered western states. His goal became the establishment of an independent Southern nation. His zeal earned him the epithet "Firebrand of the Confederacy."

When South Carolina became the first state to secede in December of 1860 "because of attacks from the North on the rights of slave owners," Alabama was not far behind. At the behest of the Alabama legislature, the secessionist governor called for a convention of delegates from all the counties, to be selected by December 24 to meet in the capital on January 7 to cast their votes on secession.

There was, however, one big problem. Alabama was a state divided! In the southern and central parts of the state, the

William Lowndes Yancey

owners of big plantations grew broad fields of cotton, and their livelihoods depended on having many slaves to plant, cultivate and pick. As the threat of abolition grew, most of the planters became secessionists.

By contrast, many of the northern hill counties had small farms where each family kept its own livestock and worked its own land. They did not grow cotton and had no slaves. As one of them put it, "We don't have no dogs in this fight."

This dichotomy existed in many states of the Deep South where the big plantations on the coastal and central flat country gave way to small farms as the land climbed into hills. There most of the small farmers were Unionists, pure and simple. They were veterans or sons of veterans of the Revolution, or the War of 1812 where they had shared the patriotism of its leader, Andrew Jackson. "Old Hickory" had deep-rooted allegiance to the United States and the flag of Washington and Jefferson.

Some had been awarded land for military service, and more came when the Indians, who occupied part of the territory, were driven out to begin their long march to reservations in the West. Alabama became a state in 1819. The northwestern frontier in the hill country was practically given away to attract settlers. It attracted many veterans who were Unionist to the core. They became homesteaders who retained their allegiance to the federal government.

Various land acts brought prices down until in 1854 Bill Looney, a former school teacher who decided to settle in Winston County,got seven thousand acres for 12½ cents an acre. By 1860, when the governor called on the counties to select delegates to a state convention to vote on secession, Looney had changed his profession and was operating a highly successful tavern on his land, the only place in that sparsely populated county that brought people together except at church. Tom Pink Curtis, who lived on Crooked Creek, got a group together at the Tavern to talk about Secession. He concluded that "What we want is to be left alone. We are not opposed to slavery as such. What we are opposed to is the strife and dissension that is sure to come into our county and our homes because of the agitation by them hot-headed secessionists of south Alabama who are not going to stop short of tearing the state from the Union."

Chris Sheats

The group selected as their delegate Chris Sheats, a young schoolteacher who had grown up in the county and kept up with things, and could be counted on to vote against secession. In the ensuing county-wide election for delegate he defeated by four to one Dr. Andrew Kaiser, an outspoken secessionist and slave owner.

The rest of the counties with small farms in Alabama made similar selections, so it was an anti-secessionist delegation that went down to the state capital, Montgomery, to meet "them hot-heads in south Alabama." What they were not prepared for was the way of life on the plantations in the South. Some had more slaves than in all the hill counties put together.

The magnificent homes with their tall columns and balconies, the landscaped gardens and roads, and the liveried carriages were all noted in passing. As Chris Sheats put it, "We who live up in the hills don't have the things we have seen on our trip." Delegate Allen from Monroe County commented, "They owe these slaves a lot. I don't say as I blame them for their interest in defending their system against abolition."

Delegate Sheats answered, "The problem confronting us is no longer slavery. The issue is secession."

In Montgomery they were to meet those from other counties who opposed secession for various reasons. Some hoped to find a compromise that would allow them to stay in the Union. Others were afraid that secession would lead to war. Collectively they came to be known as Cooperationists, numbering almost half of the delegates.

A few were plantation owners who didn't want to secede. One who was opposed to secession was my great grandfather, Dr. William O. Baldwin. He was a famous physician and scientist who lived on his land outside of Montgomery, but grew no cotton. He was not heard from, since he was not chosen to be a delegate to the convention.

He believed that secession would lead to war with the North, which the South with its weak industrial base would lose, having neither the resources nor the manpower to win. He compared Alabama to Illinois, a state of comparable size, which had entered the Union at about the same time and had four times its industrial output.

There were few foundries in the South to manufacture arms, and no guarantee that England would continue to buy enough cotton to pay for armaments from abroad. In addition there was a big transportation problem, which Robert E. Lee pointed out could be decisive. The trains didn't go far enough, nor did they connect with other trains, and they were in terrible condition. The railroad around Muscle Shoals in the Tennessee River was in such a ruinous state by 1848 that steam power was abandoned in favor of horse-drawn trains.

Although there were many railroad lines, they were short ones running East-West and not in the direction of what would be the most likely battle sites. What's more, they didn't link up. Some were broad gauge and others narrow gauge, which meant that if secession led to war, every time a trainload of soldiers or armaments came to a track that was too wide or too narrow it would have to stop, unload everyone and everything on board, and transfer what it was carrying to cars on the other line.

Another plantation owner, who did serve as a prominent delegate to the convention and opposed secession, was Robert Jemison from Tuscaloosa County. His nomination by the Cooperationists to be chairman of the convention lost out to William Brooks, a secessionist from Perry County, fifty-three to forty-five.

However, the Cooperationists did not give up. They believed that the delegates did not represent the feelings of the people of Alabama about withdrawing from the Union, and drew up a resolution mandating that the Ordinance of Secession should be voted on by all eligible voters in Alabama.

It had become obvious that many sections of the state were strongly opposed to secession, and figures from the U.S. Census of 1860, which included Alabama, explained why. Of Alabama's total population (964,201), 54 percent were white and 45 percent were black slaves, the others being Indians, freed slaves, etc. More than half (492,781) of the whites owned no slaves at all and would have nothing to gain from secession. However, there were more than enough delegates from the counties where cotton was king, and the economy rested on the backs of slaves, to pass it.

The resolution to require that the Ordinance of Secession be submitted to the electorate of Alabama got short shrift from Chairman Brooks and his committee of thirteen advisors. Before it could be put on the agenda, Brooks called on William Lowndes Yancey to speak against it. He gave a rousing address:

> This government is a representative type rather than a pure democracy. If this ordinance were passed by but a single vote it would stand. All the people in the state will be compelled to abide by and support it. If they don't, then we will revive the nomenclature of seventy-six and apply the name "Tory" to those who oppose secession, as those who favored cooperation with England were called during the Revolutionary War. All those who oppose the state of Alabama after she assumes her independence from the Union will become traitors—rebels against its authority and will be dealt with as our enemies.

Robert Jemison of Tuscaloosa replied:

> The gentleman from Montgomery tells us that the nomenclature of the year '76 will be revived—that we will be Tories as they were then. He says that if the Ordinance of Secession should pass by a single vote, all who will not submit to it are guilty of treason and must be punished as traitors. For whom and by what authority does he speak? The gentleman knows that in many parts of the state there is opposition to the Ordinance and that it will be opposed by the masses of the

people. He knows that many have threatened to resist those who try to force it upon them. Will the gentleman go into those sections of the state and hang all who are opposed to secession? Will he hang them by families, by neighborhoods, by towns, by counties? Who will give the order?

The Ordinance of Secession went to the delegates at the convention on January 7, 1861, and was approved by a vote of 54 to 46. Secession won by only eight votes. Heavy pressure and threats were brought on the 46 to change their votes so that the decision would be unanimous. This may account for the difference in the number of final votes reported from the meeting.

Delegates were told that if they continued to vote against secession they would be labeled traitors and treated as such. The opposition was reported to have been reduced first to thirty-nine and then to nineteen. Of those who agreed to change their votes, most said they would go along with secession if the vote count went the other way. Only two voted against it with no reservations, Chris Sheats of Winston and R. S. Watkins of nearby Franklin County.

"I didn't come here to sign anything and I'm not going to be forced to," declared Watkins. Chris Sheats said, "I came here as a citizen of the State of Alabama of the United States, and I don't have to sign anything to make me one. My name is already on record as opposing the Ordinance of Secession and whatever I might sign would not emphasize this or argue my loyalty to our country and our government any further."

"You'll be put in jail if you don't sign," someone called out. Sheats answered, "Let them put me in jail if they think it will serve to make a traitor out of me. But I can assure you, I'll certainly never be traitor enough to suffer for my country. I am better prepared to suffer as a traitor to the Rebels than as a traitor to the Union and to those I came here to represent."

He was seized by the arms and coat collar and rushed bodily from the hall, and was taken to jail, where he remained until the convention was over.

By February, seven states, including Alabama, had seceded. However, in none of them were the qualified voters given the choice. Subsequently we can conclude that if the people had voted, Alabama would not have withdrawn from the Union. And it is probable that neither would several other states, including North Carolina, Arkansas and Georgia. There were also big pockets of anti-secessionists in Mississippi, Louisiana, and Texas.

In February, six of the seven states that did secede named representatives in Montgomery to form the government of the Confederacy. (The Texas delegate didn't get there in time.)

Scenes in Montgomery at Davis's inauguration.

Montgomery was named the Confederate capital, and Jefferson Davis was introduced as president from the balcony of the Exchange Hotel by Yancey, who proclaimed: "The man and the hour have met!"

One border state that didn't secede was Kentucky, where my great-grandfather on my mother's side, the Reverend James Craik of Louisville, addressed the state legislature on the evening of December 19, 1859. His discourse on "The Union. National and State Sovereignty Alike are Essential to American Liberty" was so effective that thirty-five of the representatives had it printed and widely distributed at their own expense. The vote in Kentucky went against secession.

In Alabama, the state legislature moved quickly to pass an

Impressment Act that would allow officers of the Confederate army to confiscate property as needed, and to enact compulsory conscription for all men between the ages of 18 and 35. Chris Sheats was there to vote against both, and was arrested again. This time he was charged with treason, punishable by death—a sentence that was not carried out, though he was in jail for much of the time until the war ended.

Dr. Baldwin was offered a commission in the medical corps but refused it, since in doing so he would have had to take an oath of allegiance to the Confederacy. Instead he volunteered on a regular basis to take care of the wounded brought to the Soldiers Home Hospital in Montgomery. He never changed his view that it was folly for Alabama to secede, but he conceded that just as a state originally consented to join the Union, it had the right to withdraw.

His earlier misgivings as to the outcome of the war were reaffirmed when the South failed to follow up on its stunning initial victory at Bull Run, after which Confederate General Joe Johnson called for an immediate invasion of Pennsylvania before the Union had time to regain its focus. Jefferson Davis disagreed. All the South had to do, he fervently believed, was to hold its position. "Hunger for cotton in exchange for arms from abroad would soon bring Britain in on Dixie's side."

Davis didn't impose a war tax in 1861. And by the time he did, a Union blockade of ships coming and going to Southern ports had made it almost impossible for the Confederacy to get enough cotton out and armaments in. In addition, British textile workers opposing slavery made it politically difficult for the British government to sustain such a policy. The masters of private ships, which were built low to steal in and out of Southern ports in the darkness to avoid the blockade, could carry only limited amounts of cargo, so the outlook did not look good for selling cotton or for getting armaments for the South.

Dr. Baldwin's concerns mounted when his sixteen-year old son and namesake, W. O. "Willie" Baldwin, Jr. dropped out of the university at Tuscaloosa to volunteer in Alabama's 22nd Regiment. "What chance did Willie have?" Dr. Baldwin withdrew to his plantation outside the city of Montgomery, continuing to take care of the wounded brought to the Soldiers Home Hospital. He kept up with the war mostly by letters from Willie.

In the northern counties, fewer letters came from the war fronts, since for the most part men from the hills were not there. After the Ordinance of Secession was passed, many vowed never to serve the Confederacy, and after conscription was voted, they hid out.

Brigadier General Gideon J. Pillow of the Confederate forces reported that by 1862 at least ten thousand men, including some who had deserted from the Confederate Army, were in the hills. And seven months later, General Gustave Beauregaard reported that he had received word that north Alabama was full of "Tories who had held conventions in Winston, Fayette and Marion counties supporting the Union, and that federal recruiting agents were carrying on open correspondence with others in Lawrence and Blount counties who wanted to join the Union forces."

Colonel Abel Straight of the 51st Indiana Regiment said, "This is a case without parallel in American history. I have never witnessed such an outpouring of devotion and determined patriotism among any other people, and I am of the opinion that there could be at least two full regiments raised as good and true men as ever defended the American flag."

A group of farmers in the northern counties of Alabama got together with farmers across their borders in Tennessee and Georgia and proposed to form a new state called Nickajack, to be called after the old Indian name for the region. This never happened, but eventually one of the northern counties, Winston, became the "Free State of Winston" by withdrawing its representative to the capital, thus cutting its official ties to Alabama.

It was to Winston County that Chris Sheats returned after the convention, and met with his supporters to talk about what if anything could be done. They decided to call a convention of their own for July 4 at Looney's Tavern. Since time was short they sent men on horseback in different directions through northwest Alabama to invite farmers to come.

Between two and three thousand of them arrived, most from Winston but many from the adjacent counties of Lawrence, Blount, Walker, Fayette, Marion, and Franklin. Some came in covered wagons with their families, and others on horseback or mules to spend the night. There was fiddling and square dancing in the tavern, and the bar was open, but Bill Looney saw to it that there wasn't much drinking. This was a serious occasion.

A large farm bell at his cabin tolled long and loud when it came time to summon everyone to a spring where a barbecue was served, and where speeches were given and resolutions heard. Although the participants left no written accounts of the meeting, Winston County Probate Judge John Bennett Weaver, a well-respected citizen and local historian, reconstructed the meeting from the post-war recollections of three eyewitnesses. There were three resolutions:

NOTES
   Valuable back-
ground information
used in writing this
chapter was drawn
from numerous private
collections, as well as
the Alabama Depart-
ment of Archives and
History, the U.S.
National Archives, the
Records and Pensions
Division of the War
Department, with
figures drawn from the
U.S. Census of 1860
compiled just before
the war.
   There was little
or nothing, however,
in the literature
and history of those
turbulent times about
the "War Within the
War" that was fought
in Alabama and several
other Southern states
between those who
believed in secession
and those who did not.
No one wrote about
it until after the war
was over, when books
began to emerge telling
the story of "those who
did not."
   Today, these are
out of print, but can
be borrowed on an
interlibrary loan from
the Birmingham
Public Library and the
Library of Congress:
*Alabama Tories, The
First Alabama Cavalry*
by Wm. Stanley Hoole;
*Winston, an Antebel-
lum and Civil War His-*

The first commended Chris Sheats and others for their loyalty and fidelity. The second avowed opposition to "our neighbors in the South" who seceded from the Union and established a new government: "We are not going to take up arms against them, but ask them to leave us alone and unmolested, so we may work out our own political and financial destiny here in the hills and mountains of north Alabama."

The third was put as a question, "If a state can lawfully and legally secede or withdraw from the Union, then can't a county, being a part of a state, by the same process of reasoning, cease to be a part of the state?" The crowd reacted with resounding applause. Then there was a formal vote on the three resolutions, and the ayes had it.

However, the mood was not happy and victorious, but at the end of the day somewhat funereal. The people went back to their homes with heavy hearts, realizing that bad times were ahead.

The real trouble in Winston County and other anti-secessionist strongholds started with conscription, when many of the eighteen-to-thirty-five-year-olds swore never to serve the Confederacy and went into hiding. The Confederates then appointed cavalry brigades and "Home Guards" to find them and bring them in. All men of military age were warned that if they failed to report for induction within five days, they would be shot as traitors to the Confederate government.

This was the beginning of civil war *within* Alabama that divided the state, at the same time that Alabama as a state was committed to the Confederacy. The poor but proud farmers in the northwestern hill counties held out against the efforts of the plantation owners for the four long years of the "War Between the States." If anything, those in the hill counties came to hate those in the Confederacy and, vice versa, with ever greater intensity.

Hostile acts, including brutal atrocities, were committed by the Home Guards on friends and relatives of those they captured or killed. Vivid accounts in books, pamphlets, and family lore, document the intensity of this bitter struggle. Word of nefarious actions by the Confederates enforcing conscription was passed among the hill farmers in such furtive conversations as these:

"Did you hear what happened to Newt Austin? And they also got Mitch Canady . . . The father and brother of Bird Norris went to Jasper to see him in jail but after he refused to join the Confederate army he disappeared, and was found two days later dead in a ditch. A terrible thing happened to Jack Walker and his son, Bill. When the Home Guards shot at them they killed Jack, and when Bill got away they hacked up his father with an ax."

One vicious act led to another. The Home Guards targeted Tom Pink Curtis and his two younger brothers, Joel and Wash. They killed Joel and captured Wash. Acting under authority of the Impressment Act, they took everything he left behind on his farm. Tom Pink Curtis himself, who had become a probate judge, was tortured with a red hot fire poker to force him to give up money he refused to relinquish because he said it belonged to the judge's office. In another account, after the torture, he was transported to a bluff on Clear Creek where he was "executed by two shots to his right eye and his body was thrown over a cliff."

It became common practice to use impressment to strip the farms of those who were taken away. A widow, Mrs. Purdy, wrote, "They took the last cow and the last hog, and the old sow before she even weaned her pigs, the corn and fodder, the last gallon of meal, and the last middlin of meat from the smoke house, and all the spoons and forks and cups and saucers and even the bee-gum—it sure got the bees riled up."

Henry Tucker had left his hill country farm and joined the Union Army in 1861. He was cut off from his company and found at his home by a Home Guard leader, Stoke Roberts, who had sworn vengeance against him for trying to kill him in an earlier confrontation at nearby Boiling Rocks. Tucker was pulled from a meat box where he had been hidden by his wife, Callie, and taken to Boiling Rocks, where he was stripped of his clothes and strung up on a tree by his heels, which were cut for a gamboling stick, to be slaughtered like a hog. "We planned to skin him alive but our knives were too dull so we punched out his eyes and cut off his tongue and castrated him, then built a fire beneath him and burned what was left."

Retaliation was inevitable. The "Tories of the Hills" as they had come to be called, vowed to fight fire with fire and kill every Home Guard they could find. The violence continued to escalate. Jim Lewis killed Dr. Kaiser after forcing him to reveal the names of five Home Guards who had killed his father, and he shot all five before the end of the war. When they got to Stoke Roberts they left him nailed to a tree with a spike through his mouth and the back of his head.

As time went on there were fewer Tories in the hills, since increasingly they went across to enlist on the other side—if they could get there. In Winston County where 239 enlisted in the Union forces, only 112 became Confederates. In Walker and Marion counties, Woodruff Miles, who had joined the Union army as early as 1861, returned home to bring others across. At one point he had assembled a force

tory of a Hill County of North Alabama by D. B. Dodd and W. S. Dodd; *Civil War and the Reconstruction in Alabama* by Walter L. Fleming; *Tories of the Hills, The Free State of Winston*, a historical novel by Wesley Thompson; and *First Alabama Cavalry U.S.A.: Homage to Patriotism* by Glenda Todd.

A long-awaited book by historian Margaret M. Storey, *Loyalties and Loss: Alabama's Unionists in the Civil War and Reconstruction*, has just been published by Louisiana State University in Baton Rouge. It is the most recent of noteworthy books about the South.

A graphic portrayal of the "War Within The War" was provided by the recent Civil War novel *Cold Mountain* by Charles Frazier, who grew up in the hill country of neighboring North Carolina. It tells of the trials of a mountain man who was drafted against his will into the Confederate Army from the northern hills of North Carolina.

All of these point to the conclusion that if the electorate in Alabama and other states in the South had been given the opportunity to vote on secession, they would have voted not to leave the Union.

big enough to tear down a jail where the Home Guards were holding prisoners for five days to give them time to join the Confederate forces before killing them.

In Winston, Bill Looney became a full-time guide for volunteers wishing to cross the battle lines into Union territory. Looney made an arrangement with northern generals to take as many men as he could get through. He knew all the trails through the hills, where pickets were stationed, and the ravines and caves where men could hide. As word of his success spread, he also recruited deserters from the Confederate armies.

One of Looney's biggest hauls early in the war was several hundred men from different hill counties, who came to Natural Bridge, a gathering place, where he met them. He took them to join the First Alabama Cavalry, U.S.A., which signed up 2,066 white Southerners who served together as a fighting force for the North throughout the war. By 1864 when the Union armies were fighting the final battles in Tennessee and Alabama, he had delivered several thousand more directly to Union regiments and by that time had become a prime target for capture himself. But "The Black Fox," as he was known, was never caught.

5

The War Between the States

T HE WAR BETWEEN THE STATES IS WHAT SOUTHERNERS HAVE ALWAYS called what others refer to as the Civil War. And we shall do so now in recounting the final battles of some of the 260,000 Confederate soldiers whose worn and bloodied gray uniforms gave mute testimony to the supreme sacrifice they made for the South. On the Northern side, even more died (360,000), but not all of them on the battlefield. Many were prisoners of war who died in prison—13,000 of them in Andersonville, Georgia.

In Montgomery, Dr. Baldwin had been following the war battle-by-battle in letters from his son and namesake. "Willie" had been in the thick of things since he joined the Confederate Army in 1862.

By the time he was seventeen, he had become a hero for saving the colors of Alabama's 22nd Regiment at Shiloh. In 1863, he was at Chickamauga, and at Resaka and Jonesboro in the retreat through Georgia. By 1864, he was back in Alabama on his way to fight his final battle under General Hood in Tennessee.

His last five letters to his family have been preserved:

May 29, 1864, Line of Battle, Paulding, Georgia.

My dear Mother & Father,

I have written to you every time I have the opportunity, but found they had not reached you and have intended to write again. Up to the present time I have been blessed with God's kind mercy. You have heard by this time that Captain Henry and John Finley were wounded on the 25th of this month defending a line of battle.

We are daily expecting the final attack. It is one continual line of musket fire and by this time you must know of the fight between Cleburn's Division and the enemy.

For the number of men engaged, I think it must have been the bloodiest battle that has ever been fought. The Yankees left a thousand dead on the field. Most of the men were shot to pieces. One was found pierced with thirty balls.

I am so glad that the people are holding daily meetings for the success and preservation of our noble soldiers. No one can tell what our Army has suffered for the last 23 days, except the soldiers themselves. Pray on for us and God in his tender mercy will have blessed us with our once happy homes and families. Give my love to all friends. Kiss the children, and howdy to all the servants. Write soon to your affectionate and devoted son.

W.O.B.

On August 26, after receiving a box of food carried from home by Jim Hale, the plantation carpenter and his special companion growing up, Willie wrote:

My dear Mother—Jim and the box came through safely. Eggs were broken, but every thing else alright. I received the box in time to help out with a supper of biscuits made with no grease, and half done. We had *nothing* else but a few preserves. The grapes were not as badly spoiled as I thought they would be, not hard to eat by any means.

Would you believe I have seen men argue over an ear of corn?

I cannot sleep with Capt. Little while I am at Brigade Hdqtrs. because he has no blanket. He won't carry one and I always get a man who has one, to put mine with . . . Heavy firing on our right this morning. Love to all the family. Will write soon to you.

Your Aff. Son

W.O.B. Jr.

Later in September he wrote his mother again:

Yours sent by Judge C came safely to hand this morning. I wrote one the day after the battle, and another three or four days later. The probability is that we have not seen the worst, but in the end our Confederacy will come out of the dark cloud that now threatens, and envelops her, and shine as bright as the stars in the brilliant coronet of Gods lovely creation.

We will have to bear with our enemies a long time. We cannot cope with him in any field he may select, but all will be right some day. Our people at home, generally, do not evince the *right* and *true* Southern spirit. I believe two thirds of them, if they had the power would withdraw from the fray.

Don't let this trouble you so much, Mother. If I fall in battle, I cannot wish for a death more honorable. I feel and hope that I am at peace with "Him who doeth all things," for his honor & glory. If I am called upon no matter when and how, I am resigned to meet my Fathers will. Thy will be done. Oh God, and not mine.

I was today made Captain of my Company. Enclosed you will find a recommendation given to me, unasked for by Colonel Toulmin. I was complimented by the Board of Examiners. I would like you to send me a small glass of black pepper and some rice, and tell Jim to bring a couple of half soles with him. Also, would you put the bars on my jacket. It is growing dark. Kiss all the children. Howdy to the servants. Love to your own dear self. W.O.B. Jr.

An unsigned note at the bottom of this page, read. "Have I not reason to be thankful to God and proud of my noble boy?"

In October, he wrote his father, on the march, from seven miles north of Gadsden, Alabama:

We are just halted for the night and I have a little spare time to drop you a short note. General Hood has told us we are going across the Tennessee River, but where to I am unable to say. I am poorly fixed up for a winter campaign. I would like very much to get shoes, socks, drawers etc. before going but I expect it is next to impossible unless we stop at Jacksonville.

I have been remarkably well, except now and then foot aches caused from long marches. I am willing & ready to stand anything if good results will be the fruit of my labor. How do the people like our movements? Hope they are in better spirits than they have been since the fall of Atlanta. If they will go to work and try to add to the comfort of the soldiers they won't regret it.

We need blankets, shoes, socks. Have the carpets made into blankets. Keep all the wool you can find & send it to the Army.

Kiss the children, love to Mother & Brother. Write by every opportunity. I have just seen Gen. Deas. He asks that you send the books he wrote you about, with Mr. Petrie when he comes. If he cannot bring them, send them to his wife in Demopolis. Your aff. son, W.O.B. Jr.

On October 29 he wrote from Leighton, Alabama, his last letter:

> My dear Mother, The command has just halted for the night. Worn out and tired as I am, I cannot let an opportunity pass to write you a short letter. I feel a little unwell this afternoon, for the first time since we have been marching. I attribute my feelings, to the long marches. We march fifteen to twenty five miles every day, wet or dry, rain or sunshine. Up to the time Mr. Petrie left, I occasionally rode Col. Toulmin's horse, which is in my charge, but it got to be the subject of remarks & of course (since it was not the right thing to do) I discontinued. If Mr. P. rejoins us soon, I would like to have two or three pairs of socks, a pair of shoes, one pair of drawers. Maj. Armistead wishes a two bladed knife and a lead pencil (tell his sister).
>
> I have no news to write. We are near the Tenn. River—will cross tomorrow, tis thought. I hope and sincerely trust I am lending a helping hand to soon free our land from our chains and win back a portion of our downtrodden South. God help and protect you all, is my daily prayer.
>
> Your aff. and devoted son, W. O. B. Jr.

"The Boy Captain"
William Baldwin
at nineteen.

"The Boy Captain," as he was called, was killed in the battle of Franklin, Tennessee, on the night of November 30, 1864. He was leading his regiment when the color bearer fell. He raised the flag and with it mounted the breastworks of the enemy where he was shot down. It could have been that he was killed by rounds fired by volunteers from Alabama's hill country. Many of them were in Tennessee, fighting for General Sherman in the campaign against Willie's General Hood.

Jim Hale took Willie's body home to be buried in Montgomery's Oakwood Cemetery. As a child, I heard the story from my grandmother Jennie, who was Willie's sister. Standing on the wooden foot of her sleigh bed I would wave a pillow case (my Confederate flag) over my head and shout as Captain Baldwin did when he went over the bunker: "Alabama Twenty-Second, follow me!" And then with a minie ball piercing my heart, I fell mortally wounded into the deep feather mattress and dreamt of glory.

There are many Confederate and some Union graves in Montgomery's Oakwood Cemetery, which also has a place for the "unknowns." An imposing obelisk forty feet tall dominates the field with a statue of Governor William Oates, his right sleeve empty as it had been since the battle at Fussell's Mill near Petersburg, Virginia.

His inscription reads: "Born in poverty, raised in adversity, without educational advantages. Yet by honest individual effort he retained a competency and the confidence of his fellow men, while fairly liberal to relatives and the worthy poor. A devoted Confederate soldier who gave his right arm for the cause. He accepted the result of the war without a murmur."

I knew this monument, as well as others throughout the cemetery, because I played among them when my mother took me there at Easter to put flowers on the graves, and at the same time clip any asparagus that had seeded itself from the cemetery wreaths of fern left behind after funerals. She always said that the best asparagus came from around the Hill family plot: "It's a bit stringy, but it makes a very good soup."

"He gave his right arm for the cause" —monument of Governor William C. Oates in Montgomery's Oakwood Cemetery.

The family was devastated by Willie's death. His father had expected it. What he had said before the war—"We don't have the resources"—was on the mark, but it gave him no comfort. In the South there were those like old Judge Pierce, who had bragged before the war that "We can lick 'em with pop guns," and afterward acknowledged, "but they didn't use pop guns."

Jennie Baldwin recalled her father's reaction to the assassination of Abraham Lincoln. She said that when the news reached Montgomery, she and her sisters and little brother and some of their colored friends all danced around the front yard on Perry Street singing, "Hurrah, hurrah, old Abe Lincoln is dead." Their mother called them into the house. "You don't know what you are doing, children," her father told them. "The South has lost the only man who could have befriended us."

The South was devastated and desperately poor after the war. Everybody was struggling. Doctors, lawyers, and businessmen were willing to do anything that would bring in even a small amount of money. Sidney Lanier, the widely acknowledged poet of the South, worked as a clerk at the Exchange Hotel to pay for lodging for himself and his wife.

Jefferson Davis was sent to prison and it was not until twenty years later that he returned to Montgomery to lay the cornerstone for the Confederate monument in 1886. Among those in costume at the celebration that day was Jennie Baldwin (by then Mrs. Will Craik), who came as an old country woman dressed in a calico dress and sunbonnet.

The family version of the story is that when Mr. Davis saw her he said, "Jennie Baldwin, I would know you in any costume. Take off that sunbonnet and come here. You are still one of the most transcendentally beautiful creatures God ever put on this green earth."

6

Reconstruction

THE END OF THE WAR WAS LIKE A NEW BEGINNING FOR DR. WILLIAM O. Baldwin and his freedman carpenter and friend, Jim Hale, who had been marking time on the Baldwin plantation on the outskirts of Montgomery. Each had opposed the Civil War for his own reasons. For them, April 9, 1865, the day the war ended, was a time to make a new start after four long, tortuous years in which they had been "chained to their posts."

Half the population, 475,510 slaves, were free to look for paid jobs and housing, both of which were in short supply. The planters, who had formerly told them what to do, now had to pay for their labor, if they could. The alternative would be to lose or sell the plantation.

Soon afterwards, Congress established a Freedmen's Bureau in the War Department, giving it a mandate over all matters pertaining to the former slaves: justice, labor, education, relief, medical aid, employment, and, later on, voting rights. It was thought to be an orderly way of approaching the major post-war problem, relocation of manpower. However, it was not something generals were trained to do. There was great confusion. Most people were searching for answers and not finding them.

Some came back from the war with very different ideas. In Union Springs in the Black Belt in central Alabama, two brothers, Charles and Hamilton Cox, returned to their plantation from the Confederate Army, and were welcomed back warmly by the whites and blacks they had grown up with. They were soon back with their ex-slave girlfriends.

In Alabama, miscegenation laws prevented them from getting married, but they lived together openly in an interracial community on the old plantation. They called it Smuteye from the village blacksmith shop where the men used to gather on winter evenings and go home with smut eyes from the smoke of the furnace, and from the drink, according to a direct descendant, Major Cox, who still owns land in Smuteye.

Dr. Baldwin and Jim Hale were not searching for answers, but had found them in the four years they were given to think about it. They knew exactly what they wanted to do. Within a month after the war ended with Lee's surrender to Grant at Appomattox, the new president, Andrew Johnson, announced his Reconstruction plan, offering a pardon to every Southerner who could and would take an oath to support the Union, and from then on acquire no property in slaves or make use of slave labor.

Those who had served in the war or had otherwise sworn allegiance to the Confederacy were not eligible. Dr. Baldwin was eligible and on August 19 was one of the first to apply. In October, he signed the oath, which was acknowledged by Secretary of State William Seward, and on November 22 he was a citizen again.

Dr. Baldwin employed Mammy Sallie to run his house just as before, and Anne as his office nurse. He was probably already paying Jim Hale, as a freedman, to be the carpenter and his general assistant. He did not have other slaves, since he had given up planting cotton which required field hands, and grew only fruit, beans, and vegetables.

Jim Hale left the plantation for downtown Montgomery to go into business for himself as a carpenter. He had already been freed (possibly by Dr. Baldwin) so did not have to wait for the ratification of the Thirteenth Amendment for his full independence.

Downtown, where people were selling their property for anything they could get for it, Jim Hale purchased a big two-story frame house at 503 Washington Avenue. It had to be big. In addition to storage space for lumber and tools, it was where he took the family he had brought with him from the plantation, James Hale Jr., Harriet, and Clark. In the long run, he would have two more wives and altogether thirteen children, and would call the house a home for the rest of his life, twenty-two years.

Dr. Baldwin invited another physician to help care for his patients, which gave him time to work on some of the problems that beset his city and state. The basic problem was money—or lack of it. Confederate scrip was worth nothing, and there was no place to borrow any. He had a good income and his money was not in Confederate notes. He founded the First National Bank of Montgomery and persuaded some others with money to join him. He was its first and longtime president.

J. W. Durr, who owned the Durr Drug Company, was on the Board of Directors. As Mr. Durr said, "The First National Bank was the only place in Alabama where a businessman could get money." Borrowing money was a main obstacle to rebuilding the South. Many of the big plantations had been broken down into small tenant farms. The new tenants needed money for seed and fertilizer as well as merchandise.

Another approach to solving the problem was credit. In the 1870s, two Weil brothers, Isidor and Herman, immigrated from Bavaria in southern Germany and opened a general dry-goods store in Opelika, not far from Montgomery. They got into the cotton business by advancing credit to small farmers, to be paid off either in money or in cotton at harvest time. As in the case of Dr. Baldwin, they became very wealthy.

Jim Hale was successful in his new construction business not only because he worked hard at it and was known to be a skilled carpenter who could build almost anything, but because he was one of the first black contractors in Montgomery to build houses for the newly freed black men who needed places to live.

He accomplished this with the help of Dr. Baldwin. This information about Dr. Baldwin and Jim Hale was largely provided by a descendant of Hale's, J. Mason Davis, Jr., a Birmingham attorney, from oral history and written records in the family.

Baldwin moved from his plantation on the outskirts of town, and offered to "go shares" with Jim if he would subdivide it into small lots and build houses and sell them to blacks. The financing for the houses was arranged through Dr. Baldwin's First National Bank of Montgomery.

It was a successful enterprise and the newly freed families were able to purchase the houses. Jim and Dr. Baldwin and the bank all prospered. Presumably, when Jim asked the doctor where he should put his money, Baldwin advised him to buy shares in the First National Bank. I suspect he did.

It wasn't long before the bank was able to build its own three-story building at 14 Commerce Street, and there is still a predominantly black neighborhood called Madison Park on the site of the old plantation on the outskirts of Montgomery near Gunter Air Force Base.

As Jim's family grew, he acquired a second house across the street for his construction business, and bought a third house on Lake Street, which he ran as a boarding house to accommodate his staff and out-of-town customers.

Not much is known about Jim's second wife and family except that more children were added and they all lived together at 503 Washington Avenue. But a great deal is known about his third wife, Anne. Jim had first seen Anne as a child when she was purchased with her slave mother, Sallie, at the time of Dr. Baldwin's marriage in 1843.

Sallie was the household "Mammy," and stayed with the family until she died in 1901. Anne took care of the seven Baldwin children as they came along, and got her own schooling at the same time. She also learned enough about medicine to become Dr. Baldwin's office nurse after the war.

In the mid-1870s, Dr. Baldwin gave Jim a very special assignment—to design as well as build the elegant "four sister houses" for his four daughters, up the hill from his own house on South Perry Street.

A reason for this may have been that his lovely young daughter Jennie, who had married a railroad man and had been living in a remodeled boxcar and then in a rooming house in Birmingham, was pregnant, and he wanted to get her back to Montgomery where he could take care of her.

It was easy for Baldwin and Hale to work together. They had been doing it for many years. They went about it with hope and enthusiasm. Their hope began with Lincoln's 1863 plan for Reconstruction, which was slowed but not stopped by his assassination and the killings that took the lives of thousands of blacks just after the war.

As an obstetrician, Dr. Baldwin and his principal assistant, Anne, were both acutely aware of another unmet need—hospitals, and this was particularly true for Negroes, who were not admitted to any white hospital and had none of their own. It was probably with the encouragement of Dr. Baldwin that Anne made it the challenge of her own life to get such a hospital for her people.

After the war, Dr. Baldwin's immediate goal was to "heal the wounds between the North and the South," and to improve the quality of medical education. To do this, he worked within the framework of the professional medical associations, and in 1867, after an absence of five years, he accepted the invitation of the American Medical Association to attend their annual meeting in Washington, D.C. The invitation read:

"The unhappy feud which for years divided the Nation has ceased, and peace has come we trust, so we hope soon again to meet our members and delegates from the South on the platform of fraternization, and to this end we extend you a cordial welcome." In 1868, he attended the AMA meeting in Washington, with six other Southern physicians. Many of the five hundred delegates knew about him for his medical research on quinine, and one board member, a Dr. Gross who had met him and taken a great liking to him, nominated him as the next president of the AMA.

There was one upset, according to a story passed down in the family. Rebuked by a physician from Connecticut who said it would be a shame to elect "a damn rebel and slave owner," Dr. Baldwin, a very tall and strong man, simply knocked the man down. Then, turning to other delegates he said that sectional and political issues should not divide a meeting of a professional society such as theirs. "Let us again be united as friends and brothers."

He was elected as a "Southern doctor who could heal the breach."

Before the war, Dr. Baldwin had been known not only for his research on quinine but for the aggressive role he played as president of the Alabama Medical Association towards improving the quality of medical education. He carried this forward in his new role as head of the AMA.

In his presidential address he advocated the establishment of one or more national medical schools "where the appointment of professors be so guarded as to secure the very highest talents, the most profound learning, and the most fully demonstrated capacity for teaching—with the federal government assuming a proper share of the expense."

At about the same time, Jim Hale got into politics. It was the year the Fifteenth Amendment was ratified, making it illegal to deny citizens the right to vote because of their race. Jim didn't run for office himself, but 503 Washington and the boarding house on Lake Street became centers of political activity for leaders among the newly enfranchised blacks.

Jim's "boarders" sometimes came from other parts of the state where they were organizing Republican parties and getting out the vote. At Jim's, they met like-minded activists. One of these was James T. Rapier from Florence in Lauderdale, a northern county in that tier including Winston and Franklin counties that had put up such stubborn resistance to secession. Rapier had the advantage of a better education than most, having been sent to school in Canada. At home in Florence, he helped his father organize a Republican party and decided to run for Congress.

In 1870 he went to Montgomery and took a federal job as a census-taker, and in Jim's boarding house found a campaign manager in Charles O. Harris, who was himself running for a seat in the Alabama legislature. Jim Hale had the money to fund the campaigns and often did. The family was very political. Charles Harris married Jim and Anne's daughter, Frances. The Republican party in the state capital of Montgomery was practically organized at 503 Washington Avenue.

Both Rapier and Harris won in the elections of 1874, when black candidates throughout the South made gains. Altogether seventeen were elected to Congress that year, and more to the state legislatures. But by 1878, when their two and four year terms of office ended, it was a different story. Elected black officials, including Rapier and Harris, were "on the run" from the Ku Klux Klan or other hate groups, and Reconstruction for all intents and purposes was over. The last of the federal troops were not withdrawn until later, and it took more than half a century for the bitterness to subside.

In general, tensions endured between the small farmers in the hill country of northern Alabama, who were mostly Unionists, and the plantation owners, who called the Unionists "scalawags" for deserting the Confederacy. Both sides opposed the "carpet baggers" who came from the North and ran for office. Most often these were Freedmen's Bureau officials who had been brought there by the government and decided to stay. The blacks wanted to support the Unionists but soon found that while their votes were welcome, they were not. The Klan was a discouraging factor.

Jim Hale himself was not threatened, possibly because he had not run for office or been in the limelight, and continued on as a successful carpenter and business-man. His construction business actually thrived during this time.

Dr. Baldwin observed the worsening of relations between the North and the South, which pained him deeply. His feelings were reflected in a letter he wrote to his wife when he gave her a cluster of diamonds in a beautiful ring on their twenty-seventh wedding anniversary:

> Dear Wife: Please accept the accompanying ring in token of the purity and never-ending duration of that love I pledged you this day twenty-seven years ago. The afternoon shades of life are gathering fast around us my darling and time with its silent yet busy, never-resting wheel has brought us far on the journey. As I look back on that 7th of December—that bright morning of our life, fresh with all the

visions, hopes and ambitions of youth—I think of the landscape spread out before us in what then seemed the far-distant future years.

I can but too painfully realize how much of the prospect is left behind us now and lies buried with the dim and noiseless past. This period, as is the common lot of all, numbers with us its disasters, its wrecks of hopes, its disappointed ambition, and has proved to me that "The circuit vast which rounds life's dial plate hath many lights and shades," but I thank God that amid all its griefs and pains it has yet left me the darling wife of my youth to be still the guiding star and solace of the evening of my life.

Your devoted husband,
W. O. Baldwin

7

Down But Not Out

W ITH POLITICAL ACTIVISM BY FREED SLAVES CHECKMATED BY THE resurgence of the Klan, Jim Hale's behind-the-scenes role in election campaigns ended. He now became deeply involved in bringing education to former slaves.

At the Freedmen's Bureau, education had become the number one activity. This was largely because in trying to solve the employment problem, which was paramount, the Bureau advocated the signing of contracts between the ex-slaves and their new employers. However, contracts were difficult to negotiate since most of the new freedmen could neither read nor write. They had to learn how. The Bureau helped finance these schools.

As a contractor, Jim had built several schoolhouses and he had been honored as "outstanding member of his race" by the Montgomery County Board of Education, which named a school in north Montgomery the Hale School. Jim knew his workmanship was good, but he had become increasingly concerned about what was being taught inside the schoolhouses. The answer was, "not much."

A start in providing black schools had been made by northern churches through the American Missionary Association, which sent missionaries on request to teach the ex-slaves. In addition, the states were financing more schools, as mandated by the new state constitutions. But there were few good teachers.

There was a normal school that would take Negroes, the Lincoln School in Marion, Alabama, about eighty miles from Montgomery. It had been started in 1866 by nine former slaves who built the school themselves and asked the American Missionary Association to send a teacher. With some funds from the Freedmen's Bureau, it soon added a course to teach teachers.

This was most successful, and in 1873, the Alabama legislature recognized it as a State Normal School for Colored Teachers and Students, and provided several thousand dollars in financing. With some pride they claimed it to be "the oldest state institution in America established for the purpose of teacher education and liberal arts education for Negroes."

Their next move was to appoint as director William Burns Paterson, and give him enough money to enlarge its program and increase the staff. A new addition was Maggie Flack, a zealous twenty-four-year-old missionary whom he married a year later.

Will Paterson* had come up as an educator the hard way. He had emigrated to the United States from Tullibody, Scotland, to free himself from the class distinction imposed on British society by their educational system, which kept the lower classes in their place. He found himself in Hale County, Alabama, where more than half of the population had not gone to school at all. Before the war it had been illegal to teach Negroes.

Maggie Flack had come from a family of abolitionists in Ohio who were involved in the "underground railroad" for escaped slaves heading north. Her middle-aged father had volunteered for the Union army "to help free the slaves," and was killed marching through Georgia. Her mother sold part of the family farm to put Maggie in Oberlin, the first college to enroll both women and blacks, and on graduation Maggie sought a job in the Deep South "teaching the newly freed men."

In Hale County, near the county seat of Greensboro, Paterson began to teach black railway workers wherever they congregated—in a wagon or under a tree, and finally in a deserted slave cabin where they were joined by members of their families. In a short time he was asked to teach a school on the plantation of Fabius Hill, a planter who wanted to educate the four children born to him by a slave. Starting a school was a brave thing to do since soon after the war, when a missionary came to the county to teach Negroes, he was run out of town. Fabius decided to do it within the confines of land he owned.

In a year or so, Greensboro took it over and it became the Tullibody Academy for Negroes, supported by the county and the Freedmen's Bureau as well as by two Baptist churches, one white and one black. It was also supported by Hill, who believed in education for everybody, and by another plantation owner who thought that offering the newly-freed slaves an education would help keep them in the county to work the cotton fields that were the mainstay of the economy.

* The material in this section about the Patersons is taken from an article, "To Teach the Negro," by Judith Hillman Paterson in the Spring 1996 issue of *Alabama Heritage*, published by the University of Alabama Press. The information on Fabius Hill came from Nicholas Cobbs, a lawyer in Greensboro, and a member and past president of the Alabama Historical Association.

By 1878, Paterson left the Tullibody Academy in good hands and moved to Marion, Alabama, to head the Lincoln School there. By 1886 this had expanded into a university with four hundred students, whose graduation certificates took them almost anywhere they wanted to teach in the state, and were recognized throughout the South.

All went well until Reconstruction succumbed to a wave of reaction in Marion, just as it had in Jim Hale's Montgomery.

An arsonist set fire to the main building at the school and burned it to the ground, and soon afterwards, students from a local white college beat up a black student from Lincoln who refused to get off the sidewalk to let them pass.

Will Paterson, the white president of Lincoln, spoke out in defense of the student, declaring: "They clubbed him and would have killed him had he not defended himself heroically. We are prepared to repel such an attack in our own self-defense, the sooner the better. An educated man will not take the abuse that an ignorant one will."

The blacks in Marion retaliated with a boycott of white merchants that drove several out of business, and soon afterwards the Alabama legislature decided unanimously "that Lincoln school be relocated." It was specified that such a transfer would require five thousand dollars and enough land on which to locate, all to be obtained within six months, and "no place was to be selected against the wishes of the people of said place."

Jim Hale responded vigorously to the invitation and bent every effort to move the school from Marion to Montgomery. There was some minimal response from other cities, muted by whites who for the most part rejected the idea, or made fun of it. The *Mobile Register* suggested that the capital of the state, Montgomery, be chosen "where the colored students could learn the noble art of 'Shine em up, sir' by practicing on the feet of the legislators."

In Montgomery, Jim had the support of all the black ministers and their congregations, and the financial backing of Dr. Baldwin. When Jim gave money, Baldwin gave money, and when Jim gave land for a campus not far from my old home, Hazel Hedge on Carter Hill Road, Baldwin helped get the whole of John Brown Hill. This hill was a very big piece of land that was a bit larger, but in the same general location as the present campus of Alabama State University.

Emerging from the anonymity he had maintained in his political activities, Jim publicly assumed leadership of the drive to relocate Lincoln School in the state capital. He organized meetings and gave speeches, persuaded churches to take up special collections and hold ladies' fairs and bake sales to raise money. His family was, as usual, supportive. Countis Harris, a daughter of Charles O. Harris, played an active role.

Altogether, they met the six-month deadline, and the Lincoln School was moved to Montgomery and renamed the Alabama State Normal School for Colored Teachers and Students.* Countis Harris joined the faculty of the new school, which later became Alabama State University, and now enrolls about five thousand mostly black students.

When Countis married the physician son of Hershel Cashin, another forceful Negro leader in Alabama, two of the most politically and socially important Negro families in the South were joined. A generation later, another Harris daughter, Ruth,

* Much of this information on the State Normal School for Colored Students came from the testimony of historian Mills Thornton in the case *Knight v. State of Alabama,* November 5, 1990.

married Dr. Ralph Bunche, the Nobel laureate of United Nations fame. Meantime, Harris himself spent the last several decades of his life as postmaster of Montgomery, but it is probable that his appointment came from a Republican administration in Washington, as part of its political patronage.

The Patersons, who had come to Montgomery about the same time, were still living in the long shotgun house they had built at the edge of the campus when they arrived from Marion with the Lincoln School. They had also built a greenhouse and planted a vegetable garden, which proved useful when the legislature withdrew financing for a couple of years, and Will and Maggie kept the Normal School going with nine unpaid faculty members, by produce from their garden.*

From time to time, there was trouble with the Ku Klux Klan and other forces opposed to the existence of the black college in Montgomery, and on one occasion the new three-story administration building, which Will Paterson nostalgically called Tullibody Hall, was set afire. Another time Paterson awoke to find a straw scarecrow-like cross burning in the yard, with a note warning the "nigger lover" to get out of town or have his house burned down.

But he had friends. The next night Will Paterson sat on his front porch rocking, a book in his hand. He watched a group of Klansmen approach his house. Coming closer, the Klansmen saw four Confederate veterans also on the porch with their guns at the ready. The Klansmen never came back. Every year on the anniversary of the aborted attack the Patersons sent roses to the veterans, one of whom was an Arrington, according to a descendant, Bobby Arrington of Montgomery.

The nursery, now known as Rosemont Gardens, was still there when I grew up at Hazel Hedge down the road. I went there often to pick up plants and flowers bought by my mother for her garden.

Before Maggie Flack Paterson died of Bright's disease in 1904 she made a statement requesting that she be buried in the black section of Oakwood Cemetery.

When Anne left the plantation as Dr. Baldwin's nurse to join Jim Hale in his Washington Avenue house and have their own family of children, she took her dream of building a hospital for her own people with her. She must have asked Jim to build it. There is a letter from one of Dr. Baldwin's granddaughters, Etheldra Scoggins, reporting that "when Mammy Anne wanted Uncle Jim to build a hospital for the negro race, Uncle Jim would not part with his money."

Through the years, Anne did not give up. She was persistent and persuasive, and drew supporters along the way. One was Dr. Baldwin's son-in-law, Will Craik,

* Judith Paterson, *Sweet Mystery, A Book of Remembering* (Farrar, Strauss & Giroux).

who strongly believed in the need for a "public hospital that would provide patients, black and white—with better treatment, where there was supervised help and hygienic discipline."

In the *Montgomery Advertiser* he praised Anne's efforts: "Born a slave who long ago felt the true needs of her race were not in the support of a multitude of church organizations, whose aggregate cost is enormously out of proportion to the means of their numbers, but rather in a centralized philanthropy where physical suffering might be alleviated instead of mere emotional paroxysms fostered."

In the end, Jim Hale gave in. When he died he left his boarding house on Lake Street for a Negro hospital, with seven thousand dollars to renovate and equip it. Booker T. Washington had already urged the first black M.D. in Alabama, Dr. Cornelius Dorsett, to come to Montgomery. He married the Hales' daughter, Sarah, and became the first medical director of the hospital. Completed in 1889, the Hale Infirmary, a sixty-bed hospital, was dedicated to Jim and their two daughters, Sarah and Frances.

Hale Infirmary

Anne was nothing if not thorough. She had long ago arranged with a Northern hospital to bring trained nurses down not only to take care of patients, but to establish a training school for black nurses. The Infirmary continued to function for many years after the Catholic Sisters of Charity opened St. Margaret's hospital in Montgomery in 1903, with an adjacent building for Negro patients.

I remember that I was away at school in the 1930s when my grandmother, Jennie Baldwin Craik, who at seventy-four had been on the Board for thirty years, wrote me: "Did you know about my being chairman for the white people's drive for Hale Infirmary?" After that drive, the Infirmary continued for another decade or so until the building had so deteriorated it was abandoned and closed in about 1950.

Disillusioned by the failure of Reconstruction, Dr. Baldwin and most of the Hales left Montgomery. Dr. Baldwin moved to Baltimore, and most of the time his daughters were at boarding school in Philadelphia. The Hale families went about as far away as they could get—to upper New York State, Chicago and Texas. Only one of Jim's daughters, "Hattie" Davenport, and a grandson, Charles Morgan Harris, stayed behind with Jim and Anne until Jim died. Then they moved to Birmingham, where they established the Davenport & Harris Funeral Home, which celebrated its one hundredth anniversary in 1999.

Dr. Baldwin didn't stay long in Baltimore. He was very ill and soon left for New York City for medical treatment. He consulted with a well-known physician, Dr. Oliver Wendell Holmes. Just what he found out about his health we do not know, but we do know that from Dr. Holmes, he heard a lot about emancipation. Later, in the White Mountains, where he went for relief from acute hay fever, he got to know Henry Ward Beecher. Dr. Baldwin returned to Montgomery with some new ideas, and two new friends.

A few years later, when Beecher wrote that he had been asked to Montgomery to lecture on "The Inequities of Slavery," Dr. Baldwin invited him to stay at his home on South Perry Street. When his brother learned of the invitation he was outraged and said, "William, if Henry Ward Beecher passes over your threshold, I will never cross it again."

Dr. Baldwin answered that he was sorry he felt that way, but that Beecher had accepted and that he would be honored to have him in his home. Dr. Baldwin's granddaughter, Etheldra Scoggins, reported this in a letter, adding, "The day was saved by Mr. Beecher's manager who refused to let him stay in a private home. Uncle could still cross his brother's threshold."

Possibly it was the deep friendship that existed between Dr. Baldwin and Jim Hale that influenced the doctor's attitude towards race, or maybe it was that separation between the races just didn't make much sense to him as a pragmatist and a scientist. At any rate, their close relationship continued through their lifetimes.

When Jefferson Davis laid the cornerstone of the Confederate Memorial in Montgomery sometime after the Civil War, Jim Hale and his wife were among those who contributed: "We send you $5 for the Alabama soldier's monument in memory of Capt. W. O. Baldwin who fell with his regimental colors in his hands at the Battle of Franklin. We loved him from birth and know well that he loved us. James and Anne Hale."

Isidor Weil, in his eighties, courtesy An American Harvest, *Prentice-Hall, Inc., 1982.*

A similar friendship was formed after the Civil War between another successful white man, Isidor Weil, who had opened a drygoods store early in Opelika, and a freed Negro man, John Tarver. Isidor had hired Tarver in Opelika as a porter to go with him at harvest time by horse and buggy to collect the money owed to the store by the cotton farmers. Tarver would carry the money and Isidor would take the reins. If they were held up, Isidor reasoned, no one would think that a white man would trust a black man with cash. The time came when he would send Tarver out alone.

At the warehouse, Tarver was assigned to the sample room, where he was responsible for classing the cotton for grade and staple and clearing it for shipment. Although he managed the operation, he was still called a "porter" since a "head classer" supervised others, which in that time and place was "a white man's job."

One day a worker smoked in the lint-laden room, where piles of cotton are ever ready to flash. In a rage at Tarver's supposed failure of supervision, Isidor told him they could no longer work together. Tarver pushed back the painter's cap he was fond of wearing, scratched his head and said, "Mr. Isidor, I'se sorry to hear you're leaving. But I'se a fixture around here."

Tarver was over sixty when the sample room did catch fire. One man could be seen against the flames of a second-story window. Tarver rushed into the building and helped him out. "Are you crazy?" screamed Isidor. "I am old," John Tarver explained. "My children are grown. But he has a young wife and babies."

When the Weil business moved to Montgomery, Mister Isidor and John went together in the buggy carrying the money in a hand bag, while the rest of the Weils came by train. As a biographer for the Weils put it, "Isidor was the family's last pioneer. His horse and buggy symbolized the passing of an era."

William O. Baldwin died in 1886, and Jim Hale in 1888. Dr. Baldwin had co-signed with Jim for a lot for the Hales in Oakwood Cemetery not far from his own. And there they lie, these mammoth men of their times, friends who made a difference.

The Baldwins are in lot 26, surrounded by an iron fence and in the shade of a big magnolia tree; the Hales not far away in Lot 29. Between the two is an upright tombstone with clasped hands and the inscription, "Our Mother, Sallie Baldwin, 1809–1901."

Sallie Baldwin's tombstone.

8

Plantation Life and Death

D R. WILLIAM OWEN BALDWIN'S YOUNGEST BROTHER, PHILLIPS, DID not practice medicine but lived a somewhat sedentary life supervising his plantation in Union Springs, a small town forty-four miles southeast of Montgomery. Sedentary, that is, until a famous wedding that took his life. Phillips's daughter, a beautiful and popular girl also named Cecile, was engaged to be married to Walton Rainer, and plans were made for a big country wedding. Many friends and relatives from all over were invited.

Everyone was looking forward to the wedding feast. Turkeys, guinea hens, and chickens were slaughtered and cooked. Hams were boiled and baked. Salads and vegetables were prepared, some of which were brought on the day of the wedding by guests, since there were 'coolers' but no refrigeration. Dozens of biscuits, rolls, pastries, cakes, and gallons of punch were made ready.

The bride was in her wedding gown when her father suddenly became very ill. No one could understand the cause. A telegram was sent to Dr. W. O. Baldwin in Montgomery, who was rushed over on a special engine of the Western Alabama Railway. After arriving on the scene and examining his brother, Dr. Baldwin determined it was a case of poisoning. He suspected food poisoning. Phillips Baldwin, violently ill, could not recall for his brother what he had eaten or drunk. He died in the arms of his daughter. Dr. Baldwin ordered a pit dug and all the food buried and the punch thrown out. For my grandmother Jennie, who was there and wrote a letter about it, the tragedy of the death of a kinsman was compounded by the waste of all that food and drink.

The cause of Phillips Baldwin's death was later determined to be drinking from a silver water pitcher on the sideboard, which he had the habit of doing. This time, unfortunately, it contained arsenic, intended for him. It was suspected the pitcher was put there by his stepson, Wylie Turner, who presumably had refused to give up a Negro mistress he had on the place and had been horsewhipped by Phillips. My grandmother claimed she saw Wylie burn the towel Phillips vomited in.

Some say it was the Negro mistress who put the poison in the water pitcher, though it is conceded that this was extremely unlikely. Dr. Baldwin himself opined that it might have been one of Phillips's colored domestics. Another version was that Wylie thought his stepfather was cheating him out of his own father's inheritance. The family historian, Marion Augustus Baldwin III, wrote that the real problem was that the stepfather was interested in the same girl.

Wylie was apprehended but escaped while being taken away on the train. He was never caught, although the family seemed to know his whereabouts. When Dallas from California heard this story she asked, "Why didn't they pursue him?" I explained, "Not in Bullock County, unless it was a Negro suspected of murdering a white man."

That it was a Negro who had murdered the white planter was a version of the story used in the *Dictionary of Alabama Biography*, as handed down through Dr. Baldwin's granddaughter, Mildred Maxwell. She wrote in her memoirs that "Uncle Phil took a toddy just before the guests arrived. He became desperately ill and died as the guests gathered. It was thought to be from poison. His daughter, Cecile, was married by his coffin the next day. A colored man who had bought the poison was arrested. He jumped off a train while being taken to jail and was killed."

The story does not end there. Two generations later, when Dallas read in the *New York Times* about Frances Rainer, a white girl from a good Southern family, who had married Johnny Ford, the black mayor of nearby Tuskegee, Nick said, "Why, that's my cousin 'Taz.'" Dallas commented, "Everybody in the South seems to be related to everyone else in one way or the other."

Frances Baldwin Rainer, or "Taz," as she came to be called, was a direct descendant from the marriage of Cecile Baldwin and Walton Rainer. Born on the family plantation in the Black Belt near Union Springs, she played with little colored children as a child, and "threw a fit" when they were not invited to her birthday party. They later went to separate schools and saw very little of each other, but she remembered them warmly.

She went on to the state university and became a social worker. While in college she accompanied some of her sorority sisters to see the film *Guess Who's Coming to*

Dinner, in which Sidney Poitier plays a Negro who meets a California girl in Hawaii and becomes engaged to her. When they both return to California, he is invited to dinner by her liberal white parents, who did not know he was black. The groom's parents were also invited, and were surprised to learn their son was marrying a white girl. All four parents were very upset. However, the young couple was not deterred and went ahead with their plans.

Taz had been very much impressed with the film, as she was with Johnny Ford when she got to know him. Her first job was as a case worker in the welfare department of Tuskegee, Alabama, which was only twenty miles from her Union Springs plantation home. Johnny had been born and raised in Tuskegee, as the son of a custodian at the Tuskegee Institute, but had gone away after school and then worked for the Greater New York Council of Boy Scouts.

After that he became a top member of the campaign team for Robert Kennedy when he sought the Democratic nomination in 1968.

When Johnny and Taz decided to elope and get married, neither was aware of the legal implications: interracial marriage in Alabama was a felony. They were not prosecuted, however, and soon afterwards Alabama's miscegenation laws were declared unconstitutional.

According to Ray Jenkins, the reporter who wrote the story for the *New York Times*, and then a longer version for the *Alabama Journal*, the eventual reaction of some cousins and school acquaintances back in Union Springs, was, "Well, I wouldn't do it myself, but if that's what they want, that's fine with me." Some of the older people adopted the attitude of Tevye in *Fiddler on the Roof* who, when his daughter married a gentile, spoke of her as if she no longer existed.

The family was upset when they first knew about the wedding, but accepted it. One romantic old aunt commented that "it was just like a beautiful film she had just seen about Romeo and Juliet—only in black and white." Taz said, "When my mother got to know Johnny she came to love him. She learned just before she died that we were going to have a child and she was happy about it."

It was probably more difficult for the family of Johnny Ford, who explained, "I've had to educate my parents. They'd gone through life thinking all white folks were evil, growing up as they did in a strictly segregated society."

On our next trip to Montgomery, Dallas and I had lunch with the Fords in Tuskegee. I told Taz about my experience while teaching at Howard University, the predominantly Negro university in Washington, D.C. At one family reunion, an old cousin came up to me and said, "Oh, I'm so glad to see you looking so well. The way people spoke of you I was afraid you'd become an alcoholic like so many in the family. Then I found it was just that you were teaching at Howard. Nicky, I just want you to know that I'm on your side." I said to Taz, "I wanted to tell you that I'm on your side." Johnny and Taz's marriage lasted at least a decade before it ended.

Several years later when we were trying to track down the correct version of what happened that led to Phillips Baldwin's murder at Union Springs, we asked Taz, the "direct descendant," about it. She said she didn't really know. "Nobody in the family ever talked about it." It is said in the South that the blacks always know what whites, if any, they are related to, but the whites don't know because they don't want to know.

Family relationships are fuzzy. Someone not related, but close to the family, might be called "Cousin." Such was the case with Cousin Amelia and her husband, Colonel Norman Wynn, at Rosemont Plantation [not Rosemont Gardens]. The stories about their eccentricities were no doubt expanded and embellished over the years by my mother, Jean, who has been described as "the mistress of narrative embroidery."

Rosemont was only about twenty-five miles from Montgomery, just off a good highway to Demopolis, but it took Cousin Amelia and Uncle "Bum," as we called Norman, a long time to make the trip into town. The car, though not new, was perfectly good. The problem, according to Amelia, was Uncle Bum. He would tell you it was Amelia.

Uncle Bum was convinced that always driving on the right side of the road wore down the tires unevenly, so some of the time he drove on the left. He and Amelia would start off briskly enough driving on the right. After a couple of miles Uncle Bum would switch to the left without slowing down. "I wish you would drive on the right side today, Colonel Wynn," Amelia would say. (She always addressed him by his title and last name when upset.)

"I am in command of this vehicle," he would assert. Whereupon she said, "Stop the car, please, Colonel. I'll walk." So she would dismount and walk some distance behind the car, which would then move to the left side until the Colonel deemed it time to switch right again. The car would come to a halt, his wife would catch up and get in and they would proceed.

We had some very good picnics at Rosemont with Cousin Willey Gayle. Her mother was a Wynn. Mother would fix a big salad and a large thermos jug with hot crab gumbo. Father took along plenty of bourbon. During Prohibition, he generally carried a hip flask of his bootlegger's corn whiskey.

I remember one picnic in particular. Father had a flask of whiskey on his hip. Cousin Amelia followed him like a bird dog picking up a quail scent. He wasn't aware of this until mother stopped him, saying: "For Heaven's sake, Nash, give Amelia a drink." He poured her a stiff one.

Looking down at the fish pond from the veranda of the house at Rosemont one day, Cousin Amelia saw some men she did not recognize seated on the banks. She called the colored servant. "Jason, Jason!" Jason finally appeared. "Yassum," he responded. "Who are those gent'men down at the fish pond . . . I'm sure you know." "Yassum, I think they's friends of the Colonel."

"Friends of the Colonel?" repeated Amelia. "I don't recognize them." "I think somo'ems fom Birmingham, and they's all members of the Rosemont Huntin' an Fishin' Club," Jason said. Amelia ordered Jason to "go upstairs and get the .30-.30 from under my bed." "Under your bed?" asked Jason, temporizing. "Yes, you heard me, now hurry up!" Amelia commanded. Jason shuffled off as slowly as he thought he could get away with. No one had moved from the pond when he finally returned with the rifle.

Cousin Amelia carefully aimed the gun between two of the groups of men. Then she fired. The bullet whined and kicked up a little dust on the bank between the fishermen. Two of the men jumped up and looked around. Then she worked another cartridge into the chamber and pulled the trigger again. This time the dust came a little closer to the men so they scattered.

Stepping to the edge of the veranda and cupping her hands to her mouth, Cousin Amelia used what she liked to call "the country telephone." "The Rosemont Hunting and Fishing Club is herewith dissolved," she shouted. "Now you sons of bitches get the hell off this place."

9

The Romance of
Jennie Baldwin and Will Craik

T HE "FOUR SISTER HOUSES" ON PERRY STREET, BUILT BY JIM HALE FOR Dr. Baldwin's four daughters, had not been finished when the first of them to be married, Jean (known as Jennie), my grandmother, became Mrs. George William Craik on January 27, 1875. She was nineteen, he was thirty-three. He met her with her mother and sister, Mary, when they visited Blount Springs, a spa near Birmingham. Will Craik, who had come for the day from his job as paymaster of the Louisville & Nashville Railroad in Birmingham, admired her from a distance.

He recalled the meeting later in a letter to Jennie as one in which "you were surrounded by friends, and I imagined, suitors, who had every advantage for winning you; every circumstance was favorable to them, while I, an unknown stranger and mere watering place acquaintance, too bashful and proud to assert myself, stood aloof and risked losing my life's happiness."

Will originally was from Kentucky, one of eleven children of the Reverend James Craik, rector of Christ Episcopal Church in Louisville. As a young man the Reverend Craik had gone west from Washington City to take up lands on the Kanawha River in western Virginia that had been awarded his grandfather, Dr. James Craik, for military service with George Washington in the French and Indian Wars.

Dr. Craik named one son George Washington Craik, and in the next generation, George William would also have been called George Washington Craik, if his father had his way. His wife Juliet overruled him. "No, all the 'nigras' are naming their children George Washington. We will call him George William."

During the "War Between the States" the Reverend Mr. Craik was president of deputies of the Episcopal Church and as such was remembered many years later by the dean of the cathedral in Louisville as "a man of eminent stature who was instrumental in preventing the division of the Episcopal Church into two parts during that war."

Kentucky, a border state, was more Western than Southern and did not secede from the Union. Young George William, or "Will" as he was called, had been given a good education by his erudite father in Northern schools. He grew up in a Republican family without Southern prejudices. He had spent some of his summers in the far west, on a cattle ranch where he learned to milk cows and brand steers, and hunted buffalo and bears with William F. Cody, the legendary "Buffalo Bill."

When he got his job as paymaster of the Louisville & Nashville Railroad and moved to Birmingham, Alabama, he had to meet payrolls in Mobile and Montgomery. It wasn't long before he arranged longer and longer stopovers in Montgomery to see the Miss Baldwin he had met at Blount Springs.

Between times, they wrote letters, some of which have survived. In the very first one he asked for a date:

Dear Miss Baldwin,

If you have no other engagement may I claim the privilege of going with you to the entertainment at the Exchange [Hotel] on Friday evening? As it is my debut, I am naturally anxious that it should be under the most agreeable auspices, and can only promise myself any pleasure under your kindly protection. So please be indulgent and say that I may go with you.

The date evidently went well. When she heard he had been ill, she wrote him at his boarding house in Birmingham. He answered,

I received your letter and at once threw physic to the dogs. I was well in an hour. It was not the doctor stuff I needed but your delightful account of yourself in the mountains. [She was at her Uncle Ben's plantation near Verbena.]

I could picture the whole scene, with you at your rustic labours like the pretty French fan pictures we used to see, and the Dresden figures of shepherdesses. I understand it to be poetical license when you say "I ought to see you milk the cows." I'm afraid you are presuming a little on my ignorance. I milked cows on a ranch

Jeannie Baldwin Craik and George William Craik.

in the west, and my fingers ache even now when I think of learning to do it. I'll bet a hat full of peanuts you didn't draw a drop. With a hundred cows I used to make butter too, grinding a churn for a couple of hours with a copy of Shakespeare on my knee.

We do not know whether Jennie ever demonstrated her abilities with a cow, but we do know that Will pursued her with vigor. Deeply smitten, he wrote:

Why did I not see you this morning? Are you ill? How unhappy am I that I must leave without knowing. I was so agitated when I discovered you were not on the porch to wave goodbye as I passed. I cannot but think that you are dissatisfied with me. I have never known before that paralysis of expression, but my love overwhelms me, oppresses me and sometimes almost suffocates me.

With a coquette whom I should meet but once, I could make love brilliantly. To you I cannot play the lover, all tender words die upon my lips as utterly expressionless. The heart is too full and I appear in consequence as dull and stupid. You think me insensate and passionless because my feeling is so deep that it rushes all my faculties. I have no other consciousness than that delicious torture of being with you and believing at the same time that you cannot but think me a dull fool. Give me more time—when I grow accustomed to the happiness I will wear it more gaily. I am not by nature melancholy, but a man full of the life and hopes and energy that become my age, but all my energy has now but one objective—to make you my wife. Goodbye my love, my life, goodbye.

He wrote to explain why he wouldn't be at her nineteenth birthday party,

I thought it should be a purely family affair, the last of the sort. I have no doubt your father's enjoyment would be greater if he were not reminded that someone has dared to breach his family thus, and that the calamity he has so dreaded is about to happen. So, I will not come.

My dear love, it is after midnight and I only send you a line to tell you that my heart is with you all this blessed day . . . You are dreaming now, but you must learn to look the future squarely in the face; think of all the sacrifices you must make, leaving your pleasant home, your beautiful city, all your friends and associates, to come to a crude unpleasant little town (Birmingham) where the society is rude and uncultivated, is torn with jealousy and those petty quarrels that flourish so firmly in a small place where a number of people, strangers to each other, are thrown together without any knowledge of each other's antecedents.

Think of this and learn to look to him who must be to you all that can make your life happy—learn that love must be your only recompense for all you have abandoned, but be assured that a true love is the purest joy that can be vouchsafed to you on earth; that all your surroundings will seem pleasant when your heart's empire is given into the keeping of a husband who is worthy of you. I am writing this in a station crowded with men waiting for the train. The conditions are not favorable to writing a love letter, and I merely send you this because today is your 19th birthday and I want to be remembered in your happiness.

It was difficult for a young man and woman to spend much time alone together in those days, but Will devised a plan by which he would escort Jennie on a train trip she was making through Manchester, Tennessee, to Nashville, where she was to visit relatives.

I will take care of your trunks, bandboxes, satchels and reticules, your smelling salts, flowers and lunch basket, and receipt to your mother for receiving you in good order and promise to deliver you in good condition.

In Manchester, he feared he would miss her and thought of telegraphing to ask her to wait for him "but looked upon it as a sort of sacrilege to use your name over the wires." He needn't have worried. Manchester had no telegraph office. Will traveled over four railroad lines hoping to find her still there. "I hope I will not be as long en route as some of our letters are."

In one letter Jennie had some doubts about his background, asking why he did not fall in love and marry in Louisville where he knew everyone and their antecedents. He interpreted this as questioning his family background and answered that although he bore "the impress of a gentleman by birth and education," he realized these were not the only essentials for a good husband. "I am afraid that one of the essentials is to be rich, but it is the one essential without which I propose to make you a good husband." She agreed.

Finally he wrote to Dr. Baldwin telling him that he hoped to marry Jennie. He thought the answer quite favorable "not consenting, but asking me to visit his house, and promising to enquire into my character, and suggesting that I refer my suit to Mrs. Baldwin."

A few weeks later he was able to report,

> I had the pleasantest visit with your mama imaginable. I think she trusts me, has faith in me, and will speak to your father. However, I am waiting with dreadful anxiety to hear her sentence; my whole life's happiness depends on that dear lady.

He didn't have to wait long. Mrs. Baldwin wrote to tell him that she saw in him

> a sympathetic loving heart, a tender absorbing passionate love for my daughter. I pray you may find in her all that your heart calls for, but remember she is only mortal. "She has no angel's wings." Do not let her, with your indulgences, yield herself entirely to her own fantasies. She is a guileless child in the ways of the world—nothing to unlearn but much to learn. You can make her what you should have, a good wife—and to do that requires that you be a good husband, and in truth I believe you will be.

Will wrote Jennie,

> Now that we are betrothed and are one in soul I have not that wild painful happiness that racked me until Saturday night, but the sweetest peace that ever blessed a grateful heart. I can wish you no better, no more kindly fortune than that you are as happy—but how can you be when you have not you to love?

They had a quiet wedding, since the family was still in mourning for the death of Mrs. Baldwin's father, Judge Martin. The ceremony was performed in the parlor of Dr. Baldwin's house by the Reverend James Stringfellow, whom Will had known in Louisville before he came to Montgomery. Later on they were to have serious differences over civil rights for the Negro, with Will on the side of the Negro.

Dr. Baldwin gave the bride away, reluctantly. A few years later on the occasion of her twenty-second birthday, he wrote her,

> You know, my darling, I didn't like that husband of yours a bit when I first found out he wanted to marry you. I thought he would just spoil our fun by taking you away from us and didn't want to know anything about him. But since I've gotten to know him I like him first rate, I guess because he is your husband and good to you.
>
> Your mother knows I've always had a poor opinion, first of husbands, and second of sons-in-law. As to the first, I think men know how to be anything else better than they know how to be husbands, and as to the second I've sort of changed my mind, except that I would not like to give up the one I've got but still think one is enough in any family. Really, I'd rather have the other girls old maids than have four sons-in-law.

10

After the Wedding

FTER THE WEDDING, JENNIE VISITED THE CRAIKS IN LOUISVILLE, AND was described in a letter written years later by a cousin:

> I shall always remember her as being so young, full of vitality and brilliancy. She radiated wholesome fun and affectionate humor. At breakfast with intimate friends she wore a pretty blue robe, not a dress for she explained that she did not expect to see any but immediate family. She also wore a dainty little cap, saying that now she was married she could wear a cap. I shall never forget her meeting with grandmother who ran off the porch and down the path with outstretched arms. Jennie rushed into them exclaiming "Oh Mother, Mother."

Will and Jennie went to Birmingham to live first in a converted Louisville & Nashville box car on a railway siding and then in a boardinghouse. It was only when Jennie became pregnant that she considered going home to Montgomery to have her first child. Will was dispirited, and wrote her mother, "I am a little at loss over knowing what course to pursue, whether to run the risk of her becoming wearied here, or the equal misfortune of having her estranged from and independent of me, but whenever you say she should come, I will give her up resigned if not cheerful."

Not long afterwards Jennie's house on South Perry Street was ready, and at Dr. Baldwin's invitation, Will agreed to "stop over" permanently in Montgomery and take a job in the bank. The Louisville & Nashville Railroad was being reorganized and he thought he might be left out in changes to come. He saw no future for himself, and the present wasn't very stimulating. Only once was there much excitement—when he was held up by robbers between Louisville and Montgomery.

They threatened to shoot a ring off his finger, but he got it off first. He moved from Birmingham to Montgomery with little more than two buffalo robes and a shelf full of English classics.

The "four sister houses" on Perry Street were close together and quite narrow, since taxes were based on the width of the lot.

They had considerable depth, extending all the way back to an alley that led to a jointly used carriage house and barn. They were well built, with wooden pegs and mortise and tenon joints. They were Victorian in appearance, with gables, brackets and a gingerbread trim. Each house had a dozen or so rooms with shuttered windows and high ceilings to keep them cool in summer.

Jennie and her older sister, Mary, were the only two of the sisters who ever occupied their houses. Their brother, Marion Augustus, known as "Buddie Gus," lived in his house just behind them on Scott Street. He was known to be eccentric, spending most of his time reading the daily papers at a local gathering place and going to sleep on them, to the dismay of others who wanted to read them too. He chewed tobacco, and when Mary complained that "he never speaks when he passes me on the street," Jennie replied, "Well, he speaks to me—at least he nods

The "four sister houses" on Perry Street.

his head and spits."

It is possible that the powerful influence of their father, Dr. Baldwin (or "God-papa" as he was called in the family), had begun to wane by the time his three youngest, Cecile, Alma, and Abram Martin, grew up. The girls married and went to live out of state. Abram Martin, called Martin, became a banker, and when he married Miss Elizabeth Ewin of Nashville, he moved with her into a yellow brick mansion further out on Perry Street.

As a little boy I used to go to the bank with my father once in a while and Martin would invite me into his paneled office, reach into the humidor, and pull out a cigar, saying, "Have a cigar, Mr. Read." He knew I would only smell it, but he went through the ceremony of cutting off the end with the gold cigar cutter on his desk. It made me feel grown up and I still remember the delicious odor. He also gave me a ten dollar gold piece every Christmas.

Dr. Baldwin continued to live alone in the big house on South Perry Street after Mrs. Baldwin's death. He was still president of the bank, but more and more busied himself with home affairs—and with giving gratuitous advice to those in the family near enough to listen to him. Will Craik was vulnerable, working in the bank and living just a few blocks away.

Things came to a head in 1884 when, with the encouragement of Jennie, Will got away from it all and took a month vacation in England to visit the sites and scenes of his favorite books and authors. On his return, he was severely reprimanded by Dr. Baldwin, who was at that time visiting in New York. Will sent a bristling reply:

> I think that since your vacation time was for a third of a year and mine was barely five weeks, it wasn't kind of you to harbor such dreadful thoughts about my little trip. I was much amused, and could never quite determine from your letters whether you thought I had abandoned my wife or absconded from my creditors. It was quite plain you believed I had done one or both of these things, and your fear about the perils of the deep was only your delicate way of expressing to your daughter your apprehensions about her husband. He has come back, however—whether for good or evil is questionable—and his family and creditors both seem to enjoy his return.

Dr. Baldwin, still in New York, complained that he was suffering from depression of spirits. Will advised him that "the cure of this would seem to lie within yourself, for with your will power you might throw off the gloom that is merely the result of a morbid imagination." He ended his letter on a happier note, "We have your imported Jersey cow here. She has a male calf about a month old, and she is very thin, but I am satisfied we will build her up, and she will be quite well by the time you come home."

Will Craik had long wanted to move to the country, and most Sundays in good weather he would hitch up the buggy and go looking for land. Finally he found it on the Carter Hill Road, just beyond the city limits. He and Jennie withdrew some of their savings from the First National Bank and sold a few shares of Birmingham Realty stock to pay for twenty acres. Gradually they improved it, and eventually they hoped to move there.

Dr. Baldwin began to feel left out of things on Perry Street. He was no longer needed on a daily basis. He was distressed as the families of his old patients found new younger doctors. He traveled considerably, mostly to medical meetings. On one of his trips to an AMA meeting he stopped at his old alma mater, Transylvania University, where he was heralded after an interval of forty-six years as "the Great Physician of the South." But the euphoria didn't last. At home he was lonely.

He had never been a churchgoer, and it must have taken much soul searching to write to the pastor of his late wife, Mary Martin, on the anniversary of his marriage, December 7, 1898. His subject was the hereafter. Because there was a shortage of paper in the South after the Civil War, the four-page letter was hard to decipher, having been written horizontally in black ink, then turned on its side and written across the pages in red ink (the thoughtful act of a good administrator—to make for easier reading.) The letter read:

> For thirty-five years this day has been the occasion of rejoicing with my now sainted wife. This day returns to me again but alas to find her who gave life its charm and its sweetest memories, torn from my bosom never to return leaving me with a broken life and with no heart to live on alone in wretched hopelessness . . .
>
> Could I but ask her and receive from the grave her answer as to whom I should turn, it would be to you, her dear pastor.
>
> You have made Christianity beautiful even in my eyes. Indifferent as I have really been through the greater part of my life on the subject of religion, I would now like to be a Christian, and to "make her people my people, her God my God."
>
> Oh, if only I were a Christian with the Christian's hope of a reunion beyond the

grave, and could feel that I would meet her in another world, I could still struggle on with the heavy load which now crushes me to the earth.

But alas I feel that consolation and happiness will never be mine . . . I am frank to admit my skepticism. The constitution of my mind or my mode of thought has entailed upon me a load of unbelief in relation to many essential points in religion and Christianity, which I despair yet cannot overcome, and now that she has left me I fear that I shall drift on to the end of life as I began it.

Her perfect and spotless life and the silent but eloquent teachings of her own example were to me like droppings from the holiest sanctuary and did more to make me love and respect religion than all the books I have ever read and all the sermons I have ever listened to. Oh, who has enjoyed as I have the wise counsel, the sweet trustfulness and abiding love of a Christian wife and cherished the beauty of her pure, human and sinless life can fail to desire the anchorage of a spiritual faith and a Christian's hope of reunion in another world? To this end I shall still struggle . . . I trust you will remember me in your prayers.

Affectionately, your friend

W. O. Baldwin

11

The Four Little Girls

A T HOME ON 406 PERRY STREET, JENNIE AND WILL HAD FOUR LITTLE girls. The first one, born in 1877, was named Mary Martin after her grandmother, but as a baby she was such a darling that she was just called "Darling," which finally metamorphosed into "Darlie." The second was Juliet, "Judy." It was several years before the next one, Jennie, shortened to "Jean," was born in 1881. Soon after that came Cecile, who was nicknamed "Sheila" when her father, who on reading an Irish myth, discovered that "Sheila" was Celtic for Cecile so gave her that nickname. As the youngest, she was also called "Baby," then "Bini."

My mother, Jean, was called "U-Jean" for awhile, but that was just a joke. The lady next door asked Mrs. Craik about her "little boy" and when she explained she didn't have a little boy, said, "But I hear you calling Eugene."

The girls' clothes were marked on the inside with stars—one star for Darlie, who was the oldest, two for Judy, three for Jean and four for Sheila. A star was added every time a dress was passed to the next in line. There was a washer-woman who called them by their numbers. Sheila was "Four Star," the last.

The Perry Street houses were close to downtown Montgomery, with the Capitol only a few blocks away. One of the attractions for Will Craik, when he left the Louisville & Nashville Railway for the job in the bank, was that he would be able to walk to work and come home for lunch. He loved his wife and his little girls and wanted to be with them as much as possible. It was a close-knit family. Will was home every night for dinner, and as the girls grew up, he talked to them about literature and the theater, history, and current events. He read aloud from the English classics, and was a regular reviewer of books and plays in the local press.

Although it was the state capital, Montgomery was still quite undeveloped when Jean was a young girl. As a school girl in the 1890s, she described it as follows:

> The sidewalks were of hard dirt bordered with water oak trees that sent their roots across, making walking difficult, especially for Blind Bob, who sold ice cream candy that didn't taste like candy and wouldn't melt in your mouth, but had a nice name.
>
> The houses along Dexter Avenue were walled in, to separate them from passers-by. The walls were of uneven heights, some high some low. It was on the tops of these that the children chose to maneuver their way rather than use the sidewalk. Some sat cautiously on the high walls and dangled their feet as they descended slowly.

The more adventurous, including Jean, who was something of a show-off, slid down or leapt from level to level.

Every household had its sidewalk swept every morning, and Jean got to know everyone's house girl. "Some of them were so nice," Jean told. "[They'd say] 'Good mawnin' pet.' 'Howdy honey.' 'You sho do look sweet.' 'Ain't she pretty?' 'Come into this yard chile, yo petticoat is showin'. You'll jes disgrace yoself.'"

In the course of a week of sliding down walls, Jean's hands got pretty rough. Every Saturday night they were scrubbed vigorously by Mama (pronounced with an accent on the last "a," similarly to the nursery rhyme "Kiss Papa and kiss Mama and bid them all good night"). It was bath time when the long tin tub with heated water was brought into the bedroom.

"It was fun sliding down the sides until Mama painted them with white enamel to look like porcelain. But the summer heat blistered the paint and made it smell like Noah's Ark, and when the paint came off in little ridges it wasn't as pleasant as it used to be.

"In the water the palms of Mama's hands were pink with little blue veins, and she wore a wide gold band on her finger and above it a small diamond set very deep in little gold claws. What wonderful hands ladies have. Mine were grimy from jumping into the brick gutters that divide the walls to get dandelions. Mama rubbed them with vaseline. I guess there was no honey and almond cream then. The towels were laid over the fire fender to get warm."

After the Saturday night bathing ritual, the little family was bright and shining when it made its way down Perry Street the next morning to go to St. John's

The Craik sisters, from left to right: Mary Martin ("Darlie"), Juliet ("Judy"), Jean, and Cecile ("Sheila").

Episcopal Church. Few details about the church, its parishioners, and where they lived seem to have escaped Jean's notice. She later observed:

> The window just above our pew was in memory of the Phelans, who were great churchgoers. The bishop always stayed with them when he came to town. The window was in two panels, Hope and Charity, I think. Hope is leaning on something, probably a cross but in my childhood I thought it was a lawn mower, and that it didn't do much good to be an angel if you had to cut the grass.
>
> Most of the best houses were down near the church. I thought the most beautiful one across Perry Street was an Italian villa with a square tower, balconies and iron grillwork, occupied by the Freemans. For awhile, my Sunday school teacher, Miss Williams, lived there. She was very young and so beautiful with the most golden hair I ever saw. Everyone said she washed it every Saturday in champagne. She called me "her little ewe lamb." In my mind I called her Rapunzel and hoped that someday she would let down her hair.
>
> Next door to the church was the Hollinquist house. Mr. Hollinquist, who was

known as "the Count" and considered the "catch of the day," never did a lick of work. His wife was a stunningly beautiful woman who never lost her gaiety and zest, although she supported the family, as many southern ladies of that time did, by boarding several young bachelors and childless couples. She encouraged all of them to go to church, and during the sermon you could hear the turning of the ice cream freezer on her back porch as the cook got ready for Sunday dinner.

In that same neighborhood, on the corner of Jefferson and Hull, was Mr. Joel White's handsome house. Mr. White, as I remember him, looked a little like Gladstone, with long white hair. He had a remarkable book store, including some rare volumes. Collectors knew his shop well and he frequently sent books to England. His daughter married a Semple, but she always called herself Sahmple with a broad Virginia "A". She made the most delicious cordial of rose geranium leaves steeped in pure alcohol, then syrup poured on and bottled for some time. She served it to callers. Ladies in those days made calls in the morning and were given a little refreshment.

The Beals lived in that same general part of town on the corner of McDonough and Monroe. There was a porch running all around the house with the most beautiful short-stemmed, deliciously perfumed Marechal Niel Roses over it. Mr. Martin Baldwin of the bank always wore one in his buttonhole, when they were blooming.

Behind the church was the Pollard mansion on Jefferson Street, which before my day was like the castle of medieval times to the cathedral. I faintly recollect Col. Pollard, who was a warden, leading Mrs. Pollard down the aisle. She had become blind early in her married life at the birth of one of her children. After Sunday school we all went to Dr. Baldwin's big house further up Perry Street to wait for our parents coming from the regular service.

Close to the Pollards lived two women, Mary Anne Taylor and her daughter Jessie James. Mary Anne, who looked like somebody out of Dickens, played the harp with very dirty hands, and talked all the time, quoting British poets. She had married Mr. Taylor thinking he was from South Carolina. It was when he had fried chicken and jelly for breakfast instead of broiled chicken and marmalade, that she found he was from North Carolina and they parted.

One Sunday it was either Mary Anne or Jessie who did an unheard of thing in church. She heard a calliope passing, which meant that the circus had arrived in town, and she left during the litany to see the parade. She came back after the sermon to report that there were only seven elephants in the entourage, though eighteen had been promised.

Jean recalled the pageantry of Easter observances in vivid, colorful detail.

The Easter celebrations of my childhood still seem thrilling to me. It was like the children's crusade, when we marched down Perry Street in our lovely frocks and big Leghorn hats carrying banners to the doors of the church. Many of the banners were hand-painted cherub heads on silk with gold fringe, and some were inscribed "Suffer little children to come unto me."

There was a larger banner with a yellow crown on royal purple with a yellow fringe and tassels, carried by the child who had the best lessons, attendance and behavior in Sunday school. In 1890 I was awarded an edition of *Through the Looking Glass* for lessons and attendance, but I never got to carry the banner, which was as great an honor as leading the German at the Joie de Vivre club when you made your debut. There was no dancing at the Joie de Vivre Club during Lent, which was strictly observed at St. John's.

No church members ever went to the theater during Lent, not even Dr. Michael, who loved the theater better than anything except St. John's. He always carried a gold cane in front of him like a mace, and sat in the front pew of the church and the front row of the Montgomery Theater, and never missed a service or a performance. People used to tease him because as a doctor he was called out of church constantly, but never seemed to have a call during a performance of Edwin Booth or Madame Modjeska or Mademoiselle Rhea.

The greatest pleasure with Easter was going in surreys, buggies and wagons to Scott's Bend in the river to pick wild lilies. The choir went too, in a big wagon. We picked bushels of lilies and they were put in foot-tubs of water to be transferred to the church. It was also a custom for people to make garlands for the gas standard lights between the pews. They didn't have to be alike. Some made them of coral honeysuckle, some of white memorial roses, some of wild crab apple. I remember a lovely one of chinaberry blossoms.

Flowers and candles for the altar were the responsibility of old Mrs. Wylie, who had been shrouded in black crepe veils forever, it seemed. Like so many ladies at St. John's, she had gone into mourning on the death of some loved one and never came

St. John's Parish, Montgomery, Alabama, courtesy Department of Archives and History.

out. I was among her helpers. We received little gold crosses engraved with "The Altar Ten. St. John's Church" to hang on chains around our necks.

Most of the above was published in *The Life of St. John's Parish*, put together by Mattie Wood, for the hundredth anniversary of St. John's Church in 1955. In other reminiscences, Jean reflected on the anticipation and anxiety with which she approached her first boy-girl party.

We wore Kate Greenaway dresses made from Liberty cotton that came from Europe, and the ladies said, "Don't they look darlin." I remember when we went to our first party with boys. But we had to wear union suits except in summer, and although Mama safety-pinned the tops to hide them, Sheila's safety pins showed at the back and mine did too.

Papa took us to the party and when we got there we could hear a piano playing "Little Sally Walker Sitting in the Sun." How excited we were. Was that a polka or a Scottish, and do you start with your right foot or left? A hack drew in at the gate and a boy and girl got out together. A shiver ran up my spine. "Are you cold, Jeanie?" Papa asked. "No, I just got a tingling in my tail". I didn't try to explain how awful it was just to be there, and finally let go of papa's hand to go in the door.

Inside all the girls stood in one corner and the boys you had played leapfrog with stood across the room. A partly grown girl named "Pen" for Penelope who had come from Baltimore, and for whom the party was given, had a red accordion-pleated skirt and red slippers and stockings, and long ribbons on her cap. She did the skirt dance, flinging yards and yards of skirt wide out into the air like flames leaping and ducking. Nobody wanted to dance with me.

Once a very beautiful cousin whom we all loved dearly came to stay with us on her wedding trip, and I asked her very solemnly whether she had married for love or money, and when she answered, saying "For money," I burst into tears and cried, "I can never love you again. I don't want to see you again."

All of us had learned to read very early. We didn't stay long with *Diddy, Dumps and Tot*, that southern reliable about three little girls growing up on a plantation, but were soon into *Alice in Wonderland* and Dickens. We also learned to recite. Sheila could quote "The quality of mercy is not strained . . ." and "Parting is such sweet sorrow . . ." and she knew Mary Stuart's "Farewell to France" in French. When she was very little we had a French girl living with us who spoke no English.

There was a little iron trivet in the fireplace where a black pot always stayed to keep the water warm. We called this the footman. When Papa had a bad cold Mama would say "Darlin, let me make you a hot drink, and Jean and Sheila, run and get a lemon and some cloves and the loaf sugar." Then she would add whisky. Papa would give us each a teaspoonful or two and Mama always said, "Will, don't give those children that whisky."

Papa used to read to us at night, and tell us stories from history. I remember how terrible I felt when I first heard of Joan of Arc's fate. Papa walked me in his arms and sat by my bed and told me how long ago it was, and how that would never happen now. But I would go to sleep and then wake up again and feel the flames, which I didn't mind as much as the foresakeness of the young maid.

He read Dickens and Thackeray and Tennyson to us too, but most of all Shakespeare, and he called me his Cordelia. Then Mama would call from the front porch "Will, it is time those children went to sleep." How could Cordelia bear to have him leave?

12

The Craiks and Kanawha

ONE ADVANTAGE OF WILL CRAIK'S JOB WITH THE LOUISVILLE & Nashville Railroad was that it allowed him and his family to travel free. He would often take his wife and daughters to Kentucky to visit "Kanawha," the modest country home of his father, the Reverend James Craik, in Louisville.

It was a very unpretentious house, about three miles from town, built by the Reverend Craik around 1850, and occupied by the Craiks and their eleven children for most of twenty-five years. The children's lives were enriched by a fine library of books, as well as by many people of importance who stopped over at Kanawha for a night or two if they got as far west as central Kentucky.

Many of the books came from the Reverend Craik's father, George Washington Craik, who had acquired them in Philadelphia, when he served as one of the secretaries of President Washington during his second term of office there.

The Reverend Craik had been brought up in Washington and across the Potomac River in Alexandria, and had many stories to tell of the early days. When he was fifteen, he experienced the triumphal return of General Lafayette, the French statesman whose support for the American revolution had brought him to America, where in 1777 the Continental Congress made him a major general. While being escorted through Alexandria, Lafayette had the procession stopped so as to meet the namesake of his old comrade-at-arms, the wartime surgeon general Dr. James Craik.

Grandson James studied law, and socialized in Washington with late-night parties and early morning swims in the Potomac, with John Quincy Adams, among others. He had become a barrister by the time he married Juliet Shrewsbury, from Charleston in western Virginia, and built a house on land acquired by his grandfather for his participation in the French and Indian wars. After he left Charleston, their house was bought by George S. Patton, a colonel in the Confederate army, and grandfather of General George S. Patton of World War II fame. It is now on the National Historic Register as the Craik-Patton House in Charleston, West Virginia

James had practiced law until, in the course of an argument with Catholic theologians over church dogma, he became so interested in religion that he studied for the ministry and became the fourth rector of St. John's Episcopal church in Charleston. In 1844, he was called to Christ Church in Louisville. In our dining room at home we had an enormous oil painting of him with a beard that hung down to his waist. We later gave the portrait to the Craik-Patton House

Being a daughter of the civilized state of western Virginia, his wife Juliet did not look forward to life "on the Kentucky frontier, where all the men chewed tobacco and the women took snuff." However, she went along with her husband on horseback over the five hundred miles of rough roads and trails from Charleston to Louisville. Juliet was eight months pregnant with their ninth child, riding the forty miles a day side-saddle. Their eight children, household goods, and the fine library of

Reverend James Craik

books inherited from George Washington Craik, followed them in a wagon.

They called their new home Kanawha, after the river that ran by their earlier Charleston house. They planted fruit trees, built a barn for animals, and kept poultry. They were fairly self-sustaining, in part because James needed to stretch his income to support his large family.

I loved to hear my mother, Jean, tell about the trips to Kanawha. "We would go on the slightest provocation," she would begin. "Papa had his pass from the Pullman Company. He would say to Mama, 'I got a letter from mother, Jen. She said the snowdrops are in bloom and the lilacs.' I think it's time for us to go." He would take us out of school for two weeks and we would be on our way.

Then mother described the train trip from

Montgomery to Louisville. It lasted overnight and part of the next day. She remembered the sleeping car porter, Paul.

He was always glad to see us. "Here are my two little girls," he would say. There was a kitchenette at the end of the car where Paul taught us how to slice the bread. Sheila and I just took over.

We didn't go all the way into Louisville. We got off at Crescent Hill, which the train reached about ten in the morning. This was about a mile from Kanawha. We would sniff the air. One would say: "I smell Crusoe," and the other would agree. Grandmother had a very bad smelling old dog named Crusoe. Of course we were too far away to really smell him, but we imagined we could. The family station wagon would meet the train and pick us up. It was just like our station wagons today, only horse-drawn. We approached the house on a tanbark drive.

I asked Jeanie what the house looked like at Kanawha. She said:

It was a lovely house, built right flat on the ground, only two stories. How we all fit in I will never know. We had a lot of cousins, and some of them were always there. Of course there were several beds in every bedroom. There was a field of corn planted on one side and a field of grain—oats or barley or wheat—on the other with a wide lawn in front. They raised cattle and had horses. Behind the house was the barn and the carriage house.

The *pièce de résistance* was a golden coach. Inside was all upholstered in puce-colored silk, and the fittings were ivory. It was a fairy tale coach just like Cinderella's. It was drawn by two rather inferior horses. Every Sunday the family rode in it to church in Louisville. It came into the family by way of a member of the Gouverneur Morris family in Philadelphia who married one of the Craik daughters.

There was a butcher who delivered meat to the house, huge pieces of beef for roasting, juicy and tender. He would bring us children strings of wieners. But on Sunday it was always chicken, raised on the place. Uncle Sam was sort of the manager, after the death of the Reverend Craik in 1882, and he tried to manage us.

He was sort of fussy. I remember one night when one of the girls came in sort of late and he was just giving her the devil. Grandmother, who always wore a nightcap, stuck her head out of her door and interrupted him with, "For heaven's sake, Sam, weren't you ever young?"

Going to the outhouse after family prayers was one of the rituals of Kanawha. We had a swinging lantern like those used by railway men to light the way. The second sit-downers had to wait for the first sit-downers. While we waited I drew pictures on the wall of the shadows cast by the lantern. The bathtubs, to be taken to the bedrooms later, were hung on the side of the house. There was also a grape arbor. To reach the grapes, someone held my legs as I reached out the window.

The family trips to Kanawha were less frequent after Mr. Craik left the Louisville & Nashville Railroad and went to work for his father-in-law's First National Bank. As the girls grew older, they went together or alone. They came to know the city of Louisville well, going to concerts and museums—and to shop. Jean wrote home:

Minnie Craik Kilvert, George William Craik's sister.

I went to the Fall Exhibition of the Louisville Art League and spent the whole afternoon. Some of the pictures were perfectly beautiful. "Baby" [Sheila] joined me there and it was only twenty-five cents admission. I went shopping and bought a new suit. It is lined with Roman striped silk and was marked $25, but the owner said I could have it for twenty-three. He wouldn't go any lower until Aunt Fanny came in and said he ought to let me have it for $19, and after a long time he agreed.

I am taking drawing lessons. I took my first one this morning. I have a terrible time getting there. It is between Brownsborough and Chatsworth—the old Speed place. When I spoke of walking, Uncle Sam insisted upon my riding. He didn't like it a bit that I kept the horse hitched all the time I was inside drawing, and after that I had to walk.

Baby and I went mushroom hunting this morning and almost froze and didn't get any mushrooms. Mr. Speed came this afternoon and brought us a book of Kentucky poems and the *Merry Adventures of Robin Hood* by Howard Pyle, which looks to be very nice.

This was evidently young Buckner Speed, who in 1899 married Jean's older sister, Darlie.

In a dozen years many of the trees and bushes and plants around Kanawha were gone. One of Will's sisters, always referred to as "Minnie C.," who lived abroad with her husband, Max Kilvert, came back to Louisville in 1910 after a long absence and visited the old place. She wrote Jean what had happened to it.

I arrived in April in the midst of a late snowstorm, but not heavy enough to hide the dogwood blossoms and the little May apples, and I am filling my eyes and nostrils with the beauties of a Kentucky spring.

I knelt and kissed the ground of sacred memories, and touched lovingly many familiar trees and shrubs, but couldn't go in the house without breaking up. In a few weeks it is to be torn down, having been sold for $350, to be succeeded by a magnificent structure nearly 200 feet long on an English plan. There is to be a formal avenue in from the road of white crushed stone bordered by a stiff line of cedars, filling in that lovely dimple in the land.

The Blue Bells and Buttercups and Columbines that grew under the horse chestnuts are all gone, every one. And the quarry is planted in foolish conventional things instead of the ferns and wood flowers that were so charming there. The rich people in Louisville are quite mad about country homes built after the English fashion, which I think is very stupid in this smiling land of rippling hills and dimpled dales.

Will Craik never went back again.

13

Hazel Hedge Is Not a Hedge

IN MONTGOMERY, JENNIE AND WILL WENT BY BUGGY ALMOST EVERY weekend to their piece of land out on the Carter Hill Road to improve it. Will put in pecan trees and grafted them to bear bigger and better nuts. He brought cuttings and seeds from Kanawha, and planted a hedge of Hazelnut bushes around the property, which gave the place the name of Hazel Hedge. Unfortunately the bushes didn't thrive in the prairie soil. They were later replaced by rose bushes, but they didn't make it either.

Will found that only hardy plants like bamboo, yucca, and Osage orange would grow in the heavy clay soil. The latter bore a large green fruit resembling an orange. Farmers planted these trees at the edge of their fields using the trunks as fence posts since the wood never seemed to rot. They believed the "mock oranges" to be poisonous to humans, but they fed them to cattle, which ate them without apparent harm.

Mr. Craik built a brown shingle house close by an old existing well, and added a windmill to get more water for his garden. It made a pleasant squeaking noise. At a convenient distance was a three-holer outhouse, and not far from that a carbide plant which made the carbide gas that originally lit the house. The plant is remembered as smelling worse than the privy.

The four girls, Darlie, Judy, Jean, and Sheila, were in their teens when the family moved to Hazel Hedge from downtown in 1898. It was a different world. There were no neighbors within a half mile or so, and only a few small Negro shacks. The only regular visitors were farmers with produce, calling, "Get your butter beans, fresh peas, young onions, collards, nice dewberries." The Craiks didn't have to buy very much. Hazel Hedge, like Kanawha, was almost self-sufficient.

*Top: Farmers with
produce.
Bottom: Milkmaid.*

There were fruit trees and a vegetable garden, chickens, and milk cows. With the latter they started a small dairy. Judy was in charge, and eventually tended twelve milk cows. Several were Jerseys, and gave a rich cream. A light-skinned young Negro woman, Ellen Dickinson, did the milking, and made butter balls. Later on she was trained by Jennie to be the family cook, and as the senior servant came to be known as "Mammy Ellen."

Mammy Ellen presided over all the family birthdays, where the gifts were usually accompanied by verses. She enclosed one with her own present when she gave "Old Miss," as she called Jennie, a grater: "I give you this, my dear old miss. It's a very good grater, in fact a first rater."

The new milk maid, Peggy, had a drinking problem, but dismissed it with "I never gets drunk. I just takes my jug and goes to bed." Another helper was a yard man named Sam, who was agreeable but hard to understand because of his stutter. Asked how he was feeling, he would always answer "Jus tolabl, th-thank you, th-ank you. How you and all yo folks?"

All the girls had pets. Darlie, the eldest, had Pegoty, a mocking bird with only one leg, so tame it would eat from her hand. Eventually she wrote a children's book about him. She first saw him one fall day on the bough of a crooked pear tree near the *pôrte-cochére* by the front door. At first she thought his leg was pulled up under his wing. Then she realized there was only a stub, and stopped to talk baby talk to him as she went in and out of the house, as if he were a small handicapped child. He wasn't afraid, but he didn't sing.

It wasn't long before Pegoty moved from the pear tree to a new perch on the balcony of her room upstairs, and into a box where Darlie put cracker crumbs and grits. From there, during the awful blizzard of 1899, he moved into her room. In the early spring, he left the balcony for the woods, but not for long.

When she was sick in bed for a week he came back to the balcony and sang his heart out to her in trills and rich melodious whistling until she got well. By summer, he had built his own nest in a tree by the front porch, where Darlie watched a romance blossom and a young family grow.

Jean had a water spaniel named Kinky. She still talked about him when I was a little boy. I would ask, "Do you love me as much as Kinky yet?" and she would say, "Not quite yet." How I hated that dog. Judy's fox terrier was called Jack Hotfoot. He was a great ratter and it was in pursuit of a rat that he met his sad end. It was some time after his mysterious disappearance that his skeleton was found stuck between the beams inside the walls of the dairy barn.

Together, the youngest girls, Jean and Sheila, had a billy goat with long white hair and brass knobs on the ends of his horns, and a harness for pulling a little wagon. His name was Pep. One day in late February the weather turned very warm and to relieve Pep's discomfort they cut off his long hair. Then the weather turned cold again, so they made him a suit of newspapers and burlap and put him in a stall. The next morning to their dismay they found him there pink and shivering without his suit. He had eaten the paper.

On weekdays the girls went downtown to school. It was about four miles, and to get there they used the streetcar, which came out as far as the Forest Avenue Elementary School, near Hazel Hedge.

This "Toonerville Trolley" had two wheels in front and two in back with a motorman and conductor between.

When it rained hard, the unpaved road beneath the trolley would get soggy and the trolley would be derailed. For such emergencies the car carried a big jack, which was used by the motorman and conductor to lift it and work it back onto the track.

Then, in 1886, this tram became one of the first, if not *the* first, electric streetcar in the country. One wheel was connected by a steel cable to a power line overhead. Because people were afraid that they might be electrocuted, the first few runs were made at night so there would be no witnesses to any mishap.

Regular passenger service on "The Lightning Route," as it was called, only lasted about two years. One night the power house burned down and the town went back to mule-drawn cars. It was quite a few years before the electric streetcar was running again, this time as the Montgomery and Cloverdale Electric Street Railway, reorganized by the ex-railroad man, Will Craik.

Jean and Sheila took it most of the way to Girls High School at Lawrence and

Jean and Sheila

High Streets, quite close to where they had lived on South Perry. It was the first public high school for girls in Montgomery. Miss Eliza Bullock was the principal, described by Jean as

> very small, in rustic black clothes, stern, but fair, with a twinkle in her eye in spite of herself. She was a devoted Episcopalian, and the psalms she read every morning in general assembly room are the only ones that I know by heart.

We memorized numerous poems. "The Battle of Ivy" by Macauley was a favorite, as were Lord Byron's "Night Before the Battle of Waterloo" and Tennyson's "Charge of the Light Brigade." It was important that we knew the names of the authors. Now, children don't even read poems, let alone memorize them.

I remember when we were at the springs in Mt. Vale, where my mother was recuperating from an illness by "taking the waters." Before the dancing began in the so-called ballroom and we children were sent off to bed, a very elegant gentleman always recited a poem. He announced it himself, "'The Bridge of Sighs,' by request." I said in a loud whisper, "I thought it was by Hood."

Annie Mae Dimmick was one of our instructors. She had just returned from four years at Wellesley College, the first "college girl" we had ever known. My own special teacher was Miss Minnie Anderson, a very pathetic character. She had a tragic love affair and never recovered. We couldn't read a line of Tennyson that Miss Anderson didn't turn crimson and tremble. She was very Victorian. If she saw one of us pulling at a skirt or sticking in the tail of a shirt waist she would say, "You may retire into the cloakroom and adjust your habiliments."

The great event of high school was the award of the Baldwin Medal, a gold medal given by Dr. William Baldwin, who was for many years the head of Montgomery's school board. It was given for spelling, English grammar and composition. Only a senior could win the medal, but we all had to work for it and the lower grades were awarded books as prizes. In my junior year I won Tennyson's *Princess,* Miss Anderson almost blushed herself to death over the love lyrics.

Jean was one of the "Altar Ten" at St. John's church, and from Hazel Hedge had to get up at five o'clock to go in with the milk wagon to put clean altar linen on for the 11 o'clock service. Before anybody came, she had her own private service singing aloud all of the Canticles and Jubilates and Te Deums just as if there had been a full vested choir.

In the fall of 1899, a spectacular Montgomery Street Fair was held in the town square. Jean wrote about it on a lined pad, as if she were going to turn it in at school.

The girls went tearing down after school to find the place transformed. Instead of the cotton wagons with their sleepy drivers and sleepier mules, there was a town brilliant in color, animated, jocund, full of new life. All the streets were ablaze with purple and gold, the chosen colors for the festival.

There were numerous little decorated booths selling popcorn and cider and peanuts. When one thinks of it there was really almost nothing to see, a dozen or so booths in which were displayed rather commonplace wares, a few platforms for the exhibition of the usual tall man, and fat lady and a chubby armed fat boy who made me feel very uncomfortable since several of my friends had advised me to pay him a visit since they noticed a strong resemblance, but he had the advantage by several pounds.

By noon the spirit of the fair was fully upon us, the swirling crowds surged and rushed in full volume, pausing here and there in great eddies and breaking into laughing groups filled with merriment and revelry. There was a snowstorm of confetti that brought about a common feeling of mirth and good fellowship with flakes scattered into old ladies gray heads or crushed into balls and hurled at the open mouths of laughing girls. No one dreamed of getting angry. One girl hurled handfuls of colored paper at Mr. Floyd, before whom she quaked and trembled in the school room, since he was author of our final examinations.

The parade passed down Dexter Avenue. Glass's Laundry and other companies had floats, and there was a horseless carriage, and a fire engine bedecked with tissue paper. Wallace, the untamable lion, as fierce today as when captured in the wilds of Africa, a dear little pony named Dandy, and Zeno the trapeze performer were all there. The high diver gave the greatest performance, coming down 85 feet in a long easy flight and landing gracefully in a little tub of water.

I never felt so patriotic in my life as when the flag bearer was shot down and another gallant young soldier seized the standard and unfurled the stars and stripes in the breeze. Finally there was the crowning of a queen, and thus ended the week-long Montgomery Street Fair.

Most of the time the family stayed at home. There was much to be done with household chores, taking care of the animals and gardening. Except for church-related activities, they spent the evenings together. When there were guests, they often played charades, but not when Bill Cody and his markswoman Annie Oakley came for dinner—it was too exciting! Will had shot buffalo and bear in the west

The Craik girls   with "Buffalo Bill."

When the family was alone, they read aloud. Dickens was a favorite of Jean's, and when she was eighteen her father gave her all of Dickens's novels in twenty-nine small red, leather-covered volumes. We still have them.

The books were probably responsible for making her socially conscious. She wrote a paper reviewing them all, concluding: "I think Dickens's reforms and ideas are not by any means obsolete. The very conditions that he sought so earnestly to ameliorate are now being changed in just the way he dreamed of having it done."

She got her love of the theater from her father, who often took her with him when he was writing reviews for the *Montgomery Advertiser*. About a musical, *Zo*, he wrote: "The chorus sang indifferently, danced a few jigs and went through the inanities of the play without a plot, with as much spirit as could be expected, in situations as absurd as they were uncalled for."

He did not always limit his reviews to the plays.

He suggested to management that they should so arrange egress "that the swarming crowds should not be brought into so close contact with the audience from the parquette and dress circle. There is a very positive difference paid to avoid the necessity of the two classes sitting together, and it is fair to presume that they do not care to stand together for the five or ten minutes required to leave the theater."

Despite this manifestation of snobbishness, by 1896 he was reading *Nation* magazine (subscribed to by his daughter Darlie) as well as *Scribners* and *Harpers,* which consistently published articles expressing egalitarian views. He also was beginning to contribute substantive pieces and "Letters to the Editor" on economics and current events.

As a banker, he read *The New York Journal of Commerce.* Although a Republican, he wrote a long letter to the Alabama legislature approving efforts by the Democratic National Committee to limit the issue of currency to that based on the credit of the federal government, thus eliminating bank notes issued by state banks.

He visited Washington, D.C., calling at the White House to pay his respects to President Theodore Roosevelt, for whom he had considerable admiration. In an interview on his return he reported that his "most vivid impression was of Roosevelt's surprise and sorrow at the antagonism of the Southern people towards him personally."

Two days after his reelection, Roosevelt had proclaimed as one of his first objectives to "see the South back in communion with the rest of the nation." That he didn't achieve this may have been due in part to the fact that he invited Booker T. Washington to dinner at the White House, an event that was widely reported and criticized in the Southern press.

The *Washington Post* referred to Mr. Craik's visit, describing him this way: "A Republican by conviction who has voted the national ticket for many years, he has never held or sought an office, nor taken the smallest part in southern politics, but is simply a well-born gentleman, highly connected and highly placed, enjoying the confidence and esteem of the best people in Alabama, Kentucky and other southern states. He believes in the principles inherited from Alexander Hamilton and the Federalist organization."

Such public notice elicited a move to persuade Roosevelt to appoint Mr. Craik to a post in his administration, possibly as ambassador to Mexico, but nothing came of this.

The governor of Alabama wrote, "My dear Mr. Craik, I congratulate you on the example you have set, because in these days of money-getting, it is refreshing to see one who puts other things above it."

For non-gardening exercise, Will Craik took up golf, forming one of the earliest golf clubs in the country. He helped lay out the course on land near Hazel Hedge, further out on the Carter Hill Road near the Montgomery Tennis Club, which soon became the Montgomery Tennis and Golf Club, and eventually the Country Club.

Will Craik was indeed Montgomery's Renaissance man, who, long before "women's suffrage," encouraged his four daughters to think for themselves. He gave them this challenge: "Live your own lives, and while you should always be considerate of others, do not allow yourself to become morbid about your duties, either great or small. Refined and educated people living under stress of poverty need not lose self-respect nor become embittered."

14

The Reverend
Edgar Gardner Murphy

AFTER MOVING TO HAZEL HEDGE, THE FAMILY WENT BY BUGGY INTO town every Sunday to attend St. John's Episcopal Church. A dynamic new rector, the Reverend Edgar Gardner Murphy, made his initial appearance in the pulpit on January 1, 1899.

In the next three years, he had a great influence on the Craiks, as well as in the town and in the state. He spent Monday nights at Hazel Hedge as a sort of rest and change at the end of each week, and discussed social issues and books with Mr. Craik.

Jean and Sheila, in their older teens, were avid listeners. Many years later, Jean recorded her remembrances of him for *The Life of St. John's Parish*, a history of St. John's Episcopal Church from 1834 to 1955. She wrote,

> Mr. Murphy meant so much in my young life that I find it almost impossible to write about him.
>
> His work for the reform of the Child Labor Laws in the state is well known. He was certainly ahead of his time and greatly misunderstood in his attitude toward race relations. He helped found the Church of the Good Shepherd for negroes and often preached there in a building erected for them on South Jackson Street. At that time Montgomery was 50 percent negro. He was a friend and admirer of Booker T. Washington, and completely fearless, and advocated suffrage for the colored people.

The Reverend Mr. Murphy did not mince words. In the *Montgomery Advertiser*, on July 12th in 1901, he attacked a report from an official Committee on Suffrage, calling it

> a medley of obscuration, befustication and fraud, anticipated by an audience relapsed into the diversions of the tinkling tumbler and the revolving fan, under the spell of genuine beverages and artificial breezes.
>
> Equally anxious are the decent negro who has never voted, but who ought to vote, the white man who has always voted, but who ought never to vote. There is one man, at least, who seems thoroughly satisfied. He is the man who has always cast not only his own vote, but the votes of all his negroes (living and dead).

Through his friendship with Andrew Carnegie, Mr. Murphy secured fifty thousand dollars to buy and improve the Dr. W. O. Baldwin house for the Y.M.C.A. At the church he organized women parishioners into the Guild of Christian Service to assist West End Neighborhood House, which benefitted underprivileged children.

Reverend Murphy

He was also instrumental in organizing the men into a study group, the Nebulous Club, which explored a wide range of historical subjects. Mr. Craik read papers on Alexander Hamilton and Lord Nelson, and was Secretary of the club. He was still using Nebulous Club letterhead as late as 1907, shortly before he died.

Jean Read remembered that

> the Rev. Murphy formed a little poetry society, which met at the Rectory. I can hear him reading "Dover Beach" now, and from William Ernest Henley we all became "the masters of our fates and the captains of our souls." What evenings of delight these were to Sheila and me, and to Olive MacDonald, Janet Hurter and Fanny Marks. He opened our eyes to painting. For the Sunday School he introduced the postcard-size Perry pictures of great paintings, which he adapted to the Church Year to illustrate the stories of the Gospels. We had boxes of them, and even the

boys collected them in the way they later collected pictures of baseball players.

This was long before the Weil brothers moved their cotton business to Montgomery along with their fine collection of original paintings by Degas, Pisarro, Renoir, and Winslow Homer, which were hung on the walls of their modest offices. They even had a Rodin sculpture.

    I don't think the Reverend Murphy was what a congregation would call a good pastor. He didn't like parochial visiting and was rather impatient of the pettiness of a parish. At vestry meetings when the senior warden, Mr. Michel, spoke overlong, Rev. Murphy would intone, "Be brief, Mr. Michel, be brief."

    On Monday nights at Hazel Hedge, besides reading us the latest Stephen Phillips, or Christopher Fry, or T. S. Elliot, he would recite Mr. Dooley, which he did delightfully, being a bit Irish himself. We used to play a limerick game in which each person would write a line and the concluding line. He and my father talked far into the night, but before we went to bed we would sit on the lawn and look at the stars. In those days he loved them but didn't know them as well as Papa did.

    One night he said, "When I have time I shall take up the study of the stars." I remember my father said later, "Yes, and he will know so much more than I dream of." After he retired he did take up astronomy and wrote *A Beginner's Star Book*, under the pseudonym of Kelvin McKready.

He was much concerned about the poor quality of education in the South, for most whites as well as blacks, and was determined to do something about it. With philanthropic aid from the Peabody Foundation in Boston and well-to-do individuals, he established the Southern Education Board to improve the schools.

    An early project was the Evergreen School, sometimes referred to as the "Fleahop School," for poor white children, at Verbena in Chilton County. It was near Kintry, the plantation of Jean's cousin, Benjamin Baldwin, who made arrangements to have the school there. At the suggestion of the Reverend Murphy, Jean was persuaded to teach. She received fifty dollars a month.

    Her board and room cost nothing, since she stayed with the Baldwins. She was not the only one who stayed there. The big house was always filled with relatives and friends. The dining room table, which was almost as long as the room, was presided over by her cousin Benjamin, who merged saying grace with serving. At least Jean reported that you couldn't hear the "amen" for the "white meat or dark."

The first week, only fourteen students enrolled in the school, but the second week there were seventy-six. Then, twenty others—who were chopping cotton when school began—applied, but the school was too crowded to take them. The students ranged in age from seven to twenty-two, but their ages had little to do with grade levels. They were fitted together by reading levels. "A big boy grumbled because I put him in a second reader in which he was almost unable to read a single sentence. When I reminded him of that fact, he said, 'No'm, I can't read in the second, but I kin read ev'ry word in the third good.'"

Everyone tried hard. Two of the little boys got up at four o'clock each morning and worked at home after sundown to do their chores before and after school. One girl of thirteen cooked all the daily meals, morning and night, for a family of nine. Most walked from two to five miles each day in order to be present.

There were two teachers for the one-room country school, so in the beginning Jean taught her class under a tree.

My equipment consisted of a chart, a clock, and a large sun hat. Behind us hung dinner buckets from every limb. We used pine cones for adding and subtracting, and spelled everything we saw. We could hear the pupils inside doing their lessons, since in the country schools everyone studied out loud.

Then a neighboring church opened its doors and most of the older children went there, kneeling on the floor and using the pews as desks. My class moved into the school where I had a table for my flowers and books, with a chair facing straight rows of benches for the students. We also had a blackboard, and an old bucket for a trash basket. One of the boys brought me a well-trimmed white oak stick for a pointer and I had a tin pan of water for the children to wash their grimy hands and faces in.

Water came from a well outside, and there was an outhouse. From time to time someone would come in to tell me that "the Patterson boys done spit in the bucket ag'in." I got pretty thirsty. I shall never forget the first Friday that everyone came prepared to speak on something they had learned during the week. The girls had on freshly starched Sunday dresses—and shoes. A number were limping when they arrived. I spent the first twenty minutes untying hard knots, unlacing shoe strings and pulling off sandy stockings. By the time they recited they were bare-footed as usual.

One day when Jean was invited home by one of her pupils for supper, she found herself in a one-room shack with shutters but no window screens. Sitting around the table, with a kerosene lamp in the center, it was hard to see what she was eating. When she asked for some of the chicken hash, the boy's mother said, "That ain't chicken hash, honey, tha's just some moths that got into the butter."

The school year ended with a graduation ceremony to which all the students and their parents were invited. There was a program, and a photograph was taken of Jean standing under the tree where she first taught, with all the children in the branches. It is of interest that about the same time, Dallas's mother, who was teaching in a one-room country school in California, had a year-end picture taken below a tree loaded with pupils as well.

In Verbena, every child was given a present—some rings and silver trinkets from Jean and Sheila's childhood, some dolls dressed by Mama, bangle bracelets and charms from Kress's, and baseball gloves and balls and bats for the boys. There were refreshments from Uncle Ben, twenty gallons of ice cream and hundreds of little cakes.

As Jean described the scene, "Mama and the Rev. Murphy sat under a canopy, and we had music—a guitar and a banjo. I had a white dress for the occasion and wept joyfully during the whole performance. It took me days and days to get rested, as the Commencement was really a nervous strain and took a lot of work, but it was so fine and the children did so well."

Jean stayed on at her Uncle Ben's for a vacation. She wrote: "I ride through the woods, with the yellow sunlight filtering through the pale green branches and shining on the clear brown streams and the slender silver trunks of innumerable little beeches. Yesterday, at 5 o'clock in the morning over smooth blazed trails, the horses seemed to glide over the soft brown carpet of pine needles, and down to the creek bottom with the damp woodland odor I love. It gives me little thrills just to draw in the good smell of it."

She wrote a report on "Some Experiences in Teaching in a Rural School," which she delivered at a conference for school improvement. It was printed in full in the *Montgomery Advertiser* and was recommended as reading by the Alabama Federation of Women's Clubs "since it possesses all the charm of an impromptu talk, and goes right to the heart of the reader just as it came direct from the heart of the writer. No one will doubt Miss Craik's warm interest in every individual in that country school. Let every club order several additional copies of this issue and put them into the hands of men and women so that they can feel the needs of the rural schools as they are so tellingly presented by Miss Craik."

Jean was not the only family member to react to the Reverend Murphy's suggestion that they do what they could to teach others. He greatly influenced her younger sister Sheila to be a writer.

In 1903 Sheila, with a friend, Mary Fitzpatrick, started a magazine called *Tattle*, published twice a month. It was something of a gossip sheet, but with a high moral purpose, and cost 10 cents an issue.

The introduction was in verse:

> Piddle paddle, piddle paddle
> See the women, how they walk,
> Tittle tattle, tittle tattle,
> Hear the women, how they talk.

Their banner proclaimed: "Ours to Mark the Manners of the Town." Issue No. 10, in January of 1904, recorded "hot indignation at the non-enforcement of the anti-spitting ordinance, which was passed some years ago to abate an intolerable nuisance, but which has been a dead letter to this day."

A promotion gimmick offered Chirographic Fortunes: "*Tattle* will publish fortunes in order upon receipt of your Christian name in your handwriting on baby blue note paper. Gessatta will unfold your future. Gessatta never makes mistakes."

Their "office" was a table next door to a press room, "where the printer, who was often drunk, would call out, 'Copy please—more copy,' and the typesetter insisted on setting any poems that didn't rhyme, without capitals and in one line because in his opinion it wasn't poetry."

Writing one's opinion was easy, but getting enough copy to fill the fortnightly publication proved difficult. The other sisters were called upon to help. Sheila asked Darlie for permission to use one of her poems anonymously. "It could pass for Mr. Gilbert or Dr. Baker and I will never tell."

The pressures mounted, and Sheila admitted to "awful revulsions of feeling when the very name of something you have been vitally interested in brings on physical nausea."

The Reverend Murphy's influence on the family did not cease when he left

Montgomery. He urged Sheila, then the ex-publisher of *Tattle*, to go to St. Agnes School in Albany, New York, to take special training so that she could teach others. He wrote, "I long to put your hands on the tools of progress."

At St. Agnes, Sheila took Italian with a view to visiting Italy some day. She wrote Jean, "My lessons are going along beautifully. I can now ask for 'stewed beef' and say 'I love my father and my mother after God,' with which interesting filial sentiments I hope to edify all Italy. I have a lesson every night and study every day so I really ought to have enough to be of some little use to us when we get there."

The girls' mother, Jennie Baldwin Craik, had a project that lasted all her life. Mr. Murphy had suggested to that devoutly religious woman that she teach some of the old black friends who came to pray with her to read and write. She started with Aunt Haddy. After saying each letter of the alphabet, Aunt Haddy was supposed to use it to start a quote from the Bible. The lesson would go like this:

> Jennie: "A, Aunt Haddy."
> Aunt Haddy: "Praise the Lord."
> Jennie: "B, Aunt Haddy."
> Aunt Haddy: "Bless your heart."
> Jennie: "C, Aunt Haddy."
> Aunt Haddy: "Ain't it the truth."

Aunt Haddy never failed to respond through the whole alphabet, but seldom gave a quote from the Bible.

15

Growing Up and Away

WILL CRAIK'S PASS ON THE LOUISVILLE & NASHVILLE RAILROAD could be used by any member of his immediate family. The pass, honored by any participating line in the nation's burgeoning rail system, provided more choices of destinations than most major holders of frequent-flyer miles in the 1990s. Now that the girls were older he felt they should get to know other parts of the country, and go even further than his passes would take them.

He apparently reached this conclusion while traveling by boat from Savannah to New York and wrote Sheila from aboard the steamship *City of Augusta:* "I feel that this trip is defrauding you, since I long ago determined that I had all of travel that I was entitled to, and that you girls should have what formerly came to me. I am rejoiced to think that now you and Jean can travel alone, and enjoy together all the pleasures and benefits of seeing as much of the world as opportunity offers."

Sheila only went as far as Kanawha on her first trip. Her father wrote her there: "I know it's your Mama's privilege to write the first letter to our absent girls, but she happens to be in bed for the day, so the pleasant task devolves on me. Your mama had to send for the doctor this morning, and he gave her morphine, so she is much relieved at this writing . . ."

Jean went to Bridgeport, Connecticut, where she wrote her mother on her 16th birthday in 1897. "I received Papa's beautiful birthday letter and I shall answer it by coming home. It made me feel quite sad. I haven't said good bye to my childhood. I do not want to. I am sorry I am growing up. I fully realize what a happy life I have had, what little trouble I know and the thought of its inevitable coming sometimes appalls me. But you know the thought of you and Papa and the girls and my childhood will help make me good all of my life—even if I live to be ninety."

On the way home, she stopped in New York City and while she was there, she described an excursion to the Bronx, as

> crossing the beautiful, picturesque little river, where I stood on the bridge and watched a real Hopkinson Smith picture with feathery, silver willows fringing one bank and great mottled sycamores bending over the other.
>
> We followed the winding river a little way and came out at a station of the New York, New Haven and Hartford line called Bedford Park. We took the train back, and passed the most beautiful old gardens and cottages covered with grape vines, glistening in the falling rain, and beds of flowers such as tiger-lilies and phlox and crimson geraniums, and blue bells. I was quite frantic.
>
> We walked up Fifth Avenue from Grand Central Station and went into the Cathedral, and deciphered the Latin mottoes under the college crests at the University Club . . . I have just gotten three spots of ink on my white duck skirt, do you think I can get it off with ink eradicator when I get home? I am dreadfully sorry.

Jean and Sheila went together to Hampden, Virginia, where they visited Hampden Sydney College, which my grandfather and namesake, Nicholas Cabell Read, had attended before he left to join Lee's army and fight in the Civil War. While there they attended a service at a local Negro church. Jean was much affected:

> I am so thrilled and inspired. Tell Judy not to rail. I am not a Yankee yet, but the spirit that surrounded the wonderful chapel service moved me deeply. I can't talk about it, I simply choke. I was so impressed, as it was the most calm, solemn, beautiful thing. All of the old plantation songs, just as if we were at Macedonia (a Negro country church near Montgomery) but none of the hysteria, none of that effervescent religion and what's more, none of that smell. 800 splendid voices, truly praising God and giving thanks. 800 intelligent, interesting, happy faces, but modest, clean, neatly dressed, well-drilled and not in the slightest degree "biggity."
>
> They are not simply educating themselves but are learning all this to pass on to greater numbers of their race. The whole old question of slavery, all the years of discussion and strife and ill feeling came . . .

The last pages of this letter are missing; however, a letter written that same year by Mr. Craik, noted that "Jean seems to be making a study of the colored race and their characteristics."

In Birmingham, where she visited family friends, the husband wrote, "At luncheon Jean led the conversation on the subject of Negro folklore and customs and habits and was asked to sing some of their songs. She knew a lot and sang them all to the intense delight of all there. Afterwards she was begged to come to Lake George to perform."

At home in Montgomery, she sang and acted whenever she had an audience, and soon had more audiences than she could comfortably handle. She had expanded her repertoire to include a large number of old English ballads, one of her favorites being:

> Mrs. Lofty has a carriage, So have I.
> She has dappled grays to draw her, none have I.
> She's no prouder of her fine coachman than am I
> Of my blue-eyed laughing baby trundling by.
> I hide his face lest she should see
> My cherub boy and envy me.
> Mrs. Lofty has her jewels, So have I.
> She wears hers upon her bosom, Inside I.
> Her's will go with her to the grave when she dies.
> I will take mine with me to the skies.
> She has those who love her station, none have I.
> I have one true heart beside me, glad am I.
> Her fine husband has white fingers, mine has not.
> He can give his wife a palace, mine a cot.
> He comes home beneath the starlight, ne'er cares she.
> Mine comes in the purple twilight, kisses me.
> And then the difference God will define
> Tween Mrs. Lofty's wealth and mine.
> Her's will go with her to the grave when she dies.
> I will take mine with me to the skies.

Darlie's trips were usually to Kanawha on her own, for a special reason. She had met a young man there, Buckner Speed. The Speeds were an old Louisville family. Buckner's great grandfather was a friend of Lincoln's and served in his cabinet. He had met Lincoln as a young lawyer who had come to Louisville on a case and rented a room in the Speed home. If anything, this connection with Lincoln made Buckner Speed more acceptable to Jennie and Will Craik, and it rather appealed to Darlie. They became engaged. Many preparations were made for the wedding. With her mother and sisters, Darlie worked on her trousseau.

Sixteen-year-old Jean read aloud to them as they sewed. The novel, *Richard Carvel*, was a gripping one, set in Revolutionary War times, at one point focusing on the naval hero John Paul Jones, with some mention of Arbigland, the Craik's ancestral estate in Scotland where John Paul was born. Jean wrote a letter to the author, a popular American writer named Winston Churchill. Since he was a distinguished novelist, she wanted it to be a good letter and did several drafts.

These were found glued inside the hard covers of the crumbling 1899 edition of the book. In her rough draft she said that "at one time we thought of naming this place Arbigland instead of Hazel Hedge, but I think that sounds a little too grand for our pretty little croft." This was omitted from the final draft, possibly because no one else had thought of naming the place Arbigland. It was her own idea to make her letter more interesting. The author responded: "I have had hundreds of letters since the book was published, but I think I can truthfully say that none gave me such a keen pleasure as your vivid letter. I think you have marked literary ability."

Jean's letter to him had read:

I know that to the author of a great book who has received the congratulations of scholars and wits and statesmen, an opinion from a very young girl is of little value, but this is to tell you how I loved Richard and how I hate his enemies. When we came to the part about the great riding match in Hyde Park, Darlie's fingers were so wet she couldn't pull her needle through, and Sheila and Judy both squealed from sheer excitement.

I had been reading so long & so fast that my throat was quite dry and Mama had to take the book. At lunchtime we were in the midst of the duel fought in the forest at Vauxhall and we didn't dream of putting it aside, so Mama and I took turn about. When Papa came in he found us all breathless and we stopped to tell him the story.

My sisters have forbidden me to open the book and see how it ends but I can't think of everyday mortals until I know. Many times I have taken the history of John

Paul Jones from the shelf in a bookcase that belonged to General Washington at my grandfather's home in Kentucky.

I have always known he was the son of a poor gardener on my ancestor Craik's estate of Arbigland in Scotland, but it was such a surprise to find it all written out in your novel. I was very proud and read it over twice, and Sheila and Judy cried out, "That's us!" I marked the margin of this page with a very hard pencil though Darlie told me not to.

It was such a disappointment when Richard Carvel and John Paul walked towards the gardener's humble little cottage and met an old gentleman in black. I knew it was Mr. Craik and bristled when Mr. Craik passed John Paul with his head in the air, refusing to recognize him. Did the old gentleman really do this? I hope you just made that up for I have always had great respect for my ancestor.

Mr. Churchill's answer confirmed her suspicions. Mr. Craik didn't really do that, but the author added it, knowing that John Paul was snubbed by the townsfolk when he returned to Arbigland on a visit to his gardener father; the rumor was that he had been responsible for the death of another young man from Arbigland who had gone to sea on a merchant ship under his command, and been brutally punished, which led to his death.

The book was finished and the trousseau completed, and Darlie became the first of the sisters from Hazel Hedge to be married. She and Buckner moved to Arizona where Buckner was a civil engineer for the Southern Pacific railroad. Darlie came back to Hazel Hedge for the summer.

Her father wrote a friend, "She has grown to be a broader-minded woman, quite free from prejudices, and is able to go with her husband where his business takes him. She has slept in section houses and boxcars and gone across a hundred miles to a mining compound, and is thrown with Indians and Mexicans and Chinese."

The Speeds soon left Arizona and moved to Berkeley, in the San Francisco Bay area, where Buckner invented an eighteen-inch pipe that could carry oil and water at the same time, keeping them separate. It made both him and the Southern Pacific quite a bit of money. Then he tackled the problem encountered by ferry boats traveling through dense fogs across the Bay, and soon they all had Buckner's fog lights penetrating the gloom.

Before Darlie had her first baby, her mother went to Berkeley to be with her. Will missed Jennie terribly.

Now that you are there brings home to me the desolating and depressing knowledge that for all the weeks to come our own home is to be without its soul and inspiration. It is not that the sweetest girls in the world do not look after my comfort and happiness; but it is not physical or material things for which I hunger, but for the companionship of her who has become my own very life.

There has been no quarter hour of the day that I do not catch myself wondering why you have not come out of the house, for of course, I have not been indoors since I ate my breakfast, and read the paper. First taking the cows to the vetch; then padding around the pasture and over the new golf links; then cutting away the crepe myrtle and many other useless and inane things.

Will sent almost daily letters. "Jean has taken up a new passion—the West End settlement work. She goes there every day, loaded with milk and bread and cakes. I have purchased a new cow named Countess to replace Amanda, handsomer in every way. Judy, who still runs the dairy, says she is just crazy about her."

After the baby, William Craik Speed, was born, Jean went to Berkeley to help her sister Darlie, and Jennie came home. Will continued to send letters west, but now they were to his daughter:

"I finished yesterday a happy and enduring work, having received a huge box of shrubs, and with the help of old Joe from the Country Club, put them out in my own famous way. There were a number of broad leafed evergreens and many deciduous plants, beside a live oak, a magnolia, a mountain laurel, and a holly. But with every plant I wished for my sympathetic helper. I am enclosing two dollars, and your mama sends one dollar."

His garden was a labor of love, his job at the bank something to be endured: "Alas, on Labor Day I labored, not at sowing turnip seed, which is the highest form of pleasure, but at the drudgery of the bank, where we have become so enamoured of building up the business that our holidays are cut down to about the observance of Christmas and the 4th of July."

In Berkeley, the Speeds got a Chinese servant, and Jean took a class at the University of California from Charles Gayley, the head of the English Department, who had married a Montgomery girl. His textbook, *Gayley's Classic Myths*, became famous and was kept by my bed as a child, along with the Bible. Jean read the myths to me, and my grandmother read the Bible.

16

Jean Falls in Love

J EAN, WHO LOVED ENGLISH LITERATURE BETTER THAN ALMOST ANY-
thing, met one of Professor Gayley's younger colleagues, Martin Flaherty,
who had co-authored *Poetry of the People* with him. On the flyleaf of the copy
he gave Jean was written, "We have gathered here a posie of other men's flowers,
and only the thread that binds them is our own. M. C. Flaherty."

Dr. Flaherty invited her to audit one of his classes. She agreed and attended,
but was disappointed that it was on composition rather than literature. She wrote
him a short letter protesting.

He answered on official university stationery in December 1903:

> I received your jolly little note this morning. You are a bad girl to laugh at me and
> merge my identity with "parallel construction" and other unmentionables. Besides
> you have broken Faculty Rule No. 8293, which reads: "And should any student
> poke fun at any member of this august faculty, said student shall immediately be
> summoned before the Academic Senate and shall then"—Well, I forget the rest of it
> but I know it's very dreadful. You will find it on page 713 of the Regulations three
> lines from the bottom.
>
> Yesterday morning one of the questions in the exam was "Write a formal accep-
> tance of an invitation to dinner." Please don't tell me that you've forgotten your half
> promise about our dinner in San Francisco? And you didn't tell me in your note what
> evenings you are at home. But that won't save you since I mean to call anyhow.

He did call and they saw each other often during the seven months she was in
Berkeley. She left in the middle of July. They never met again. We do not know

why. At thirty-one, he was a young professor at the bottom of the academic ladder, not making much money. Perhaps he thought of her as having a schoolgirl "crush" on him.

All we know is revealed in their letters over the years. Many of hers were pencilled drafts of letters she wrote but possibly did not send. At least, there was a note on top of the drafts to the effect that "I've come upstairs to collect all of the letters I've written. I hardly know what they say. You'll have to give up college for a week to read them."

What they tell us was that Jean was in love with him then and for many years afterwards—possibly for all her life. His letters to her, which came for the next thirty years, were somewhat reserved, and usually marked important times in her life and his—when her father died; when Flaherty left Berkeley for Tucson, Arizona; when she married; when I was born; when he retired; and finally when, at the age of sixty-one, he married.

Only the first one, to thank her for a picture she sent him in 1908 before she left on a long-planned trip to Europe with her sister Sheila and a friend, gave any clues as to their parting. He wrote:

> Dear Little Girl, I have no words to tell you how much I thank you. Perhaps you know without my telling, and I would rather leave it so. And the note you took the time to write in the hurry of your going was all very dear and sweet and very characteristic of you. And though in writing this I may seem to have turned aside from the path marked out for me, it is just to acknowledge freely and very inadequately, the gracious thing you did.
>
> Good bye, sweet Jean. Life holds many beautiful things in store for you, and yet none so beautiful that it should not be a thousand times more so, did it come within the power of my wishing. As ever, M.C.F.

She sent him a letter from Europe.

> I am sometimes so apart from the talk of French and French literature and the things that absorb my sister and our friends that I smile and think how little they really know, not having known you. I have known a hundred things from you—St. Francis of Assisi, Lamb, Carlyle, Mathew Arnold, Newman—and times and places. Sometimes when I hear their discussions I think how much more you know, and

want to react the way I used to at school when I'd tell my teachers, "My Father wouldn't agree with that," and discuss it no further.

She had evidently hoped that he would come to Italy that summer, and when he didn't arrive she wrote:

> I had planned to get up very early and have breakfast with you when the garden was dripping and cool and the valley was gray with mists, and peel your figs myself and make your coffee on the spirit lamp. It's very silly of you not to want to know our villa—it's the loveliest in Italy—but you aren't coming. I was too confident.
>
> I know that now, as I have really known all summer, that you were right and that we will never see each other again, but the threads that you have woven into my life you cannot pull out, and the pattern is there, a very small one as regards space, but it quite dominates the whole, a most exquisite one like those in the Gobelin tapestries. They will never fade, and when I am quite old and solid and fat and untidy there will still be that beautiful patch of perfect workmanship in one corner of my life.

Martin Flaherty

After she returned from Europe she wrote again:

> It is taking more courage than you know to write this, but it wouldn't be right not to tell you. I have grown up at last. I am not a "little girl" any longer. Remember that horrid time when you teasingly said "I couldn't really love you, at least only as a little girl, not as a woman." I've been trying to be just what you wanted. I am of course myself, mostly, but now I am a woman.
>
> You are like no one I have ever known. I am grateful to you not only because in knowing you I was saved from madness and mistakes that would have made my life wretchedly unhappy. You were the first person that opened my eyes. I tried quite pathetically to change myself—but I am such a stupid person that it takes long drilling & practice and beginning all over again & being trained. You only gave me a few suggestions.
>
> Do you know you are the only person I have ever

been suppressed or reserved with? I was so afraid that you would find out, would discover me and realize how little I knew. I think I almost helped you to, by my fear of it. I was always in a panic about it, and wanted you to know before you were sorry . . .

After her father's death in 1908 she suffered from painful neuralgia. While she was ill with terrible headaches and lying in bed with a bandage over her eyes, she thought a great deal about Martin Flaherty, and tried to analyze his feelings towards her. "He held me very lightly indeed and he's made me count myself as less than a moth, a moth that can be blown from one's hand after it has died against the light."

This did not end her deep fondness for him. Four years later, on July 14, the anniversary of one of the last times she saw him, she wrote:

> I waked today at 6 o'clock, just as I used to on my birthdays. Now it is the best anniversary of the year except the 16th, and I always begin to count the days until it comes. Then, I looked for my presents at the side of the bed—the books I wanted most from Daddy—and although there was nothing there today I was quite happy listening to the mockingbird and watching the long shapes of yellow light on the lawn and the sparkling dew, and thinking about how it would be, going to the City tonight for dinner with you.
>
> Instead, you will sit on the terrace and watch the lights go on across the bay in your beloved San Francisco and over in the City there won't be even a ghost of a memory of us at our table. I always pretend that you remember me these two days and that you will take out my picture and look at it. It's the most agreeable delusion I permit myself.
>
> July 16th. It's afternoon—five o'clock, the time to move from our seat in Piedmont Park near the street, and the grass sprinkler, and the children, and the ladies embroidering, and go from the hydrangea bushes by the little footpath along the canyon and sit on the bench under a palm—a wonderful magical bench that changed the whole, whole world.
>
> I remember it was there I told you that I was like a cake where the icing had been picked off but that the cake was all there for you to eat. Only you just nibbled and backed off—and now I've scattered all the crumbs to the few persistent birds that haven't flown away.

Back in the Berkeley days, her sister Sheila was the only one she told about Martin Flaherty. We do not have Jean's letter, but we do have the answer she received from Sheila: "You've got your face turned west, and your dear heart turned to some new land of promise full of peace and happiness where you may not look back. This time you must listen. Remember you are entering a new phase of your life and must determine what lies in yourself to make it happy."

Her father knew something had happened to lift her spirits. Before she left home she had been depressed. He said:

> Your last letters have made me very happy, for I think I see in them the return of your old buoyancy. I well understand what Darlie means when she says they are just crazy about you. So am I dearest, and I know you better than any of them.
>
> They know you as a charming, high-spirited, beautiful, entertaining girl. I know you as that and more—so vastly more—as the girl who never in her life knew a selfish motive, who loves her Daddy as Cordelia did old Lear, who does a thousand good deeds and never suspects herself of doing one, whose very faults and mistakes are fine, for they come from a tender heart.

He did not know that it was a young professor who had lifted her spirits. It was only many years later, when I was about the same age as Jean was then, that she wrote me a very special letter in which she alluded to Berkeley and said she regretted not pursuing someone she had found there and wanted very much, who would have changed her whole life. I found out later that it was Martin Flaherty. She said I should always pursue what I wanted most.

On November 1, 1913, after he had moved to Tucson, Arizona, Martin Flaherty received the announcement of her wedding to Nash Read, and wrote her:

> When I went to the post office this morning there were some eight or nine letters awaiting me there that had been forwarded from Berkeley. Usually I put letters in my pocket and wait till I get back to my room before reading them. But one was post marked Montgomery, Alabama, and that one I opened and read where I stood.
>
> Something in the shape of the envelope gave me more than an inkling that it contained the announcement of the happiness of one whom I have known and loved since she was a young girl. I know it won't offend you to have an old bachelor whose mustache is turning gray speak in this fashion. He is so much older than you

that he permits himself liberties, but my heart is over-flowing with sincere wishes for your happiness.

They aren't wishes merely; they are a kind of prayer, the deepest and most fervent I have ever known. The words will find their way to you in benedictions that will follow and bless you all the days of your life.

Shortly after writing this letter he received another from Jean, written to him in Berkeley a month before her wedding, but forwarded tardily. We do not know what Jean's letter said, but we have Martin's answer:

This is just a line to say that your October letter reached me in Tucson a few days after I wrote you. When I saw the date on which you wrote I felt angry with the Gayleys for not having sent it sooner. But maybe things were better as they happened.

When it came I wrote you a letter that I felt I must not send, nor yet another that I tried, and so both have gone to join some unwritten ones that have never reached you. I am sending you today a watercolor by Sydney Yard just for remembrance. It is of the stretch of marsh near the Alameda shore. We passed the place together, you and I, on a trip we made to Los Gatos in the days of long ago. [The Sydney Yard watercolor hung at Hazel Hedge.]

If wishes could invest this little gift with talismanic powers it would speak for me the things that I may never say now, and which you alone could understand. It would do more than that. It would freight the on-coming years with the realization of your dearest hopes, and would open straight before you the land of your heart's desire. As ever, M.C.F. Please burn this.

In 1923, he sent her a book he had written, *How to Use a Dictionary*. It was inscribed:

To J.C.R. from M.C.F.
Not Rosemary, Yet, 'tis for remembrance.
Berkeley, March 1923

It was ten years before she heard from him again. In 1933 he wrote her on the occasion of his own marriage:

It's years and years ago since I was here in Tucson. So long ago that a whole lifetime seems to have elapsed. Yet I remember it all as if it were but yesterday. It was here that I received the announcement of your marriage. I remember that I wrote you a letter that morning. Just what I said I can't recall, possibly it was incoherent—it could easily have been—for it came more from the heart than from the head. It was my swan song, and here I am today writing to you again, to say something that will sound very strange to your ears.

I was married yesterday to Mrs. Mina Butler Beyer. I'm 61 and she is 59. I have known her for many years and if my sister is alive today it is owing to her constant and tender care. There is no romance. Life does not promise to stretch out far ahead for either of us. You are the only one I shall write to, for you are the only one who would feel a real interest in whatever I did. I hope you will destroy this note as soon as you read it. The writing of it seems almost traitorous, but it won't seem so to you.

Good bye, dear Jean.

As ever yours.

M. C. Flaherty.

17

Carrying On

JEAN LEFT BERKELEY RATHER ABRUPTLY WHEN MR. CRAIK REMINDED HER that her railroad pass would run out, and that she must use it immediately to get to Mexico City where she was scheduled to meet her sister Sheila and visit her Aunt "Minnie C." (for Craik) and Uncle Max Kilvert. They had made elaborate preparations for the visit. So had the girls.

Still at Hazel Hedge, Sheila was getting out her last issue of *Tattle* before Lent, and at the same time working with a seamstress on clothes for her trip to Mexico. They were doing a flowered muslin on organdy, and a blue silk dress with a sheer grey over-veil, and four chemises, all for forty-six dollars. "I also bought a pair of shoes and a corset."

Uncle Max wasn't stationed at the Embassy, but knew everyone there and they knew him, if for no other reason than his magnificent moustache, which had pointed ends that extended several inches outward and upward. He was said to have kept them straight and firm by putting them in a moustache-trainer at night and waxing them each morning.

Jean had arrived on schedule, and from then on was scheduled. She wrote home:

> I have been seeing everything, and have even been to jail. I haven't told Minnie C. about that because she would be provoked with me for going to Chapultepec with Mr. Haber. It is terribly exciting when you get arrested here. We were coming down the steps that wind up the hill and I went into ecstasy over a great trailing mass of pink geraniums covering the rocks. Mr. Haber said he would pick one for me because it went so nicely with my blouse.

He did, and out of nowhere sprang a giant—no, it isn't the story of beauty and the beast—oh, such a mean stern old fellow with a dog, who marched us off and out of the gate where we naturally thought he would leave us in peace. No sir! He kept us straight in front of him and took us right to jail. The judge came and I said "*Buenos Días*" and kept on talking in my broken Spanish, and saying "*Turistas*" and finally they let us go and I said "*Adios*" to the judge and "*Muchas Gracias*," and that was the end.

Sheila couldn't join Jean in Mexico until she finished the latest issue of *Tattle*. When she finally arrived, it was a continuous round of teas and parties and "at homes" for the two of them.

She wrote her father:

I have very little time to write for I am sleepy. Everyone has come to meet us—fat, sweet-faced old English ladies, badly dressed English girls & young American married women who might have been in some society play with their long trains of *crêpe de chine* and boas and furs and violet perfume and silk petticoats. Then there were big-nosed English men who say "just fawncy" a great deal but are really awfully nice, and who wear beautiful silk socks invariably.

The old ladies arrive and kiss each other on each cheek, and the men and girls shake hands when they come and when they leave and when they are contemplating leaving and every other time they feel like it. We have met only one American, a bacteriologist, who told us that with every cubic inch of ice cream, we swallow six million microbes.

We were invited to a party by Mr. Waswick, who is the loveliest giver of parties I ever knew. At noon we got on a tram and rode through garden country and saw a beautiful view of Popocatepetl, and passed through numerous little villages until we came to the garden where Jean said she was chased by about 50 gardeners and 100 dogs.

We stopped for lunch. Mr. Waswick had said he would have a few sandwiches for us. Let me tell you what we had, with everything in courses. Cantaloupe, fish salad, roast beef, veal loaf, aspic of turkey with lettuce, ice cream in moulds, black coffee and champagne and frappe. Topo Chico water all through the meal.

Mr. Craik answered her:

In your recent letter a Mr. Clifford, or was it Turner, was your faithful servant always at your bidding. Now it is Mr. Waswick. Has Clifford run his course, or are they now both your slaves, or do you allow a week each to your admirers and then refuse them to promote others, and are they really fine fellows or flannelled fools and dull oafs, and what is Jean doing in the way of conquests?

I am sorry to hear about the trouble with your teeth, and think for that and other reasons you had better turn your faces homeward; a month is enough for a visit even for so long a journey, and I am sure you have learned a great deal since you went away.

The girls left soon afterwards for New Orleans, where railway passes were waiting to take them the rest of the way home. Mr. Craik had missed them and was delighted to get them back. He described them in a letter to an old friend:

You impose a somewhat delicate task asking me about the Craik girls, as they are known collectively, for it is a theme I can scarcely treat dispassionately.

The frank comradeship that has always existed among the members of my family has grown and the girls are my best friends as I believe I am theirs. Their first thought is always of me so I am a pampered and spoiled old Papa.

I have written you of Darlie, who as you know is married. Next in line, that little rascal Judy has long been a social favorite, but is intensely practical with all her triumphs, wise and tactful in her relations with people and has scores of friends. She is about to abdicate in favor of her two younger sisters, who will make their formal entrance into society next month by means of a little function here at the Hedge.

They are both very pretty and really charming, quite unlike but passionately attached to each other; well educated and well read, with already many friends; they have never been in the society of boys, but have seen a good deal of men and women, our friends and those of their elder sisters; they have traveled rather more than most young women of these parts and are very perceptive; their minds are acute and they talk delightfully. In a word, they do not in any way disappoint me, and I am very fastidious.

We are all enchanted with our country life. Mrs. Craik sells butter and eggs and fruit and vegetables and we try to make the farm support itself. We have a dozen cows, of which five or six are registered Jerseys, and have several hundred fowls.

I have not achieved either fame or fortune, but I do not regret either for I have
that which neither fame nor fortune often brings.

Contrary to Mr. Craik, Jean had indeed been in the society of boys before she
went away. In a letter she wrote to Judy, after noting that it was so cold in Montgomery that "Baby and I have put a great pan of banana ice-cream out to freeze so
I don't care how cold it gets," she reported that she had just gone to a matinee to
see a horrid French play by Dumas, that was "so terrible and vile I was glad I was
with my sister, and not with Edward who had asked me to go. I couldn't have sat
through it with a man."

Before she left, Edward gave her seven dozen daffodil bulbs, but after she got
back, she severed their relationship. "He only talked of silly things." Silly or not,
he was smitten.

He wrote: "I am sorry to have been so rude to you last night but I was hardly
conscious. I didn't fully understand my feelings until I got home and saw your pictures on the mantle. Something seemed to come in my throat and I could hardly
breathe. I believe I will always love you. Devotedly, Edward."

In Berkeley, Darlie had a second baby, Jane. After that, things began to go badly
with the marriage. Darlie was as intensely interested in religion as she later became
in socialism. The pragmatic Buckner was interested in neither. After a few years,
they parted and eventually were divorced. This was a bold thing to do in those
years, especially for a Southern girl. Darlie returned to Hazel Hedge and brought
the children with her. As a boy, Craik, as he was called, devised a stick with wires
on one end so that his grandmother could gather pecans without bending over.
His grandfather noted that the boy seemed to have inherited his father's inventive
ability.

Craik was still at Hazel Hedge in 1907 when his aunt Judy relinquished the
task of managing the dairy and married a young Montgomery physician, Charles
Teed Pollard. Judy was very pretty and Dr. Pollard was regarded by many as the
handsomest man in Montgomery. Years later Craik recalled what he remembered
of the wedding and his relatives:

Everyone traveled to the church downtown, in carriages called "hacks." Uncle
Charlie and Mama rode in one. He borrowed the buffalo robes from the house
and they were all wrapped up snug. Uncle Charlie had a gun in his pocket which

surprised everyone, but he said they had to go through Bouge Homme (pronounced Bougahuma and translated as boogy man) at nightfall, a Negro section at Decatur and High Streets considered dangerous.

Many relatives came to the wedding. As I recall, Jennie had three sisters. There was Alma who had married a Mr. Bolton who was a mining engineer in Charlottesville, Virginia, and Cecile who was a carver, married to a Mr. Maxwell in Charlotte, North Carolina. The oldest was Mary who still lived in her house on Perry Street. She was married to William Ethelred Williams. I remember them because they had two daughters, one called Baldwin and the other Ethelred.

One of the old ladies' favorite pastimes was to get together at Hazel Hedge and sew on their funeral gowns. My grandmother Jennie was pretty strict. There was no sewing in that house on Sunday. It was sinful. Speaking of strict, one of the few spankings I ever got in my life was when I came back from kindergarten where I had heard the word "lousy." My grandmother was so outraged I got a spanking. Well, I use the word "lousy" whenever I can now.

The Pollards were so conservative they were prudes. Sex was considered to be a dirty word and was never mentioned, although they must have had some, since they later had a little daughter named Jean. These were Victorian times, when a maiden aunt was quoted as saying, "I've never seen how a lady could do it."

Dr. Pollard had little influence in that family, but was a good and kind doctor who visited his patients regularly and hated to send bills. His favorite patient was my grandmother Jennie. He would drive by in his Hupmobile almost every day, and hold her hand and ask, "How's that old heart today?" One day he had trouble starting his car. He cranked and he cranked and he cranked. An old Negro man watching him inquired, "How far do she go on one winding, doctor?"

18

The Tuppenny Tour

I N 1907, JEAN AND SHEILA WITH THEIR FRIENDS, OLIVE MACDONALD and Janet Hurter, were to sail on a cotton boat from New Orleans to Europe, on what they called "The Tuppenny Tour." Mr. Craik helped plan the trip, and it was out of the ordinary. Other young ladies in Montgomery had gone to Europe, but chaperoned and guided by Miss Margaret Booth, an imposing six foot tall head mistress of a private girls' school, who went along to explain what they were seeing and to watch their manners and morals. They wore white gloves and hats and curtsied.

No one curtsied on the Tuppenny Tour, either on the boat going over, or in London or all the places they went from there. They had inside cabins that were too warm, with only hatches at the top to let in air, and these were closed when the decks above were washed down at dawn. Olive in the upper berth was accused of using up all the cool air before it came down to those below her. They left their berths in the middle of the night to sleep on deck.

In the morning they were brought hot water, and coffee or tea at 6:30, had breakfast at nine, walked around the deck seventeen times, had bouillon and biscuits at eleven, lunch at one, read books in the afternoon, had four o'clock tea, and dinner at six. After eight days at sea they saw land. Then a most unexpected thing happened. Jean described it:

> We had passed the white cliffs and a Marconi station when we came on a battleship and three cruisers and their flags were at half mast. They were taking John Paul Jones' body from France where it had been buried almost 100 years ago to the United States. It was the most stately, impressive funeral procession I have

ever seen in my life. And to think that he grew up in Scotland on the estate where our great grandfather was born!

Their biggest problem before they landed was figuring out how to divide the ten dollars they had reserved for tips among all the people who seemed to expect a tip. From the beginning they had moved their own deck chairs, and asked for no favors, but everybody seemed to expect something: "I'm afraid we are going to have to skip some."

In London and the rest of England, they sought the places familiar to them from Dickens and Shakespeare and routed themselves so as to intersect with places they had been invited to spend the night. Abram Baldwin, who was by then president of the First National Bank, had written a letter on the bank's stationery paving the way:

> The young ladies bearing this letter, the Misses Jean and Sheila Craik, are traveling in England without the escort of a gentleman. Should the opportunity present itself for extending them any courtesy, or the occasion for them to seek such favors, I trust this letter may secure them especial consideration; their identity may be vouchsafed by their signatures.

In Devonshire they admired the villages and downs and relished clotted cream and fresh strawberry jam. In Cornwall they scaled some of the great sea cliffs. There was no one to tell them not to. Jean did charming sketches along the way, and put their experiences into a manuscript for a book, to be called "A Tuppenny Tour." In due time it was submitted to, and rejected by, the Century Company publishers in New York. A polite letter complimented her on her "bright and refreshing style, but the subject has been threshed out so often."

Sheila stayed on in Paris. Jean was wild about Italy, where she saw the originals of many of the paintings she had first viewed in the postcard series Mr. Murphy introduced in the Sunday school at St. John's Church. She bought a full-sized casting of a Della Robbia, which she painted for the garden at Hazel Hedge. She wrote long letters home describing the trip, wishing only that her father could be there to enjoy it with her.

He answered:

Your concern for my happiness fills me with tenderest emotion, knowing it is not a sense of duty that activates either of us but affection. Duty is a cold, stern forbidding sort of virtue sometimes necessary in the absence of loftier sentiments, but a poor substitute for the sort of love we feel for each other, which is not instinctive love of father and daughter nor the love of lovers, nor the regard of friends, but a love made up of the best part of all of these.

It was a sad homecoming. Mr. Craik was quite ill. He had prepared them before they got there:

Your imaginative letter made your dear old daddy and your always young mudder so broken of voice, so wet of eye, and choky of throat that neither of them could finish your marvelous story at one sitting. The only specter that haunts me is the thought that I can leave you so little, and sometimes this makes me very miserable. I have so little time to work, and I accomplish such insignificant results, that I am often oppressed with the belief that I have been faithless to the trust given to me.

Jane Speed with Nick under the Della Robbia at Hazel Hedge.

Mr. Craik died on Easter Sunday in 1908. There were many editorials and letters of sympathy. *The Advertiser* mourned "the loss of a man whose civic achievements were matched by refined and scholarly attainments blended in exercise of the noblest faculties of the heart."

Edgar Gardner Murphy wrote a moving tribute to his qualities of mind and character and his dedication to causes he believed in—such as the Republican Party as the party of Lincoln, and the emancipation of the Negro. He emphasized Will's dedication to his family. "Hazel Hedge was not a mere house of wood, but a pure entity of love and grace."

The Daughters of the Cradle of the Confederacy sent their standard resolution of sympathy to Mrs. Craik:

> Whereas, the angel of death folded its heavenly wings around her beloved Husband and their devoted Father, George William Craik, and carried him beyond the skies, Chapter No. 94 of the Alabama Division tenders our loving sympathy.

Jean was devastated. With her father gone, and her association with Martin Flaherty suspended, she was at a loss to find her way. Her neuralgic headaches returned and went on frightfully. She looked for new directions for her boundless energy.

Reverend Murphy advised her, "Give yourself in your very heart, dear Jean, to rest and calm. That we must always be 'doing things,' even unselfish things may often be utterly wrong for it sometimes represents the impatient conviction that if there could only be enough of us to go everywhere and do everything, it all would be perfect and no one else would be needed atall."

Jean began to realize that her life had been very protected and sheltered within Hazel Hedge, and now she must make a new one. Her best friend, Olive MacDonald, married and moved to Boston, where she filled her time with the theater and opera—and a few lectures.

At one of them she heard Mrs. Pankhurst speak on "women's suffrage." She wrote enthusiastically to Jean in Montgomery, where Jean and Janet Hurter caught the torch. They began to think about women's rights, but in a debate, "Resolved that co-education is beneficial," the Wiley Literary Society rendered a negative decision.

In a letter dated 1910, Olive was highly critical of a mutual friend "who is as ardent a suffragist as Mary Partridge. And what does Mary P. think of Labour Unions after the McNamara disclosure?" Two brothers, John and James McNamara, had admitted dynamiting the *Los Angeles Times* building to demonstrate against the newspaper's anti-labor policy. Twenty persons were killed.

She ended her letter, "I can't follow you and Janet into Socialism. Never!" Jean and Janet met to talk over Olive's letter, the labor movement and women's suffrage at the Cassimus Restaurant where "we had the most delicious oysters and Floating Island for dessert." What they ate was worth reporting, not what they said. The McNamara brothers were passed over lightly.

Both had become active in a young women's club named "Tintagel" after the birthplace of King Arthur, and renowned in Tennyson's *Idylls of the King*. Along with the others, they gave readings and wrote reports on books and writers. Jean wrote one paper on "The Friendship of Walpole and Gray" and one on "Stevenson's Letters."

Such activity comforted Sheila, who was deeply worried about her sister, who stayed at Hazel Hedge in deep mourning for their father for almost a year. Sheila herself had returned to France to study French at the university in Grenoble. Once she had mastered the language, her goal was to go to Paris and become a newspaper correspondent. Sheila wrote her mother, "I'm glad my precious sister is having such a good old time—her days with the girls and talk and a free woman's life sound utterly perfect." Not perfect, but helpful in getting Jean away from the mournful atmosphere at Hazel Hedge, and into a real world of work.

She opened a shop downtown where she sold items she had brought back from Europe and things hand-crafted in Montgomery by herself and others, such as lampshades and Christmas ornaments. She also began to go out again, and while reestablishing connections with an old love, Steve Partridge, a newspaperman in New York, she was also making connections with a new one, the publisher of the *Alabama Journal* in Montgomery, Frank Miller. In her letters from Boston, Olive had opinions about both:

"By this time you will have heard from Steve. Does he comfort and satisfy you? You are not going to fall in love with Mr. Miller. That is too much. I can't under- stand your being able to spend an hour with him, him, him!" Jean kept seeing Mr. Miller because she thought having him for her best friend would "make her more of a man's woman." "I don't altogether approve of him myself but he's made me grow up too. I would almost marry him but I don't love him."

Meanwhile, Montgomery was changing, and Jean was changing too, but not everything came out even. Bicycles were in, but the girls couldn't ride them. Their clothes were too restrictive, and although bustles were on their way out there were still corsets, and skirts were too long. Telephones were coming, which was making communication easier.

When the United States got into the war and men were sent overseas, more jobs were open to women in Montgomery. A new cotton-picking machine was invented by a Mr. Todd of Chicago and several large cotton mills were built in the city. There were improvements.

The lower part of Commerce Street was overrun with wagons and drays putting down paving which consisted of six-sided stone blocks that had been used as ballast when the boats taking cotton to England came home empty. Now there was something better under foot than dirt and mud.

Some attention was also being paid to the condition of the jails, and the Montgomery jail was described as one of the nicest and cleanest in the state. There was not much concern for the plight of convicts in chains who not only worked on public roads, but were contracted out to private companies. For example, the Coal, Iron and Railroad Company budgeted $8,486 for the hire of a number of prisoners each month. J. O. DeLacy, pit boss at Pratt Mines, was publicly charged with manslaughter in the deaths of ten prisoners assigned to a bad section where they died from an explosion of fire damp.

Negroes were beginning to stand up for their rights. In one encounter, a Negro who entered the first class car of the train from Selma to Montgomery was accosted by a white man, "Don't you think you are in the wrong car? This is for white people." The Negro refused to move, "I paid the $1.50 price," he said. He was applauded by the *Montgomery Advertiser* for his manly stand, "When you are right, stand your ground." Two new newspapers emerged edited by Negroes—the *Montgomery Argus*, devoted to the moral, social and financial interests of colored people, and the *Normal Reporter*, advocating their educational advancement.

19

The Man from Corsicana

J EAN'S "FREE WOMAN'S LIFE" DIDN'T LAST LONG. IN 1912, WILLIAM NASH Read came to Montgomery, representing his uncle's fertilizer business in New York. He was handsome and charming, and a widower. He arrived in a seven-passenger Stevens Duryea car made of aluminum, with brocade seats and vases for flowers. There was a glass divider between the front and the back seats, and a white chauffeur named Gannon from Baltimore. It was quite a sight. It was the only Stevens Duryea in Montgomery, and no one had ever seen a white chauffeur before.

Nash was in his early forties. He had grown up in Corsicana, Texas. His father, my grandfather, Nicholas Cabell Read, had withdrawn from Hampden Sydney College in Virginia to join Lee's army, and after the war left the state for good. His ancestors had held seats in the Virginia House of Burgesses since before the Revolution, so it was a big move. He went to Mexico and bought a coffee plantation, saying he would never live under the Union flag.

Things went well until 1867, when the Mexicans turned against all foreigners in their country. They beheaded Emperor Maximilian when he was named to govern them by Napoleon Bonaparte III. My grandfather was forced to decamp.

A cousin, Marion Rous, wrote about his escape:

> He beat it for the coast, riding his best horse, with his parrot on his shoulder, and carrying in his purse a quantity of gold pieces. On the way he was taken ill and fell by the road, helpless. Along came a Catholic priest named Father Leon, who took him into his house and tenderly nursed him back to health. Father Leon refused to take any money, even for the medicine he had bought for the invalid.

When Nicholas was well again, Father Leon put him on his horse, with blessings for a good journey. He had not gone far before he was attacked by masked bandits, who took his horse, his money, and his clothes except for his shirt. He was allowed to keep the pet parrot. As the bandits rode off, the mask slipped from the face of one of them and revealed Father Leon!

"Oh, Father Leon," cried Nicholas, "You did not have to rob me! I would gladly have given you everything I had!" "As a priest I am one thing," retorted Father Leon gaily, "as a bandit, another. Adios."

That this may have been apocryphal is suggested by the fact that virtually the same story was told to Dallas by her grandmother, a pioneer in California, but the role of the priest was taken by Joaquin Murietta, a western bandit.

Nicholas proceeded on foot to the coast of Mexico, crossed the Gulf of Mexico and headed for Corsicana, Texas, where lived a former neighbor from Virginia, Francis Peyton Wood. After the war, Wood had sold his Poplar Hill Plantation in Prince Edward County, Virginia, with its worn-out tobacco lands, and having been shown a cigar box full of rich loam from the Brazos River Valley, moved lock stock and barrel to Texas. It wasn't the rich soil, but a pretty young daughter, Ellen, who was the reason young Nicholas headed in that direction. We found the poems he had sent to her from Mexico in Jean's collection. He described her in "Some One I Know":

> I know an eye whose cloudless blue
> Is darker than the summer sky.
> I know a cheek whose ruddy hue
> With the half-opened rose may vie.
>
> I know a cheek whose rosy glow,
> The sunset's dying flush might shame
> And oer it smiles and dimples go
> Like sunbeams on a laughing stream.
>
> I know a voice whose music sweet
> Can banish sorrow, pain and care;
> I know a footstep, light and sweet
> As the quick tread of mountain deer.

I know a heart that's warm and true,
And purer than the driven snow.
In fine, I know a woman, who
Is good, and pure and lovely too.

They were married, and Nicholas opened a law office, "Davidson & Read, Attorneys Collecting and General Land Agents." Ellen helped support the family by giving piano lessons. They had three little boys, John Archer, Nash and Isaac. The boys were still young when their father died, and Ellen was their sole support. Her buggy was always on the go. "I was hard brought up and little thought of," my father Nash used to say.

Ellen's sister, Frances Rous, came from Baltimore to comfort her, and help out. She brought her son, Peyton, close in age to the Read boys. They became friends and took turns hitching Ellen's horse, Dufunky (who was said to have one, if not two blind eyes) to the buggy that carried her to her piano pupils.

The Rouses returned to Baltimore, but several years later, when Peyton was threatened with tuberculousis, he returned to spend a year curing his weak lungs in

Ellen Read and her sons Isaac, John Archer and Nash.

the dry air of Texas. It was like coming home. Everything was the same, from the century plant in its great iron vase in the front yard to the peach tree from which switches had been cut on occasions "that fortunately were rare." At the side of the house was the funnel-top of an old-fashioned locomotive filled with blooming petunias and bordered all around with green bottles stuck neck-downward.

Mostly, there was his beloved Aunt Ellen, "who warmed to each and every occasion in our lives and indeed helped me out of what I thought was a love affair but that she declared a piece of foolishness, as indeed it turned out to be."

My father Nash got his first job as a cowpuncher on cattle trains going to Chicago. From there he went to Brooklyn, where he stayed with relatives and worked at the Read Fertilizer Company in Wall Street for his uncle Isaac Read. He walked across the Brooklyn Bridge twice a day to save the nickel fare. On the way he may have met Dallas's grandfather, who was walking across the bridge at about the same time to get to Manhattan where he was starting a tea business.

It was on a visit to Peyton and the Rous family in Baltimore that Nash met and fell in love with Marie Sullivan, the only daughter in a prominent and rich Catholic family. They were married despite the disapproval of her brothers, who objected to the fact that Nash was not Catholic.

A year or so later when Marie died in child birth at Johns Hopkins Hospital, and the baby shortly afterwards, it made a great deal of difference. The Sullivan wills had been rewritten. Money inherited by Marie could only be passed on to her children, not to her husband, Nash. Peyton Rous, by then a resident in pathology at Johns Hopkins medical school, was among those who could verify that Marie had died first, leaving her inheritance to the baby, which was then passed on to Nash.

After the double tragedy, Nash was inconsolable. To get him away from Baltimore with its reminders, Isaac sent him south to represent his fertilizer business in Montgomery. It was there, in 1912, that he met Jean Craik and her circle of friends. Soon they were going out together. Within a year he proposed.

Not everyone approved. A letter came from Sylvia Beach who said of Jean's interest in Nash, "I think it very important for you not to marry a man who owns all of O. Henry. That means he's such an average American, when I'm thinking up some great genius for you to marry. You must promise not to rush away with anyone without consulting me."

Another letter from Sylvia started off, "Why did you call me Sylvia in your last letter and not Sylvie? You must be furious with me for something. Your planned marriage and neuralgia have turned you against me! This marriage with Mr. Nash is quite an important step, but isn't it nice to take steps in any direction, and he will be interested in getting 'expert opinion' all over the world on your wretched neuralgia. And as to not reading the same style of books, instead of doing as I did and keeping my books together, here I am in the United States and all my books in Paris because I couldn't decide which to bring. Now, if you get a separation, he could take away his O. Henry's and you hurry off with the others."

Whether Jeanie consulted further with Sylvie is not known, but it wasn't long before she broke up with Mr. Miller and became engaged to Nash. She wrote to him, "Oh! Nash Darling, this is complete surrender. Will you always, always decide everything for me—except what theaters to go to. I think you are lots nicer than college professors and 'cultured Johnnies,' and I want you to not change a single taste—and I'm going to prefer O. Henry to Galsworthy and Kipling to Browning—if I can."

Sylvia evidently forgave her: "I should have been very surprised if you had remained unmarried . . . Has your neuralgia gone away entirely? There are only about one and ½ nice men existing at all. Please congratulate him for me on having such a wonderful, lovely girl and one of the few geniuses in a population of so many millions."

Jean and Nash were married October 23, 1913, at St. John's Episcopal Church in Montgomery, with a reception under the elm tree at Hazel Hedge. Jean was thirty-two years old. The sketches she did of the wedding do not show the rain that fell from the sky, but do record the shower of old family silver that poured in upon her. Some of it may have been buried to hide it from the Yankees during the War Between the States.

Jean's sister Sheila was maid of honor, and Marion Rous, Peyton's sister, who wrote the account of N. C. Read's trip from Mexico, came from Baltimore to represent the northern family at the wedding. She was a concert pianist and played for the guests. The newlyweds went to Maine on their wedding trip, and moved into Hazel Hedge on their return.

Nash had bought the old shingle house from Jean's mother, Jennie Craik, and added two wings, with a large drawing room on one side and a spacious screened porch on the other. Hazel Hedge became the "place to go" in Montgomery, with costume parties and other festivities by the fireplace in the winter, and in summer parties and lunches outside in Jean's garden.

Jennie Craik lived there for more than twenty years in rooms off the garden and near the front door where she received guests. She didn't need a street number. Her mail was addressed to Mrs. Will Craik, Montgomery, Alabama, until she died in the 1930s.

Jean's main concern was the garden, which had never done well in the "prairie soil" that covered much of Hazel Hedge. It was a limey white clay that baked hard and developed cracks in the summer, and became a sea of sticky mud in the winter. Houses didn't like it either. They shifted ground with the seasons.

Her elderly cousin, Mildred Maxwell, who lived not far away on Country Club Lane, climbed under her house in dry spells to dampen the soil around the foundation. When Dallas first came to visit Hazel Hedge, she looked up in the drawing room and said to my mother, "Could that be blue sky I see through the corner of the ceiling?" Jean replied, "It's just a crack. It will close up when the rains come."

As an anniversary present, Nash wanted to give Jean a diamond bracelet. "What I really want," Jean said, "is two wagon loads of manure." To this she added twenty wagons of rich soil, and

Top: Jean Craik wedding drawing. Bottom: Nash and Helen Rous.

replaced the hard clay, which she had dug up and carted away. Around it all she put a masonry brick wall finished to look like a wall she had admired in Sorrento. She installed a Pan fountain in the wall, and put the Della Robbia copy she had brought from Italy under a tiled roof over the old well.

When the well was cleaned out, the remains of a horse and rider were found at the bottom. They had probably fallen in when the land was a pasture and wooden boards covering it had rotted away. Horse and rider were probably taking a short cut through the fields on their way home.

All kinds of flowers and plants were put into the new garden. I remember especially the roses, a Silver Moon that draped over the wall, and a Lady Banksia that climbed to the top of a bay tree and every spring gave a spectacular show of yellow blossoms.

Jean used the garden as a setting for her social life. When her field of daffodils was about to bloom, she invited her friend Mrs. Doubleday, of the book company, from New York for a visit. At the end of the long-distance call, Jean asked the operator, who of course had been listening in, "Do you think I was cordial enough?" The operator answered, "Miz Read, you was plenty cordial. If she ain't comin' for that, she ain't comin fer nothin."

The night before Mrs. Doubleday arrived, a hard freeze was predicted. Jeanie gathered armloads of daffodils and put them in a bathtub of cold water until morning, when she took them out and stuck them upright in the field. Later that morning, she preceded Mrs. Doubleday through the daffodils, gathering the flowers for a large bouquet.

20

Sheila Becomes Cécile

BEFORE THE WAR BROKE OUT IN EUROPE IN 1914, SHEILA LEFT Grenoble, where she had been studying French, and returned to Hazel Hedge to be the maid of honor at her sister Jean's wedding. Afterward she went to New York City, where she continued to study French, using one of the new "crystal sets" called radio. It was her objective to return to Paris after the war. She hated the Kaiser, "his terrible moustache" and what he was doing to France.

She kept in touch with a young man, Paxton Hibben, whom she had met when he was the acting *Chargé d'Affaires* of the U.S. Embassy at the Hague in the Netherlands. Afterwards he resigned to become a foreign correspondent for *Collier's Weekly* in Germany. That is what Sheila wanted to do in France—become a newspaper correspondent. But she didn't know where to begin and had no money to support herself.

A friend in Paris wrote that there was a volunteer job in the Section for the Wounded in the American Ambulance Hospital in Paris, run by the Red Cross. She wrote her mother, "I would love it. If I could sell what I wrote about it, I would go in a flash." She approached the *New York Sun,* asking if they would take an article a week, with her name signed. "The *Sun* won't make any agreement but asked me to submit articles." She decided that in France, she would use her given name, Cécile, with a French accent. However, she signed most of her letters home "Bini" or even "Baby," her nicknames since childhood.

In the end, her mother, Jennie, financed the trip, and early in 1915, two years before the United States entered the war, she was in Paris working in the Dental Surgery Operating Room of the hospital. The hours were 8 a.m. to 5:30 p.m., which meant she had to leave her apartment at 7 a.m. to get all the way across town from where she lived at 54 rue Notre Dame des Champs. She didn't get home until after 6:30, which didn't leave much time for writing.

"Home" was a two-room apartment she found and furnished, just one block from the Luxembourg. She wrote her mother:

> I am so excited at being a *locataire Parisienne*. You cannot imagine what a solemn and terrifying step it is here in France! I wish I could send you my lease. It stipulates that I pay one franc for each window and door (not for having them washed but just for having them), two francs for the right to put garbage out, three francs for the carpet on the stairs—and a million other absurd things.
>
> The apartment itself is only fifteen dollars a month and I thought it would be so cheap, but all these expenses are rather frightening, so will you please reassure me by telling me that I may call on you if I run over before my allowance is due?
>
> It is the cunningest apartment in the world, quite as much of an establishment in its small way as Hazel Hedge. The rooms are freshly painted and papered, a nice little kitchen and a really scrumptious W. C. with a chain that pulls. My windows look into a tiny courtyard, very sunny, where there is an adorable little statue of the Virgin, which is very old.
>
> The Bergers (old friends) are going to lend me a bed and there is a nice bathtub and wash stand, and I shall buy some willow chairs and a table and pretty curtains and a secondhand desk, all of which I can get very cheap.

In the spring of 1915 she wrote her sister,

> I would be so happy if you could read the French newspapers. Nobody who does not read French and who is not here can have any idea of what this war really is! These are *les grandes heures*, and everything that is not real seems to have been cast off in this wonderful France and she stands calm and sure and sublime. In America we simply have no idea of the price the French are paying, so simply and un-blusteringly. Here everything is so different—so breathlessly close to the great and simple things of life and death—so far away from Billy Sunday.

Her work at the hospital was emotionally as well as physically exhausting. She described the soldiers brought back from the front with terrible head wounds. She wrote her mother:

I wish you and Dr. Pollard could be having the benefit of all these hideous and wonderful operations instead of me. If I could only send you a few of the photographs of men who have had their whole faces blown off and some who have come in without the slightest sign of a chin and leave with only a few scars and new chins grown on them. All of this surgery is the result of the trench fighting—there have never been such hideous nor so many face wounds as there are in this war, when as soon as a man sticks his head above the trenches, he gets it blown off or apart.

In these last three days we have received over 200 wounded, having evacuated some 100 into nearby convalescent hospitals. All night long the ambulances come in, bringing the wounded from the trains. In my department the work is simply breathless. There is never a moment to sit down. During the luncheon hour the horrible stench of the wounds I have unbandaged is so strong in my nose I cannot eat. I did not know it was possible for men to have such wounds and not die of gangrene.

There were breathtaking moments. "The Queen of Portugal came to visit the hospital. I showed her the photographs and she brandished them in the air and made dramatic utterances about God's vengeance on the Kaiser and sending him to Hell. She is very nice looking and has a grand smell."

Outside the hospital Cécile volunteered to help French refugees from the war zones. On February 23, she wrote home:

Yesterday I spent nearly all day at the *Croix Blanche*—such heart-rending cases we had. One poor woman, the saddest of all I think, had come all the way from near Combrais on foot with her husband and two children, all of them in their night clothes. It took six days for them to get here.

She told me between sobs and in such a delicious way—"Oh Madame, we left everything behind, a fine café, everything. And when I think of my little girl's first communion dress, which cost 40 francs, hanging in the wardrobe, and her flower crown and her gloves and white shoes! Oh it is hard to bear. To think that some dirty German has sent dress, crown everything back to that awful Berlin! *Chez nous* we had everything; we wanted for nothing and here in Paris we never know where we are to get our next meal and none of us have a garment, except what we have on our backs."

Cécile began to ask friends and relatives in the United States to donate clothes and money for the refugees. Nash sent fifty dollars. "Tell Nash that I never in my life have enjoyed so much spending money on the poor, and please, to keep on playing golf as he has no idea how much his winnings are needed here. For fifty cents I got enough cotton goods to make my poor woman of yesterday three chemises, and she was so grateful that she almost forgot her unhappiness about the first communion dress!"

Jean contributed clothes. Not all of them got to the refugees. Cécile wrote, "I have had the little old paint-stained $10 dress you gave me for the refugees beautifully cleaned and wear it with deep, ravishing, ruching with great effect. Heaven knows what I am going to do about buying clothes, as Sundays and nights are the only times I am free."

That fall, she had more to say in a letter about the French— "who are so calm and almost solemn in their wonderful days of victory. I think so often of what General Joffre, when after the Battle of the Marne was asked about celebrating the victory in Paris with illumination and flags, said— '*Non*, there are too many dead.'"

She asked her mother to request that an old friend, who had lived for a long time in France, introduce her to some French families, as she was surrounded by "Americans and know very few French people, and am fast ceasing to speak any French at all." On October 15 she wrote of family things, "It seems so trite to say how terribly sorry I am for Darlie, and you will think I am only being malicious if I say that being rid of Buckner is good riddance! I don't think he is any crazier than he was when he told me last year that he had outgrown Darlie—that was his immortal word!"

She mourned the death of her aunt, Minnie C.:

> It has *bouleversed* (upset) me more than I thought possible. I was only waiting for you to send her address to forward a letter I had written her. About ten days before her death I was at St. Cloud with a friend overlooking the view of Paris and rather lost in the loveliness of the afternoon. Suddenly I had the most extraordinary impression of someone who had been there and left.
>
> I turned so pale, with tears in my eyes, that my companion asked what was the matter. I tried to explain. "Was it your sister?" he said. "No, it was my Aunt." I didn't know until I said it that it was Minnie C. I have thought about it so unceasingly

ever since, that it has grown a perfect obsession—this presence, which suddenly went out, ceased—and I knew then it was for good!

If the *estragon* (tarragon) I sent Jean is still alive, tell her to serve it on top of beefsteak (*filet de boeuf* here), butter creamed with *fresh estragon* chopped in it. Of course the meat must be extra hot. I wish I could give you the receipt for sole, cooked with truffles and almonds that I ate the other night at Chez La Perouse, that baffles all description! . . . My dearest love to you all. Cécile.

In February of 1916 she wrote her mother,

If you could see this lovely world all covered with snow—the only snow I have ever seen in Paris that didn't melt away into mud as it fell. This noon I bought a sandwich and a cake and went to walk in the Bois (which is not very far from the hospital). It was unbelievably lovely—like an enchanted woods—and so still and sparkling with the sun turning the ice of the Cascade into a million rainbows!

With German zeppelins overhead almost every day, are you still saying not much is happening? I haven't written you since the last dreadful air raid Monday night, the first time our quarter has borne the brunt of the attack. It lasted three awful hours and my house was so shaken that it seemed actually to stand on its hind legs at moments.

I finally fled to the cellar as everybody else had done and stayed there until it was over. I shan't return the next time as there is great danger of panic in such places and in case our house fell it really would be worse than dying calmly in my bed. Fortunately, the bombs fell on houses of the very rich, who were not made homeless.

Still my French friends think the war will be over this summer—and it will! I am already invited to the *defile* [parade] from the *terrasse* of the *Club de L'Epataut* in the *Place de la Concorde*! When I think of that day—to which the whole world is moving—and the statues of Lille and Strasbourg are wreathed in flowers and not funeral crowns and the glorious remnants of the *Fusiliers Marins* and the military music which has been silent for so many months and all my *grands blesses* knowing that what they have given has not been in vain—I lose my head altogether. I just swoon in a sort of ecstatic dream of glory! Jean must already begin to look in Vogue for a dress for me—it must be the most beautiful dress in the world!

Ola! Tell Jean to try to get *Parmi les Ruines* translated into English. It is the best thing I have read on the war—and I have read about everything. It hasn't anything to do with the causes, but just an account of a trip through the Champagne, and all the invaded provinces—but wonderful.

If coal and meat and petroleum are expensive in Paris, the Spring flowers are cheap enough to make up for everything. Every Friday afternoon when I leave the hospital, I go to the Marche de la Madeleine and buy all the pink double tulips and frescias and anemonies in the world and come home in an open horse taximeter. I must stop this letter as I have work to do now . . . For ever, Cécile.

She read the French papers for the war news, and had little patience with family or friends who expressed doubts about how things were going. "Really, your talk about a German victory is the maddest thing I ever heard of! Don't you know anything about what is going on in France?"

One night she was awakened in what seemed like the middle of the night "by an agent from the *Prefecture de Police* who came to ask me for all my papers. I didn't mind his visit except that it was so *boche* and unlike the French to get nervous about spies."

Mail from home reached her intermittently, sometimes in batches and often not at all, as ships changed their routes to avoid submarines. Off and on she received packages with books and food and clothing. "The tea and coffee hasn't come yet, but another little handkerchief arrived with yesterday's letter, and my need for these continues. They simply disappear in the laundry. Now if you could only send me sugar, vinegar and oil, and beer and meat, I should be less terrified at the soaring prices."

She wrote Jean of her increasing interest in Paxton Hibben, the progressive young journalist who had developed his craft in the United States in the muckraking days of Lincoln Steffens, Ida Tarbell, Upton Sinclair and John Reed. He was now reporting for the Associated Press in the Balkans.

She couldn't tell too much in her letters home because they were read by the whole family. She asked Jean "where can I write—just to you? There are some things I must say. Please tell me—it will make me feel less heartbreakingly far away. I love you so everlastingly much, and that is all there is to say."

The interference with the close relationship of the two sisters was acutely felt by Cécile—so far away not only from Jean but from the whole family.

She was getting more hardened to the work and the long hours, but she still got very, very tired. When summer came, she escaped for an overnight to St. Germain "away from the choking smell of iodoform, and where the forest is the most lovely thing in the whole world. I lay there all day curled up in my steamer rug on a mossy bank, looking at the unbroken roof of green over my head."

She urged Jean to ask Nash to bring her over for a visit since

at present things are very quiet here and almost half the patients are convalescent, because there is so little going on at the Front. It takes France 21 days to mobilize all her troops. Not until October is a great *coup* expected.

You could shop for antiques. So many people are selling their furniture, and Paris fashions are riotously exciting. The new high up *coiffure* is going to be most lovely on you. There are some very fine hats in Paris too! And doesn't Nash like polo? There is good polo at *La Bagatelle* . . .

22 JULY 1915. To dearest heart (Jean).

Mama's letter arrived this morning enclosing the communication from *The Sun*. I suppose the *Sun* won't even use my name, and newspapers seldom pay more than $5 a column. It was a funny idea for you to send the manuscript to the *Montgomery Advertiser*. I wonder if you think that all I want is just to see what I write in print? The only good that could come out of having it published would be to cut out the article when it appears and paste it neatly on a sheet of paper so that it won't look all dog-eared, and when you get to New York, take it with you and see some editor about placing my stuff.

That is of course if you don't mind my cheekily asking this of you. I am afraid it is an awful nuisance, especially as I scold you when you do it wrong, but there is no use asking a literary agent to place my stuff as long as they don't know me and I don't see any chance of their getting to know me if I am to write unsigned articles for the Sunday *Sun*. And so—I do hope that as you are to act as my agent, you will help me seriously in trying to get a start.

This morning I got up all the nerve I have and asked one of the ward nurses if I could come in and watch the decoration of a soldier (an officer of course) with the Legion of Honour. It was the simplest and most thrilling thing you ever saw. The little Lieutenant being white in his bed, his eyes full of tears while the General touched him on both shoulders with his sword and then kissed him and pinned the Cross of the Legion of Honour on his shirt:

"For steadfast courage since the beginning of the war, for inspiring his men with hope and confidence in the darkest days of the campaign, for leading 20 volunteers up a hill under a rapid permanent fire and taking a house in which there were 45 Germans, and for bringing his wounded Colonel from the field of battle after he himself had been desperately wounded and under heavy fire."

Today again I have had a *bouleversement*. The soldier, of whom I am most fond of any of my patients, is leaving the hospital tomorrow and in a little while returning to the front. He is a strapping big fellow, so awfully good looking with such nice blue eyes.

He has been wounded three times and now he is returning to the front for the fourth time. "Every time I have gone back," he told me, "I haven't the slightest misgivings. I knew I was coming back alive. This time I know I'm not. It isn't of the slightest consequence of course whether I do or not, I go just as I went before, only this time—*Ça va y être!*" And that with the most perfect sangfroid. Oh, they are wonders, these Frenchmen. Did I tell you that my job is a very exalted one with nobody over me at all and nobody to quarrel with if I am late mornings or early in leaving? However, I haven't yet been late a single time . . . My dearest love to Mama and Nash and please, please come over here and motor in this beautiful France. Please come, Bini.

July 30.

Dearest Mother, How did you get that lovely smock here in such a hurry? I didn't have to pay on it, and not being at home when it arrived I didn't even have to give two sous to the postman. Thank you *so* much for it.

I have been ruining myself buying *N.Y. Suns* for the past week and yesterday I saw my article. It made me sicker than ever to see that they had published the thing without my name. I can't see for the life of me why I send it to a newspaper. I am very much discouraged as I did spend a lot of time on that thing and I think it was good—(*The Sun* thought so too or they would never have given it the place they did). As it is, Jean might just as well have taken it to the *Montgomery Advertiser* where at least they would have used my name.

My work here continues to be interesting and with my refugees who come to me in the evening I am about as busy as anybody could be who has only 19 hours a day at their disposal. I also have a prisoner to whom I send a package every week. Poor wretches, they are starving to death there in the prison compound and what one sends is to keep them alive, not to pamper them.

The other day I talked with a French Red Cross man who had been a prisoner five months. It simply makes you despairing to hear the life they lead there in the camps. He was in a camp with 1500, which was a very small one. They were in a great bare field where there wasn't a tree or a blade of grass and the whole thing surrounded by many barricades of barbed wire.

The perfect apathy of the life—the endless empty days are broken only by the three nauseating, insufficient meals, the bodily suffering and the anxiety, just make you think that these prisoners have the most tragic fate of all the victims of the war. This doctor told me that during the five months he was prisoner, the much-vaunted "meat three times a week" had never been anything but a terrible sickening soup made of a great deal of water, no salt, and pieces of chitterlings or tripe floating about in it.

I take it for granted that my prisoner isn't finicky, so I don't send a very fine quality of groceries—just prunes, a sort of biscuit especially prepared for the purpose, concentrated milk and canned meat, from which the silly Boche make you take off the label, if it happens to be an English brand. The parcel post fortunately is gratuitous . . . Oh, I do wish Jean could come over. With all my whole heart, Cécile.

Nash and Jean didn't make it over for the reason that Jean had become pregnant. Cécile was overjoyed, and immediately began to look for suitable gifts for the new baby (me) due in April.

She wrote that her very first check for eighteen dollars from the *Sun* would be used "to buy christening clothes." Since Jean couldn't come to France, she decided to go home to Alabama to see all of us. Much was to happen before she made the trip, before we entered the war in the summer of 1916. Most of all, she had fallen in love with Paxton Hibben, who was now an Associated Press correspondent in Greece.

By the time she got to Hazel Hedge, all of us were in Montgomery —her mother Jennie, Jean and Nash and of course me, as well as Darlie (now separated from Buckner) with her two children, William and Jane. Judy with Dr. Pollard and their daughter, Jean, lived just down on Perry Street.

Most of all, Cécile wanted to talk to her sister Jean. The two sisters had almost never made a move without consulting each other. Now she had something important to discuss—her possible marriage to Paxton Hibben. She was falling in love with him but even at twenty-nine needed Jean's reassurance when it came to cutting her ties with home. She may still have been undecided when she left Montgomery in August, although she packed more than she would normally have taken back to Paris. On her way, she stopped over a few nights at the Brevoort Hotel in New York City, and there encountered Buckner Speed, who was on the verge of being divorced from Darlie. Cécile, ever loyal to the family, described how she handled the situation:

> Tell Mama not to worry about what I failed to do to B. Speed! It was in the basement of the Brevoort and Nash knows how crowded that is, at lunchtime. I had just had my hair waved and had on a lovely little dress and everybody was looking at me because I was standing in the middle of the room and there was no place to sit down. When Buckner spoke to me, holding out his hand, I just looked at him slowly from head to foot and then said to the waiter over his head, "*Je ne peux pas attendre toujours, sacré bleu!*" ["I can't wait forever, for goodness sake!"] and turned on my heels. Everybody saw him being cut by an attractive looking woman and that was a good deal better than if I had told him any plain truths—to my mind!

Instead of returning to France on August 21, Cécile took the SS *Konstantinoe* to Athens. The boat was crowded with Greeks. She reported that "the only Americans on it were a young newly married couple from North Carolina—very nice, very country—the bride being a little thing from the small rural town of Youngsville, who until she got aboard the *Konstantinoe* never knew that all the nations of the earth didn't live off butter beans and corn and waffles and chicken!"

There was not much socializing, and she was alone for much of the crossing. She had two long weeks to think about her future. By the time the boat docked she had written Jean, "It is so wonderful—so utterly thrilling to be sailing straight into the arms of happiness this way! It makes up a thousand times for all the pain of leaving you and Mama—and God knows that *is* pain! It seems sometimes as if it were the first time I had left you in my life. In the middle of the night, in my little black cabin above the snoring of the old woman in the berth below me, my tears were hot and heavy for you."

21

The Paxton Hibbens

I N ATHENS, CECILE (WHO HAD DROPPED THE ACCENT ON HER NAME), found Paxton quite ill—and very frustrated. She wrote home: "Paxton is exhausted. He has been fighting hard to get the truth out about Greece, giving impartially both the King's position and the other side's. The King wants to keep Greece neutral. The Allies, of course, want Greece to join them."

The leadership of the country was divided. King Constantine was determined to keep the country out of the war. His prime minister, Eleutherios Venizelos, was strongly opposed, openly siding with the British in his efforts to get Greece to yield to the pressure of the Allies. Paxton attempted to report both sides. Cecile wrote home:

> Because Pax also reports the King's position, the French and the English, headed by Compton McKenzie who is utterly unscrupulous, are now accusing him of being a German spy. This would be ridiculous if it were not so enraging—he who has given more material proof of his devotion to the Allies than most of the Ententistes themselves, and is more French than Joffre and almost as much so as I myself.

It did not help that one night when Pax was having dinner with a German acquaintance, a Frenchman Pax didn't know came to the table and accused the German of being "an assassin." Pax remonstrated and was challenged to a duel. He thought it was a joke until his friends put on silk hats for the occasion. The Frenchman took two shots at him that missed. He had fired his own pistol into the ground.

A little more than a month after her arrival, Cecile wrote Jean:

I know you will think I am the original duck-billed platypus—for after all, I have decided to be married. Sunday was the first day of publishing the bans. They should be published three times but the nice old French priest is going to let us do with twice. He tried to assure me that it doesn't hurt and that the much-dreaded marrying is over in five minutes—but it sounds so like painless dentistry that the resemblance may go further and it will only begin to hurt when it's all over!

They were married on October 17, 1916, in a Roman Catholic church in Athens. It was probably the closest thing to an Episcopal Church that Cecile could find, and, she wrote,

it fitted in with Pax's feelings on religion. He had no affiliation but said once that if he were to embrace any, it would be the Catholic Church, as its structure had more in common with socialist principles than any other. In spite of our best intentions it wasn't the quiet wedding we had meant to have. The witnesses made quite a small army in themselves. My witness, George P. Waller (on the Embassy staff but originally from Montgomery), published the day and hour so effectively that there were nearly seventy-five people there. He came in his frock coat, and very pie-eyed from a little drink he had been accumulating for the occasion.

Paxton's newspaper colleagues were in their usual dirty collars and shabby sack coats; Count Mercati, who represented the King, was resplendent in burying clothes. The Minister, Mr. Droppers, was miserable and uneasy at being inside the chancel of a Roman Catholic Church and making responses to Latin that he didn't understand.

Cecile added a P.S. asking Jean to tell Mama,

Please to send my November allowance here as most of that fortune all of you gave me has gone for hotel bills before I decided to get married. Living is incredibly expensive and it is just by the skin of his teeth that Paxton's salary pays our daily expenses, so I am thankful that I shall have my allowance for my personal needs and grateful beyond all words to Mama for it. For she did mean, did she not, that it was to continue? Otherwise I should never have taken this reckless step—and I would so much rather have it than a trousseau or fussy wedding.

There were many festivities when Paxton was awarded the decoration of Grand Commander of the Order of the Redeemer, for his stalwart defense of neutrality for Greece. Cecile wrote, "I began to think that after the King, we were the most important people in Greece, with cinema photographers lying in wait for us when we went out of the hotel and demonstrations before our windows. Paxton even had a street named after him. I think Rue Paxton Hibben is very cunning, don't you?"

By November there was more than a frost in the air. The Allies set up a blockade and recognized a provisional government that Venizelos established in Crete. Cecile wrote:

> The situation is intolerable. With the blockade on in earnest, the suffering is heart breaking. People are dying of starvation and I admit that I have been hungry for two weeks. The prices in restaurants have gone up so alarmingly that nobody can eat quite as much as they would like. Oh, shall I ever get the taste of mutton tallow out of my mouth and the sickening smell of it out of my nose! I miss my little apartment in Paris.
>
> McKenzie is back in greater glory than ever with all his whores and his Italian boys and his morals of Oscar Wilde without the genius. Really, if the poor unsuspecting British taxpayers only knew what they were paying for! [To this letter she added another P.S.:] I'm afraid you are going to think by my mentioning my house in Paris that I like that solitary life better than matrimony! If you only knew how utterly supremely happy my husband is making me and how I can't even think of Paris or anywhere else unless he is in the picture too.

In December she wrote,

> We are still here, but the crisis is not over yet. Meantime, I have asked a dozen unattached males, George Waller and several from the American Embassy here, for egg nog on Christmas Eve. I am sending this letter by way of George in the diplomatic pouch, but you must not speak of it since it is against the rules. When George goes back to Montgomery he will take the tablecloth I bought you. Please be very nice to him. He may be able to bring a few things to me when he returns here.

According to letters written home by Cecile, Pax was called back to New York by the Associated Press when his stories couldn't get through the blockade. The encyclopedia puts it differently: "He was recalled for his criticism of the Allied diplomatic course with regard to Greece." By this time, the United States was almost an ally. Paxton had to draw two months salary to get enough money to bring Cecile home with him. It cost $125 to go from Athens to Naples. In New York City they stayed a few nights at the Brevoort, then found a tiny room under the eaves large enough for Paxton to type on a corner table and for Cecile to write on the edge of the bed.

Paxton wrote a roundup story on Greece for the Associated Press that his editor called "great," and it attracted attention. He then took a month's leave to write a book on the situation in Greece.

Cecile wrote Jean: "Pax and I sit here in our funny little room all day and nearly all night, and he writes while I pound on the typewriter. We are both working hard and it is great fun and now the proofs are coming home every day, which is thrilling!"

Pax couldn't get away, but Cecile went home to spend some time with her sister and mother in Montgomery, her first visit since her marriage. Afterwards she wrote Jean, "Oh my darling dearest, how I miss you. Paxton realizes all the joys I gave up to come back to him and he tries hard to be you and sunshine and moonlight all in one, poor dear. Oh, sweetheart, it was such a perfect visit."

In Cecile's absence, Paxton attended several conferences at which he drew some criticism for stating King Constantine's case for Greek neutrality. An article in the *New York Times* reached Montgomery and embarrassed the family.

In answer to a letter from Jean, Cecile wrote home,

> Your and darling Mother's troubled letters arrived today. I am sorry I have been so bad about writing, but really I am busier than anybody you ever knew. If you could see me cooking two meals a day and doing Paxton's typing and keeping his files and having company and calling and darning and gardening you would wonder that I even found time to sleep!
>
> I am sorry the *New York Times* article troubled you so much. Of course I hated it, but I am the only person here who takes the thing seriously. When you read the account of his speech I am sending you, you will see that he did not attack the Allies—in fact he is too much occupied with our getting the best we can out of this war to think about either the Allies or Greece. You don't know anything about

public feeling in this part of the country when you say that nobody will tolerate any criticism of the Allies.

Please read Richmond Pearson Hobson's article in last Sunday's *New York American*. He says that it is England's cynical egotism that is losing the war, and more along that line. Also read an account of Francis Hackett's speech at the Foreign Relations meeting the same day Paxton made his speech. He for one did not mince matters about what he thought of England's hypocrisy and inefficiency, and you will remark in Paxton's speech there was nothing of that sort.

Also, he has spoken at nearly a dozen club dinners lately and everywhere he has talked perfectly frankly about what he considers the most important thing in all this business for us: that is, not telling ourselves lies—neither about the actual situation with our enemies or our allies, or their real aims or their chances of victory or defeat—and everywhere he has not only been enthusiastically received but has received twenty-five dollars for these little after-dinner speeches!

Behind the attack on Pax, according to Cecile, was a campaign to discredit the book by Eleutherios Venizelos, financed by the British. He was later successful in engineering the ouster of Constantine and became the premier after the abdication.

If you could see the letters Paxton has received from the distinguished men, you would not think that his views were "not being tolerated."

You say you don't agree with Paxton when he says it doesn't matter whether the Greek King is pro-German or not (he is not).

You have got to agree with him or else we have got to stop talking about making the world safe for democracy, and the rights of small nations to have any form of government they choose, so long as it represents the "consent of the governed." The truth is that nobody (I mean the British who do all this howling about it) really cares a rap about the rights of small nations, and it is up to us to see that it isn't just empty phrases.

After he completed the book on Greece, Paxton volunteered for the U.S. Army in his home state of Indiana and was assigned to an officer training camp there. Cecile wrote,

It does seem such a waste of time for him when he speaks nine languages and could be really invaluable abroad—but I can't hope that the Department will have that much discrimination. However, he is going to try for that sort of work before he goes to Ft. Harrison in June.

He took me to a reception at the Princeton Club to meet his relative, John Grier Hibben, the president of Princeton, but I am terribly afraid of having to go to Indianapolis to meet his immediate family. He wants me to go there to stay with them, where he can see me once a week while he is in training. But I positively will not do it as I think it would be the greatest mistake if I ever hope to remain on friendly terms, staying for two months as a first visit—especially as they are rather difficult and it is a household all disarranged by illness. Don't you agree with me?

I have planted sunflowers and coreopsis in the garden and the moon flowers and morning glories are up two inches already. I have bought three yellow lanterns like yours and we are going to have dinner out-of-doors now as well as luncheon. We shall be very glad to see the Peyton Rouses, since Peyton is in touch with what is happening in Washington, and Pax will be going there next week to see some people in the War Department about doing interpreting work in the Army.

The book (on Greece) is to go on sale Saturday. Alas, I am afraid you will have a great deal more to suffer from notoriety and blackguarding than you have already! I hesitate to think what the *Times* book review will say about it, but you can make up your mind that there will be some more mud slinging by Venizelist propaganda people, as they will stop at no infamy to discredit the book.

Cecile decided to wait out Paxton's training by going back to her old job at the Red Cross Hospital in Paris. She reasoned that it would only be a couple of months before he would be sent overseas, and she would be there waiting for him. In September she sailed aboard the SS *Rochambeau*, "with everybody's nerves on edge going through the submarine zones."

By the time she left, Pax was already in officer training camp at Fort Harrison, and he was commissioned as a lieutenant before Christmas. However, it would be a year before he would get to France as finance officer in an Army camp not far from Paris, and in that time he and Cecile drew far apart. Sometimes it would be weeks between letters. She was lonely and alone in a situation she could not handle. She needed comfort and support desperately. She ended one poignant letter to Jean:

"Oh, my darling, I suppose I must say good-bye. I love you, love you, love more than I can ever tell you. Some day I may tell you what has happened. Sweetheart, sweetheart, go on loving me please—some far off day we shall yet be together. My whole torn and loving heart, Bini."

There were separations and sessions with French psychiatrists, and when Pax was finally discharged, Cecile returned to the United States alone and went to Jean and her mother in Montgomery. Paxton left for Moscow to cover the Russian Revolution for the *Chicago Tribune*. Whether they would ever get together again was questionable.

There were ten months of reconciliation and breaking off by mail. In the meantime Paxton had gone to work for the Russian Red Cross, as co-director of Near East Relief. Finally, Cecile rejoined him when he took a new assignment in Constantinople. Afterward they returned to Greece by way of a romantic interlude in Italy where she became pregnant. She stayed in Athens when he went to the Caucasus to cover the aftermath of the Russian Revolution. While he was away Cecile was never quite sure where she would be going next, but she was well treated by the royal family and the Greek people.

She wrote her mother:

> I am expecting a cable from Paxton telling me he is back from the Caucasus. I shall be eager to hear what our nice Georgia was like under the Soviets. No good booze for one thing! I sent him a letter charging him solemnly to bring back some black caviar for Jean.
>
> Day before yesterday I was invited to tea, to be presented to the Princess Royal (Princess Elizabeth of Roumania). I was quite unprepared for such dazzling beauty, very tall with marvelous deep gold hair and violet blue eyes. She wore a loose kind of drapery, a sort of cloud of grey chiffon, cut absurdly low for an afternoon dress, and a small grey tulle toque with pink roses coming nearly over her eyes, and the most gorgeous and barbaric jewels I ever saw.
>
> I am certainly in luck being looked after by old Dr. Louras who is the busiest man in Athens and most adored, and he comes to see me a couple of times a week although I am really quite well. I daresay he has his orders from the queen. When I had that stomach attack he was all for my coming to his private hospital for a few days, which he let me know tactfully, would be free.

The Hibbens returned to New York City, where Cecile became Sheila again and gave birth to a daughter. She was named Jean Constantine Hibben—Jean for her Aunt Jean, and Constantine for King Constantine of Greece. He became her godfather, and sent her a gold cross and a suitably inscribed silver bowl. She was soon nicknamed "Jill," and later as a young woman she dropped the Constantine and substituted Paxton as a middle name. So, by degrees she became Jill Paxton Hibben—and when she grew up and married, added Hellendale.

22

A Baby Is Born

*T*WAS BORN ON APRIL 19, 1916, IN A GREAT FOUR-POSTER CANOPIED BED in the pink room at Hazel Hedge. Jean, at thirty-five, was many hours in labor. To celebrate my birth, Anne Goldthwaite painted a picture of the four-poster draped in mosquito netting, behind which presumably were my mother and me. Outside the netting, waving a large fan to stir up the air was a little Negro girl.

Years later, after Anne Goldthwaite had become quite famous, a local gallery considered including this painting in an exhibit of the work of famous Southern artists. However, it was rejected as being too much of a reminder of slave labor.

Even before I arrived, father became leader of a Boy Scout troop, and took me as a baby to be shown off to "his lads." He was very pleased when Jean suggested that I be named after his father, the Nicholas Cabell Read of Corsicana, Texas. She was no doubt happy that his and my middle name was to be Cabell, after a Virginia relative, James Branch Cabell, a well-known novelist of the time.

Cecile, writing from France, had advice. "It is very important that you call the baby Nicholas and not Cabell—and even if you don't see it my way, please agree to my request. Truly surnames as Christian names are so mid-Victorian and utterly out of fashion, and the only way to do it is to make servants and everybody begin calling him 'Nicholas' now."

She also gave advice as to my future career. "What do you think about diplomacy for Master Nicholas? Of all those stylish titles I think I like 'His Excellency' Nicholas Cabell Read best. Of course he will never make any money at it, but there are better things than that."

I was much welcomed. Cousin "Tea Cake" wrote from Kintry, the Ben Baldwin plantation in the country, "You have been mothering this whole big world a long, long time—dear Jean—and it is time that you have this real, true motherhood." Jean sent pictures of me to Sylvia Beach in Paris, who answered: "You colored them, didn't you? I have them in gilded wood frames along with you in your wedding dress and dear Nicholas in his bed at the age of a few hours and no one looking after him but the Della Robbia Madonna you took home from Italy. He looks very beautiful! I would give my picador on horseback on Triana pottery to see him. What career do you think he'll take up? I should have him identify himself with the 'Internationale' like Kropotkin."

A few months after my birth I was baptized with water from a silver christening bowl that is still in the family. From the beginning I was surrounded by people who adored—and spoiled—me. My mother and father were in the forefront, and the servants competed with one another to please me. I resisted only one, my Mother's friend Olive Macdonald, who called me divine and gave me wet kisses as she clasped me to her ample bosom. Some of my first words were "Moosh, Olive, moosh far away."

Painting by Anne Goldthwaite of Jean giving birth to Nick in a four-poster bed.

My grandmother Jennie was the only holdout. She loved me, but did not spoil me. She read the Bible to me and went by what the Good Book said. At an early age she taught me to say my prayers. From her I learned all the virtues (not that I always practiced them). My prayer was: "Oh God, give me clean hands, clean words, clean thoughts . . . Build it well what you do, build it straight, strong and true . . . Good night, good sleep, good rest from sorrows." To guard against sorrows, when I began to walk Jennie had a cover put on the old well so that I would not be tempted to go over the edge.

I was only a year old when the United States entered World War I in 1917. My father was over-age for military service, but he asked Sam, the yardman, to be his substitute. Sam said he would like to be, but explained why that was impossible: "There's one thing I've been voidin' all my life, boss, dat's death." Later on, Nash persuaded Ben Miller, our houseboy, to join the service. We have a picture of Ben in his uniform, but he didn't get overseas.

Nash himself volunteered for civilian service with the War Labor Board. Just what he did remains a mystery, but he didn't write many letters. At least a very large supply of U.S. Department of Labor stationery was still around as late as 1927, though my mother had been using it regularly to write long letters once a week to her sister Sheila.

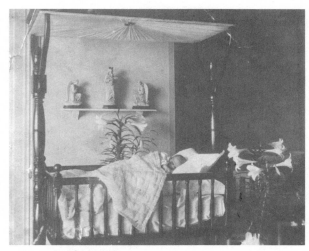

Top: Jean and Nash with baby Nick. Bottom: Baby Nick in an antique crib.

What my father did do during the war was to perfect his golf. When he came to Montgomery he joined the golf club, one of whose founders fifteen years earlier had been Jean's father, Mr. Will Craik. Nash played golf in plus-four knickerbockers, and was usually accompanied by his dog Vopsa. Eventually I was old enough to take Vopsa's place, but I was too slow. "Stop suckin' the hind tit, son," he would say. He finally switched to short pants for the 18-hole walk about the course in the hot summers. There were no golf carts then. The first tee was near the old clubhouse on the north side of Carter Hill Road, which was then unpaved and devoid of traffic except for a few buggies and wagons. The green was on the south side. As traffic increased, which was very obvious to father since it passed Hazel Hedge, he advocated buying land south of Carter Hill, moving the first tee to that side and extending the whole course in that direction.

He put his money where his mouth was by purchasing one of the first Country Club bonds to finance the move. We still have it. It says it is worth one hundred dollars. There was some opposition by neighbors, including Files Crenshaw Sr., who believed it would hurt property values. Only when the old shingle clubhouse burned was father able to make much progress with his idea, but from then on he spent many hours a day on the plans and the construction of a new brick clubhouse at the end of Fairview Avenue.

Top: Nash in rocking chair. Bottom: Nash with hunting dog.

He was a very good golfer, usually winning, but he helped along the way by comments designed to throw his opponents off their game. For example, if an opponent's putt was short, my father would smile at him and say: "Faint heart never won fair lady." If it happened again he would say: "It will never get well if you pick at it." Chances were that the man would hit his ball well past the hole on his third putt. Father would express sympathy.

He had enough money and plenty of time, having retired from the fertilizer business shortly after he married Jean. He was one of the few people who knew what to do with leisure. He taught me golf, as well as how to hunt and shoot. He was a very good shot himself, having learned as a poor boy in Corsicana, where the cost of every shotgun shell was reckoned. He seldom returned from a hunt without a number of ducks or quail, doves and snipe.

His friend, George Westfeldt of New Orleans, who founded the Whitney National Bank there, invited him to join the Delta Duck Club, a prestigious sportsmen's group where he outshot most of the members. He had three bird dogs—two setters and a pointer—who when not out hunting were kept in the dog yard. They were not allowed in the house.

By contrast, Figaro, a French poodle Sheila had bought in France, had the free run of the place. Father thought his dogs were being discriminated against and brought his favorite setter, Dan, into the dining room. The experiment was not a success. Dan stayed close to Dada all the time, watching every move. His eyes would follow a fork or spoon of food up from the plate and just as it reached his mouth Dan would open his own mouth and make a noisy gulp. He was soon returned to the dog yard.

Ben serving al fresco.

Meanwhile, Jeanie continued to improve her garden. She built a white-columned pergola and a fountain on the west side of the house, and connected them to the screen porch by a path lined with old plantation bells turned upside down and planted with shrubs. Another path led to a stone sundial, which showed the time of day when the sun was shining. She put a small rectangular pool about three feet deep in the yard to the west of the elm tree near the replica of a religious statue, "Rebecca of the Well," and a marble bench with the inscription: "I know a lovely garden, a calm retreat. It is not entered by feet of flesh, but by the feat of love."

My mother began to have dinners out by the pool, dining "al fresco," as she put it. Of these Nash said, "I've eaten more cold gravy than any man alive." Ben, who served the food, commented, "I don't mind carryin' things to the pool. I fills my finger bowls as I go by." The gravy may have gotten cold, but the food was always good. Occasionally Nash used expressions Jean hated, "Good belly don't bust" and "That's what makes the cheese more binding."

Nash played golf a lot with an enthusiastic young lady named Eva Mae Clark, which in Montgomery was cause for gossip. When he became chairman of a beauti-fication program for the club, he told his committee that he wanted more "Lonicera Fragrantissima." They knew that such a horticultural term must have come from

Jean, but that it was a honeysuckle the locals called "Kiss-Me-at-the-Gate." They all had a good laugh.

During the war Nash met a colonel who was being posted overseas and arranged to bring his young son, Francis Burdette, to live with us and keep me company. He was with us for a few years.

We also entertained young soldiers from Camp Sheridan, the military post in Montgomery. Jean recalled serving two of them artichokes. One just stared at his. The other, after attacking a few leaves, turned to his buddy and said: "Go on and try it, Joe, it ain't bad." "Naw," said Joe, "It ain't worth it." Jean persuaded one of her Army Air Corp guests to take her up in a plane, and fly out over the house where the servants stood gazing upwards and making such remarks as, "Look at Miss Jean, ain't she grand?" When the war ended, in Alabama there was a lot of catching up to do, and there was not much money to do it with. The great new Dixie-Overland trans-continental highway was stalled for want of a bridge to replace a ferry across the Tombigbee River near Demopolis, about 100 miles due west of Montgomery. Frank Derby, from across the Tombigbee in Sumter County (named for "Game Cock" Sumter, a Revolutionary War General), promoted the idea of raising the money to build the bridge by having an auction of gamecocks.

That was the summer of 1919 when the "Big Four," President Woodrow Wilson, British Prime Minister David Lloyd George, French Premier Georges Clemenceau and Italian Premiere Vittoria Orlando, were meeting in Paris to negotiate an armistice. Derby referred to them as "the Game Cocks of today."

Frank wrote about his idea for the auction to his Congressman, who showed the letter to Secretary of the Navy Josephus Daniels, who relayed it to the "Big Four." It was well received as something all of them could agree upon. Each said he would give a rooster, as did Generals Foch and Pershing—to be named for themselves.

President Wilson himself brought the foreign roosters across the ocean on the liner *George Washington*, and presented them with great fanfare in Washington, D.C. Much laughter arose when the president said he thought Lloyd George's cock "looked sick." In the nation's capital more cocks were given—by Josephus Daniels, Admiral Benson, and Treasury Secretary William McAdoo. When they were brought down South, awaiting them in the bridal suite of the Tutwiler Hotel in Birmingham, were roosters Fatty Arbuckle, Mary Pickford and Babe Ruth, with one little hen from Helen Keller.

Anyone could give a rooster by paying a ten dollar fee. Literally hundreds came into Demopolis from all over Alabama. It took two days, August 14 and 15, 1919, to auction them off before an estimated 40,000 people crowded into bleachers built around Confederate Square. The biggest barbecue ever held in Alabama was served off a table 12,000 feet long.

A special edition of the *Montgomery Journal* was flown in and dropped by parachute from an Alabama Aviation Repair Depot plane. Some birds went for one thousand dollars. The big-name cocks were held until last. Woodrow Wilson was no doubt highly pleased to learn that his namesake was bought by a syndicate of Alabamians for fifty-five thousand. The Union Stock Yards of Montgomery purchased Clemenceau for ten thousand dollars. An astounding total of three hundred thousand dollars was promised.

Unfortunately, less than one-fifth of the pledges were ever paid.

The State Highway Department, with some federal money, completed the drawbridge in 1925. Officially it was named Memorial Bridge, honoring the boys from Marengo and Sumter Counties who had died in the war, but everybody called it the Rooster Bridge. In 1959, the governor signed an act making the name official. Eventually, when traffic on Highway 80 got too heavy for the metal-frame bridge, it was turned into a one-way bridge, and in 1980 it was torn down. There are still markers on both sides of the river, honoring Frank Derby and listing those who donated roosters.

It didn't take an auction to get people to Jean Read's parties, which were staged either with special food or special events. In the summer they were in the garden; in winter, and traditionally on Christmas Eve, before a roaring fire in the drawing room. The holiday party was a big one. All our friends and their children came, and to these Jean added anyone she knew who might not have somewhere to go on Christmas Eve.

She customarily did things that other people didn't do, and got away with it. I had a dream once. Someone said: "Have you seen the holes in Jean's curtains?" And someone else said: "That's the style now. Jean always sets the style. I'll go home right away and slash mine." Another voice said, "Be sure and hit the soiled spots."

Her activities were many, from arranging the flowers for weddings and services at the new Episcopal Church of the Ascension in Cloverdale, to founding and running the Montgomery Little Theatre. In this she was supported by Nash, whose hearty laugh could be heard from the audiences at each performance, and whose generous pocketbook along with that of Mr. Fred Cramton (known for founding Cramton's

The Little Theater, in a production of Noel Coward's Hay Fever.

Bowl stadium) supported the construction of the theater on Julia Street.

The Little Theatre had professional directors, but everything else was done by volunteers. Jean helped select the plays, having learned a lot about them from her father, Will Craik. He was a theater buff who wrote reviews of touring company performances for the *Montgomery Advertiser* and often invited actors home.

When the Shakespearean actor Ben Greet appeared with a touring company in Montgomery, he was entertained at Hazel Hedge for dinner. After a couple of bites of dessert, he turned to Jennie Craik to ask: "What is this delicious concoction?" To which my grandmother replied: "Mr. Greet, you have just named it." (The recipe for "Delicious Concoction" is on page 265 of *American Regional Cookery*, written by Sheila Hibben many years later).

At the Little Theatre, Jean was the number one volunteer, involving her friends, looking for talent, acting in plays, and designing sets—usually with some furnishings from Hazel Hedge. With all the wear and tear, antiques and pictures, as well as furniture and silver, were often damaged.

After Jean's death, the silver was appraised before it was divided among the grandchildren. As the appraiser examined each of the forty or fifty pieces of hollowware he made the same pronouncement. "If this piece wasn't damaged it would be worth a lot more."

When Mr. Corbett—or was it Mr. Monk, the carpenter—came to do some repairs one day, he suggested planing off the dents and scratches on a long table behind the sofa. Jean said, "Oh no, they've been there since the sixteenth century. It's a Queen Elizabeth table." He answered, "Well, she sure had some mighty bad children." Jean refrained from telling him that Elizabeth was a virgin queen who didn't have any children.

The theater had a heavy schedule, as printed programs, all of which are in the Alabama Archives, attest. Several were performed each year, ranging from *Arms and the Man* by G.B. Shaw and *The Circle* by Somerset Maugham, to *Ruint*, a folk comedy about a North Carolina mountain woman.

When Jean was cast as a "lady of refined appearance" in *Serena Blandish* by S. N. Behrman, a newcomer to Montgomery, upon being introduced to her, said: "Mrs. Read, I'm so happy to meet you. Everyone says you are so talented." "Well, I have a lot of energy," Jean replied. "In Montgomery that passes for talent." Indeed her energy knew no bounds. Or, as Nash put it, "You can't keep a squirrel on the ground."

Evidence that Jean imbued the theater troupe with her dynamism can be seen in her description of how they triumphed over what could have been a disastrous natural calamity: "We gave *Lysistrata* three nights between torrential downpours. It opened Thursday after a great rain that filled the punch bowls and sopped the tablecloths and wet the chairs. We got bath towels and dried the chairs. The setting and lights and music were wonderful. The punch was magnificent. In three nights we

A "Fleahop School" picture, after Jean cut out her own face.

used 89 bottles of sauterne, two cases of champagne (French), one case of cointreau, oranges, lemons and fresh peaches. We had about 250 people each night."

In her leftover time, Jean made items for her shop, did much of the cooking and gardening at home, sewed clothes and curtains, filled jars with artichoke pickles and bottles with plum cordial. A new yard man, Joe Lee, told the cook he was having a hard time with Miz Jean. "She say, 'Dig here, dig here, do this, do dat. Clip this, prune that. I cain't keep up wid her." Mammy Ellen answered, "That sho is Miz Jean. Cain't nobody keep up."

At the request of an elderly distant cousin, Elizabeth Tinker Elmore, who was practicing to be a painter, Jean agreed to let her do a portrait. When asked how he liked it, Nash said, "Well, it doesn't quite capture Jean's vitality." "Oh, I can take care of that," the cousin answered, and added a little touch of red to each nostril. Jean looked like a fire-wagon horse breathing smoke and flame.

Nash showing off infant Nick to his Boy Scout troop.

Jean cut it up. She had a habit of doing that when she didn't like something of herself. In an early photograph of a young people's party at Hazel Hedge she cut out her face, as she did in a photograph with her pupils at the "Fleahop School," and she even cut up a portrait of herself by Anne Goldthwaite. "I needed the frame for something else," she explained.

23

The Birthday Parties,
School and Ben

WHEN I WAS VERY YOUNG, JEANIE BEGAN TO GIVE ME BIRTHDAY parties to which family and guests would come in fancy dress costumes based on the book being read to me at the time. Jeanie made my costumes. I remember a particularly disagreeable one when I was Puss 'n Boots. Mother glued whiskers over my upper lip and with a safety pin attached a tail to my pants behind. The glue smelled awful and the pin stuck me in the bottom.

There were a lot of books. We didn't enact them all. Years later, when dusting my bookshelves, Jean reminisced in a letter to me: "Cleaning your books and the filthy book case took so long because I would stop & look at each one & remember when you were reading it & how you looked & what you said. Your first books were *The Cock, The Mouse and the Little Red Hen,* and *Roly Poly Pudding.* Your grandmother Jennie gave you the children's Bible, and read to you from it every night in her feather bed. Celie [my nurse] learned *The Little Red Balloon* by heart. Others were *Mother Goose, Water Babies, Dr. Doolittle, The White Company, Lorna Doone,* and of course *Robin Hood.*"

Robin Hood was the last role I played in the birthday enactments, except for "Black Jack Davy," which our family performed every Christmas Eve. Eventually I grew old enough and tall enough to play the role of the dashing highwayman, who carried Jeanie away from her husband. Dada was a sultanish-looking deserted husband, and Jean wore a conical hat as his wayfaring lady. The words were:

Nick as Caroler.

Nick as Black Jack Davy.

Oh the Black Jack Davy came riding along
So merrily, so gaily
And he rode so straight and he rode so strong
That he charmed the heart of a lady.
"Will you forsake your house and farm?
Will you forsake your baby?
Will you forsake your husband too
And go with the Black Jack Davy?"
"Yes, I'll forsake my house and farm
And I'll forsake my baby,
And I'll forsake my husband too,
And go with the Black Jack Davy."
The husband he came riding home
Enquiring for his lady,
And the servants they made answer thus,
"She's gone with the Black Jack Davy."
"Oh saddle me up my iron gray mare
My roan is not so steady.
I'll ride all day and I'll ride all night
'Til I overtake my lady."
He rode all day and he rode all night
'Til he came to the banks of a river,
And the tears came trickling down his cheeks
For then he saw his lady.
"Last night I slept on a couch of gold
Beside my lord and master. Tonight
I sleep on the cold, cold ground
In the arms of the Black Jack Davy."
"Will you take off your sky blue gloves
made out of Spanish leather,
And give to me your lily white hand
And say farewell forever?"
"Yes, I'll take off my sky blue gloves
made out of Spanish leather,
And give to you my lily white hand

And say farewell forever."
Oh the husband he rode sadly away
A mourning for his lady
And the moral of this tale, they say,
Is just a little bit shady.

Afterwards, there were carols. Nancy Smith always played the Steinway, not easy to do since the strings inside were festooned with leaves and burrs from extravagant flower arrangements placed on its flat top through the years by Jean. Serving the strong Christmas punch was Ben Miller, a majordomo of a black man who used his judgment, and didn't serve more punch to any guest he thought had enough.

Ben had come to Hazel Hedge when he was sixteen and known as "Boysey," from the Oliver Plantation in Mt. Meigs. There, he had been brought up by his father, an ex-slave, who had earned a federal pension for his services to the Union during the Civil War. Just when he started fighting or where, is not known. "I just fit, and fit, and fit," he said. It was a white man's war in the beginning until Massachusetts broke the color ban by mustering a Negro regiment into the Union Army.

Congress had passed two acts in July 1862 allowing African-Americans to enlist, but official enrollment did not occur until after Abraham Lincoln issued the Emancipation Proclamation, and the Civil War became a war to save the Union *and to abolish slavery.*

By then several Northern states had formed colored regiments and some Southern states authorized the arming of able-bodied ex-slaves. Within the next year, fourteen Negro regiments were in the field, and many had engaged in battle.

But it was 1865 before a battle was fought in Alabama in which nine U.S Colored Infantry Regiments, possibly including Ben's father, had "fit and fit and fit" and earned their pensions and some self-satisfaction in knowing that they had participated in the war that eventually freed their people. Approximately 180,000 Negroes served in the Union Army and many more in the Navy.

Ben and his first wife, Clairisy, lived in quarters over

Nick as Robin Hood.

the garage at Hazel Hedge and had a daughter Ruby, about my age. I worried about Ruby because as I explained to Mother, "She was so ignant." I didn't understand the "separate and unequal" doctrine of the Southern educational system. There were colored schools but they didn't teach much. However, Ruby was a quick learner and was encouraged by my grandmother who read aloud to us. Eventually, she went to normal school. When she graduated, she moved north to White Plains in New York State. We still exchange Christmas cards with fond remembrances.

Quite a few years after Ben and Clairisy were divorced, Ben married Mary Martin, a school teacher. When he told Jean what he was going to do, he said, "It ain't goin to make no difference." It didn't except he moved into a comfortable house with Mary in nearby Belair, a colored section and became "Uncle Ben" to her children—all of whom went to college. One was Bert, whom we got to know best. He taught in the drama department at Alabama State University nearby, where he directed plays and acted. He often dropped by to see his "Uncle Ben."

Ben wasn't there one day when Bert came through the kitchen door and asked to see Miz Read. Jeanie was on the screen porch with Willey Gayle Martin, an artist friend who was given to making derogatory remarks about Negroes. Dallas, recently arrived from the North, didn't invite him out on the porch because she was afraid that Willey would be rude to him. She need not have worried. Only "red necks" do anything like that.

Kids eating watermelon.

Ben came every morning to Hazel Hedge in time to make and serve breakfast on the round marble table on the screen porch under the ceiling fan. Usually we had soft-scrambled eggs and grits, slices of fresh tomatoes, and wonderful crisp bacon done in a heavy frying pan that got blacker through the years. For a long time, Dallas insisted on using a burned old pan to make "Ben's kind of bacon."

Aside from breakfast, Jean did the cooking. Ben cleaned the kitchen and did the brass and silver, and kept Dada's Stutz Bearcat in a fine state of polish. He also did some garden work, and in the winter laid the logs in the big fireplace. He had a strong sense of propriety, except for whistling in the house, which my

grandmother said was unseemly, but he never gave it up. He was a sporty fellow. He hunted, and cleaned and picked feathers off the hundreds of quail, dove and snipe that he, as well as my father, shot. He liked fine horses, and had a fast-paced one of his own, named Mamie Smith, which he kept in our barn.

How proud I was to ride in a sulky on Ben's lap, allowed to hold the reins under Ben's big hands as he guided us out the Pineleaf gate at the back of Hazel Hedge into Belair, where the streets were unpaved and soft under Mamie Smith's flying feet.

Ben would stop and see his friends, and I got to know their little boys. Since they lived close by, they became my best friends.

There was Jimmy Porter, the son of our postman, and Booker T. Blair, whose father ran a small dry-cleaning establishment, and through them I met Clayton Marcus, who everyone called "Peewee" because he was so small. I liked him immediately. He was the only boy my age who was smaller than I was. He had the brightest smile, and could sing and tap dance and was very funny.

Clayton "Peewee" Marcus, dancing.

In the summer Mother would buy a big watermelon and a fifty-pound block of ice, which would be broken into little pieces to cover and chill the melon in a metal tub set on a marble table by the little pool. When it was cold enough it would be cut in long slices and divided between about twelve of us, who put our faces in the melon and our feet in the pool. It was a good place to wash off the sticky juice. We spat the seeds into the grass and broke the rinds into chunks for ammunition in throwing and dodging contests.

Not long ago, Peewee telephoned me from New York City, where he said he had been on the stage, after entertaining at the Hermitage in Nashville for a number of years. He was a little short of cash, which didn't surprise me since several of our family are in the theater, and are always short of cash. Over the telephone Peewee reminded me of the "beautiful times . . . they will never come again."

When I was six years old I started the first grade. The new brick Cloverdale Elementary School was not yet open, and I attended a temporary one in an old white frame house on Carter Hill Road near Narrow Lane, which we called "The Chicken Coop." There were no Negro pupils there, so it was the first time I got to know white boys very well.

I had bobbed hair and was dressed by Mother, who liked everything English, in a

Christopher Robin smock with a sort of skirt, which hardly showed the abbreviated shorts underneath. I carried my lunch of cucumber sandwiches wrapped in waxed paper, in a little basket. Almost immediately I got into a fight with a boy who called me a girl. My suit was dirty and my basket broken by the time I returned home.

Everyone at Hazel Hedge was out to welcome me and ask how I liked school. "How did you like your teacher?" my grandmother asked. "All right," I muttered. "How did you like your classmates?" asked my father. "All right," I replied. Then mother asked, "How did you like your lunch?" I exploded. "All I want is a cold sweet potato wrapped in newspaper like everybody else."

As soon as the Cloverdale School opened I went there. Mother had cut my hair and put me in boys' clothes. My teacher was Miss Birdie Belser, a chesty little woman who brooked no nonsense. Miss Belser called by the house to speak to my grandmother about me. She got off on the wrong foot. "The trouble with Nicholas is . . ." she began. She was stopped before she went further.

Nick, dressed in a smock, with bobbed hair.

"There is no trouble with Nicholas," said my grandmother, who knew there was plenty of trouble with Nicholas, but she wasn't going to let Birdie Belser tell her. Whether it was due to the influence of my grandmother or Miss Belser, my beginning grades of mostly threes and fours (fairs and poors) moved steadily upwards to all ones (superior). My mother and grandmother prodded and complimented me in turn. When I was in the third grade, a short essay I wrote (with help) was printed in the local newspaper:

THANKSGIVING

NICHOLAS READ, GRADE III, CLOVERDALE

> Thanksgiving was first celebrated by the Pilgrims.
> The Pilgrims landed at Plymouth Rock in 1620, and
> had many hardships. They had to fight the Indians.
> The corn crop was very good, and that is the reason
> we give thanks to God on Thanksgiving.

I liked the fact that there were girls at Cloverdale. I still have one of the letters everyone was required to write me when I broke my arm. I was about ten years old. "We hope you will be better soon. The girls missed you a lot. One girl said she missed your winks at her."

We always had two or three cows in the small barn at Hazel Hedge. Ben milked them and Mammy Ellen, the cook, churned for butter. She repeated over and over again, "Old Aunt Kate waiting at the gate, waiting for the butter, come butter come." Sometimes she would let me lick a little butter off the dasher, while she made butter balls between two wooden paddles. I liked to swipe a butter ball, run to the dog yard, and hide in a dog house to eat it.

We also had curd presses so there were curds and whey. The curds were eaten as a dessert, sprinkled with ground nutmeg and sugar and served with cream. Mammy Ellen also made beaten biscuits on our beaten biscuit machine—two steel rollers and a crank with which to mash the dough flat. They were served with thin slices of Virginia ham at parties.

One of our cows was named Daisy. She was a good-natured Jersey. Sometimes I would lie on the floor of Daisy's stall and Ben, while milking her, would squirt the warm milk into my open mouth.

The other cow I remember with no pleasure as "Red," was a mixed breed and mean. She would chase me when I went into what was then the pasture. I was allowed to accompany Ben when he led the cows down Carter Hill road to be serviced by a bull, which was both interesting and frightening when the bull mounted the cow. I thought he was hurting her, but Ben reassured me.

My mother introduced me to the theater when I was very young. She made puppets and manipulated them on a small portable stage. There was Limber-neck and Benjamin, and on my first birthday I received from Paxton Hibben a Peter Paxton Rabbit. For my seventh birthday, Jean put on a marionette show, "Snickerly Nick." It had two settings, the first all snow and ice and then a transformation into flowers and grass.

My portrait was painted by the eminent artist Anne Goldthwaite. I was in the garden wearing a yellow smock. Jean loved the portrait, but didn't like my hands, so she washed a little paint over them, to hide them.

My grandmother, Jennie, was my conscience. She bought a brooder and one hundred baby chicks for me to raise, her objective being to start me in an enterprise at which I could earn money for my "Mite Box" at the church. The chicks were not very bright and I was bored with them. Unless they were kept out of the corners of the brooder room, they would smother one another to death, and I had to grease each chicken's head with an ointment to keep it from getting the "sorehead."

Nick with his roosters.

The project came to an abrupt halt when Atalanta, a German Shepherd named for the huntress in the Greek legend, broke in and killed half my chickens. Mammy, in the kitchen, saw him do it. "It waren't Mobile, and it waren't St. Louis, so it had to be Atalanta."

Granny lost out permanently when my father took me to a cock fight. The two cocks "pitted" against one another were unlike any roosters I had known. They were lean and strong and bred for combat, with "gaffs" (curving steel spurs) strapped on their legs. From the time the referee commanded: "Gentlemen, pit your cocks" to the final lethal blow it was an exciting action-packed contest.

After the fight I met a man who offered to help me get started raising game chickens and told me about *Grit and Steel,* "the magazine of game fowl fanciers," with articles about different breeds. I chose Roundheads, and learned how to tie little leather "boxing gloves" over their natural spurs which had been sawed off to about half an inch long, and to spar them with another cock of about the same size to give them experience and confidence. In a regular fight in the pit, both cocks would be wearing gaffs, and the fight would be to the death. My first fighter, a beautiful red and bronze cock, won his first twelve fights, and in doing so won a fair amount of money for my father. He was retired to service game hens after his thirteenth fight, which he won but was badly hurt.

The fact that he escaped death was fortunate for me since the death of my cock would have meant bringing him home to the kitchen. The birds were "conditioned" for battle and were very tough. They ended up as chicken hash to be served with waffles. I liked the waffles but could never eat the chicken.

The most popular pit near Montgomery was on the Crommelin place near Wetumpka. I remember a fight there when a plane flew low over the pine trees surrounding the pit. We all thought it was "the law" (the sport had been declared illegal) and we scattered into the woods. In a short time a man in a khaki naval uniform came forward on foot, asking in a loud voice, "Where's the chicken fight?" It was Lt. John Crommelin, Jr., U.S. Navy pilot who had flown up from the Pensacola Air Station to see the fight.

During prohibition, "Red" Chambers, the family bootlegger, would deliver charred oak kegs of corn whiskey to Hazel Hedge in a mule-drawn wagon covered with loose cotton. These would be carried to the lumber room, a kind of attic. Father would add dried peaches through holes in the top of the kegs, and sometimes charred oak chips. After aging in the keg he would insert a rubber hose similar to that on an enema bag, suck on one end, and start a flow decanting the whisky into glass jugs.

Father never failed to send a jug to Judge Clayton at Christmas and New Year's. This was very prudent and proved quite helpful when Red was later arrested for bootlegging. When his case came up in court, Judge Clayton questioned him about how he made his whiskey. After being satisfied he used no impurities, the Judge fined him and sentenced him to three years in Kilby prison. My father paid the fine. Then, in an aside to the clerk, the judge said, "Remand that sentence." I don't think Red ever served time.

I had my own business arrangements with Mr. Chambers. I needed some "walks" for my game cocks and Red would help me place them on farms in the country. These were generally Negro families. He would buy their "dung-hill" rooster, kill it, give it to them to eat and leave my game cock with their hens. My bird was literally the cock of the walk.

24

The Roaring Twenties

IN THE 1920S JEAN WAS HAVING RECURRENCES OF HER TERRIBLE headaches, which she called neuralgia. A letter from Sheila feared "that you are having day-and-night hysterics again." In the middle of one night she awoke and scribbled a terrifying note:

> My Darling (to Sheila)—I may die tonight as I took some chloride pills left in a glass by mistake in the dark. I'm awfully sorry on account of Nicky, and you and Mama. Nicky needs me now. He is very difficult. Nash can never bring him up properly. He is so like me. Won't you help him? I leave all my possessions to Jill Constantine except my books to Nicky. I love you so. Goodbye.

It could have been this frightening message that propelled Nash to try to get Jean away from what was troubling her—Hazel Hedge. It had become a daily reminder of what she had not accomplished in life. Its beauty was transient, not lasting. What did it amount to when she might have become a writer, or a poet, or a real painter? Something more permanent than running a little theater, spending so much of her time producing other people's plays.

Jean was so unhappy she was thinking of leaving Hazel Hedge permanently. Sheila, among others, was deeply concerned:

> The whole tragedy of your going is just overpowering me. This afternoon I ran around to see Anne Goldthwaite, and she was almost as unhappy as I about your saying you don't want to come back to Hazel Hedge. She just buried her face in her hands and howled. I had no idea that she had such an appreciation of the lovely

life you have created there . . . she said that what you have done there is rarer and greater than any painting or any music ever made.

Perhaps Jean's unhappiness had its beginning in an exchange involving her and her old friend Janet Hurter. Jan had become a painter after the war and opened a studio in an old mill just outside Boston. Jean was wild about her work and had persuaded some friends to sit for portraits. At Jan's invitation, she was planning to take the family and stay in what came to be called the "Old Mill" studio for a few weeks. One friend, Callie Hubbard, didn't like her portrait, and demanded that it be redone. Jan wrote, "Tell her for me that I do not care to paint her another portrait. Have her return the one I did, minus the frame for which she paid. I would not accept her dirty money. She had a pretty picture well worth $50."

Jan wrote to Jean:

> From now on, the subject of painting will be taboo between us, and I shall no longer refrain from saying, that outside of Montgomery circles, I think you make yourself rather ridiculous by your comments about art. Knowing nothing about painting, you of course don't know the code about touching up another fellow's work, which you did when you repainted Nick's hands in the portrait Anne Goldthwaite did of him. You should have seen her face when I told her that you had done that.

Portrait of Nick by Anne Goldthwaite, with the hands touched up by Jean.

Jean's reply told a great deal about herself:

> I am always so miserable because I can't paint, or write, or have any creative self-expression. It has been such a real, poignant ever-present unhappiness to me, and it does no good to remind me of what I do in the garden with my fleeting flowers—or even in the theater, since these things can't be compared with real artistic achievement.

Jean had done sketches and water colors all her life, but no serious art. Twice she tried to write for publications. Her first effort was an illustrated manuscript on the Tuppenny Tour, which was rejected by a publisher who said it was good but he already had some travel books on England.

For her second effort, she took a solo trip to Spain to isolate herself from family and Montgomery demands on her time and wrote a short novel entitled *A Spanish Cavalier*. She sent it to Sheila for a quick reading and punctuation.

Sheila thought it "a charming piece of writing," said not to worry about the punctuation, but suggested that she take out her descriptions of a side trip to Italy, since they detracted from the central story. She did not try again. Her life was too full of what she considered to be unimportant things and uninspiring partners. She got no inspiration from her sportsman husband, Nash. What would it have been like if she had married someone who shared her interests?

She had never forgotten the young English professor, Martin Flaherty, with whom she had fallen in love when she was twenty years old in Berkeley—and there were others. The scribbled first drafts of her letters which she left behind included one to an unidentified beau, which began, "I think this last week has been the most miserable & lonely I have ever known. How I wanted you to be tender and sweet to me. I never dreamt you would tire of me so soon. I am writing from the wicker sofa behind the door. It will miss us both." And there was always Steve Partridge, a journalist suitor who had shared her love of literature for many years. It was long after her marriage before she finally told him she would not see him again.

Our trip to Boston to stay at the Old Mill was canceled after Jan's letter, and instead we went abroad. I was six years old, and was to take notes on what I saw. Quite a few years later, I used my notes to write about the trip for an assignment:

A drawing of Lambo by Jean.

We sailed on the White Star Steamship Line's SS *Adriatic* and landed in Southampton, then went to a small hotel, Bayliss House, outside Slough on a golf course. Father spent his time on this course, and the longer course at Stoke Poges. Mother was reading a book to me about a little boy, named Tommy Traginnis in a Cornish fishing village. It prompted us to go to Cornwall where we found lodging at a Miss George's in Polpero. Adopting the name "Tommy" I made friends with the boys in the fishing village. It was fun.

In England we stayed at the estate of Vyvyian Harmsworth, of the Northcliff family who owned the *Daily Mail*. My mother was in rapture over their English lawn, and said several times, "The grass is so green!" Young Master Harmsworth finally turned to his mother and asked, "What color is the grass in America?" Lady Harmsworth answered, "A dirty brown."

From England we went to Austria. I remember eating veal, and Father having to get an extra suitcase to hold enough paper money to pay the hotel bill, because of inflation.

Then we went to Italy where Mussolini was coming into power, and there were crowds of black-shirted young men standing in the streets.

My most vivid memory of our stay there was a trip we made in a carriage from Sorrento along the Amalfi Drive. We had gone along for awhile at a brisk trot, when the horse stopped. The driver unhitched him and walked up and down the road looking worried. My father fumed. Mother, who spoke a little Italian, found the trouble—it was the horse's bladder. He had not urinated for some time.

She picked a long piece of grass at the side of the road, stooped down, and began tickling the horse saying, "Swish, swish." This had no effect on the horse, but it did on me, and when the horse saw my stream of urine he really let go a mighty flow. The driver picked me up saying "Bravo, bambino, bravo Nicolino." From then on he took me along on many of his drives.

We didn't get to France, where Jean wanted to see her old friend Sylvia Beach, who started the bookstore Shakespeare and Company after the war in Paris. She wrote Jean,

> I was so sorry to have missed you. You would love my book shop. It has not only the classics but the works of English and American writers of today, and has become a gathering place for English and American writers who stayed in Paris after the war.
>
> Those who join our book lovers club, *La Maison des Amis des Livres* get a special 20% discount. I now know so many authors personally that it quite prevents me from having time to read their works, God forbid. It's a little like the gamine Irma who is an errand girl in my friend Adrienne Monnier's book shop. Andre Gide, the writer, said to her "You are fond of books, are you not?" She replied, "Oh, yes, I like them well enough but I prefer the grocery business."

Sylvia Beach did read James Joyce's manuscript of *Ulysses* and when no one would touch it as being too risque, published it, and became quite famous.

Sheila must have been satisfied that the trip abroad was doing mother good. In a letter from New York she wrote, "Your letters make me so wild for Italy that I could almost swim there." She bemoaned the fact that she had no time for anything since Pax's return from Moscow and the publication of his book, *The Famine in Russia.* "There are too many people who want to talk to him."

> Louise Bryant, who had followed John Reed to Russia and had just returned from his burial in the Kremlin, has been here to tea. Down underneath she is heartbroken, but on top she is so amusing and surprising that she doesn't seem radical at all, but very worldly and smart. John Dos Passos, on the other hand, is ill-at-ease and embarrassed as ever but he inscribed my copy of his new book *Three Soldiers.*
>
> We are dining with the Bullitts tonight (He had just made the first Russian report to President Wilson). Louise Bryant will be there too. She is quite good looking, but the most sad person I ever met except the Queen of Greece. She gave Paxton an introduction to Prince Bibesco (Mrs. Asquith's son-in-law) who she says is as nice as can be and utterly unlike a Roumanian.

Fortunately, Jean did not receive a letter from Darlie, reporting that their mother had suffered a heart attack, in time to worry.

Jennie herself wrote, "All the family ought to learn by this time that I always get low in mind and body at the close of Lent [the anniversary of Will's death]."

We returned to Montgomery that summer. I had enough of travel, and was glad to be home again, where I could see my friends, and ride with Ben behind the fleet-footed Mamie Smith. There were other excursions in the family car, a sporty seven-passenger Paige, painted green with yellow "wire-spoked" wheels. The Stevens Duryea had long since been put up on blocks in the barn.

The Paige had its problems. A wire-spoked wheel would occasionally come off its axle. One day Ben was taking my grandmother and her two sisters, Mamie and "Tante" Alma, for a drive, when the right front wheel went spinning down the embankment into a patch of sugar cane. He managed to keep the car on the road, but "Tante" Alma got all the credit for keeping it upright. She was a heavy lady seated in the rear on the opposite side of the missing wheel, and when Ben called out "Lean to the left," Miss Alma did, and the car righted itself.

There were not many cars on the road then. A few other families had them, including the Weils. My mother approved of the Weils. At one point she told me that they were the "only other cultured family in town." The story is told about the elder Mrs. Weil, who left her car parked in front of a downtown department store, blocking the entrance. When a clerk located her in the store and asked her what kind of car she had, she answered, "I'm not sure, name some." He guessed, "A Cadillac?" "That's it," Mrs. Weil said.

Once in a while we would go in the Paige on one of the ferries that crossed the Alabama River. The ferry consisted of a rectangular wooden platform built on two boat hulls attached to a cable, which could be paid out or slackened as the current pulled it towards the opposite shore. Today the only reminders of these ferries are the roads that led to them, such as "Ware's Ferry Road" in northeast Montgomery.

Sometimes we would go to nearby Mitylene to hear the preaching and singing at the New Home Baptist Church. First came the collection with the spiritual:

> God's gonna meet you in the heaven, Oh Noahra.
> Kimbo yourself, Oh Noahra.
> Put your hand in your pocket,
> Put your finger on your nickel,
> Walk spotted like a leper and
> hand it to the preacher, Oh Noahra.

If the collection was falling off, the Reverend Benny Robinson would tell his congregation he wanted each one to "Bring a dime and a rusty nail the next Sunday. The dime represents the thirty pieces of silver Judas took; the nails in the cross." Baptisms took place at the creek with the congregation seated or standing on the bank singing "Wade in the Water." Two deacons took each candidate down to Reverend Robinson, a tall man standing chest high in the deeper water for total immersion.

It was Ben's church, and the congregation always seemed glad to see us. We must have looked well fed. Most of the congregation were poor sharecroppers, who thought it would be very nice indeed to have eaten a great deal more. Once when we took visitors to the church, one of whom was quite plump, someone in the congregation said approvingly, "Ain't she fat and purty?"

A self-described "walkin', talkin' preacher," who came to the back entrance of Hazel Hedge, was "Gitright Buddy." He got a cold glass of buttermilk at the kitchen window from our cook Mammy Ellen, and then started preaching to anyone within earshot. Within earshot besides Mammy Ellen, were usually Ben Miller, my nurse Celie Dennis, a gardener Joe Lee—and sometimes Mammy Ellen's brother, a "policy" man who came to get insurance payments from the servants.

Celie always had two things on her mind: dirt and dying. She was a determined cleaner of the house—and of me. Every week she paid some of her hard-earned money on her burial insurance policy. It was her ambition to be buried in a wardrobe casket. She tried to convince my mother to get one. "It's got a mirror and a light. It stands in your bedroom and you can hang your clothes in it, and it fits you fine to be buried."

Mother said all she wanted was a simple pine board coffin. "I could get Nick a pony for what a wardrobe casket must cost." Celie looked at her disapprovingly as if she shouldn't joke about such a serious matter. "No, Miss Jean," she said, "what pleasure do you think Doosome [her name for me] would have riding that pony knowin' he kept his mother out of a wardrobe casket?"

Celie had a brother, John Dennis, who had been in the Army. We never met John. Celie got word that he had died in a Veteran's Hospital up north. She wanted John buried in Montgomery and the V.A. was so notified. Some weeks later the telephone rang for Mother, and an unfamiliar voice said: "Mrs. Read, that fellow you've been expecting has arrived." Mother could think of no one she was expecting. Then the voice on the phone continued, "and in surprisingly good condition." It was Mr. Loveless, the Negro undertaker. John had arrived. There was no wardrobe casket for him, but he did get a fine funeral, which we all attended.

Death was recognized as an occasion for courtesy between the races.

There were other traditional occasions. Cramton Bowl, the big outdoor stadium, had always been used by Negro schools for their Thanksgiving Day game and parade. When Police Commissioner L. B. Sullivan threatened to cancel this arrangement, the *Montgomery Advertiser* editorialized:

> Such a repression would be unfaithful to Southern tradition, and would be an injustice to our colored citizens. What the white citizens of Montgomery ask is that the apartness of the races—separate but equal—be maintained as the best way of living together. So long as that separation exists, the stated creed of the white man is that he wishes with kindness in his heart to see the colored man do well in a world that is hard enough for both.

This was a nice thought and pointing in the right direction, but it was more of a creed than a practice. When Jean went to see a Mrs. White, a missionary who had come down from the North to open a small school in her own house to teach young black girls whose parents wanted them to learn more than they would in their public school, Mrs. White burst into a torrent of tears. "You're the first white person who has come into my home," she explained.

My father held no grudges, but obviously had the same prejudices as many of his fellow Southerners. He wrote from New York City on a picture postcard of the Chrysler Tower, where he had taken me high up to see the sights of the city, "We are looking over more Jews than Jerusalem ever produced. Last night we saw *Green Pastures*. Very wonderful but too many Harlem niggers with 'hard r's' in it." The "hard r" was favored by most Yankees. Southerners slurred over the "r."

Mainly, Nash was a sportsman—playing golf, hunting birds, going fishing, cock fighting, and teaching me how to do the same. If he had a cause he believed in, it was raising money to improve the golf course or build a new clubhouse. I saw a great deal of him, and loved him a lot. In a note to my Mother I wrote: "Dear Mother, I hope you have a good night. And by the way I want to tell you to tell dad to sleep with me."

It was agreed that I would get more discipline if I were transferred from Cloverdale public school to Starke's University School, a military academy. Professor Starke was a hard-shelled Baptist who believed in the literal word of the Bible and the importance of Latin and mental arithmetic—as well as corporal punishment. I received my share of licks on the palm of my hand by "Fessor" when I gave incorrect answers. I don't know why he gave me a Certificate of Distinction.

After school was out, I was sent away for the summer to Winnepec, a boy's camp in Wisconsin. Granny wrote to me every week from Hazel Hedge, sending a dollar and candy now and then, and reminding me of various things like not to share my sleeping bag because two in it might split it—and it was borrowed.

She reported that our cow Daisy was giving more creamy milk now that her calf had been weaned . . . that the Carter Hill Road in front of our house was finally finished . . . that she had been given two new records of hymns for our Victrola, and was anxious to play them for me . . . and that the Pollards were buying an electric refrigerator but couldn't agree on what kind to get. Judy wanted a Frigidaire, Uncle Charley a GE, and their Jean a Kelvinator.

When I came home I was told that I would be entering the First Form at Kent

School in Connecticut in the fall and that my best friend, Brannon "Bo" Hubbard, would be going there, too. At twelve I didn't want to leave home, although it was a relief not to have to go back to Starke's. In addition to putting me where I would get a better education, the family had other motives. My father wanted to get me away from the Communist influence of family members, Darlie and Jane. My grandmother thought that a religious school with an Episcopal priest as headmaster would increase my interest in the church and curb my interest in cock fighting.

25

Kent, Church, Chickens
and Communism

MY FATHER DROVE ME NORTH TO KENT. I WROTE MY MOTHER about the trip. This was the first of the weekly letters I wrote her from Kent, and the hundreds of letters she received from me during her lifetime. It began, "Darling Mummie" and as I grew older progressed to "My Dearest Jeanie" with an occasional "Darling Daughter" thrown in (mimicking my grandmother who always addressed Jean that way.)

Jean's salutations to me ranged from "Darling" and "My Dearest" to "Precious Boy" and "My Only One." On my birthday she wrote, "I have thought of you—since very early this morning when I woke in the same bed where you were born and I was all bound and strapped and so tired, but you were the sweetest thing I had ever seen. I miss you so, my lamb. Ever my heart, Jean."

Her answer to my last letter from Kent was perhaps the most poignant, "Your letter was so sweet. Oh my darling, how sweet, better than any love letter I ever got. I want to hold it in my hand when I am dead—please put it there."

Describing the drive with my father to Kent, I wrote:

> We passed through Quaker country, with the finest barns you can imagine, and stopped at one place to inquire the way. An old, refined lady in a black dress and bonnet called her husband who was an old man with the longest and thickest whiskers you ever saw, dressed simply with a broad brimmed flat straw hat. There were no automobiles. They all drove covered buggies.
>
> We stayed at "Ye Old Village Inn." I had a great deal of fun the next morning

bouncing up and down on the beds. I could almost hit the ceiling. The country wasn't very pretty until we got up through the Delaware Water Gap. Kent is right in the heart of the Berkshire Hills. It is very cold, and I am going to snuggle with Dada tonight. We took a walk up a country road. The maple trees grow huge and there are lots of little streams that flow into a river called the Housatonic.

Grandmother was certainly right about the religion at Kent, and I participated, though somewhat involuntarily. I wrote her about this new experience:

> I made my confession and took Communion.
>
> I wonder if a confession really does one any good, because one does the same old things over and over again and it really doesn't take a load off my mind because it makes me think more about my sins and when I do this it makes me sad, because I know how weak my will is and I know that I can't keep the fight against sin out very long without weakening.
>
> I wonder if it wouldn't be better just to forget them like I do at home. There, I never bother about my conscience, but just go on saying my prayers as if I was a Saint, and it doesn't bother me at all. This is much the easier thing to do. Our headmaster, Pater Sill, said a definition of a saint is a Sinner who keeps on trying.

Nick on the stoop at school.

When I left for Kent I put my fighting cocks in the care of "Net" Burdette, who knew them well. He had lived at Hazel Hedge long enough to become involved in most of the family activities. When I was away, he went to cock fights with my father. He became stage manager for some of Jean's plays, and a political follower of Darlie and Jane.

About the chickens, Net wrote: "All the chickens are in good condition. Tommy is still in the eating coop, pending verdict of the jury. We're trying to get a walk for the white rooster at one of the sharecropper farms. Mr. Chambers promised he would get one. He was to come around last Sat. morning but he failed to. There was a fight last Friday. Uncle Nash went to it. Mr Whittle's chicken won quite a few. He said he had around 80 little chicks now."

He described a big garden party Jean gave for actors and other volunteers. "It was a grand one. It was cloudy but the rain held off. There's another show at the Little Theatre this week, 'Service for Two,' a light comedy. I'm the stage manager. Next week we will be taking it down, returning all the properties we borrowed and sending the rented costumes back to New York."

In one letter sent to my mother, I protested these demands on Net's time: "To Mrs. N. Read (Private please): This will have to stop. Do you really know what Francis A. Burdette is at Hazel Hedge for? Well, it's to take care of MY CHICKENS. He has written me that his time is so limited that he can scarcely take care of his personal needs other than brushing his teeth twice a day. I think that he should be compelled to STOP and I don't mean maybe. This letter was instituted for the reason that F.A.B. devote what time he has TO DOING WHAT HE WANTS TO DO. My best wishes. N.C.R."

"My Precious Boy" was not forgotten for his first Thanksgiving away from home. Grandmother wrote:

> I am afraid we got the Thanksgiving box, or boxes, off too soon. Although Mammy Ellen had been ill, she came by & made you an angel food cake & kept saying "It's the cake my boy loves—I hope it will reach him all right." We were so afraid the turkey would mash it that we sent it in a separate box.
>
> We thought you would have plenty of cranberry sauce so substituted guava jelly & artichoke pickles, as well as parched pecans & candy. Father insisted on sending you a wild goose so mother gave him a box all to himself! He is going for partridges tomorrow & mother hopes she can have one broiled to get there in time for your Thanksgiving breakfast.

I thanked everybody for Thanksgiving, and said "Tell all the servants—Ben, Joe, Johnie May and Mammy Ellen that I send love, and I hope Mammy Ellen is on her feet by now." I was homesick, and missed them. To cheer me, Dad bought a new red and bronze rooster "who looks a lot like 'Red.'" To cheer himself, over the loss of old Sam, his favorite hunting dog, he bought a new one, "Taffy." This didn't cheer Jeanie, who came home from a dinner at the Hubbards to find that Taffy had pulled out her new white hat and eaten every shred of it, two pair of silk stockings, one pair of silk pants, a bunch of artificial violets and a silver-colored belt, "everything in the drawer but the corset."

Before I could get home for Christmas, there was a family tragedy. Paxton Hibben died of pneumonia in New York City at the age of 48. My mother and father came up to be with Sheila and Jill, who was just seven. I was left at Kent in nearby Connecticut since I didn't really know my Uncle Paxton very well, and there was to be no funeral in New York.

It was only years later, when I read his obituary and countless documents and news stories that had been preserved by Jean, that I pieced together the following paragraphs for this book.

The obituary and articles about him embraced major happenings in his life—from his high school graduation in Indiana with the highest honors ever won by a pupil at Shortridge High School, to being named to the Officer Order of the Redeemer by Greece, the Chevalier Order of St. Stanislaus by Russia, and the Order of the Sacred Treasure by Japan during and after World War I.

Accolades reflected a high regard for Paxton as a reporter "who told the truth wherever it might lead him." One churchman wrote, "Facts are like lions from which many run away, but he never ran away from a fact. When he found it to be the embodiment of truth he took it and made it a part of his life." He was heralded as a champion of civil liberty "who suffered for his belief as few of us have done."

Starting with his defense of King Constantine's efforts to keep Greece out of the war, when Paxton himself was accused of being pro-German, each of his books in turn brought its own problems.

Even his much-admired book, *The Famine in Russia*, written after he served as Co-chairman of War Relief for the Russian Red Cross, gave him some trouble. In connection with its publication, a picture in the *New York Times* showed him laying a wreath at the grave of John Reed, a fellow journalist who wrote *Ten Days that Shook the World* and who became a Communist. It followed as the night the day that some thought Pax was a Communist too.

The book was in evidence in 1924 when he was questioned by a military board of inquiry as to his fitness to retain his title as Captain in the Officers Reserve Corps, ostensibly because of laying the wreath on Reed's tomb, but also because of his sympathetic writings on the Russian situation.

As a young man he had witnessed the cruelty and oppression visited on Russian people by the Cossacks, and it influenced his writing. And although he was successfully defended in the military court of inquiry by General John Bradley

(Omar Bradley's father) and retained his title as Captain, a short time later at his twentieth reunion at Princeton University, his classmates staged a mock lynching and called him a "red."

He got into an entirely different kind of trouble over his biography of Henry Ward Beecher, the abolitionist brother of Harriet Beecher Stowe. He was writing the book on contract with Doubleday-Doran, and noted that Beecher had been publicly accused of adultery. This generated widespread publicity. Doubleday, an abolitionist himself, wanted Paxton to omit reference to the adultery in the book. Paxton refused "because it had happened," and defended Beecher as a "liberator of his generation from theological fears and from shackling conventions."

I remember that my mother, who was a good friend of Mrs. Doubleday, wrote to her on Pax's behalf. However, Doubleday withdrew from the contract, and there was considerable delay before George Doran published it in 1927. By that time, several more books on Beecher by other authors had been published and there was little demand for Hibben's book. Financially, it was not a success.

He continued to write book reviews for the *New Masses*, and his last defiant act was to help Pat Jackson, a labor leader whom I came to know very well, organize a demonstration in Boston in defense of Sacco and Vanzetti in 1927. These were two poor Italian immigrants who despite evidence to the contrary were sentenced to death on a murder charge, not because they were guilty but because they were anarchists. Up front in the demonstration were such well-knowns as the journalist Heywood Broun, the poet Edna St. Vincent Millay, Katherine Anne Porter and Felix Frankfurter, who within a decade would be appointed to the Supreme Court by President Roosevelt. The case became a *cause célèbre* internationally, but the demonstrators didn't achieve their objective. The condemned men were executed.

When Pax died in 1928 he had almost finished another biography, published posthumously, this one on William Jennings Bryan. Royalties from sales were so meager following Pax's death that Sheila was hard-pressed to pay hospital and funeral expenses.

Ashamed of what had happened at the class reunion five years earlier, Paxton's Princeton classmates wanted to make amends and give him an appropriate funeral. Sheila would have none of it. Instead she accepted the Soviet government's request that his ashes be sent to Moscow where he would be buried with honor.

On the cold winter day of February 7, 1929, several thousand Russians gathered in Red Square before the mausoleum of Lenin to hear eulogies delivered by Russian officials. Full page obituaries under banner headlines "*Izumitel'nyy Amerikanets*" ("An Exceptional American") "of sterling idealism and rare intellectual attainments, who although not a communist became the butt of persecution and hatred for avowing sympathy for the new social ideal." They also paid tribute to his heroic efforts as co-chairman of the Russian Red Cross which saved so many children during the great Russian famine.

Paxton was buried in the Novodevitchi Monastery among other writers and some political figures, eventually to include Khrushchev. The Pax plaque reads: "American Journalist and Member of the Soviet Red Cross." My father tried to help Sheila financially, but she was determined to make it on her own. She supported herself and Jill mostly by working at a politically progressive magazine, *The New Leader*, started by her old friend Suzanne La Follette of the Wisconsin political dynasty. Sheila was listed as treasurer, but spent her time doing whatever Suzanne needed to have done, including some editing and book reviews. She also used the office to do freelance assignments.

I began to see a lot of Sheila and Jill in New York since Kent was so nearby. They were my sounding board, and Sheila passed on what she learned to the family in Montgomery, which they pieced together with the weekly letters I wrote home. Everyone knew I hated Kent, because it was so cold and strict, and Father Sill was such a hard task master. In addition to our classes and several church services a day, we all had regular housekeeping duties, with punishments for various infringements such as being late for breakfast. Since I was always late, they called me "Speed" and gave me extra jobs to do.

My father learned from Sheila that Darlie was continuing to send me left-wing propaganda, and my grandmother found out that although religion was making a big impression on me, it was not enough to curtail my love of cock-fighting: "When Nick stopped by to see us in New York, he was carrying a copy of *Grit and Steel*, the cock-fighting magazine. He even tried to get Jill interested in cock-fighting, but she said she wasn't comfortable even picking up a chicken, let alone watching them fight."

Granny's feeling about the sport didn't keep her from being sure my birds were well cared for in my absence. "I suppose Net has written you that many of your chickens have the sorehead. The vet said that 'Sore Head Salve' is the best remedy. I have ordered some from Burke's drug store. Don't think so much about your chickens and buckle down and keep the rules as far as you can. It will all go to build up your character."

She was reassured about my character when I wrote with much enthusiasm about the new chapel,

> It is quite grand inside with carved seats like those in theaters, and the holy sacrament is being kept up in the oratory so we won't have to bow our knees so much. An organ has been installed as well as chimes in the tower, and great oak doors and stained glass windows are being added.
>
> We are preparing for All Saints' Day, and have been given Father Sill's *Rules of Life for Kent Boys,* and are supposed "by the Grace of God to keep them." There are fourteen in all. Many I want to keep, but if No. 11, "I shall avoid loose and foolish talk" means not talking after lights or getting to my job on time, I don't think he ought to ask that of us.

My father seemed to understand how I felt about Kent, and soon after I arrived wrote to say "if you feel that your school life will amount to nothing and are not happy in it and if by Christmas you are not content, you can come home and go to high school here, but it is a decision you must make for yourself." He said that he had lunch at the Harvard Club with a relative, Max Kilvert, who suggested I get in with the rowing crowd. Max said that because of my size, I could become coxswain, which is the most responsible position in the crew.

Granny's weekly letters kept me informed about everything and everybody at Hazel Hedge:

> Mammy Ellen is much better & is up today. I read your letter to her, and she sends you more messages than I can write. She was here today with her friend Lizzie Snow to pray with me, and I read them prayers out of the "Great Physicians" book. They got so happy while I was reading that they nearly shouted!
>
> Net has joined a small class of big boys at Sunday School and is going tonight to the Young People's Church League . . . Father is in Atlanta attending poor Uncle Percy's funeral, who died in a home for incurable, unhonored & unknown, all from the curse of drink! He had a brilliant mind & a splendid education & a lovable nature but was weak . . . Your dog, Bugger, has decided to be a hunting dog! She

caught a rabbit yesterday . . . We found another possum, quite young, in the pool that had no water in it. Fortunately, Ben got it before Bugger did and has put it in a cage to get fat for his own Sunday dinner.

We have all been busy gathering pecans, especially your mother.

I wish you could have seen how handsome she was last night in a yellow satin evening dress she got in Paris. She and Dad went out to dinner at the Oates.

We are so proud of your nice letters and miss you, oh so much & love you more than anything in the world.

God bless you. Granny.

I had taken Max Kilvert's advice about joining the crew and it began to change my outlook on Kent. I reported to Dad that "a lot depends on me, since I must call the strokes for the crew members and guide from the stern. The Housatonic River is swollen now on account of the rains and there are many logs floating down and the current is quite swift so the cox has to be very careful. 'Knock on wood.' So far I've done pretty well. Last year we won the regatta."

After Pax died, Jean spent as much time as she could in New York City, providing moral support for her dearest sister, Sheila, and being with Jill when her mother was away at *The New Leader*. One day after she left, Jill asked her mother, "Where is Jeannie?" and without waiting for an answer, added, "Oh, I wish she were here to take me to school so gaily." It was arranged, that next time Jean came she would invite Jill to come to Hazel Hedge with her for a visit.

It was the first of many such trips, sometimes for short holidays, and always for summer vacations. Going in either direction, Jill was laden with packages. Jean regularly asked Sheila to shop for her in New York, and everybody at Hazel Hedge sent edibles to Sheila. Mostly they were from Jean and her mother ("Mama's first ham was a little salty, but the second was superfine, and the gumbo was heavenly"); and the bird hunter, Nash, usually had a box of his own containing whatever game bird was in season. And everybody picked pecans.

A letter from Sheila to Jean said something about everything, "When I got your request about the lamp shades I found the most beautiful Japanese paper I ever set eyes on—six sheets and a tube to put them in only came to $2.85. It will make three shades. The partridges Nash sent arrived in as fine condition as Jill. I take it Jill's blue coat is following by mail. I hope it does not take too long for she will have to wear her good brown one, and sliding down rocks in the park and playing in mud will ruin it."

Jill's vacations with us gave her mother more time to write, and she got a regular assignment doing the "Markets and Menus" section of *The New Yorker* magazine. A great cook herself, her culinary skills enriched its pages and in 1932, Harpers books asked her to do a national cookbook. *American Regional Cookery* was published in 1932, dedicated to her mother, "Miss Jennie, the noblest cook of them all," who had made up many of the recipes and adapted others. But they had never been written down.

To get the ingredients in the right proportion, Sheila had to watch the family cook, Mammy Ellen, as she put them together in the kitchen. It wasn't easy. Mammy Ellen never measured anything, and when questioned as to what to put in and how much, she would say, "Some flour, and a little milk and enough butter to make a good dough, and season it to make it taste right." Or if asked, "How long does it cook?" would answer, "Until it's done." Sheila, with pencil and measuring equipment in hand, stood at one side taking notes.

The cookbook came to the attention of Eleanor Roosevelt, who invited Sheila to the White House to advise on meals for the poor. While waiting in the reception room, Sheila started to pick up something from the table, and was nipped in the ankle by a German shepherd. When the Negro maid cried out, "Miz Roosevelt, Miz Roosevelt, Major done bit Miz Higgens," Mrs. Roosevelt came in to say, "Mamie, we must keep some Band-Aids and a bottle of iodine in here." Mrs. Hibben, no admirer of the New Deal, commented later, "Just like the Roosevelt administration, applying a Band-Aid to the economy."

She felt that although Mrs. Roosevelt, an indifferent gourmet, commented favorably on her recommendations at a press conference, she wasn't really interested in the food. Sheila remarked that the dishes were meant to be eaten, not printed.

My grandmother sent me ten dollars and said I should use it to go sightseeing in New York. "Go to the museums, the galleries, the aquarium and the Statue of Liberty," she advised. I also wanted to see some of the people Jean and Sheila had talked about.

I made a somewhat formal call on Suzanne La Follette, who I found to be very intense, enunciating too forcefully; and on mother's old beau, Steve Partridge, who I liked much better. I knew he had a drinking problem but he seemed to know

Nick in a Kent school photo.

everything about the city, and took me on an exciting tour of the *Daily Mirror* where he worked as a reporter.

Afterwards I sat in the sun in Union Square and talked Communism with two small Jews. One knew a great deal and argued nobly with the other younger one. I had learned quite a bit from Darlie, and held my own. In fact, I was on the receiving end of a great deal of left-wing opinion, which I shared with my classmates, most of whom were from affluent northern families. It must have surprised them, coming from a southerner.

Francis Burdette, who had followed Darlie to New York, and was working with the American Committee Against Fascist Oppression, made his first street corner speech on Fascist trends in this country, and sent me a three-month subscription to the *New Masses*. I thanked him, asking that he "tell Darlie I've been giving the boys at my table an earful on Socialism. I just wish she wouldn't go sailing off to Paris, because I've just got to get some hot dope on the subject this summer."

My acquaintances in Union Square injected some bad doctrine, declaring: "Conditions, not leaders bring revolutions. Hitler can't last in Germany because he has nothing to offer." An ex-Servicemen's League speaker announced that there would be a bonus march on Washington. A crowd began to gather, and a cop told us to disperse.

Back at Kent, though my ankles were weak, I learned to ice skate. And when I sent for my sailor cap, and asked Net to "look in the hall table to get my first baseman's mitt, as well as a baseball that looks old and dark but is a good one. And please send my boxing gloves" was a clue to everyone at home that I would stay at Kent. In the spring I played a lot of tennis, and even began to enjoy studying.

The school work was hard. I wrote home, "Darling Mummie—I am terribly, terribly busy. Exams start Monday and I'll have to WORK, WORK, WORK." The results didn't put me at the top of my class. I got 79 in French, 78 in English, 82 on the Bug (biology), and 67 in Virgil. However, my 99 in Chemistry didn't mean that I knew any real chemistry, but that I had memorized the review sheets before the final exams.

School was out and I was on my way back home to Hazel Hedge. Jill joined me when I went through New York, to spend her vacation in Montgomery. We had a good time, going down with a basket of food packed by Sheila, and coming back with another packed by Jeanie. I described the food in a letter written on the train, "Mummy Darling, the lunch you packed was perfectly sumptuous with its tomatoe chicken and beaten biscuits, and Hopjes (a favorite candy from Holland)."

The summer passed quickly, and it seemed no time at all until we were on our way back again. "We sat at the rear of the train last night and saw the last of Montgomery. 'Pill' (my nickname for Jill), poor darling, was much affected. Gosh, how she loves Hazel Hedge. Today we pulled down the seats and stretched out full length and read *Sons and Lovers* by D. H. Lawrence alternately aloud."

While I was at Kent, Darlie and my cousin, Jane Speed, became increasingly interested in social problems, and in 1929 they went to Austria, taking a Montgomery girl, Miriam Arrington, with them. This was after Dolfuss came to power. Darlie and Jane soon became Socialists, and eventually Communists. Darlie's son, William Craik Speed, was going in a different direction. My father had helped him get a job in New York, where he became an inventor like his father, Buckner, and very wealthy. He worked on Vitaphone for the first talking picture, *The Jazz Singer* with Al Jolson, and was in Paris for Paramount when his mother and sister visited Vienna. He didn't see them. "They were Communists, and I was a dyed-in-the-wool Capitalist."

In Vienna, both Jane and Miriam married Austrians. They eventually brought their husbands back to Montgomery, where they were to find the southerners a strange lot. Miriam's husband, Victor Block, is remembered for a remark he made when told that the circus was coming to town. He asked "Vy?" (for "Why")—thinking that Montgomery was something of a circus in itself.

When Jane's husband, George Seigelbauer, departed, Jane remained behind with Darlie to fight for causes. They stayed at Hazel Hedge, talking the party line and passing out Communist literature. The conversations at dinner could get pretty sticky. One night, one of Jean's guests, Clifford Durr, who headed the New Deal Federal Communications Commission, asked Jane, "What would happen to me—a Liberal—come the Revolution?" Jane answered, "Oh, we would have to shoot you." It may have been after this remark that Nash avoided the home gatherings and would go to the Country Club for dinner.

The family often learned about Jane's comings and going from outsiders. Howard Pill, manager of WSFA, the radio station, phoned Bill Gunter, the Mayor, saying that Jane Speed had just come in from New Orleans and wanted to talk. What should he do? Bill Gunter replied, "Howard, I was in school with her mother. Let her talk, but turn the static way up so no one can hear her."

Jean wrote Nick about the broadcast:

> Sunday night we had supper at the Pollards and at 10:30 Jane Speed made a speech over the radio on Communism but we had a hard time understanding her because of the static. Her voice is terribly hysterical and she seems to have no control over it. She advocated equality for the negroes, not only in voting and on juries but in everything.
>
> We tried to locate her but she was probably staying with her negro or Communist friends.

She had evidently been in Louisiana organizing a hunger march in Baton Rouge to confront Senator Long and the Governor on the plight of the tenant farmers.

Jean heard from a cousin, Etheldra Scoggins, who lived in New Orleans, that Jane had rung the doorbell one night. "There she stood: long pants, red braids wrapped around her head, with a marvelous dachshund named Vopsa in her arms." She asked if she and her husband could pitch their tent in our backyard.

The whole neighborhood was entranced. "Vopsa stayed with us until after Halloween." This was undoubtedly my father's old golfing companion whose place had been taken on the golf course by me. Vopsa evidently "joined the party" with Jane.

In New York city Sheila was told by Ben Stolberg, a leading Communist there, that the New Orleans leaders wanted to get Jane out of Louisiana because she was making trouble for them "by her crazy performance—going to the governor screaming and yelling."

"If only she and Darlie could have remained balanced liberal members of society, they could have done so much more good. Instead, they helped organize a sharecroppers' strike north of Montgomery, against land owners in Tallapoosa County. And from there Jane went to Birmingham where she opened a workers' bookshop featuring Marxist literature." Interestingly enough, the store had formerly been headquarters for a white supremacy group.

Jean, who loved bookstores, visited the Jane Speed Bookstore, and reported that "it was very nice indeed—a lovely little book shop filled with Revolutionary literature—and despite what a reporter had said, none of it was hidden away."

26

Jane Goes to Jail

IN BIRMINGHAM ON MAY DAY IN 1933, THE HEIGHT OF THE GREAT Depression and a heyday for social protest, Jane was arrested for speaking at a United Front Unemployed rally, sponsored by the International Labor Defense (ILD), a tool of the Communist Party. Most of those present were underpaid black workers from the iron and steel plants, who lived in squalor and made scarcely enough to feed their families.

Her appearance at the rally was described by Catherine Fosl in *Life and Times of a Rebel Girl: Jane Speed and the Alabama Communist Party,* published by the University of Alabama Press in the spring of 1997: "When young Jane Speed jumped on the running board of a car and addressed a mostly black crowd she needed no microphone to be heard, 'Fellow workers, this is the way they do us. We refuse to starve quietly in our homes.'"

Jane's act was a striking challenge to Southern race, class, and gender mores. Red-haired, flamboyant, a "born rebel" according to those who knew her, she was a leading figure in the Alabama Communist party, mainly a working-class black organization. Neither black nor working-class, she was a renegade Southern aristocrat whose mother's family, the Baldwins, were among the elite of Montgomery, while her father's family held equal sway in Louisville, Kentucky.

She described the experience: "The cops rushed in and dragged me into a police car twisting my arms. They threatened me and cursed me in the vilest, most obscene language calling me 'a dirty nigger lover.' They also arrested two black men who tried to defend me, and had blood running down their faces, and took the three of us to jail."

Technically, Jane was arrested for speaking without a permit to a public assembly of mixed races without physical barriers of separation. One of the men was charged with assault and battery with a large stick, the other with carrying a concealed weapon. The police claimed they had taken a four-inch blade from him.

When my father, Nash, offered to go Jane's bail, she refused unless he paid bail for all the Negroes arrested with her. Called as a character witness for Jane was Rabbi Benjamin Goldstein, who identified himself as having been a resident of Montgomery until he was "severed by his synagogue for participation in a meeting to protest the Scottsboro case, and now would be going back to New York." In 1931 the Scottsboro case in Alabama had brought charges against nine young Negroes, for allegedly raping two white girls in a freight car. Eight were sentenced to death, the ninth got life imprisonment.

From Kent I had written my mother about the Scottsboro case,

Jane Speed in the garden at Hazel Hedge.

Can't anyone save those poor Negro boys? I believe them perfectly innocent. When they got into that freight car where the white boys and girls were, naturally the white boys got mean and wanted them to get the H. out. I think, from what I know of the attitude of "poor white trash," that although out-numbered they started a fight so as not to be shown down before the girls. Then at the next station the girls made up the story (about being raped).

A death penalty, my dear Mama, and the boys are only 17, 17, 18, 19—none over 21, and two under 16 who will share the fate of many other little Negro boys. Their young lives will be soured and corrupted by a reformatory. Soon *I* will be sixteen, a great event I've been told but I can't see why. It just means I'll have one less year to live. A lot of years for such a small potato.

Although the Supreme Court had concluded that since Negroes were not allowed to serve on juries in Alabama, the Scottsboro defendants had been denied adequate defense, the Southern courts continued to find them guilty. It was only in 1937 that four were released, and not until 1966 that a judge in the case released confidential information that exonerated all of them. Several had been in jail for almost thirty-five years.

A Roman Catholic priest wrote a letter in Jane's behalf to the Birmingham Police Commissioner. He described himself as a liberal Christian clergyman dedicated to the American principles of free speech:

> I have great sympathy for a young person in her predicament. I believe her motives were the highest, and in identifying herself with a situation in which the racial element entered, she offended certain southern sensibilities.
>
> As a southerner, and the grandson of an officer who lost his arm in the war between the states, I understand this. At the same time, it appears to me that the young negro arrested with her, Ned Goodwin, was acting the part of a man simply trying to defend her.
>
> Miss Speed is very young and youth is always impetuous. They have something of the idealism of the early Christian teachers who suffered prison and persecution for their convictions. I am asking your indulgence, Commissioner Taylor. "The quality of mercy is not strained."

Jean wrote to her cousin, Judge Mortimer Baldwin, in Birmingham, telling him of Jane's plight and asking him to talk to her. He had some trouble locating her through the southern district office of the International Labor Defense, which had sponsored the rally in the park, but they finally said she would be in the office at ll o'clock and he went there and arranged to meet her at 4 p.m. in his office. Their conversation, which lasted for three hours, was reported in a 10 page handwritten letter from the judge to "My dear Jean."

The judge reported that

> in the beginning I kept the conversation on the family to get better acquainted, and when we came to the major topic I told her that I was willing to admit everything she had to say about the condition of the poor, oppressed workers under our system, as well as under every form of government now or heretofore—tribal, monarchical, aristocratic, oligarchic, democratic, communistic, etc.
>
> She took issue as to Russia. She thinks it is ruled by the masses and not by Stalin and his committee backed by the Army & Navy which they control. But that is immaterial. I wanted to know her remedy? It was to overthrow the present capitalistic system and end its control by the present ruling class. I told her that,

while her objective might be eminently desirable, that she was going about it in the wrong way, at the wrong time and in the wrong place.

Neither she nor her co-workers had a monopoly on the desire and efforts to better the lot of our fellow men, and that on our side we were proceeding along what we thought was the best course as shown by the history of this country and every civilization. I pointed out that considerable progress has been made here by forward-thinking persons, foundations and government in the matter of wages, education, housing and working conditions and that more is to be expected—in the form of old age pensions, unemployment insurance from the New Deal administration.

If done her way, it would certainly lead to violence and blood-shed and could not produce revolution since we are a self-governing people and there are not enough discontented with the courage to even raise a flag against a small company of National Guards. She said that if trouble or violence comes "we will control it." She would not or could not tell me who she meant by "we."

I then made reference to her case and said that I might be able to help her get a moderate fine and no imprisonment, since I know the Police Commissioner and the Judge, if she would agree to discontinue her agitation here. She said she knew they would like to get her out of town, but she was going to exercise her right of free speech whenever and where she wanted to. "Most of the others have served jail sentences for the cause, and I am ready."

She seemed rather anxious to suffer the jail penalty. I told her that a speech in court would do neither her nor the cause any good, and she agreed that she wouldn't speak "unless the *necessity* arose." Of course I do not know what she will do.

From what I have said you might think our conversation was not altogether pleasant, but not so. We listened to one another but talked quietly and plainly and straight to the point, and parted as friends. I am sorry, Jean, I could not do something. The length of this letter is to show that I tried.

M.M. BALDWIN

Jane spent fifty-three days, including her twenty-third birthday, in the Southside Birmingham City jail. Her cousin Fanny, who was head of the Colonial Dames and the wife of Judge Baldwin, was driven there regularly by a Negro chauffeur to take Jane her meals. Miss Fanny explained, "No Baldwin could survive on that jail food."

Darlie was in New York City where she had given an interview to the *New York*

World Telegram, stating that she had been driven out of the South because she "had dared to work for the Scottsboro boys and the Tallapoosa sharecroppers." She said her conservative family, with its Little Theater president (Jean Read), had asked her to go North and stay there, but that one prominent relative had admitted that "things are so bad down here we dare not let the truth be known." She identified the relative as Judge Mortimer Baldwin.

In Montgomery, the city fathers passed an ordinance directed at Jane and Rabbi Goldstein for their activities in behalf of the sharecroppers, making it a crime for two persons or more to meet together to read or possess radical documents. When some of the sharecroppers were killed and others put in jail, my mother, Jean, got into the act. She was spokesman for a committee including Rabbi Goldstein who went to see Governor Miller to ask for an official investigation. She reported the results in a letter to the editor of the *Montgomery Advertiser.*

> We pointed out that the attorney for the arrested men was not allowed to see them except in the presence of the Sheriff, and that two of them, Judson Simpson and Milo Bentley, were lying seriously wounded in jail. The Governor stated that no Sheriff had the right to prevent an attorney from conferring with his clients, and that the attorney could appeal for a court order restraining the Sheriff from interfering. However, this court order would have to be executed by the Sheriff himself.
>
> The Governor refused to order an official investigation, replying that the committee could investigate on their own. A member of the committee then asked the Governor for a letter to the Sheriff permitting such an investigation and giving it his approval. The letter was refused. The most he would do was to assure them that if they got into any difficulty, they could telephone him for assistance.

When he left Montgomery, Rabbi Goldstein wrote my mother a letter: "You cannot begin to know what you mean to Margaret and to me. To know that one like you, whom we admire more than we can tell, feels as you do, atones for everything that has been unpleasant. Our admiration has turned to love. Ben."

Jane had gone from Birmingham to New York, where she gave a press interview describing the working and living conditions of the Negroes in Birmingham: "Relief when given to negroes amounts to but $2 a week—that to cover big families—one step above starvation. They live in shacks with great gaping cracks in the walls and broken window panes through which the winter cold pours. Often only one faucet of water supplies a whole neighborhood, and the gas has been turned off, and there are no sanitary arrangements. And who owns these shacks? Whites, always whites."

In New York her activities took on an international aspect. She protested the Italian invasion of Ethiopia by a visit to the Italian Consul, where it was alleged that she threw ink at him. The story in a New York tabloid quoted a bystander at the trial, commenting, "Just Trying to Make an Ethiopian of Him." According to Jane, the consul made a move to have her thrown out, and the ink was spilled by accident when she picked up the inkstand to emphasize a point she was making to protest war and Fascism: "I wish I could go to Italy and tear the black shirt from Mussolini." A secretary seized her wrist and the ink went everywhere.

Her mother Darlie wrote Jean:

> I brought Jane up with these ideals, but she has long since taken the lead. I only follow. She begins where I leave off. Surely you can see the meaning of such a protest against fascism. Just today war was declared by Italy. Fascism necessarily means war and war means that Nicky and Brannon and millions of other young men will have to fight and suffer and die when they had much rather be peaceful and happy and live.
>
> You say that by your gracious living you have brought more happiness to people than we can ever do. Yes, as an individual you have, but we belong to a great movement that will do more to liberate millions of people than you could with a hundred Hazel Hedges. It is needless for me to go into the details of a socialist state. All I say is that a practical plan has been formulated and carefully worked out by Marx, Lenin and other economic experts. This plan is the only one capable of ending unemployment and the exploitation of the working class.
>
> You are right, we should not stay in Montgomery. No Communist can be a true Communist when his friends are among the well-to-do *bourgeois*. We belong with those we can help to freedom.

Mother wrote to me,

> I think you are too hard on Jane. She is perfectly sincere in what she is doing and I don't believe she threw the ink because she said she didn't, but the part I mind is her dragging her family into it.
>
> Let her do these things independently if she believes in them, but she doesn't

have to keep dragging us into it by saying she's related to a prominent Montgomery family, or that she's the great, great, granddaughter of Dr. James Craik, the surgeon general of the Revolution.

What all of us resent is her stirring up the negroes, giving Ben and all the Hubbards' servants literature, and sending you books and ruining Francis Burdette's career. Meanwhile, she and Darlie are living in one of the cottages at Hazel Hedge, bathing and doing their week's wash, and eating there along with their Communist guests.

Jane had a huge picture in the Birmingham paper captioned "Southern Girl Retains Negro Lawyer." That part is thoroughly disgusting, and right now when we all have all we can bear, she so easily could have spared us this.

Jean, as she had done most of her life, retreated each night into her world of books. She read a wide variety, usually going to sleep under an electric light hanging from the ceiling directly overhead. She highly recommended that I read *The Story of Genghi (or Ghenghi)* by Lady Murisaki. "It's a 9th or 10th century translation which is the best book I ever read and the most charming. Prince Genghi is the most delightful fellow, very poetic. He had as many affairs as Casanova but he never forsook or went back on his ladies at least he always had a tender sentimental feeling for them."

But she changed her mind about what I should read. "For you, history comes first, and if you go to England you must know something about what you are seeing. And you should read Charles Beard's book, *The Rise of American Civilization.*"

Basically, Jean was not interested in politics, except as they affected her immediate family. She opposed Communism largely because of the loud and strident talk of Darlie and Jane's friends, and by what she considered to be their bad taste.

About a play recommended by Darlie she wrote: "It was the most awful thing—can you hear their voices? If that's what the Communists do to the theater, the Capitalists should keep it."

Only my father and my grandmother wrote letters with no political or sociological overtones. My father's letters were usually about hunting.

I went to a water hole last Saturday and had a piece of luck. My gun hung up on me so I could only shoot one barrel. As I was approaching a small pond for doves, a flock of teal ducks came by and I fired but only killed one and couldn't fire a second round. I got down and hoped they would come back. They circled and circled and finally came from the sky with a great swoop. I rose as they neared the center of the pond and as they bunched, fired and got four with my one barrel.

Taffy is going to make a fine retriever. One fell in the middle of the pond and he swam out and brought it to me. He finds every one I have killed, and he really is lots of fun, so keen and joyous. Keep well son. Work hard and try this year to establish a little more system in your work. You will find it pays.

From grandmother:

My Nickie Boy, I was so glad to get your letter, but you must not let my letters overburden you now that you are so busy and have other members of the family to write. I'm sorry I have not better news of the pecan crop. It has been a failure as to size and quantity. What the trees need for quantity and size is cultivation and fertilization with cotton seed meal, but I have enjoyed gathering the small crop in spite of my hay fever, which has been pretty bad, owing to the ragweed under the trees.

Uncle Charlie Craik sent me the *Recollections & Letters of Gen. Robert E. Lee* which I am enjoying very much. I hope you will read it when you come home. He writes to one of his children who is off at school, "You must study hard, gain knowledge and learn your duty to God and your neighbors. That is the great object of life."

We have a baby squirrel in a basket on the side porch. I crack nuts for him and made a "tit" to suck by putting some soft bread in warm milk and sugar in a little bag made from the finger of a glove, which he is thriving on. Jean calls him "Nutkins" in memory of your pet squirrel. God bless you my beloved.

Darlie came for a last visit to Montgomery to have her ear operated on by Dr. Thigpen. Neither my mother nor father were at Hazel Hedge. She wrote mother describing her stay:

I did not dream that my coming would drive Nash away, and I am more sorry than I can tell you. He has been so wonderfully good and kind to me through all these years, and I wish I could repay him in a better way than bringing disgrace on the family, but one must be true to one's convictions & ideals, gratitude notwithstanding.

Mama came over on Sunday afternoon in one of her 10-cent taxis, and considering the tragic and emotional way everybody is behaving regarding this disgrace brought on the family, she is remarkably composed and sweet and kind to me. To my mind there are lots of us who are not "riff-raff," and Jane has done a courageous and important piece of work towards the new economic order, and when the history of this period is written she will be recognized as an outstanding and distinguished pioneer.

My last letter from Kent was somewhat upbeat:

> I've been having some close talks with a friend of mine here and we've decided on a lot of things we're going to do to improve ourselves morally and physically. There are so many things I want to learn this summer. Mechanics from Net, and how to avoid diseases and take care of myself from Uncle Charley.
>
> You and I will read lots of books and talk over my future, and work on my character and will-power. Granny will take care of my spiritual and religious life. If only Darlie was going to be home I could talk over a lot of things with her and get a good philosophy of life.

Jean answered, "Darling, I do want you to have a good life and get all there is out of it—to live is the main thing—be alive and conscious of things—not just of injustices and the underdogs—but conscious of sensation & beauty—and get all the fun that's going around."

They didn't see Darlie and Jane again. Jane left the United States permanently in 1939 for Puerto Rico, where she married Cesar d'Andrieu, a leader of the Communist party there. They had one son called Nicholas. Jean was sure he had been named after me. Not so. He was named for Nikolai Lenin.

27

The Depression

LIFE AT HAZEL HEDGE WAS GREATLY ALTERED BY THE DEPRESSION. IT wasn't long before Ben Miller was the only full-time servant, doing gardening and serving and cleaning up—and working with Jean on all of her projects, from setting up scenery at the Little Theatre to polishing brass for the Altar Guild. After Mammy Ellen left, Jean did all the cooking. She also kept the house filled with flowers and the table filled with guests.

Some of these were paying guests, invited to stay at Hazel Hedge because they could pay and were friends, or friends of friends.

For a long time Earl McGowan, a state senator, lived there when the legislature was in session. Jean commented, "He is very intelligent and has a good deal of culture in spite of the fact that four years at Oxford and much travel have not eradicated 'inny pinny' from his pronunciation. Mary Webber, a social worker who became head of Alabama's WPA, stayed for several years. Loula Dunn, head of the state child welfare department, was there intermittently.

Taking in boarders was not without precedent among "good old families" in Montgomery. It was a survival tactic carried over from the Reconstruction. Through the Depression, Jean had many paying guests. She selected hers carefully, and always made them feel it was a privilege to be staying at Hazel Hedge. I knew them all, and from Kent always sent "the boarders" my love. Among those who became Jean's life-long friends were an Army Air Corps general and his wife from Maxwell Air Force Base. They occupied the big pink room with the bay windows and a fireplace, and a ceiling-high four-poster bed.

Jean described her new role as landlady: "I get up every morning early and have breakfast with my lodgers. We eat on the big, round marble table on the side screen porch overlooking the garden, and share our crumbs with a chipmunk who lives overhead in a lantern that he makes swing in a most daring fashion. Then I do flowers and put bouquets on the mantel and Ben lays coal in the grate so they can have a fire on cold mornings."

She did the shopping and planned dinner, which usually included extra guests. Then, there were drinks beforehand ("I have just found a good bourbon for juleps at only $1.65 a quart."), to be served with beaten biscuits and thin slices of Virginia ham. A favorite light supper was scalloped oysters and grit souffle with hot bread and a salad. In summer the beverage was iced tea, and when it was available, dessert was honeydew melon with a lime. When a guest brought some there was wine.

A description of Hazel Hedge at that time was given by one of Jean's favorite guests, Ben Baldwin, the son of the Benjamin Baldwin who had the plantation at Verbena. Years later, after Ben came to national attention as one of the foremost designers of interiors and gardens, he wrote in his *Autobiography in Design* that Jean Read was his inspiration:

Without her, the Hazel Hedge house was simply a big wooden ark on the out-

The garden at Hazel Hedge.

skirts of Montgomery that was being actively eaten up by termites and dry rot. In winter the heat was unpredictable and the pipes froze. There were always repairs under way—on the big rambling roof, the floorboards and the porches. In summer it breathed in the air from the shaded lawns that encircled it, pulled through the rooms by a big attic fan. Architecturally, no one would have looked at it twice. But with Jean there, it became an ever-changing set for make-believe and magic.

It was surrounded by a dense hedge of yucca, bamboo, and pink roses. In the front yard was a small pool near an enormous elm whose branches covered most of the yard like a giant umbrella. In the spring, masses of daffodils and rain lilies bloomed . . . and garlands of pomegranates ringed a screen porch on one side of the house. Lambo, a black poodle, had pushed holes in the screen going in and out to the garden.

A long arbor, covered with wisteria and roses, led to a fountain. Mounds of pink azaleas, lilies, and big rice-paper plants lined the hedges, beyond which were beds of roses and a high garden wall with yellow banksia roses cascading over it and climbing up into the tall cedar trees. Near the porch was a well with a bucket and a painted Della Robbia plaque; a column of Confederate jasmine twined up to the eaves and mixed its fragrance with that of a huge clump of white ginger lilies.

The drawing room of the house, which gave the place its English country feeling, was full of sunshine, filtered through gold gauze in winter and cooled by green gauze in summer. On both sides of the fireplace books spilled out of the shelves onto tables and chairs. The furnishings—a big overstuffed sofa tufted in worn brown velvet, a cane chaise and chairs, a long carved wooden bench, a small Steinway grand, and bowls full of flowers—were all casual and comfortable.

In the springtime, huge branches of cut pear blossoms touched the ceiling and long sprays of yellow roses in amber Venini vases, and paper-white narcissus in green pottery bowls stood next to small vases of pink camellias.

In summer the room was like an enchanted place under the sea. The gold gauze curtains were changed to green and the vases filled with tropical-looking rice-paper leaves. All the furniture was slip-covered in green and white and the rugs put away in cedar closets. During the Christmas season, when Jean gathered her many friends of all ages to sing carols and drink her lethal punch, the room danced with golden candlelight and with shadows from the fire of oak logs. The house was full of laughter.

Jean was full of delightful conversation and wonderful stories made even more

THE DEPRESSION   225

fascinating by bits of inaccurate information, and she gave herself with complete enthusiasm to living life and to giving people pleasure. I went to Hazel Hedge whenever I needed to reinforce my feeling that life should be full of wonder and beauty. She and Hazel Hedge taught me the greatest lesson—that living and working are part of the same thing and must be done with joy and total awareness, that a house is a shelter in a garden and that living there is what makes it beautiful.

Many years later, "paying guest" Connie Wash, the wife of the general, wrote Jean, "Time cannot alter the sheer magic of you! All my other friends grow stale and stuffy and drab with the years and you are dynamic, lovelier, more stimulating each time I see you."

It was fortunate that Jean was dynamic. Not too long after the stock market crash in 1929, which took away much of their income, she began to convert various structures on the grounds to cottages and built others to rent. She did seven in all, working with B. B. Hawkins, a contractor and carpenter ("I never uses cured wood").

First to be done was "Mammy's House" just in back of the big house. Next was the barn, which became "*Casa de Vaca*" (House of the Cow) when Jean used Mexican tiles bought years past in Dolores Hidalgo in Mexico to copy the front of a fireplace she had seen there. She put a *papier mâché* cow's head over the door, which was borrowed from time to time for performances of "The King's Breakfast," a Mother Goose rhyme which Jean modified to include a cow—so as to use the *papier mâché* cow's head. Father played the part of the king, Kathleen Wilkerson who lived in "*Casa de Vaca*" was the dairy maid, and whoever was handy was the cow.

"Arbor Cottage" was built near the end of the Scuppernong arbor, and "Daffodil Cottage" was in the daffodil field. "Lane House" was erected on a new driveway from Carter Hill Road called "Hazel Hedge Lane." Its first occupants were C. and Grace Lane. Then there was "Green Mansions." And one of the last cottages built was a brick structure, "Blanding Castle." World War II had begun, and I had been drafted and sent for training to Camp Blanding in Florida, where I drew the floor plan—hence the name.

To be a tenant required more than rent money. You had to have good manners. Intelligence and a sense of style helped. Reading good books was a plus, as was having an interest in the theater. Or being a romantic newly married couple, or a friend of mine. Jeanie got to know her renters well, dispensing plants and flowers, bric-a-brac and decorations, books and edibles—as she collected the rents—that put me through school.

The list of brides and grooms who started their married lives there and later became prominent in the civic and social life of Montgomery is a long one, including Truman and Joyce Hobbs and Sally and Gene Millsap, Barnet and George Wood and Dot and Joe Moore. Dot Moore remembers coming from the hospital after her son, Russell, was born, to find all the other tenants, including Mary Lee Stapp, in her garden at an elaborate tea party—with martinis—supplied by Jeanie to welcome her home.

Some of the renters were controversial. In the 1950s, when a reporter from the *Advertiser*, who was living at Hazel Hedge, was accused of writing for the Communist *Daily Worker*, public opinion, not Jeanie, forced him to leave. She characterized him as "a very charming person and well read."

Hazel Hedge was also a stopping place for old friends returning to Montgomery from big jobs in the Roosevelt Administration. Such a one was Aubrey Williams, who had been head of the National Youth Administration, and came back to edit the *Southern Farmer*. Dallas remembered his name appreciatively for the part-time NYA job that helped pay her way when she was getting her master's degree at Columbia University.

Friends of mine from the University of North Carolina, Gould and Mary Beech, moved into "Green Mansions." As Gould described living there, "It certainly helped to be at Hazel Hedge. Being a resident of one of Jean's cottages set you apart—as if you were a member of an exclusive club. The houses were simply built. The setting and Jean made the difference. When you said you lived there it was more of a distinction than saying 'I'm a friend of the Governor,' or 'I'm a cousin of the Mayor.'"

Tenants were encouraged to "do their own thing" out of their homes, as long as it was attractive or tasted good. For awhile Gould and Mary operated a small business from their garage, filling blue glazed jugs with sugar cane syrup, sealing them with red wax, and selling them. Sheila described the syrup in her *New Yorker* column and the orders—quite literally—poured in. One letter came from Katherine Cornell, who reported that the red wax had cracked, and the syrup got into the mails. It was a sticky business. She complained and asked for a replacement.

George Stoney, a friend who at the time was in charge of the southeast for the New Deal's Farm Security Administration, documenting the dehabilitating effect of the Depression on rural people, lived with the Beeches for about a year. On one trip to poverty-stricken Georgia he visited a commissary where mill hands had to buy their food with scrip issued by the owner. When he visited the commissary he wondered aloud why there was such a large supply of dog food. The storekeeper said, "You'd be surprised at how good that stuff can be—at least that's what these folks around here tell me." He also noticed a large stack of liquid Dyanshine shoe polish, and was told, "When you can't get whisky, people buy that and pour it through a loaf of bread. It takes the black out."

Jean continued to operate her small shop in downtown Montgomery, cooking items she could sell over the counter, as well as supplying food "delicacies from the South" described in Sheila's column. Sheila made connections for Jean, such as advising her to write the buyer at Charles & Company, Vanderbilt Ave. at Forty-Third, "about the artichoke pickles you can supply." She wrote, "If you read my Christmas list, you will see that most of the ideas I make up, and then get the shops to stock them."

Jean became a good supplier: "It's 12 a.m. I've just come up to bed having made 12 pounds of plum pudding and 24 jars of pickles, and a dozen jars of artichokes." She sold the puddings for $1.40 a pound.

The cottages took a lot of time. A change of tenants often meant a change in decor. When "*Casa de Vaca*" was rented to the Ballards, it was a complete redo. As Jean said, "The Ballards are so colorless I thought I would give them a real treat. I rearranged the furniture and made new curtains and repaired the terrace. It is just about the cutest place I ever saw."

In addition to maintaining the houses, she was up early digging, planting, trimming and watering, since she had no gardener. She was too tired to give many parties and allowed herself to be absorbed into the social life of her old friend Minnie Reynolds Saffold and Minnie's daughter and son-in-law Georgia and Will Oates, who entertained often and lavishly at Belvoir, their estate not far away on Thomas Avenue.

When the strain got too much, Jean would just go to bed for a few days. At one point Granny wrote me at Kent, "Just a line, because Jean is not able to write & I know you miss her letters. She does not even want to sit up. Judy comes out every afternoon with Charlie and brings her the most wonderful supper, and spreads a feast for the rest of us. She will write you when she can sit up."

There were always things to do from her sickbed, such as updating her financial records. She was pleased when Nash complimented her on the way she kept her books. "I'm really getting to be a very good business woman," she wrote me, "and your father is a good provider from his hunting."

Dad verified this: "Our shooting season opens tomorrow and Jessie Rawlings and I are going down to the preserve. We will get some doves. A few weeks ago I came back from the Delta Duck Club where I killed 50 ducks and 12 geese. Last Friday I brought home eight doves and six partridges. We will organize a quail hunt when you come down next time."

The Depression was hard on my father, who could no longer provide the income that had taken such good care of us. I wrote in a notebook I had been keeping, labeled "Private Diary":

> It was not so much the loss of money but the loss of his claim to importance that went with it. It hurt him with me too. How could he tell me about stocks & business, when he had nothing to report? He survived, I think, with a great deal of dignity.
>
> His position was a hard one—one I could not endure. What philosophy or implicit spiritual powers has he relied upon? When I discover what inward stamina he has (& I should have long ago) I may respect him more than any man I know. I knew that he was deeply unhappy.

He had written me: "I lie awake a great many nights and worry and worry over the future, particularly your future. I review my past and see the mistakes I have made and what I might have done; so very futile, but depressing and disheartening, and I feel I have made a very poor showing. I keep a brave front, for Jeanie has been in such a state of health and nerves, I must boost her up. I have been terribly worried about her."

I wrote him, "You, Dad, must not worry. We are all going to be all right. If you made mistakes, it was by way of doing what you thought was best for us, and think of the men that have made mistakes, thousands of them, and many have given up the game. Wealth will not mean so much, and no one is going to be very rich in a few years. The times are troublesome, but they are equally interesting, and we can in many ways make life worthwhile—without money."

I analyzed the relationship between my parents: "Love rests largely on respect.

We don't love someone we can't respect or admire, and respect rests partly on accomplishment. If my father were a very important something—it doesn't matter what—my mother might have stayed in love with him. The fact that he was retired, and had nothing to do, made the loss of his money, which was his chief claim to self respect, poignantly tragic."

He was a sweet and generous man and preserved Hazel Hedge for her, and made possible its development as a background for her own dramatic undertakings and social and cultural life. She adored literature and poetry and the theater. He was a sportsman who loved hunting and fishing, football and cockfighting, golf—and the country club. The country club "Chatter" said that there was one adjective applicable to him in all his ways of living—hearty! But I don't believe my mother respected him for these things.

At one time, after she had been complaining about Ben's faults and went off to Birmingham to get away from it all, my father took it upon himself to fire Ben. When he told my Mother about it, she returned forthwith, and went to find Ben and bring him back. "I could do without you," she said to my father, "but I couldn't do without Ben."

28

Jean and the Saffolds

D
URING THE DEPRESSION, JEANNIE STOPPED GIVING PARTIES BE-
cause the strain of keeping up Hazel Hedge, the rental cottages, and
the garden with only Ben to help, wore her out. She transferred her
social life to Belvoir, just a few blocks away, where her old friend Mildred Reynolds
Saffold and her daughter Georgia Oates held sway. They welcomed her almost as
a co-hostess, and gave plenty of exciting parties.

Jean had known Mildred Reynolds since she came to Montgomery from Bullock
County as the bride of the well-connected Mr. Saffold many years ago. "Minnie" had
grown up as the daughter of an overseer on a cotton plantation, not poor, but not
from an old established plantation family. In the South, where almost the first question on meeting a stranger was "Who are your people?," this was a drawback.

In Bullock County, Minnie had made it on her own. Being smart, pretty, and
popular, she was a stellar attraction for young men at the parties and hay rides young
people attended in those days. She married well and came to Montgomery to live
in a big house on Hull Street. There she had her six babies easily, in fact so easily
that Dr. Gaston had difficulty getting her to the hospital on time. One was said to
have been born on his raincoat. There were four girls and two boys.

No one remembers much about Mr. Saffold, who stayed in the background.
There was little said about the boys either, but Minnie, who later came to be known
as "Rosie," and her girls shone.

The one that shone brightest was Georgia, a pretty blonde who married Captain
William Oates, the only son of the governor of Alabama. The governor, who feared
nothing and nobody, was given to saying outrageous things. Once when a heckler at a
political rally baited him with "What do you do with your bastard nigger children?,"

the governor shot back, "I educate mine, sir. What do you do with yours?"

His son, William, went to West Point and married Georgia before World War I, when he was a captain in the artillery. When he came back he took a law degree, and became secretary-examiner of the Alabama State Securities Commission.

They had one daughter, Marion, who came to be known as "Oatsie." Their elegant estate, Belvoir, on Thomas Avenue, was quite the center for social events. Georgia was said to have eight extra services always laid at the dinner table, "just in case."

I know that my mother often had dinner there—always in evening dress, if not in costume. A description of one ball, where the guests came in the costumes of their distinguished ancestors, was recorded for its historical significance in the quarterly publication of the State Department of Archives and History.

Will Oates began to drink heavily and he and Georgia separated. He moved into a guest house in their garden and his already failing health worsened.

My mother Jean, who was probably Georgia's best friend, described him in a letter to me. "He was so repulsive-looking. In fact, death is a very undignified thing—the dissolution of the body. People talk of the dignity of death. After it's all over there is dignity & peace, but the going is pretty terrible—just as the process of birth is. Of course, he will die soon."

She went to see Georgia and found her with Will.

> Georgia seemed more affectionate than I had ever seen her with him, calling him "Billy" & submitting to his kisses gracefully. But the very next morning four people called before 11 o'clock to say that she was getting a divorce & was going to marry a millionaire from New York.
>
> I lambasted them, saying what a lousy gossipy town this was. One of them, Mrs. John Kohn, repeated what I had said to Grover Hall who wrote in his editorial, "Why don't people stop gossiping & tending to other people's business & pay their poll tax instead?"

Soon afterwards, Jean got a telephone call from Georgia, who said that she would get her final divorce decree the next week. "Heaven knows I don't blame her. Twenty-six years with a man who is drunk half the time and has no moral responsibility about anything is pretty tough. Of course this rumor about the millionaire suitor is all bunk."

It was only a short time before a letter came and I was informed that

> Will Oates died this morning. He was only 55. It is really like a Chekhov story.
> No one would believe, although, poor Georgia, I think it is more the gossip that is
> affecting her than anything else. They are saying that she locked him out in the rain
> and that he got pneumonia as a result. Another story was that he was exercising and
> struck himself in the head with a dumbbell. Another was that she was planning to
> leave him and marry a rich man from New York.
>
> It certainly was unfortunate as long as she had waited all these years to divorce
> him that she hadn't waited just a little longer. Of course, no one knew he was go-
> ing to die. He is lying in state at Belvoir now. I just finished fixing a little lunch
> for Georgia and took it up on a tray. Rosie Saffold was there, and said to me, "We
> could ill afford to lose Mr. Oates."
>
> Afterwards, Nash, Mary Webber and I took a picnic lunch to Reynold's Mill. It
> was a perfect May day. We wore summer clothes & didn't take any rugs or sweaters,
> and had a fine steak cooked on charcoal, and a wonderful salad and beer and coffee
> and warm, white fruit cake. I read a book aloud and we all dozed in the sun. Taffy
> swam all day & then rolled on pine needles.

It wasn't long after Will's death that Georgia married Philip Gossler of Long
Island and Nassau, a very rich older man. She wrote my mother, "So happy! To
tell it on paper impossible beyond the limit of any letter—Philip lifted me over
the threshold of my new home-to-be and it is hard to take in what is unfolding—a
beautiful new life here. I am the happiest woman on earth."

I was visiting in New York when Georgia invited me for lunch at the Stork Club,
and I sensed her relief at having someone from home. She didn't seem happy living
in Manhattan, and after a few cocktails unburdened herself. She was redecorating
the town house, and having "undressed" one room, taking out its Chinese decor,
was afraid she would make a mess redoing it. However, her biggest problem was her
inability to communicate with Philip's friends, and I can understand why.

She invited me to spend the weekend with them at the Piping Rock Club. I
described it in a letter to Jeanie:

> No less interesting to me than the luxury of this swank horsy club was the state
> of Lady Georgia's private affairs. Her new life is complicated by two problems: one

is her husband, the other her husband's friends.

Philip, it seems, demands a great deal. For example, he wants Georgia to sit on his lap when he makes long distance phone calls to business associates. Georgia, you know, likes to choose her laps. As for Philip's friends, they are not a bit interested in Belvoir and the "Deep South." Even Marion told her mother that it was very boring talking about Belvoir and Montgomery. Unfortunately, Georgia knows nothing at all about horses—which are the big subject at the Piping Rock Club.

I agree with Oatsie, but I will bet a hat that some of those horsy people are twice as dull talking about withers and foals and geldings ad infinitum. Poor Georgia doesn't know a bay from a sorrel. At dinner at the Club, there were eight at our table, four young people, a girl named Cozie Noyes and her beau, a rather nice young rich boy whose Dad owns a string of papers in New Jersey. The Gosslers' friends were Mr. and Mrs. W-something (the man's brother was Claire Booth Luce's first husband).

The club was packed with people. I liked the men in long-tailed red coats, each with a different colored lapel to denote his hunting club. Considering the number of cocktails that everyone must have had, the conversation was rather slow. It was Marion's birthday and I proposed a toast and stood up. No one else stood up. They said that the toast was a good idea, but made no effort to make it a successful one. Ms. Gossler's new life has its complications as well as compensations.

Philip is quite short, and wears a scowl behind his pince nez.

Georgia told me privately that he is failing (getting old). In front of him, she kept saying, "Isn't he the youngest looking thing!" I think he looks Jewish. The next day I had some time alone to talk with him and found him a dull conversationalist. Although he is slightly deaf, he heard me when I told him the South should forget about the Civil War and that a great many southerners already had. He turned to Georgia and said, "This is the most intelligent person I have met from Montgomery, Alabama."

I wandered over to the horse show. What a magnificent spectacle! A long tent of white and blue cloth, behind which were other tents in the woods, where food and drink were served. Cars were drawn up around the ring. Old gentlemen and ladies sat in their Rolls Royces and young sporting bloods perched on the tops of rakish Packards. I stood humbly at ringside in awe of the magnificent jumping, but left about 3:30 for an engagement in town with Ann van Doren, to see *Pins and Needles*.

Oatsie is thriving in her new environment. She says it is just what she wants—for awhile. I do not think she is really in love with Morris Baldwin in Montgomery. According to Georgia, she had some swell beaus abroad, royalty in Scotland and England rushing her, etc. And she wants to be rushed some more. Morris Baldwin was there when I called, but he is a hard working boy and Marion is a deb.

For her, every day adorned with orchids, it's the Stork Club, where our lunch cost $10, or the Rainbow Room, or El Morocco. As Oatsie said, "It's a lot better than Snow's drug store in Montgomery." And I agree.

Cholly Knickerbocker described her in a syndicated press column,"These Fascinating Ladies," as:

[a] beautiful creature, twinkling brown eyes in a gardenia face, statuesque grace . . . no wonder the cameras clicked, as they did at the fashionable opera opening, in a merry frenzy whenever this photogenic glamour girl put in an appearance. Where the stag line is thickest and the cutting-in rampant, there you find her twirling through every number. She would be a ballet starlet today if she hadn't sprouted so high, so fast.

Southern belle, Alabama-born, she was grown up before she realized that "Dixie" isn't the national anthem. Attended Margaret Booth's school in Montgomery and after her mother's marriage to Gossler, went to Miss Broadbent's in Belgium. Then, by permission of Cardinal Faulharber, she was the only American and only Protestant to have entered the Kloster St. Joseph of Zangberg in Germany, where royalty and titled students have received their education for generations.

She made her debut in December at the St. Regis, in a white tulle frock embroidered with sheaves of gold and topaz oats, befitting her name. She has given many hours to charity, serving as a mannequin in benefit fashion shows etc . . . Her dearest girl friend is her mother, Georgia Gossler, and she and her grandmother Saffold, the authoress, are cronies.

Inheriting the desire to be an author from her grandmother, writing is her ambition. She has no place in her vocabulary for slang—never "makes a date," but keeps an engagement. Is almost never present at cocktail parties, prefers to have her friends in her own home for tea.

At the family camp on the Canadian Restigouche River, she is the pet of the guides because she casts so proficiently and last Summer caught the largest salmon there. She gets to Alabama annually for the month of April.

The Gosslers lived part of the year at their house, "Harborside," on Hogg Island in Nassau. Georgia wrote urging Jean to come for a visit.

I've got to entertain the Duke and Duchess of Windsor who are here at Government House, and cannot bear to think of it without you. Bessie Merryman (Wallis Simpson's aunt) says they can play cards but prefer not to.

Presumably the Duke is difficult to talk to, but likes to be amused. I suspect they would enjoy something southern. If only you could come as the adorable mammy you were at my ante-bellum party, and tell your billy-goat-ate-the-newspaper story, you could be the Court Entertainer.

I gave a small luncheon for Aunt Bessie Merryman and in her honor arranged an elaborate mint julep table on the lawn, with crystal decanters and Philip's silver mint julep cups. I went through all the ceremonies, crushed ice and all, and made them myself. It took some time as you can imagine, and of course, I served mine last.

I noticed the ladies, many of whom had never tasted a julep before, putting down their glasses one by one. When I tasted mine I nearly dropped dead! It was awful!! The ice made from water here is brackish and the whole MESS tasted as if someone had put in salt. A MINT JULEP SHOULD BE SERVED IN A SOUTHERN GARDEN. This, child, is the land of rum and gin!

We went to a dinner for the Windsors at Government House and I sat beside the Duke. Afterwards when the Duchess announced that the guests would play bridge or poker, I had to confess that I played neither, and the Duke quickly said, "Don't leave me, come sit by me." Since we were not card-minded, we broke up the poker table by making limericks. The best one was "Ada from Decatur ate a raw potato, when he tried to date her she said, 'Can't, I'll have to see you later.'"

When I saw him later at the annual dinner of the Porcupine Club on Washington's birthday, where the acting Governor and His Lady were honored guests, I said, "Sir, how is Ada from Decatur?" He repled wittily "I'll have to see you later." It is customary in speaking to the Duke to use "Sir" whenever addressing him. This I found a little difficult, as I was crazy to call him "darling." He was adorable in his kilts. After the toast to the King was drunk, the lights were lowered and a piper played the bagpipe around the table—a most impressive ceremony.

The Duchess was simply but exquisitely gowned in white organza with gold embroidery, slippers and gloves to match huge gold jewelry. Her voice interested me tremendously; the fret-work of it is more Carolinian than Maryland, to which she has added some French and a decidedly soft English accent.

I have seen a good deal of Sir Harry and Lady Oakes; Sir Harry and I were discussing the need of a restaurant here that would specialize in native cooking. I told him about you and Sheila, and he said he would back anybody who was equipped and interested.

You meet everyone here. A charming Mr. Robertson from Richmond, who had been stationed at Taylor Field in Montgomery, said, "You are southern and remind me of the loveliest southern girl I met in Alabama." Without a moment's hesitation I said, "Was her name Willie Gayle?," and it was.

I have had a series of Sunday buffet luncheons, having already entertained some 300 people this way and not yet covered my obligations. Next Saturday I am having a buffet luncheon for Mr. Salzado, the harpist, and his wife. As a patron of the Forum of Arts, I was asked to do this, but remembering him so delightfully through the Montgomery Concert Course, I am looking forward to it.

Georgia did not object to Jean's antics or liberal opinions, although I was told she regards both of us as somewhat left-wing. Normally she avoided controversy, never having a serious opinion, unless it is about the race question, which she considered off limits for discussion.

She once wrote to Jean: "I am very much upset about Helen Hayes acting the life of Harriet Beecher Stowe, not that the question of slavery will come into it. But in these days of Harlem Park atrocities and with the public school rowdyism—colored mothers beating up white teachers (no school here is without police protection)—and with Mrs. R's visits to Tuskegee, and the Eleanor Clubs destroying our southern feeling, I think the whole business is exceedingly untimely and I believe will lead to racial disturbances that will actually be dangerous. What can we do about it?"

As time went on she began to carve a niche for herself in musical circles, by playing and composing music for the harp. She gave concerts and had her music presented at St. Thomas Church in New York, and at The Homestead in Hot Springs, Virginia. In 1943, Robert Kitzin, a Russian violinist, played two of her pieces at Carnegie Hall and she was made a member of the League of Composers and Conductors.

She said of her music, "It has always been a source of self-expression, which I have never taken seriously, and now I am told that because it is fresh, original and uncontaminated by any school, my ignorance of technical knowledge is the better for it." A story about her in the Cholly Knickerbocker series picked this up, "Though she doesn't know the notes, she has composed over a hundred songs, the first one executed at the age of four being 'We live in a white house. The shutters are green. We have cabbage for dinner.'"

One Christmas, Jeanie made a creche in a hollow gourd and sent it to Georgia in New York, who was ecstatic: "On the night of the 24th, after dinner, we turned out the lights and set the creche on a pedestal, and I played 'Holy Night' on my harmonica. Nearly all of us cried—Philip for one did—and we drank a toast to you, to Hazel Hedge, and to the memory of Belvoir. Bless you for sending it."

At that very moment in Montgomery, "Rosie" Saffold was undoubtedly at Jeanie's Christmas Eve party. She had lived at Belvoir since Georgia moved to New York. Mr. Saffold had died many years before, at which time she had gone to Europe, viewed mourning clothes in the house of one of the great designers, and refitted herself. From then on she wore black for the rest of her life. "It becomes me," she said. I remember what she said, when as a teenager, I admired the evening dress she was wearing, "Child, what I have on is a nightgown, a black satin one. It clings

Jean's drawing of the Christmas party.

beautifully, and is cut low in front so that I can reach down into my bosom for a white lace handkerchief."

Her daughter Georgia's marriage to Philip Gossler was richly rewarding, as was her granddaughter Oatsie's to Tommy Leiter, the rich scion of a Chicago family. They also had one daughter, Victoria, and were divorced. Oatsie received a generous settlement although as in the case of her mother, it would have been even bigger if she had waited, since he died shortly afterwards, leaving his fortune to Victoria.

However, Oatsie rebuilt a beautiful historic house in Washington D.C.'s Georgetown with Victoria's inheritance, for Victoria's upbringing. It also became the setting for her own climb to prominence in Washington's political and social circles. Oatsie became a major Democratic hostess, but when Ronald Reagan won the next election, she changed sides and became Nancy Reagan's close friend and guide to social life in the nation's capital.

Victoria rebelled against family and tradition, and broke her engagement to an eligible bachelor in Newport, joining VISTA, the domestic equivalent of the Peace Corps. In VISTA, she met and fell in love with a young man of modest background. Her mother gave them a splendid wedding reception in a huge tent in the garden of the Georgetown house. It was attended by an odd mix of young people from VISTA wearing casual cottons and blue jeans and sandals or going barefoot, and elegant ladies and gentlemen from Newport. There were several blacks in the wedding party, including the daughter of the cook.

The mother and father of the groom felt a little out of place with both the dominant groups, but kept their poise. Once, when the groom's aunt reported to his mother that "they are saying he married her for her money," a guest standing nearby said soothingly, "Don't worry about that. They can't help it. The whole family has always married for money. They don't really know that anyone can marry for just love."

29

Sheila and Jean

IN NEW YORK, SHEILA WAS DOING WELL. SHE HAD FINISHED HER SECOND book, *A Kitchen Manual.* She explained in the foreword that it was not really a cookbook and expressed concern that

> letters will come complaining that it has no index, gives no clue as to how many raisins go into a Lady Baltimore cake, and is dark with prejudices deep and personal.
>
> I hope my publishers (Duell, Sloan and Pearce) will not quail but will break a lance or two for me. They have known from the beginning that my intention was to write a new kind of mystery story, a book of secrets, a homily on the hang of the thing. We agreed on a work to be read between meals and meditated upon.
>
> I would like to think that my words might persuade the writers of next year's cookbooks that cooking is neither to be left to those who believe that the end of all culinary endeavor is the making of a white sauce without lumps, nor to those precious amateurs who self-consciously bandy about the rather down-at-heels title of gourmet.

Later on she wrote two more cookbooks. One was *Good Food for Bad Stomachs*, in collaboration with Sara M. Jordan, M.D. The introduction was by her editor at *The New Yorker,* Harold Ross, whose painful peptic ulcers had inspired the book. The other, *American Regional Cookery*, had recipes from every part of the country—including Baked Alaska from Manhattan, and Huevos Rancheros from Santa Fe, New Mexico.

She wasn't as famous as M. F. K. Fisher, but was a favorite of Mrs. Fisher's, who admired her books. Unlike Mrs. Fisher, whose focus was on French cooking, Sheila was interested in American cooking, which she was afraid was being inundated by the "graceless routine of eating out of packages and cans."

As they had all their lives, Sheila and Jean not only sent recipes back and forth, but consulted each other about what to wear and what books to read. Sheila wrote, "Be sure to return *High Wind in Jamaica* and tell Nash to read Jake Baker on *How to Run a Speakeasy.*" Sheila wrote a book review for the *New Republic* on *Their Eyes Were Watching God,* by a Negro woman novelist, Zora Neale Hurston.

She drew from her own Southern background to appreciate Hurston's description of the "vibrant negro lingo with its guitar twang of poetry, and its deep vivid humor—-the flowers of the sweet speech of black people are not quite so full blown and striking as in her earlier books. On the other hand, the sap flows more freely, and the roots touch deeper levels of human life."

As Sheila made more money, she bought "a very good second hand Ford sedan coupe for $50," and a little house across the Hudson in New Jersey, which she called "Mud Fence." She continued to do Jean's shopping for her in New York, and relied on Jean's seamstress in Montgomery for help with her wardrobe. "I would love to have the violet chiffon made into a dress just like your blue one. The yellow is much too long and should be taken up."

Many of Sheila's writer and editor friends got to know Jean and visited Hazel Hedge, as did friends of mine. Joseph Auslander and Louis Adamic were such visitors.

On one visit, novelist John Dos Passos slept in the four-poster bed. As Ben was serving breakfast the next morning on the screen porch, Jean was casually perusing the *Montgomery Advertiser* when a story caught her eye, "It says here that this year it is predicted that a nigra will win the Irish sweepstakes. Oh Ben, wouldn't it be wonderful if you won? Let's see what we could do with the money? We could fix up the kitchen, and repair the pergola and mend the broken wall in the garden" to all of which Ben responded with his customary noncommittal "Yassum."

But when she got around to repairing the garage, which was leaning at a disturbing angle, his tone changed. Ben had a room above it, and must have been concerned for his own safety. This time he said, "Yes maam, it sho do need fixen."

Dos Passos had said nothing, but when Ben went to the kitchen for more hot biscuits he turned to my mother and said, "This is peonage, Jean, absolute peonage! This man has won the Irish sweepstakes and you have spent his entire fortune on your estate!"

Ernestine Evans, next occupant of the four-poster bed, tolerated no interruptions. She came to report on social conditions. Her work included graphic descriptions of desolate mining towns out west "where the owners just closed down the mines and left whole towns of miners stranded on the hill sides. Then someone goes in, buys up all the little cottages and moves the people off. They just disappear, off to the city bread lines, no doubt."

Jean mixed her guests with no regard for political opinions. For one dinner honoring Stanley High, a well-known liberal writer from New York, she had the conservative Marion Rushton. "We had a lovely time. 'High' was the most delightful person I ever met, of course very intelligent and liberal, and so humorous. And Marion Rushton never talks politics."

She planned to have one of her plum puddings for dessert, and when she discovered she had no rum for the sauce, and Nash was still at the Club, she called his bootlegger and asked him if she could talk business over the telephone. "'Shoot,' he answered, so I knew I was talking to the right man." He even brought it by.

Another time she put my friend George Stoney, who was a writer for *Survey Graphic*, the liberal sociology publication, together with Dick Hudson, the very conservative publisher of the *Montgomery Advertiser*, and Willey Gayle Martin, the portrait painter whose attitude towards Negroes matched that of her brother, the mayor of Montgomery, who put Rosa Parks in jail for sitting in the front of the bus. Mother wrote me that they had a very pleasant time, talking about world conditions and Anne Morrow Lindbergh's book.

> You would never suspect that I cleaned the kitchen stove with lye today, and that I didn't have a fine cook in the kitchen. I never had to get up—or see after anything. We had baked oyster soup and plenty of doves and rice croquettes and creamed spinach and little individual baked squash and hot biscuits and a chocolate roll with whipped cream, and drinks before dinner, and wine with dinner.
>
> I got some red leaves from the curb market today—sour wood—as lovely as any Canadian maple and they were stunning in the drawing room against the gold curtains, and in front of the lamp on the piano, they looked as if the room was on fire.

When Dorothy Thompson—Mrs. Sinclair Lewis—arrived in Montgomery to give a lecture, Jean got into trouble. The lecture series was being sponsored by a Jewish organization, but except for the lecture, Dorothy spent her time at Hazel Hedge. Nash in particular enjoyed her. He wrote me: "I wish you could have heard her talk. She is most brilliant and entertaining. She hasn't much opinion of the Communists: she said she was one once but they converted her to a reversal of that faith."

The Jewish ladies organization was upset because they felt Jean had taken their star performer away from them. In a letter to me Jean wrote, "Now my shop is being boycotted by the Jews. Not one has put a foot in the shop since." This was not the only time Jean raided a lecture series. She gave an elegant luncheon for another speaker on the very day of the lecture, and was upbraided by the chairman of the event who told her, "You had no right to tread on our rights."

It's no wonder that the speaker accepted Jean's invitation. "It was the most perfect Sunday supper I have ever tasted. I had oyster gumbo in the big silver tureen and a great silver dish of hot rice. Then a small cold turkey. Stuffed eggs in jellied bouillon in individual moulds, and a mixed salad of lettuce, tomatoes and alligator pears and tarragon tossed together. And the most delicious dessert—nuts and dates and eggs all cooked up like a macaroon and broken up and soaked in sherry and afterwards touched with whipped cream. With dinner, we had Chablis."

When Scott and Zelda Fitzgerald returned to Montgomery after an absence of many years, they were treated to a picnic with cold martinis and hot crab gumbo. Richard Burton came to appear in the repertory theater and never forgot to send a Christmas greeting thereafter. And she gave a theater party celebrating the return of Tallulah Bankhead to the area. Tallulah had many lovers and no inhibitions. She stood on her head at one reception given for her, with nothing on underneath her dress. She had surprised everyone by marrying an inconspicuous actor named John Emery. I asked her, "Why?" Tallulah replied, "Because he fucks like a rabbit, dahling."

One old acquaintance who didn't get to Hazel Hedge was Gertrude Stein, whom Jean had known in Paris, and who came to Birmingham on a lecture tour of the United States but didn't have time to get to Montgomery. However, she did *me* a favor by writing Jean that of the twenty universities she visited, Chapel Hill was one of the best.

John Dos Passos made a second visit after an absence of many years and was again met at the door by Ben. He told Jean, "Your man has a remarkable memory, after all this time, he recognized me." What Ben said was "Lordy, looka who's heah!" That's the way he greeted everybody. And when they left he said, "Y'all hurry back."

30

A Time To Weep

THERE WERE SAD TIMES. MY FATHER, NASH, LEFT FOR FLORIDA TO TAKE his brother Isaac, who had been very ill, on a last fishing trip. My grandmother wrote, "Everything has been done to make it perfect, but he looks so ill and changed that it would not surprise me if they returned sooner than they had planned." Isaac died soon afterwards.

A few years later, Hazel Hedge lost its oldest and best loved inhabitant, my grandmother. Jennie Baldwin Craik, that delightful and industrious wife of Will Craik who planted the hazel hedge that gave the place its name, died in 1935. Her obituary stated that she gave much of her time to humanitarian causes, principally the Hale Infirmary for Negroes, founded by Anne Hale, who had been her nursemaid when she was a little girl.

The funeral in Montgomery was conducted by a cousin, Bishop James Craik Morris of New Orleans. He wrote to Jean, "I do not need to tell you how truly I loved precious Aunt Jennie and what a privilege it was to read the service. There was no one like her, and several people said to me at the church door that hers was the finest influence in Montgomery. She was the best example I know of the 'childlikeness' which our Lord said was the mark of a Christian and a disciple. She never grew old, and her interests and sympathy were so spontaneous, so winsome, that they were as irresistible as they were beautiful."

Jean wrote me:

> I want you to read some of the letters I get about Mama. How many people loved her. I feel badly that dear Uncle Charley, who nursed her so many years, was left nothing in her will. She left me her engagement and wedding rings and said

she hoped you would use them when the time came. She would have been 80 in October. I had a letter from Miss Jessie Parkhurst of Columbia, saying if her book amounted to anything it was because of Mama's inspiration and that she had never met anyone in her life who had meant as much to her.

Negroes and whites, young and old come every day to tell me more of her sweetness and what her life meant to them. I have been going through Jennie's things and she was certainly the most spiritual person I ever knew. She lived her life so close to God and Christ. She had a little book with your name on it filled with quotations, and a list of people she prayed for. I am sending you her picture for your desk.

Miss Lizzie Snow, the old Negro woman who used to come and pray with Granny and who always answered when asked how she was, "Wells I jes lives in the past, and the past aint fattenin," died soon afterwards.

Mother wrote about it: "I drove out to take a great bunch of flowers. She was lying so small & dark on a snow white tufted silk casket with an electric light in a fancy pink & gold shade just over her face. It looked incongruous in that little

Jennie Baldwin Craik

white-washed cabin. The funeral was at Macedonia at two, but I had to do lunch and help Callie make punch for a garden party."

My beautiful young cousin, Jean Pollard, had been ill for some time. She was named for my mother, and was the only daughter of my mother's sister Judy and Uncle Charley. They lived not far away from Hazel Hedge in one of the "four sister houses" on Perry Street, and spent a great deal of time with us. It was the first serious illness in my generation and was deeply felt by me. At Kent, I had prayers said for her recovery.

Judy was quite different from the other three sisters, being equally strong-minded, but going in a different direction. She was conventional and frighteningly ambitious for her only child. At young Jean's bedside, her mother kept her baby book with the words she said at ages one, two, three, and four, and there were numerous photographs with maxims written below them such as: "I want my daughter to be a lady by inheritance, by birth, by nature, by education. Genius is push, push and ambition. Remember! A man never does anything that a woman won't stand for."

Jean Pollard was brought up to be a Southern belle. She was never allowed to think for herself, to make a decision. When she went abroad on a tour with Miss Margaret Booth's young lady students, Judy made a chart of all her clothes and the accessories she was to wear with each outfit. This was tacked in the lid of her trunk. After she made her debut, her mother decided which lads she could see, and monitored her activities.

Jeanie gave her a cocktail party before the Spinsters Ball.

> They came at 9 o'clock & it had turned cold so the house was the most marvelous combination of Xmas Eve and springtime I have ever seen. Just close your eyes & imagine it—fires and *all* the candles—and the drawing room a mass of pink azalea—deep rose pink—long sprays of Banksia rose trailing over the sconces—lilies in the mantel vases—bowls of purple iris—the hall & dining room were in boughs & trees of dogwood & hawthorn.
>
> I had a punch bowl in the drawing room & one in the dining room, coffee & a birthday cake (it was young Jean's birthday). The punch was superb & there were ham sandwiches & cheese sandwiches & stuffed eggs, olives etc. It was too pretty for those little snips.

A new social organization had been formed in Montgomery called "The MOR" (Mystic Order of Rebels). As in New Orleans, each year a queen is selected, usually by people with influence. Judy saw to it that Jean became the first queen. She had a beautiful picture on the society page of the *Montgomery Advertiser,* and for a time was quite popular. But her mother made her admirers so uncomfortable that they soon dwindled in number.

Judy had stage ambitions for Jean, who auditioned for a Montgomery Little Theatre production, but her mother would settle for nothing less than the leading role. Since Jeanie had started the theater and my father helped pay the bills, it was expected when Jean tried out that she would get the part. Instead it went to Louise Mohr.

Judy was furious. "Why didn't Jean Pollard get that part?" she demanded. "Because the director selected someone else," my mother replied. "Yes," screamed Judy, "the wife of that Jew!" This offended mother and caused a permanent estrangement between the sisters.

Jean wrote mother a sad little note, "Let's try to forget all about the unfortunate affair. I did not have myself under control, and gave way to my temper. The disappointment meant more to me than you realized. Much truth always hurts, and that you should have called me 'a temperamental little fool' before everyone did hurt me; but I want to forget it, and that I was in the play at all. I do thank you for all that you have always done for me. Love, Jean."

When Tallulah Bankhead was giving her performance in Montgomery, her aunt, Marie Bankhead Owen, arranged to invite Jean Pollard to attend the play and come backstage and meet the cast. It was a thrill for Jean, but she never tried out for another play. It was a household full of conflict with Jean. She was, in fact, in rebellion against both her mother and father.

In one letter, Granny wrote me: "Poor Uncle Charles leans so on your mother for help and comfort, that I don't know what he would do without her. He telegraphed her yesterday afternoon to ask her to come at once. Jean found him utterly broken down, with Judy gone and young Jean having hysterics. Strong man that he is, he wept. Judy had left home because she couldn't endure it, and he had a baby to deliver in an hour or so."

My mother described the situation:

> He doesn't believe that Jean is just a self-indulgent, selfish little minx, which she is, but has absurd fears about insanity. I took charge and gave her a long needed talk, even adding a little religion, which was nervy of me, but she is a great Lent keeper with three crucifixes in her room. I stayed until 7 p.m. We discussed many things.
>
> Judy had never told her that menstruation had anything to do with maternity. She thought it was a purely arbitrary inconvenience of nature. I pitied the poor little self-consumed empty soul with all my heart. How can she help it? Why, oh God, should Judy have the privilege of bringing a daughter into the world and training her for life in this way?

Dr. Pollard's fears about insanity were realized. Jean had a nervous breakdown and got the notion that it was wicked to look at beautiful things, so wouldn't let any of the flowers sent to her come into her room. When she refused to eat anything except an occasional banana, she was sent to a private sanitarium.

My mother wrote that when she came home for a time, "she cried day and night and kept saying that her parents had ruined her life by sending her to that place and that she could never again hold her head up in Montgomery. She isn't really crazy, at least not so that she should be kept with really crazy people. But she will be unhappy anywhere she is. The poor Pollards are in terrible shape. Judy is almost crazy herself and Charley looks like death. It is so tragic it is ghastly and will soon blow up." Jean was finally sent to Shephard Pratt and then to the state mental institution in Tuscaloosa. She died in her late twenties, and within a few years, Judy and Charley were gone too.

It seemed the end of an era to Jean. When I graduated from Kent, she was restless and suggested the possibility of renting Hazel Hedge for the summer or longer. She was deeply concerned about my future.

Precious Heart you are so much of an individual with such Socialistic ideas for the good of the working classes, and so unconventional in your opinions. Nobody knows how the world is going. It's crazy as hell right now and everyone in Europe is ready to jump at everyone else's throat.

I think you might get into political economy, lecturing and writing and talking over the radio, which will be used more and more in the future. But how should I advise you? I haven't made any great success of my own life, except having got you, but I have learned this—it's best to be after the thing you like best & go for it & do that thing well, no matter what it is.

31

Not Harvard, but a State University

T HE GREAT DEBATE ABOUT WHERE I SHOULD GO TO COLLEGE BEGAN long before I graduated from Kent. Mother wanted Harvard, where I was accepted on early application, and as mother put it, "where you would meet and know men in New York and make the right connections that would lead to something when you leave college."

When I didn't acquiesce immediately, she suggested other alternatives. "Talk to Father Sill about Columbia. Carl Van Doren told me that Columbia was excellent. Couldn't you get off some Saturday and go over to New Haven and give Yale the once over? Don't let Sheila, who is prejudiced, keep you from Princeton. I've written Baldwin Maxwell at Ohio for his opinion. He is a college professor and will know a lot about it . . ."

Mainly, it was not what Jean was for, but what she was against—state universities in general and North Carolina (my choice) in particular.

State universities, as a rule, can't have the same standards of education that Harvard, Yale, Princeton, Williams and Dartmouth have. The standards, after all, are set to meet the qualifications of the mass of boys who go there.

You don't have to go to a second-rate college, and you do have a better chance for a job if you have a good college behind you. I don't think you know anything about North Carolina, certainly not enough to decide to go there. Its dramatic department has a reputation but that's all. If you were a city boy, a small town college might be all right, but being a small town boy, I think Chapel Hill is too southern and too provincial.

Jean stopped telling me where I should go, after her friend, the writer Ernestine Evans, wrote telling her off:

What an idiot you are, and what a snob! Where did you get such a heaven high notion of Princeton and Harvard graduates? And how do you know that North Carolina isn't by way of becoming one of the great universities? And how dull to convey to Nicky that you think he is going to an inferior school.

What's the matter with your point-of-view? Isn't half the trouble in the world this terrible desire of everybody to be top dog, not a common desire to participate in a decent enterprise? By and large, one can hold Harvard and Princeton graduates responsible for the mess. Nicky will share the fate of his generation, with honor and integrity and skill, and far more, will do it well because of a joyful life at Hazel Hedge, than anything that can harm him now.

Jean wrote to me:

I am terribly worried about what I have done. I wish to God I had kept my mouth shut. Please act as if I had never said a word about your college. I am sure Harvard would be too cold for you. Please write me that you will decide entirely according to your own needs and wishes. I don't want you to be distinguished or prominent or even contribute something to our country—just be normal and sane and happy. "Accomplishments are the ornaments of life." They come second.

I answered,

Darling, I shall be very angry if when I decide on going to a college you say that you made me go there & it was a mistake. If I choose Harvard it will be because I want to go there & the same thing applies to N. Carolina. At least I have decided that I don't want to go to Columbia. After enjoying such a floral paradise as H. H., how could I bear to live in "iron-shod" New York. It isn't so damned important where I go, but . . .

I want you to stop worrying about everything. If you think you have made mistakes, and heaven knows everyone has made them, stop thinking of them. They're past, done with. If you must worry about something, worry about your health. You should take better care of it. If you want me to be a success and to get somewhere & have a glorious life, then take time out and relax. If you should die, the life and spirit in me would also die. So, promise me two things: stop worrying, and be careful of your health, if not for your own sake, for mine.

Jean didn't stop worrying about my future, but now directed her advice to my career after college:

> I do think diplomacy, or newspaper correspondence in a Big Way, is the career for you. Grover Hall, the Editor of the *Montgomery Advertiser,* read the article you wrote about Ruby Bates and the Scottsboro case, and said it was the best discussion he had read on the affair and "that there was no use asking what Nick's going to be—he already *is* a newspaperman."
>
> Do send a copy of the Scottsboro piece to the Hon. Josephus Daniels if you haven't already. It should come from you with a note, not from a fond Mother. Keep all the connections you make.

Jean's letter was interrupted by her conversion of a basket of pears that had fallen to the ground that day, to sweet pear pickle, "which needs my attention right now."

In the next letter, she asked why I had given up the idea of architecture. "It's much better than engineering, I believe. And if Communism does come, which isn't going to be the way Darlie believes, all the old tenements and apts. will come down and we'll have to build new ones."

I refused to make any decision about what I was going to be, but firmed up my choice of North Carolina, a deciding factor being the reputation of its president, Dr. Frank Graham. I got some unexpected support from Charles Beard, whom Sheila had consulted. He knew Frank Graham and said that Chapel Hill was okay.

Jean consoled herself, "You'll be nearer home of course at Chapel Hill," but she had not quite given up. "You'd be further away in New England but closer to the Eastern women's colleges, where you could meet a lot of awfully nice girls during your four years of college."

For the summer between Kent and college, it was decided that I would go to Europe. Mother suggested I go with the Kent crew, which was racing at Henley in England. Round trip would be only $107. I countered with "going on a cotton boat from New Orleans would be almost as cheap, and you could go with me and on the boat I could catch up on reading a history of England, and once there, with just the two of us, we would be invited to stay with so many people."

Jean answered, "Life is not long enough to read all we want to, and I won't leave Dad alone for the summer with only Granny. He can't play golf or drink & it would be very boring since Granny talks about 'her loneliness' all the time, and I hardly ever leave her."

In the end I went with two boys from Kent, but Jean joined me in France. There we visited an artist friend, Madeleine Sharrer, who had lived at Hazel Hedge where she enjoyed the dubious honor of painting a successful portrait of my mother. I say "successful" since Jean didn't cut it up, as she did several others, including one by Anne Goldthwaite.

Madeleine's daughter Honore, whom I remembered as a child, was with her in Paris and I wrote my grandmother that "she has grown very pretty, and is a painter too, and although I have not seen any of her work, Jeanie says it is remarkable and that she surpasses Mad and is already launched on a successful artistic career."

I described to grandmother our visit to Chartres. "It was the loveliest cathedral I have ever seen. The inflamed colors of the stained glass melting with a perfect harmony into the shadowed arches of transepts, the lofty spires pointing like a lady's delicate jeweled fingers towards heaven."

It must have been difficult for me to keep my gaze going upwards to the lofty spires for long, since I had received a painful bee sting on the bus and came into the cathedral with a veritable salad affixed to my neck. At the suggestion of the driver, I had applied vinegar on a handkerchief, and at someone else's suggestion, added parsley, which stuck out from around my ears, giving me a druid appearance, and kept me looking straight ahead.

I didn't get back to the United States until the middle of September, just in time to pack and make arrangements to dispose of my fighting cocks and enroll at the University of North Carolina. I stopped in New York to buy some clothes and see Sheila and Jill, mother's old beau Steve, and Maxie with his pointed moustache. It seems Maxie was no longer a Mr. Micawber and hasn't the slightest scheme up his sleeve nor any enterprise just around the corner. "Tell Jean," he said, "that I don't know where I'll be or what I'll be doing next fall—if anything."

I stopped over in Washington, too, to see the Pat Jacksons. I won't attempt to describe my thrilling and lovely visit. I arrived at a time of great excitement when the New Deal was setting up all the alphabet agencies. I got the inside dope on the back stage work connected with Rex Tugwell's writing of the Agricultural Adjustment Administration Act. Pat was a very close friend of this prominent member of Roosevelt's "Brain Trust."

Everywhere I met the most interesting and significant people, and I saw the Nation's Capital. Dode and Pat were the sweetest and most hospitable of people. I thought Washington a stirring, thrilling city. It's alive and moving, though very few seem to know the next step.

I had a successful trip down to Chapel Hill on the day coach. Talked all night to a brilliant research historian taking his Ph.D. at Duke, who spent the last year and a half in Russia on a Guggenheim Fellowship. His stories were gripping, spellbinding episodes of Russian history during Kerensky's regime after the overthrow of Tsar Nicholas. I also met a very jolly crowd of girls and boys going from Greensboro on the train to Durham and then by bus to Chapel Hill.

I wrote home: "And here I am at the loveliest place in the South. I can't expound on that sweeping statement, because I have only just arrived, and as yet haven't seen Chapel Hill except for the Inn and the houses and buildings on the main street. I will be bubbling over with comment and praise (I know it will be praise) when I get home. I have nothing to wear so I'll be at Hazel Hedge, in a couple of days at the most, and that ain't all that's bringing me home. You know who it is, or ought to—Amorum ad infinitum, Nick Read, Your Son."

I was too full of my new life to be sad about the loss of my fighting cocks. However, I didn't forget them entirely. When I got to the university, I used the facilities of the library to do research on fighting cocks and found they had originated in India thousands of years ago and were mentioned in the records of China, Persia, Greece and Rome.

It had been ten years since I acquired my first "Round Head." Now, "Red" Chambers, the moonshiner who had always transported my cocks back and forth from fights to farms, took them away for good. He was just out of jail for beating up a Negro. The verdict was "not guilty." I doubt it.

At Chapel Hill, I joined a fraternity, Delta Psi, also known as St. Anthony's. When someone wrote my mother that the Delta Psi chapter "was one of the swellest at Yale," my father predicted, "She will begin to see some good in Chapel Hill and will change her mind about your going there." He was right, she did. However, she took no chances on the quality of the education, and sent me books and subscriptions to such magazines as the *Atlantic* and *Harpers,* to feed my mind.

Father sent golf sticks and a little extra money to buy a tuxedo and to go to the

University of Virginia football game. Jean said that she had never attended a football game and didn't intend to. Father instructed me to keep track of my finances "on a sheet marked Disbursements and Receipts, to be filled in and returned."

Sheila wrote that Michael Straight, the son of Frieda Kirchwey, the editor of *Nation* magazine, had enrolled at North Carolina and would be someone I should know. Mother reminded me that my cousins, the Shephard Strudwicks, who lived in nearby Hillsboro, were a talented family of artists, writers, and actors, and I would enjoy seeing them.

She also told me that Polly Read (a cousin several times removed) was at Black Mountain College (shades of Louis Adamic!) and since it was near Chapel Hill, could drive down with me for Thanksgiving. She did, and after that Polly and I became very close friends.

Father was glad I had decided to move from the dorm into the fraternity house "where the food would be better and more nutritious," and Granny was delighted that I was going to have "that charming young man I met, Phil Hammer, as a roommate." I liked it because I was able to have my dog Bupser, a dachshund whose registered name was Volderman Von Schintz, in the fraternity house with me.

Phil and I were the only "liberals" in the fraternity. I remember one night in particular after an anti-war meeting. We were studying when Parker came in quite drunk, wearing only his pajama top. Parker started ranting on American Student Union radicals in general, "Joe Sugarman, Communism, shits, kikes, bastards, you are lowering yourselves to associate with them." I asked him if he ever took part in any activity to bring credit to the hall. He cried hysterically. I realized I touched a sore spot.

Phil preceded me in almost every activity I undertook, except for my first, which was to run for president of the freshman class, which I lost. He had been secretary of the YMCA, as I was later, was prominent in campus politics, became an anti-war activist, and was also an editor and writer for the *Daily Tar Heel*.

When I became a reporter for the *Tar Heel*, I subscribed for my grandmother. She wrote that she read every word of it, but that "it doesn't quite take the place of letters." When I began doing long pieces for *The Carolina Magazine*, I sent them home. Jeanie would comment favorably, but often made suggestions:

"It was very interesting & well done, but you had 2 glaring grammatical errors: The first was in the 12th line 'He was helpless & afraid like he had been near the end of the exam.' This should have been 'as he had been.' The second was 5th line from the bottom 'He felt like he was sinking right through the pavement.' It should be 'as if he was sinking.'" Not to be outdone I fired back, "'as if he were sinking.'" Dad said that Jean had corrected him so often for using "like" in place of "as if," that he found himself saying "I feel as if Hell."

At the magazine I was in good company. One of the other contributors was a quiet fellow named Walker Percy, who later became a novelist. Another, known as 'Bunny' Royster, became V. C. Royster of the *Wall Street Journal*. E. C. Daniel, later known as Clifton Daniel of the *New York Times*, who married President Truman's daughter, Margaret. The crew also included Don Shoemaker, who became editor of the *Miami Journal*—and Shelby Foote, an eminent historian.

But the best writers were two geniuses whose post-college careers were unhappy failures—Joe Sugarman, an aggressive little Jew from Newark, and Nelson Lansdale, a self-conscious elitist from Pennsylvania. Both went to New York, where they died young—Lansdale from alcohol and Sugarman from heartbreak.

One of my friends at the fraternity was Eulas Mason, the black caretaker (or janitor). He was known as "Sap," a nickname I didn't like to use, but there seemed to be no way out of it. He was a hunter and suggested I "send for my 'Little 20,' since there are more doves in the county this year than ever before and in November, we could get them in the pea field." We went hunting regularly during my four years at college.

Eulas took a leading role in trying to make it possible for Bupser to have progeny. Bupser, a dachshund, was built too close to the ground to perform successfully with any of the female dogs who were ready and available. With the enthusiastic help of several of my fraternity brothers, alternate approaches—a hole in the ground for the female, or a wooden superstructure from which Bupser could hit the target—were devised. Bupser would have none of it.

I was very close to Eulas, who would come to my room and we would talk about what I was learning in class. I kept in touch with him after college. It must have been twenty years later when he telephoned me from North Carolina one night at our home in Chevy Chase, Maryland. He said he had gotten into a little trouble and needed to get away for awhile.

My wife, who had met him on one of our trips south, heard me say, "Well, why don't you just come up here and stay with us until it blows over?" When I hung up Dallas asked, "When is he coming, and how long will he be here?" Eulas was here all summer. This turned out to be most fortunate. Dallas and I had planned to go to Scotland where one of my films was being shown at the Edinburgh Film Festival. We almost canceled the trip when my wife's eighty-year old mother, Lyda, who was getting pretty vague, unexpectedly arrived from California. But when Eulas came he took over "Mother's" care.

From the moment she came, this Native Daughter of the Golden West wanted to go home. Every day or so she would pack her bag and get ready to leave. Eulas just said in his polite sweet way, "Now, it's too hot to go right now, Miz Lyda. You just sit down and tell me some of those stories about crossing the plains in a covered wagon and fighting the Indians." He would get her a long cold drink of tonic water (possibly with a little gin in it) and listen to her stories. Then he would unpack her bag and get ready for a repeat performance the next day. And so it went through the long hot summer. By the time we got back from Scotland, Eulas had not only kept Mother relaxed about going back to California, but had even painted all the bedrooms in the house. Whatever was bothering Eulas in North Carolina had "blown over," and he went south and Lyda went west.

At North Carolina I had become associate editor of *The Carolina Magazine*. A good friend of mine, Billy Hudson, was editor, and on the staff was a girl reporter. I wrote home about her:

> Jeanie Darling, No longer can I wait to write. Lessons, the world, everything can go to hell . . . I AM IN LOVE. Madly, head over heels in love with the most magnificent obsession. She is the only girl in the world who has ever suited me in every way. In short, she is wunnerful and her name is Ellen Deppe.
>
> Yep, it's Ellen and she's in love with Don who isn't in love with her. That's how I got that way—just helping her get over Don, and dammit if she falls in love with me it will be rebound and I'll have none of that. She thinks I'm one of the swellest persons she's ever known (she doesn't say that but that's what she thinks). Jeanie, you will adore Ellen.

Whether or not Jean ever adored Ellen is doubtful. We do know that my romance with her faltered after Jean eliminated her from a proposed trip to meet my relatives in Savannah. "I do think you could have a much better time in Savannah alone. There are lots of girls there and you and Polly could have a good time together and everyone wants to see you. Do you realize that if Deppe is with us we won't be able to stop with relatives there or in Augusta? I know Deppe is a lovely girl, but . . ."

I do know that eventually I got a new girl named Ruthie Crowell. I don't know whether it was Ellen or Ruthie about whom my mother wrote in a letter to a friend in Savannah, but it couldn't have been flattering.

I read the answer: "My heart aches for you. What would I do if my son fell in love with such a person. Your description is so vivid that I am sure I would know her anywhere. And there are oodles like her." On the other hand, when Sheila met Ruthie Crowell, she wrote mother the sweetest things about her. She and Jill both liked her tremendously.

In Montgomery, Mother and Dad were fully occupied with other problems. There were terrible floods. Father wrote, "The waters of all the rivers have risen and risen, and things look very serious. We filled the bathtubs and demijohns with drinking water as it was believed that the river would overflow into the reservoir. We stayed inside playing gin and listening to Charlie McCarthy on the radio. The flood waters didn't reach Hazel Hedge and the cottages didn't leak."

Rain or shine, Jeanie had her own agenda, the Little Theater and a renewed and active interest in poetry. She spent considerable time with a couple of young local poets, Myra Hall in Montgomery and Diedre Shannon from Florida, encouraging them and helping them publish their work.

Two guests routed to her from Sheila in New York were Mr. and Mrs. Joseph Auslander, who came to Montgomery to meet Mrs. John S. Tilley, the niece of Sidney Lanier. Writing under the pen-name of Audrey Wurdeman, Mrs. Auslander had just won a Pulitzer prize for *Bright Ambush*, a book of her poems. After supper, they picked pink camellias in the garden, and when Jeanie found two pomegranates still on the tree and peeled them and passed around pieces, they formed a "Pomegranate Society."

My friends Pat and Dode Jackson stopped for lunch, on their way to a conference on sharecroppers in New Orleans. Jean wrote me,

"I had oyster gumbo and quail and salad, with figs and shelled pecans for dessert. Pat talked about his defense of Sacco and Vanzetti in Boston. Both seemed so alive and thinking without being Communist."

The next weekend Dad and Jean took a little trip to Pensacola. Jean said that she had to sing the whole 197 miles to keep him awake. They brought back several beautiful king mackerel. Jean boiled two in spicy garlic-onion-bayleaf water, and took some to each cottage. "On Monday we had a picnic on that mountain in the state park, Cheaha, the highest point in Alabama. It was really beautiful up there, but too cold to swim in the lake. No trees out, but violets everywhere and azalea in the canyons."

When I broke off with Ruthie much later I wrote, "I feel awfully sorry for Ruth. It pains me to see her looking so badly—so tired and so sad. The trouble is she must love something very intensely. She will never make a conscious compromise. When she had me, the Cause didn't bother her too much. She has the makings of another Jane Speed. She is also a most lovable and intelligent person, and with gentle handling would make a fine wife. I wish I hadn't broken with her. I could have helped her a lot. I was scared she would become too dependent upon me."

With no one to love, that year I began to take my studies seriously, possibly inspired by the accomplishments of my father's cousins, Marion and Peyton Rous, about whom my mother wrote a great deal.

In 1937, Marion, a concert pianist who by then had become Director of Greenwich House Music School in New York City, received accolades for setting standards by which college entrance credits could be given for a knowledge of music, history and literature. Mother reminded me that I could get more studying done if I followed Marion's example when she was studying piano in Italy, and just had a raw egg beaten up in orange juice for breakfast.

Her brother, Dr. Peyton Rous, a research scientist at the Rockefeller Institute, discovered that a virus could cause cancer—and had one named for him—the Rous sarcoma. He was made an honorary doctor of science at Cambridge University in England, and later awarded the Nobel Prize.

I decided to make a contribution to mankind:

> I have resolved to fit myself for a career that requires more training and a broader grasp of knowledge than perhaps any other kind of work. My task is a difficult one, I know, and a pleasurable one, I hope. I swear by my sacred emblem, the "Game Cock," that I shall tackle it with "Grit and Steel."
>
> I am resolved to become the statesman of the South, serving my state and nation in the interest of my fellow men. Public office shall not be the end in itself; my goal will be intelligent service and leadership . . . I will turn away from my "playboy-intellectual" philosophy of life to intensive work in government, economics, sociology and philosophy—as well as pursuing my present major in American History.

I also said I would "give up high pleasure frolicking, and have dances and dates in a limited number."

My mother wrote congratulating me on my resolution:

> The only other document that has ever moved me as much was Edward the VIII's abdication speech. His was simple and pathetic and he was a damned fool, but yours was splendid and courageous and young and very fine. The only thing about a career of that sort is other people who aren't fine. Some are low and corrupt. You simply must read Lincoln Steffens. He was a muck-raker, and can tell you all about it . . .
>
> I'm giving a buffet supper New Year's Eve for you. Who will you take, Jill? You'll have to take Marion Oates to one party. Darling, please don't go too serious on me—and let the world rock along. It will never be reformed and it only crucifies reformers—so please enjoy life as much as you can. Your college activities are just as good for you and in many ways better, than just the intellectual things. I love you so much and am so proud of you.

Mother didn't have to worry about my enjoying life, and I'm afraid I didn't give up frolicking. Not long afterwards I wrote:

> Last week were the German dances. I had resolved to study and save the $7, which the bids cost. But on Saturday taking Dave Murchison to Durham to get some liquor, an idea occurred to us almost simultaneously. Dave wanted to go to a Zeta Psi party given for the S.A.E's, and we thought up a ruse. If I went as a girl, I might get him in.
>
> An hour or so later I emerged as Daisy Mae Twitchet, dressed in a blue wool dress, over which was a coat, because the dress wouldn't button when my false buzoom was installed, and wearing a fetching hat and veil put on at a rakish angle over false curls and earrings. Dave chickened out and the "date" I was meeting at the party was a substitute—Bill Daniels. Two other students, dressed appropriately as my parents, brought me to the party. My "father" carried a shotgun, which he menacingly pointed at Bill Daniels from whose coat pocket draped a silk slip.
>
> No one at first noticed our entrance, but when I raised my skirt to hitch up stockings attached to men's garters, I was discovered amid great mirth. I received the attention of numerous admiring males, and was invited to go to the tea dance.

After the bets that I couldn't get by the door, nothing could have kept me away. Soon I was getting a terrific rush on the dance floor, whirling round and round so that the blue and white decorations looked like a barber pole.

Then the dance committee banished me to the balcony where I was determined to stay, but nature called and I had to go to the little boys room (or little girls), and to avoid getting too involved, Bill and I went across the yard to Saunders Hall, but I couldn't get back in since girls are not allowed to leave the dances and then come back. When I dropped sober and exhausted into bed at 2:00 that morning, I considered that I'd had more than my share of fun for the price of getting put on dance probation.

32

Setting High Marks

THERE WAS ENOUGH RESOLVE IN MY GRANDIOSE PROCLAMATION TO become "the statesman of the South" to enroll in a course taught by Billy Hudson's father, the eminent professor Arthur Palmer Hudson. I did papers on such subjects as "Landlord-Tenant Relations" and "Relief in Alabama."

I bought my first movie camera, and began to put on film what I saw. It was the beginning of my interest in cinematography which eventually led to my career as a documentary filmmaker.

My "outside activities" at college began to get serious. I participated in the peace movement, and helped lead a mass meeting where a delegate was selected to go to a conference in Washington, possibly to meet with President Roosevelt. I was not the delegate, but on campus I became chairman of an anti-war committee, and organized a strike against war.

I told Dr. Frank Graham about my plan. "He said: "Fine, boy, fine, I'll ring the bell, let everyone out of class." I begged him not to, "It wouldn't be a proper strike if you did that." "Yes, it would be a better strike," he said. So he rang the bell and I made a speech from the steps of the South Building. We had loud-speakers. Girls stood on the top step with me and carried signs: "Get a Lift with a Bomb" and "We're Putting All Our Boys in One Casket." We abandoned the idea of a parade when it rained and about a thousand students moved into Memorial Hall to hear the speeches with a debate and open forum for discussion that lasted until 10:20.

I was a strong pacifist for several years, writing home that I "thoroughly approved of Chamberlain and even of fascist absorption of Austria, not because I liked the fascists but because any other policy would have led to immediate conflict." Germany may be a threat to Britain's possessions and prestige, I reasoned, "but better lose both of these than another two million young men." In a few short years I would be in boot camp as one of the early draftees into the Army from Alabama.

At UNC I was elected President of the University Club, where my first task was to welcome the Navy football team coming to play us at Kenan Stadium. What I remember most was what Kate Smith said after she sang "God Bless America," and before the game began: "May the better team win." Her grammar impressed me.

I made a trip to Washington to see Phil and Jane Hammer and Dode and Pat Jackson. In a letter to my mother I wrote,

> I went on the spur of the moment, but found a room that cost only $1 a night and had a good dinner for 45 cents—roast beef, mashed potatoes, peas and custard (with a little too much vanilla) plus a nickel for a package of fudge."
>
> The senators and the president weren't getting on very well; no one knew what committee had the farm bill or in what form it would come out (some of them hoped it never would). No one knew the score in foreign policy, and some heretics were already calling the "recession" a "depression."
>
> I went to the Senate gallery—too late to hear Borah's second tirade against lynching, but in time to hear old Carter Glass accuse Bob Wagner of filibustering. It was fun watching the senators wander around and every now and then get the floor for their two cents worth. I was reminded of watching monkeys in the zoo. Of course some of them work tremendously hard.
>
> I dropped by La Follette's office but didn't see him. He evidently goes like a dynamo day and night. In contrast, I had no trouble seeing 'Our own Bob Reynolds,' who is known as the only Senator in Washington who never shuts his door. He spends most of his time greeting visitors.
>
> At the Supreme Court, a temple of marble that dwarfs the common man, the only humanizing touch was the queer assortment of chairs that the justices had brought over from wherever they were before, contrasting strangely with the magnificent dais behind which they sit.
>
> It was late afternoon by the time I got to Pat and Dode's in Chevy Chase. I was greeted by four dogs and a crackling fire and Dode asked me to dinner and told me to invite Phil and Jane. The supper was grand—beefsteaks, preceded by cucumbers in sour cream, and a fish-spread on toast. After dinner the conversation went from Dr. Graham to the CIO and the United Mine Workers, where Pat works for John Lewis. He met Lewis through his work on the share-cropper problem.

Pat was fascinating and amusing. He is deadly earnest in his radicalism. I am convinced that he is no mere parlor pink. But his politics are delightfully tempered with good humor, which is so often just good sense. He has discovered that he is on all the fascist organizations' blacklists as "Barbed Wire #367264." He has written La Follette asking him to find out, if he can, whether barbed wire means a concentration camp.

Back at Chapel Hill I got to know Gould and Mary Beech. He was in graduate school, and I met a lot of interesting people at their house. One was Thomas Campbell from Tuskegee, who was employed by the federal government as Director of Agricultural Extension and Home Demonstration for Negroes in the Southeast.

He has done wonderful work in Alabama with a movable school for black farmers.

I wrote in a letter home,

He is a big man, with large, strong rough hands and long fingers that are used to work. He has a straight-forwardness and a naturalness which, coupled with his perfect manners, puts you at ease. I lay on the studio couch listening to the conversation with half-closed eyes.

"We must stop pitting the tenant against the landlord and stirring up one against another . . . the trouble is in the system, in the wasteful way of life they must both try to overcome together." Could this be a Negro talking? I looked at the huge colored man across the room by the tea table to reassure myself that he was black.

Could he be of the same stock as the ragged little Negroes that hold your mule when you are hunting in Pike County? Yes, not only the same stock but he was reared in just such an environment. Until he ran away from home, where he had been hired out by his father to white people for a few dollars a month, and reached Tuskegee, he had only a few months of schooling in his life.

After thirty years of work among poor Negro farmers he has retained his sympathy and his sense of humor and his belief that progress has been made and will continue to be made . . . SLOWLY. He was not bitter, he was not a visionary. He was a realist.

On the campus, I was initiated into Amphoterothon, a campus organization presumably composed of about thirty of the best-informed men on campus, interested in national and international political and economic questions. I became active in the North Carolina Political Union, which invited political leaders to the campus to speak. I got into trouble almost immediately with my mother, when I proposed that we invite Huey Long of Louisiana as a speaker.

Jean wrote: "I most earnestly hope you will not make the colossal blunder of inviting such a person to address the Union. I am inexpressibly shocked that you should think of doing such a thing. To be an exponent of liberalism is all right, but to give countenance to a Political Mountebank—a man devoid of honor—is another thing. I simply can't get over it. He is such a horrible person—a liar, a demagogue, unscrupulous in every way."

Things got worse later on, when we decided to invite Trotsky to come up from Mexico to speak on campus. Our Chairman, Alex Heard, was turned down when he asked the State Department to grant Trotsky a visa. Jean wrote: "I'm glad Secretary of State Cordell Hull turned you down. You'll be asking Jane Speed to speak next."

This was of course said in jest. She knew from an earlier letter how I felt about Jane and Communism now.

> Jane would be both pathetic and amusing were it not that she is in our family, and that being the case, it is disgusting. Aren't the Communists childish? It makes me boil to think a cousin of mine possesses a mind that is so easily saturated with silly ideas. Her ideals may be big, but her I.Q. is rock bottom.
>
> Remember Pet, that whether I fulfill your high hopes of becoming a power & an influence, I shall always strive to be intelligent, liberal and fair. I know already that there is no one absolute solution to the world's problems. One solution may create a hundred new problems. On the other hand there are facts, and it is up to my generation to draw logical answers from these facts and apply our knowledge to solving the problems, which are fast piling up.

My mother got so angry at Jane and Darlie that for a while she was critical of any and all liberal or left wing influences on me. She wrote, "Darlie will use any means to see you become a Communist. God knows I believe that lots of Communist ideals are right, but they sacrifice too much for it. Now don't you listen to Gould Beech. He is a great dear and Mary is even greater, but he's awfully Radical. You didn't miss anything by not hearing Hugo Black's speech. He didn't say anything. I think he is smart enough to become a fine judge, but I believe he is an opportunist with enormous personal ambition."

My father wrote about election day. "Well, the great day has come and gone, and so did Thomas, Browder and Lemke. They all went down in no uncertain manner. It seems funny that we should have been agitated about the Communists here in Alabama; one vote in Montgomery County and a total of 39 in the state was all they got."

He congratulated me for the part I had played as an editor of *The Carolina Magazine*, exposing a cheating ring at the University. "Glad you had the moral courage to assume the duty as one of the investigating committee on the shady situation," and consoled me afterwards when I wasn't elected to the Honor Court.

"You will find many such experiences of ingratitude as you go through life, as in my own experience with the country club. When the old club house burned and plans for a new one were about to fall through, I formed a syndicate—put up my personal check for $17,500 and bought 30 acres to round out the property and locate the new building on its present site. Three years later, I was kicked off the Board of Directors and some little whipper snapper who hadn't contributed a dime was elected in my place."

My twenty-first birthday was celebrated in 1937 with a big costume party at Hazel Hedge. Poems were read and glasses raised and Mildred Reynolds Saffold wrote and dedicated a song "on Nick's coming of age." Everyone sang it to the tune of the Bonnie Blue Flag. It had six verses, starting off:

> Just one and twenty years ago
> Before the break of dawn
> A doctor and a nurse proclaimed,
> "A son to Jean is born."
> "Hurrah!" said Nash, "for the finest son on earth."
> While Jean said feebly from her couch,
> "Nash, you're not the only one."

Nancy Smith wrote a shorter rhyme:

> You are young, Nickie Read, the old duchess said
> You have scarcely as yet come of age
> And yet you incessantly say the right thing,

What makes you so awfully sage?
In my youth, Nickie said, as he shook his dark locks,
I chanced on a wondrous advantage,
I picked the right parents to born myself to
And the rest has been easy to manage.

Life went on pretty much as usual at Hazel Hedge. Nash played a lot of golf and went hunting. He was a regular supplier of birds to Delta Psi. Just after explaining that he wouldn't be going out for a time because of rheumatism in his knee, he added, "But I'm sending you half a dozen doves in today's mail." He ended that letter, "I miss you more than I can tell you and you are always in my heart."

He was deeply saddened when his favorite bird dog, Taffy, died. Polly wrote me about it:

> Your father must be completely lost without Taffy. They understood each other far more than two humans do. I can't imagine Hazel Hedge without both of them together. They looked on the world with the same gentle eyes.

A costume party for Nick's twenty-first birthday.

Oh Nick, your Father is the sweetest, biggest-hearted person I ever met. He's kind and good—and that counts for everything. Your most beautiful expressions are your Father's.

Jean had dozens of things to keep her busy. She filled the house with guests and good food, and helped with other people's parties. She did the decorations for May Baldwin's coming out party, and helped with Carolyn Clark's. She had stationery headed "Jean Craik Read, Decorator." She even participated in a garden club competition, admitting that "it won't be much of a competition since I am sure to be named a judge, and in all fairness my entry will get the prize."

Sometimes she arranged picnics on the bluff with gumbo and grilled chickens, and entertainment. "Sweet Peter and about 10 young Negroes came to sing some of the most interesting spirituals I have ever heard—with mouth organ accompaniment. You would have gone wild about the harmony and syncopation. They danced so well, too."

There was an excursion to New Orleans where Jean, inspired by Ramos gin fizzes, made up a verse that was sung to the tune of "Stand up, stand up for Jesus":

Hail to thee New Orleans,—to thee I kiss my hand.
Thou art the fairest city in all the fair Southland.
Tis here the festive oyster, Rockfeller, reigns supreme.
The only city on God's earth where gin is served in cream.

Another holiday took them to Natchez in Mississippi. Father drove, and his passengers besides Mother were Mary Webber who lived with us, Georgia Saffold Oates, and a lady from Birmingham, Rosa Earle. Everything was full at the hotels, but Mr. Bowman at the bank who used to live there found rooms in one of the beautiful old houses. They visited more than a dozen of the mansions, and went to the ball and saw the tableaux, and before they headed for home, Jean slid down a bannister and Nash broke a rib from a fall in the bathtub.

At UNC I was depressed. I wrote father,

Dearest Dada: Your devoted son hasn't done much to prove his devotion since he has gone back to school. Well, as the saying goes "Life's just one damn thing after another and love is just two damn things after each other." A melancholy visits me more often as the time remaining before graduation shortens. I hate the thought of leaving this soft life. Taking stock of myself, I have to make some painful admissions. I am not even decently educated. I know so little history, and must cram to pass the comprehensive.

This is, of course, my own fault. The information is here, quite accessible in professional heads and on library shelves but I have never bothered to get it. I might have been forced to absorb a little more at a northern school where grading standards are higher. I have a terrible laziness, but I have not acquired a distaste for learning. On the other hand, Chapel Hill must be credited for giving me a sincere desire to get an education, and more than a suspicion that I haven't got one.

My spirits lifted when I was selected for the Order of the Golden Fleece. I sent a wire to my parents, "Last night I was tapped by the Order of the Golden Fleece, thereby receiving an invitation made to those showing the most leadership and character."

I am not sure that I showed much of either in the festivities preceding graduation. I wrote home:

The past weekend was a stupendous one. I don't know when I have had so much fun. It began Friday with a trip to Durham to pick up Fred Bunting's sister who came from Sweet Briar, and the necessary fuel at the A.B.C. liquor store. We skipped the tea dance to get up steam for the dance that night. I took Coo Westfeldt and Geoff took Barbara McIlhenny, who had both come from New Orleans. After that we went out on the Durham road to a little shack where an old man cooks wonderful fried chicken.

Next morning we were happy to meet "The Hon. Thomas Collins" at the Phi Delta breakfast dance, and in the afternoon got together with Fred and Ethel Jane Bunting and searched for the May Day in the Arboretum, but it was rained out. Instead, we had drinks at the house, and just to sober up for supper, I climbed the 200 foot water tower. Coo, who remained at the foot of the tower, was in a much more uncomfortable situation, when the matron of a little house nearby came out and asked what she was doing. "Just waiting for a friend," Coo said.

At that moment I was high up in the stratosphere, glorying in the raging wind and lightening flashes, thrilling at the sight of the orange moon, eerie phantom of a lower region rising slowly in a cloud rift on the eastern horizon. With pounding heart I looked down on the twinkling lights of the town, but I didn't fall down, which would rather have spoiled things.

It sobered me when our cousin, Marion Rous, who couldn't make my graduation, sent me as a present, the manuscript of my great grandfather F. P. Wood's address, when he graduated from Hampden Sidney nearly a hundred years ago. Young men then were beginning to think about the prospect of Secession. When I graduated with my class of 1938, I was only thinking about making an interesting living, and still didn't know what I was going to do next.

In my senior year I had applied for, but unfortunately didn't get, a Rhodes Fellowship for graduate work at Oxford. I wrote Mother, "I'm not sure about my plans. If I go to Harvard Law or Virginia Law in the fall, I should like to spend the summer at home, or with you somewhere. If not, I would love to land a job on *Time*. What do you think? If we stayed home I would do some work on biographies —Ala. characters, beginning with Alexander McGilervaray."

I went back to Hazel Hedge to rest up and think about my future. Everyone had opinions. Mother favored graduate work at Harvard University law school and suggested she could go up and take an apartment with me. She didn't explain what would happen to Dad. Ernestine Evans thought I should go into politics. Sheila wrote that "Nicky shouldn't have to study law against his will," but later altered this opinion when she read Ernestine Evans' letter: "I don't see what could stop him from being president. I hope he studies law as a first step."

Everybody worried about the possibility that I might just take a job in Montgomery and enjoy the comforts of home and mother. They had reason to. Mother often alluded to not having seen anything of me for the twelve years I had been away at Kent and in college. She and dad were, of course, looking for something that would bring me back to Montgomery, including work on the *Montgomery Advertiser*, and even explored buying another paper, *The Southern Farmer*, which was printed in Montgomery but distributed in other southern and southwestern states. They talked to Gould Beech about working with me.

Sheila counseled against my staying in Montgomery. "Nick sounds so miserable and unhappy about you and Nash being alone, in fact he used the very words you did to me about not having seen much of you all those years he was away at school. Poor, dear boy, of course that isn't true, but the fact that he suffers for the pain you feel is true enough. But I don't think both he and you realize that you would be even more unhappy if he just came home and settled down to some small job which didn't develop all that is in him."

A letter from Polly to me put it on the line:

> Don't lie around Hazel Hedge all summer and let your mother wait on you. Not that you haven't been working like hell all winter, but it still isn't good for you. One smug dull person in the family is enough. It's my part to be in a state of coma—you lay off. Do something, or you'll be the most uninteresting, self-centered fool in the world.
>
> I say get out of Montgomery and prove somewhere else that you're the white hope of the world, God's gift to women and the most wonderful person born to mortal parents. You might get someone who can write, help you get the high school style out of your own. You could be good, if you weren't so sure of it now.

I left Montgomery for New York City to find a job.

33

Job Hunting in the Depression

ON MY WAY NORTH TO LOOK FOR A JOB, AFTER I GRADUATED FROM college in 1938, I stopped briefly in Washington, D.C., where Sheila's friend, Jake Baker, tried to be helpful. He got boys in his office to look up the various men on papers I might see, and gave me some tips on approaching each one. One I called was Mr. Morley, an editor at the *Post*, who was tied up but referred me to an assistant editor. Mr. Norver was a nice young Jew, who said, "No job, not even a prospect—go back and work on a small paper."

In Baltimore I saw Frederick Nelson, one of the higher-ups at the *Baltimore Sun*, to whom Jeanie had written. He asked me where I was staying and when I said I had telephoned the YMCA but would have to call back later since they had no vacant rooms, he invited me to stay at his house. Their yard was full of Kefir pears, and they didn't know what to do with them. I remembered that Jeanie had made chutney of hers, and wrote for the recipe. It was a small price to pay for such elegant lodgings.

The next day I got the royal treatment. I was introduced to Hamilton Owens, editor of the *Sun*, who called in Gerald Johnson, a fellow graduate of mine from North Carolina, and we went out for lunch. Afterwards I was introduced to the managing editor and the city editor, Bill Knighton. He took my name and address, and shook me warmly by the hand, then he told me goodbye.

Jean was concerned about my going to New York City to look for a job. She warned me about seeing Joe Sugarman: "Don't let New York City get you all worked up about Communism again. If you are going into politics eventually, that won't help."

When I got to New York I went to the *Herald Tribune* with an introduction to Lewis Gannett. There, the assistant city editor saw me briefly but didn't even ask for my address. I wrote home: "The possibility of landing a newspaper job here is pretty slim. There used to be 14 papers in New York; now there are seven and lots of experienced men thrown out of work by mergers and failures are still around."

The letter Mary Webber gave me for the managing editor of *Time,* Mr. Gottfried, paved the way to my taking "the *Time* test," a collection of news stories and supplementary material to be boiled down into five hundred words of interesting reading matter suitable for *Time.* I put in a good deal of work on those three-and-a-half typewritten sheets and checked them out with Sheila before turning them in to a Mr. Prouty at *Time.* I waited in a high state of excitement while he read them. I got an "A."

Mr. Prouty said that my piece did not sparkle, but was well told. "You have cut out the hay and kept the essentials. It shows you can write. *Time* is always glad to get real talent. You have a chance to get a job."

We talked of the South and briefly of the affairs of the nation. He asked me what I really wanted to do and I said, "Write about things that make a difference." He advised me to see more of the country, and suggested the Midwest. "Go to Oskaloosa, Iowa"—a town *Fortune* had made an economic study of in its April issue. "I can give you some letters that will get you in there. I don't think it makes much difference what you do in the next three or four years just as long as you are learning and observing and writing. Keep your tools sharp."

The *Time* test, it seemed, did not get me a job. It simply put me in line for one if things opened up, with other young men who made "A." We did not have to compete with women, since *Time* did not hire women for writing jobs. "You will be notified when we want to interview you," he explained. "It may be a month, it may be five years." I felt better when his secretary whispered that very few people made "A"s.

But five years seemed a little long to wait. I went on job-hunting. Everyone tried to help. At the *Daily Mirror* I saw Jeanie's old beau, Steve Partridge, but to no avail. When I made a date for supper with Peyton's musical sister, Marion "Tiger" Rous, she said, "I'll take you to a restaurant where journalists hang out. We'll stalk the prey at the watering hole. The proprietor is a friend of mine. He will deliver the unsuspecting into our hands." There were no deliveries.

I wrote home: "New York is filled with southerners and Jews. The Jews have the jobs, leaving the southerners time to cuss and play. I spent a weekend at my old school in Connecticut. I came back sore from touch football, but it was grand to go back to that beautiful country where I have many happy memories. However, I like Kent better as an alumnus than I did when I was there. I really believe I am beginning to like New York, even the noise and smell of it. I hope I shall be here this winter."

I moved into St. Anthony Hall, the headquarters of my old fraternity Delta Psi, on Riverside Drive. There I shared a room with Bill Fackner, whom I had known at UNC. It only cost fifteen dollars a month, and I could have had all my meals for twenty-four dollars more. But I knew I would be eating out a lot, at Sheila's and with relatives and friends from Chapel Hill and Montgomery.

Tonight I am dining and theatering with Peyton and Marion deKay Rous. The intellectual companionship between Peyton and his wife is almost as important as the children in that marriage. Little Phoebe at 15 has a husky voice and won't look at men under 20. She's a knock-out. She pretends she is 17 and gets away with it. Marion Jr., at Swarthmore, has received the only graduate appointment at Cambridge ever given to a woman, and will be going to England to write children's books. Their younger sister, Ellen, is very shy.

The other day Mary Losey called up and said her brother, Joe, was doing some film work and might have a job for me. He is doing an industrial film on the petroleum industry for the World's Fair and wants someone to take charge of his production schedule. The job sounded so big that I told him I didn't feel qualified to handle it. He asked me if I was interested in making money and I said, "No, not particularly." He said that was too bad because he wanted someone who was. I told Mary that if the desire to make money was a prerequisite for the job, I could easily remedy that flaw.

In my next letter home I had big news! "I've got a job. It's only a temporary one for the *Daily News,* going around Brooklyn and Queens ringing door bells, doing a straw poll on the governor's race between Lehman and Dewey. Six of us will work together. We will have a car and drive out every morning at 9 and work 'til we finish the district assigned to us for that day. We work seven days a week for 17 days, getting $5 a day, with extra for overtime."

At night I was also ringing doorbells and seeing old friends and new ones, and going to plays.

> Last night I went to Sheila's for supper. Suzanne La Follette, looking very lovely and no older than when we saw her five years ago, was there and we went to her house afterwards. Freda Rivera (widow of Mexican painter Diego Rivera) came wearing a Mexican costume, and sang Mexican songs.
>
> The next evening I had dinner at Dorothy Doubleday's. After dinner I brought on myself a discussion of birth control. Dorothy talked for two hours. Much of it was interesting, but two hours was too long. She is knitting some socks for me.
>
> The play I liked best was *Abe Lincoln in Illinois*. It made me realize how little I know about Lincoln. I took Jill to see *Outward Bound* and afterwards we went to "Tiger" Rous's for her *Twelfth Night Revels*. She had quite a galaxy of musicians and music lovers. People came in costume. Aunt Frances Rous was marvelous-looking as Catherine de Medici. We got there in time to put out the food and stayed late enough to carry out the dirty dishes. "Tiger" enjoyed herself tremendously at her party, her only regret being that she hadn't had time to comb her hair.

Plenty of my own contemporaries were in New York. I double-dated with my oldest friend from Montgomery, "Bo" Hubbard, who was at Princeton. Alex Heard from UNC dropped by, and I bumped into Rod Nachman in the Public Library. I gave a party for everyone—about forty-five in all—at St. Anthony Hall. Mac Smith and his girl, and Randy Berg and Carey Vaughn were there. I had Coca Cola and one bottle of bourbon, but had to send out for Scotch, the favored drink. My prize hors d'oeuvre was shrimp on toothpicks stuck like porcupine quills into a cabbage, the top of which was hollowed out for mayonnaise.

A friend from school, Howard Davison, introduced me to skiing and the Oxford movement on a trip through a blinding snow storm in his fine Cadillac convertible sedan to the Red Pheasant Inn in Millbrook, New York. It was a pleasant enough trip but I didn't learn to ski very well, nor did I join the Oxford movement.

One night "Tunie" (Petunia) came in from Sarah Lawrence to have supper with me. We had a hard time meeting in Grand Central Station, being almost swallowed up by a huge political rally for Lehman. I took her to Yar, a nice Russian place where we had a good dinner with wine afterwards. Tunie was terribly embarrassed when she discovered the 11:55 train back to Bronxville didn't run on Sunday and we had to wait for the one o'clock. I wouldn't have minded anyway; she was so pretty and so much fun.

The night before wasn't so pleasant. I went to Frances Stephenson's new apartment for her first real meal using her wedding silver. By the time I got there at 7:30 after work, she was a little tight, having had drinks with some people who dropped by earlier. I tried to catch up with too many martinis too quickly, and paid for it the next day. The meal was good but it would have been better if her new husband, Frank Pryne, could have controlled his dictatorial impulses. I would come to the defense of "Little Net" but a few minutes later he would lash out again with a "Don't interrupt me, Frances!"' or "I am talking!" I don't like Frank.

I had a hangover the next day which didn't help with the poll-taking. I had expected that house-to-house canvassing would introduce me to a variety of New Yorkers. I soon learned that depending on what district I was assigned to, I would have all Italians one day, and the next day Jews, and the next mostly Irish. The poll ended the Saturday before the November election, with Dewey given a lead of about one percent over Lehman. My final check for the two weeks came to $107, including $19.50 overtime.

My feet rejoiced that it was over, but I felt rather sad that the six of us who had been working together without an argument and with a great deal of laughter and good spirits were to go our separate ways, probably never to meet again. We gave ourselves a little farewell party at the McAlpin bar. I contributed a bottle of champagne and a long and very bawdy poem commemorating our "City Crew 2."

I started job hunting again, troubled by my failure to find anything permanent. I went to Macy's and spent my overtime money on a suitcase. I wrote to Jean, "I think I shall be heading south pretty soon. I have a few irons in the fire up here, but they are not hot. I wonder why I came up here at all." It didn't take my mother long to suggest that I come home to stay in Montgomery and get a writing job on the *Montgomery Journal,* or go to Harvard for graduate work. I didn't entirely close the door on either.

I went to Boston for a weekend with Phil and Jane Hammer, where Phil has a fellowship and is doing advanced studies in economics. My letter home read, "Harvard is not grand—it is magnificent. I'm glad I didn't take undergraduate work here, but I look forward to the time I can go for graduate study. We went to the Fine Arts Museum—lots of Copleys & Stuarts & Sargents. I don't like Copley's technique, but he certainly could paint clothes. I had a fine time with Monet, Degas, Gauguin, Matisse and Cezanne. I think Boston is mighty ugly. "

Sheila was emphatically against graduate study. She wrote Mother: "Nick needs more than anything else to get out in the world and on his own. Another year of sheltering life at college would be bad for him. He has depended on you so long that it's awfully hard for him to make even casual decisions, but if he could be absolutely unadvised about anything—either what clothes to wear or what social engagement to make, I am sure he would be a lot surer of himself and acquire a lot more independence of spirit in everything."

I stayed in New York looking for a job, and filled in the time with social engagements. Many evenings were spent with "Coo" Westfeldt, the daughter of my father's bird-shooting friend, and a banker, "Sonny" Westfeldt of New Orleans. It was fun to go out with "Coo" because neither of us were serious and we had a rollicking good time. Usually we were accompanied by Bill Flaxner.

Once in a prankish mood, we sent Coo's sister, Jane Bunting, a screwy message, "Getting married St. Johns, Newfoundland. Wish to avoid red tape. We can live on love but can you spare a dime for honeymoon?" The answer was appropriate to our joke, "Fatigue and financial worry detrimental to marital happiness. Go to Niagara and sleep on Simmons beds. Sending a dime by freight to ease your financial pain."

It was when we began to get a raft of congratulations that we began to worry about it getting into the newspapers. We sent a lot of telegrams to straighten things out. After leaving Western Union and dropping off Coo, Bill and I stopped to see Alex Heard who was in Columbia University Infirmary with flu. I showed him the wires, but he was a little doped up, and didn't know what to make of them. He congratulated me. "To be on the safe side, I will have it annulled," I said. "But aren't you afraid there will be biological complications?" he asked, very concerned. "No," said Bill Flaxner solemnly, "I was with them all night."

Another Southern anchor was Marion Oates, "the beauty of France and Alabama," who was making her debut in New York. She couldn't come to the phone but said for me to come right over. I walked the fifteen-to-twenty blocks up Fifth Avenue for the exercise and arrived at the mansion of her stepfather, Philip Gossler, to find a formal reception for "Oatsie," as she was known, in full swing.

I described the scene to mother:

Limousines were pulling up at the awning outside and fur-wrapped ladies were stepping out. I went through the agony of a receiving line. My shirt was green and my face was red, but the house was very beautiful. With flowers banked against the walls, Marion was in a Carlotta dress, and her mother, Georgia, in something fine, and Ms. Saffold in 7th heaven at the end of the line. Ah, it was a touching scene.

How long, how many trying years had Georgia waited for this!

I grabbed a glass of champagne and found Kate Baldwin and "Little Net," and got another glass of champagne to give me courage to speak to the most famous debutante of the season, Brenda Frazier, who was there, and kiss the honoree, Marion, who made me feel no longer uninvited. But when I left the party I was rather sober and this was due to Mr. Hamilton.

Mr. Hamilton, to whom I was introduced by Mrs. Saffold, was obviously of great importance in the business and political world. Mrs. S. spoke of our mutual friend George Waller, now a diplomat in Luxembourg, and by way of conversation I mentioned that Luxembourg was probably on Hitler's wish-list for its steel output. I casually gave him some production figures. "Where did you get those figures?" quizzed Mr. Hamilton, and when I stammered "from various trade journals," he corrected me and demanded "Why do you talk about something you know nothing about? Know everything about something—I don't care what it is—and talk about what you know."

I will not forget Mr. Hamilton, or his advice.

On November 17 I had an interview with W. A. MacDonald at the *New York Times*. He heard me out and said the same things everyone else had said about there being hundreds of applications and no jobs. But he differed from the rest: he promised to try to get me a job elsewhere. "I have friends on Paramount News. Call me next Tuesday." I called Mr. Macdonald and he said his Paramount friend, Mr. Park, might have a job.

34

From the Underground Up
in Filmmaking

M R. PARK OF PARAMOUNT DID HAVE A JOB FOR ME. I WAS TO BE A film librarian. As such, Mr. Park said, I would learn all about storage of films, and eventually how to cut and edit and write narration. He was a little vague about the pay. He said, "It will be enough, enough." I wondered what his idea of enough was, but was afraid to ask.

I wrote mother that, "Under the circumstances I do not think it wise to come home right now. Jeanie, why don't you take a trip to California? If you are waiting for me to get settled you may wait for years. I've got to swing this thing alone so for God's sake go now."

I asked her to break off her negotiations in my behalf with the powers-that-be at the *Montgomery Journal,* in view of their recent stand opposing Negro participation in a Southern conference. "At Chapel Hill when we had a conference, Negroes took part. This doesn't mean equality socially, but a meeting of minds on common problems." A few weeks later I reported for work at Paramount. I was there Monday morning at nine a.m. sharp, to meet Mr. Park, who was too busy to come in until noon. I wished I were so busy I didn't have to get to work till noon.

The first thing I had to do was join the union. It seems that Paramount had a "closed shop" contract with A. F. of L. Local 702 of the International Alliance of Theatrical Stage Employees and Moving Picture Machine Operators of the United States and Canada (IATSE). A "closed shop" meant that all employees must join, but first I would have to be admitted to the union. This required going before a

Board of Admissions and arranging to pay a fifty dollar initiation fee at ten dollars a month deducted from my salary.

My title was assistant film librarian, and I was to work in the basement where the inflammable film was stored. My job was to log rolls of negatives as they were delivered to the vault, and when called by those upstairs, bring up 100-foot rolls of 35 mm "library shots." Some of this was edited into news sequences to be shown in movie houses. There were also orders from Hollywood and other film centers for news footage to give authenticity to feature films. I felt I was nothing but a "gofer" between the basement and the top floors, and said as much to my mother.

In fact, I spent a lot of my time in the vault sleeping. I was keeping late hours, going with a very pretty actress, Eleanor Doolittle, a roommate of Celeste Holm. With the iron door to the outside closed, I had absolute quiet. When they wanted me upstairs, after some angry calls for that "son of a bitch 'Speed' Read," they would beat on the iron door with a steel pipe. I felt secure in my job because I had joined IATSE, which made it very difficult to fire me.

From the first day I was a regular contributor to the employee suggestion box. I learned later that the Monday morning board meeting often opened with "Well, let's see what 'Speed' has to suggest today." I had only been there a week when, after considerable thought, I decided it was a deadend job because:

Nick with an old film machine.

1) The newsreel, only about 1,000 feet of film, is too short to adequately inform; 2) Even if I were writing the narration, the voice is supplementary to the pictures and cannot give much information; 3) There are millions of feet of non-release film here that will in all probability never be used, since Paramount Films is not set up to produce new films.

I knew that Mary Losey was working for an organization backed by the Rockefellers, a clearinghouse for educational films, and the thought came to me: Why not make short educational reels from the film Paramount has on hand? I talked to Mary, who told me that Mr. Montague of Paramount had the same idea. "I'll tell him about you. Meantime, your present job is as good an entree into film work as anything you could have."

As for the future of educational films at Paramount, I learned from Mr. Montague that the words were an anathema around the place. They were even refusing to release footage to outside organizations making educational films for schools. Mr. Montague said that it would be two years before anything was done in that direction. He suggested that in the meantime, I learn all I could about the process of making a motion picture. What I thought, but didn't say, was "That's all very well, but when your job is to stay in the basement and type cards or dig into the vaults, you don't learn much."

Mother had answered my earlier letter about my dissatisfaction with my job, by a long impassioned plea to give up New York and come home. I had the strength to write back:

> It is entirely too soon for me to be passing judgment on anything. I have had the sense to be quiet as a mouse at Paramount. Perhaps Mr. Montague will have some cheese for me. At any rate, I am going to stick.
>
> You must remember, Jeanie, that you have gone through this thing before, and that thousands of mothers have kissed their boys goodbye for thousands of years. You must not consider it a tragedy. If you do, it marks our relationship as being psychopathic. You must not consider yourself a martyr. You must realize that events are taking their natural course, events that all of us, I, someday with my children, must face.
>
> To oppose those events for the sake of our mutual pleasure at being together cannot lead to happiness in the long run. Neither of us would be happy if we knew I had thrown away an opportunity to find real creative and important work in order to stay at home. This may not be that opportunity, but I must have a chance to find out, before you wail, "Mistake, mistake," and before I get disgusted.
>
> It seems to me that I have found a job that may lead to very important things and you should rejoice and be glad. Celebrate this Xmas my debut in the world of affairs. We will celebrate it together. I have decided to come home for Christmas. I am to be a Xmas present from Sheila, Jill, Aunt Callie, and probably Dad. I will arrive Saturday morning tied up in red and green ribbon. I consider the matter closed.

I wrote my father, "I hope I can add your name to the list of contributors. Sheila has put in $30, Jill $5, and Aunt Callie $50 and I will put in $10. That leaves about $15, unsubscribed. I got a letter from Jeanie today urging me not to come for so short a time, that it would reopen a wound. I don't think the wound has healed. I can only have three days at home, but if it gives Jeanie a happy Xmas, I think it is worth coming for."

When I got back to New York, I enrolled for the remaining seven lectures of a course in motion pictures given by Columbia University and sponsored by the Museum of Modern Art. The first lecture was by Alfred Hitchcock. Later we heard a lecture by W. H. Auden, who had got into film by doing the narration of an English documentary for a producer named John Grierson, for whom I would eventually work at the Canadian Film Board in Canada.

Another speaker was a great authority on phonetics. He said the broad "A" is relatively new in England, affected by those who wanted people to know that they had been to Italy to have their clothes made. When Dr. Johnson heard it for the first time he said it was the most God-awful sound he had ever heard. The lecturer said that Americans speak much more like Englishmen of the seventeenth century than do Englishmen today.

I bought a good Royal Standard typewriter for ten dollars to take the place of my little portable, which hadn't been in decent shape since I tried to fix it. I really needed one to work on a film script I was doing on used cars, for the "Getting Your Money's Worth" series based on *Consumer Reports*. I got into this through Mary Losey, who introduced me to Julian Roffman, who had already made two films for the series. The first, on shoes and milk, had been seen by about 500,000 people, and the second, on razor blades and cosmetics, had been running at the Film Art Theatre on West Fifty-Sixth Street for about three weeks. It had already attracted the attention of J. Walter Thompson, the big advertising company.

Julian was a film cutter by profession, director by ambition, and full of ideas for doing movies. He was penniless because every cent he made he spent on film and cameras. Two other young men, one a cameraman, shared his ambitions and his poverty. Perhaps I would be a fourth.

I cautioned my parents to say nothing about this, since I wasn't yet firmly entrenched in Paramount. In fact, I had yet to meet with the Board of Admissions of Local 702 of IATSE, to be officially admitted to the union. They finally asked me to meet with them one evening after work, but as it turned out, that was the night I had been invited to dinner weeks previously by my mother's cousin Augusta, a friend of Sara Delano Roosevelt's, to meet Mrs. Carnegie, who was said to be interested in film.

I wrote Jeanie what happened:

When I telephoned Cousin Augusta to say I was going to be a little late, explaining "why" over the phone was impossible. About all that penetrated her deafness was the fact that I would be late. I didn't know I would be an hour late.

However, she didn't tell me that she was taking me to a banquet at the Astor Hotel where she had been given a table by Mrs. Carnegie to help raise money for the Presbyterian Board of Education's Sesquicentennial Fund for Christian Education. On the phone all she said was I should come to Mrs. Carnegie's table, No. 16, in the grand ballroom of the Astor Hotel.

When I finally arrived, all the lackeys at the Astor seemed to be expecting me. I was met and welcomed by the doorman, the chief bellhop, and the head waiter in turn, each of them saying, "Are you Mr. Nicholas Read? Mrs. Augusta Hope is at table 16." Their tone was that of the "Ca . . . ll for Phi . . . lip Mo . . . rris" man. I could see that Mrs. Hope, as substitute hostess for Mrs. Carnegie, had made a profound impression.

My seat was next to Cousin Augusta in the center of the room. The vacant chair seemed to frown at me as I hurried in embarrassment to the table. It seemed to say, "Mrs. Hope and I are extremely vexed." Explaining the cause of my delay was impossible. A union meeting indeed! Unions one could approve of theoretically because "dear Franklin" approved of them, but not when they kept a guest from being on time for dinner.

I didn't know until I read the program what I was in for. We were to hear Dr. Lewis S. Mudge on "The Great Program of the Sesquicentennial," as well as the Rev. Robert Andrus, Student Pastor of Columbia University and the Rev. J. Maxwell Adams on "The Universities and Christian Education," and sixteen other leading Presbyterians.

I had no time to contemplate my martyrdom. "I don't think you will get any supper," said Cousin Augusta. The sickly smile that I had affected died at these words and the sight of the fruit cocktail in front of me. Grimly I began on the cherries at the top. "What do you think of the German debt situation?" boomed Cousin Augusta. I swallowed a piece of pineapple I had been chewing.

"I don't think anything of the German debt situation, Cousin Augusta." "Don't you think they ought to pay us?" she pressed.

"Cousin Augusta," I replied very coolly. "I don't think anything, one way or another, about the German debt situation." The truest words I ever spoke. I was thinking of food. Thanks to the good waiter, I got the filet mignon and the dessert too.

After the ordeal, which lasted till about 11:30 p.m., a fellow sufferer at the table, Max Holloway, suggested (out of earshot of Cousin Augusta) that we have a drink. We had several and a good talk. He was a curator for the New York Historical Society, and had been invited by Mrs. Carnegie. It seems that unless they are on the program, sponsors like Mrs. Carnegie do not attend these functions, but give their tickets to friends who ask friends, or unsuspecting visitors from Alabama. I hope I am not on a permanent list.

In my job, I had some interesting assignments, one being to pull out roll after roll of film for the Czech story. Some of it may have been used in *The Crisis*, a report on the rape of Czechoslovakia, which played in many theaters. It brought what was happening in Europe much closer. I joined a discussion group called "The Dissenters," led by Roger Baldwin. We met in a private dining room in a Village restaurant for a dollar dinner and hours of heated debate.

On my first evening, two very smooth young Englishmen crossed swords on the Munich Pact and Chamberlain. The Chamberlain champion showed some interesting advertisements that appeared in the *Daily Mail* at the height of the crisis—ads for gas masks, for bombproof cellars, etc. There was one priceless one: "Feeling nervy? Wrigley's chewing gum will soothe you."

My father had forwarded a letter from Vyvyan Harmsworth in Scotland, who had gone there with his wife and grandchildren to get away from the bombs in England. "My eldest son is at sea in a big sticky job. Both the others are in the fighting line. I see by some of the American papers that they don't think the war has started yet. I would just like to take the gents who write such bosh for a turn or two around this tight little Island.

One of the grimmest naval battles in history is taking place. "I think we are holding our own. I am helping keep the home fires burning by shooting for the pot, my game keeper having joined up. I have also my mare and 5 dogs to look after. This show cannot last less than two winters in my opinion and may well last a great deal longer. We are not expecting an early finish."

I wrote Dad my opinion:

Chamberlain is inherently Fascist rather than consciously so. He is the spokesman for the English bankers, and as such, is neither hero nor villain. Stooge yes, but no villain. Whether Munich would save capitalism, or perhaps just give England time to prepare for war, is the question.

Hurling troops against Germany's line to stop her drive against Czechoslovakia would have been at terrific cost. Will Germany fight Russia or is there some truth in the rumor of an alliance? Can England count on the totalitarian nations turning on each other or will they make a united and simultaneous attack—Japan in the Far East, Italy in the Mediterranean and Germany in the Ukraine? If Chamberlain achieved "peace for our time" is it an armed peace tottering on the brink of war?

I had honed my thinking about the European situation in an argument with a taxi driver focusing on Hitler and the Jews (he was pro-Hitler). We sat in the cab with the meter off for an hour on Twelfth Street, until I noticed it was 8:15 and had to be at Town Hall to go with Helen Rous (the artist sister of Peyton) to a folk dance and song festival. I urged Dad to read Charles Beard's *We're Blundering Into War* in the *Mercury*. Dr. Beard pointed out that we are still selling war materials to Germany, Italy, and Japan. I agreed with him but doubted whether any of us will be as logical when war comes. I had already gone to the Seventh Regiment in New York to look it over with a view to joining up for military training.

I closed my letter by thanking him for the doves, "which arrived in much better condition than the quail. I have been having them for breakfast, and am late to work every morning as a result. Today came two jars of marmalade from Jeanie. How glad I am to get them. They tried to sell me some in the shop where I bought oranges today, but I said 'Nix, Brudder, me old mama makes de best in de woild.'"

Quite suddenly, we were all out of work at Paramount. There was a strike. It was not ours, but the projectionists' Local No. 306. We couldn't cross their picket line since our Local 702 belongs to IATSE, the same International. The projectionists called it to try to force about seventy-five unorganized theaters in New York to use union projectionists.

First, they tried to get the producers and distributors of films to withhold films from the theaters involved. However, the producers and distributors had contracts with those theaters and would be liable to damage suits. So they decided to shut down the labs and exchanges, including Paramount, by throwing up picket lines. When we left at the end of the day, I couldn't get back in to get a pair of rubber shoes I had left behind. How long it will last, no one could say.

The projectionists in 306 constituted one of its most powerful Locals. They charged a huge initiation fee of around a thousand dollars. Even with that, you had better have a brother or an uncle or some influential friend to join. The attitude of those in it was simply this: "We are in, let's keep the jobs for ourselves, and to hell with those that are out. The fewer jobs, the better pay." This is an attitude that prevailed in many A.F. of L. craft unions.

Here, it seemed to me, was the real danger to freedom of enterprise, one of the fundamental concepts of democracy and capitalism. Businessmen, editors, and the poor deluded middle class that howled in unison against the "communistic" CIO, needed to take a look at the good old A.F.of L. tactics, which they, of course, learned from business.

I shed no tears when one monopoly clashes with another. The history of the Paramount Company is one of the most fantastic tales of capitalistic pyramiding ever recorded. If Adolph Zukor could combine theaters and studios and have one hand in the pocket of Kuhn Loeb, the labor chieftains realized they could do a little combining themselves. The theaters are largely controlled by the producers working with Wall Street. The local unions are controlled by IATSE.

Studying labor problems and being part of them were quite different. I learned a lot more about unions than I did when I finished Mr. Wolf's course in labor problems at Chapel Hill.

The strike gave me "time off" to apply for a Rockefeller-backed fellowship from the Film Center, which would provide me with a stipend of $120 a month to learn about documentary films. When I told Mr. Slesinger, the director of the Film Center, that I was interested in doing agricultural documentaries, I had no idea I might be sent to Minnesota. That's where I went on May 18, 1940.

Jeanie set up her usual hue and cry. Why couldn't I have been given an assignment in the South, a place I knew? Sheila wrote her: "Please read my letter again. I did not say it was necessary for Nick to get 'weaned away from home'. I said 'weaned,' which is very different and meant that he must grow up and be on his own feet before he goes back home. I simply can't understand your attitude about this job. The value of this study is for him to learn something that he does not know, not given an assignment in the South, which he does know. It seems to me the greatest opportunity, and I can't see why you don't realize it."

35

Getting to Know the Midwest

MY FIRST ASSIGNMENT ON MY ROCKEFELLER FELLOWSHIP WAS TO the Visual Education Service of the University of Minnesota where I reported to Mr. Robert Kissack, the director. I was to work with another fellowship winner, Hilda Gruenberg of New York City. We were assigned to do a film on Minnesota—a very broad subject.

We certainly did not realize the difficulties of organizing such an assignment for the camera. A film on farming, or on industry, or on labor organization, or politics, or even any particular period of the State's history, might have been manageable. But fitting together what had happened in Minnesota from early steamboat days to the eclipse of the Farmer-Labor party was beyond our reach.

Hilda and I labored at our jigsaw puzzle under handicaps. First of all, we were strangers to Minnesota. I for one must admit I hardly knew where its boundaries were. Secondly, we were not acquainted with the potentials or limitations of the camera, and of that great instrument of the cutting room, the Moviola.

Our first responsibility was to get to know Minnesota. Because of the importance of agriculture in the state's economy and thus in our film, and incidentally because the Visual Education Service closed down for the month of August, I decided to look for a job on a farm. I hitchhiked as far as St. Cloud, and then caught a freight. There were no "empties" as I learned to call the empty cars from Bob Raymond—a down-and-outer going west—who taught me to ride a tank car.

Mr. Rockefeller probably never envisaged one of his fellows riding a Standard Oil car—or I'm sure he would have made the board over the wheels a little wider. I managed to hang on until I was deaf and my teeth were all loose. We got off in Evansville and spent what was left of the night in a vacant section of the foreman's house. I shared Bob's ragged quilts on the floor and with my pack for a pillow, slept soundly until morning. We bathed and shaved with rainwater, which had poured into the barrel outside while we slept.

My next ride took me as far as the North Dakota State Fair where I met George "Smokey" Maas—drunk as a coot. George was a small man, but a big liar. He told me and a couple of people in the dairy cow exhibit that he was buying cows—hundreds of them. He bargained for and finally promised to buy a huge Holstein bull for two hundred dollars. "I just have room for him on the car of cattle I have on a siding. If you don't believe me I'll pay your taxi fare down to the railroad and you can see for yourself."

No one believed him or accepted his offer. However, he told the truth when he said I could get a job with his boss, Fred Ziegler, who had brought him to the fair. I was hired to shock and bind fodder corn, at $1.25 a day. I got the job by claiming to be a cotton picker from Alabama.

I wrote home:

> I only hope picking cotton isn't as hard work as pitching corn bundles. Mr. Ziegler raises wheat, flax, barley, corn and hay. He has 3 tractors & 3 horses, beef cattle and 2 milk cows, and lots of fine hogs. There are no chickens, nor is there a vegetable garden or flower garden.
>
> We are right on the Red River. The house is painted, but has few comforts. The steps to the attic where I sleep with George, Ray, and the other farm hands, are rickety. The house has electricity & a telephone, but no bathroom. God, it is hard to get clean with a coffee can of water. The kitchen is the most important room in the house, with an electric refrigerator and enameled range. We eat four meals a day: breakfast at 6:30; dinner at noon; lunch brought to the field at 4:00; supper when we knock off at 7:00.
>
> The Zieglers and farm hands think I'm a bum going from harvest to harvest. The boys have given me some fine tips & asked some embarrassing questions. I will be here about 5 days.

My next venture was with Hilda through southern Minnesota—Rochester, Austin and Winona—where we saw the work of the Soil Conservation Service. We talked to several farmers, who praised the Department of Agriculture for its soil conservation program. At first they had been suspicious of the project, but later wouldn't try any other way of farming. The government supplied the machinery and labor for terracing, which in that hilly country was often necessary.

Mother and I had passed through Winona when we drove up from Alabama, but it was late and we didn't see much. This time I described it for her in a letter: "The red tiled roofs of St. Teresa College, shining in the late afternoon light, and the pinkish crags to the west of the town reminded me of Monterey. The streets are red brick and lined with elms. The houses have neat yards and along the lake are several elegant residences. Watkins Medical Supply Co. is the largest single employer, and the town appears to be prosperous."

In St. Paul I went to a meeting of the Farmer Labor Association (Party), where a panel discussion went on all afternoon. There was a great deal of criticism of then Governor Harold Stassen, interspersed with talk about unemployment, natural resources and farm problems. A former mayor of St. Paul, Bill Mahoney, spoke on "How to End the Depression," his scheme being to supply the unemployed with the means of production. He quoted a university professor's reaction to his plan as, "Why, Bill that's socialism," and the Mayor replied, "What solution do you have?"

I got to know some schoolteachers from the range country. The father of one of them had worked all his life for the mining company and was "blasted" five years before he could retire on a pension. His son was not bitter, but said, "That wasn't the right thing. He's old now and all he knows is mining. He can't do anything." The situation was pretty bad. Conveyor belts had thrown hundreds of men out of work. Those that had families and homes didn't know what to do. There were few jobs anywhere.

Before the depression, a lot of the young men went to industrial centers like Detroit and Cleveland, but many returned. One who did come back and became a teacher said, "I'm not going to stay in this stinking work much longer. Getting a thousand dollars to take care of some one else's kids! Not for me." The one whose father had been blasted said, "You're not married. You don't have two children like I do. You can talk that way." The belligerent boy replied, "No, thank God, I'm not married." The other one said mildly, "But it's natural to get married. Every man wants to have a family and a home."

Men out of work, men starving slowly on WPA, their souls starving before their bodies, men getting rusty like the earth. Old men lying awake at night studying how to save their little homes and the savings of a lifetime, their minds turning this problem over and over and getting nowhere with it. Young men at the drug store wondering if they'll ever have families and homes of their own, and then turning their minds to the more immediate problem of getting a pint and going to a dance or having a party.

A big WPA strike occurred while I was in Minneapolis, because of a new regulation that threatened the union wage scale. The WPA administrator reacted by trying to bully the strikers by threatening to hand out dismissal slips, unless they returned to their WPA assignments in five days. One worker was killed, and the mayor declared he wouldn't give any more police protection and would close the projects.

Hilda and I went to the funeral of the worker, Emil Bergstrom, and about five hundred of the most depressing people were milling around the entrance to the central labor union office. The coffin was brought out soon afterwards. The crowd broke up and the flashy hearse followed by old cars paraded down Second Avenue to Second Street, where the man had been killed in front of the WPA sewing project, where he had worked.

I wrote home,

> Then the whole crowd marched off again; the most filthy, ragged, stinking human vermin since the days of the Bastille. If this were an article I would not use these words. You know what I mean. Another might think there is arrogance and hate expressed by them, the hate of the aristocrat for the "scum." There is in me no hate for such people, only pity.
>
> I do not despise them as do some of our prosperous citizens. They are the urban Okies. In their hearts there is hate stored by poverty and despair. It is a sad thing to contemplate.

Hilda and I drove out to the cemetery. Red roses were sent by IOOF Local 54 and white roses by Local 544, and pink ones tied by a green ribbon marked in gold letters "Workers Alliance."

That was a depressing day, but I interspersed my sociological studies with a lot of good weekends in the Midwest. Aunt Callie in Montgomery was from the Clark family of Kimberly-Clark in Neenah, Wisconsin, where I spent a few days. I played golf with "Uncle Bill," a delightful person with a quiet humor that puts you at ease and an honest directness that compels your respect. I think that more than any person I know, he had a sort of nobility. I didn't think of him as an extraordinary businessman, which of course he was, nor did I begrudge him his wealth.

He seemed to come by it naturally. "Aunt Jessie" made guests feel at home—and served delicious Old Fashioneds.

In St. Paul I saw a bit of Berry Richards, who four years later married my friend Bo Hubbard and came to live in Montgomery. She oriented me to the city by taking me sight-seeing from the Minneapolis-St.Paul airport in a plane that flew over the cities. This was followed by dinner at the Sheik's, canoeing on Lake Calhoun, and to Charley's Exceptionale for a midnight beer. We were stopped there for looking too young. The doorman, who was Charley, said, "You can't come in. You are underage." We had to show our driver's licenses. Berry's read "sixteen." "Ah, ha," said Charley, "What did I tell you?" "Look at the date!" said Berry. The license was three years old.

Berry's father was a doctor. They had a lovely house on White Bear Lake across from the golf course, where we spent some time. It was a sultry afternoon, but there was a breeze, and after the sweaty golf went swimming. Dr. Richards mixed the best martini I have had since the City of Norfolk and we had a delicious supper. It didn't take much persuading to make me spend the night. Dr. Richards provided me with silk pajamas and shaving equipment. Berry and I went to *Confessions of a Nazi Spy* at the village movie. It is an excellent piece of anti-Nazi propaganda.

I had followed the progress of the European war on my radio, a low point being the German-Russian treaty of non-aggression, but the war became more personal to me the next day at lunch with Berry's aunt and uncle. They had as a guest a young Frenchman, who was in this country studying steel production. He expected to be called home immediately to go into the service, and said, "So every day here before I go is of special meaning because I may not be back."

My own assignment in Minnesota was drawing to a close. I had learned a lot about filmwriting and visual continuity, and handed in a number of scripts, none probably very good. In my report to the Rockefeller Foundation in New York I wrote:

"Just how profitable learning at the Visual Education Service was, is hard to say because I never saw any of my impressions translated into film. I had not touched a camera. I do know that Mr. Kissack's method of developing a film by little sketches which he adeptly drew upon the wall, came to nothing more than an illustrated lecture.

"I also learned that in a documentary film you shouldn't try to tell everything about anything or something about everything. Pick the dramatic highlights, and tell the story in simple, human terms." I didn't have a chance to put this to much use, since none of our work was ever put on film before Hilda and I finished our assignment in Minnesota and parted company.

This probably pleased Jeanie who had already begun to show concern, as she always did when I spent much time with an attractive girl. Usually she questioned their "background and breeding" or their "good taste." Not so with Hilda, whose mother Sidonie Gruenberg, was a sociology pioneer in family planning and whose father, Dr. Benjamin Gruenberg, was an eminent biologist. About Hilda, Mother wrote, "I am devoted to her—I like her more than anyone you ever seriously liked and I don't mind her being a Jew, but . . ."

I returned to New York City where my fellowship was renewed. I was then transferred to the Canadian Government Motion Picture Bureau, in Ottawa, Canada.

36

Getting to Know Canada

CANADA WAS ALREADY AT WAR IN LATE 1939, AND I HAD A HARD TIME getting across the border without an official piece of paper from the government accepting me as a Rockefeller Foundation fellow assigned to the Canadian Film Board. Some fast talking in the correct tone of voice enabled me to transfer from the train in Montreal and catch an early morning connection to Ottawa.

At the station there, when I attempted to call the Film Commissioner, the pay telephone was occupied by one-and-a-half-people. Inside was a man. Beside him was a woman standing half inside and half outside the booth. "I'm trying to get John Grierson," came the agitated voice from within.

"So am I," I said to the young woman, who was quite pretty. Before her husband had located the inaccessible Mr. Grierson, I had gotten to know the persistent caller's wife fairly well and had contributed my share of coins to the machine. They arranged to meet Grierson for lunch; I took a taxi to his office.

A feisty Scot, Grierson was much less ingratiating than the couple, and I knew better than to be ingratiating with him. His first words were: "Can you run a projector?" He might as well have asked if I could fly to Mars. He found out in five minutes all I had done and in half that time all I didn't know—about cameras, sound projectors, lighting, etc. I hadn't even edited film.

He lapsed into deep concentration. His bushy gray eyebrows lowered over his piercing eyes and his little gray moustache clamped down over his lip before he said, "No more blathering about what you didn't learn in Minnesota." He called for Stuart Legg, the filmmaker he had brought from England, and told him "to start me from the ground up." A few hours afterwards, I was running the Moviola for Legg and papering film. I telegraphed home: "Commenced work today under Stuart Legg. He's keen as a razor and twice as friendly. It looks good for our side."

I had not yet found a place to stay and was routed to some rooms that I thought were too gloomy and uncomfortable. Legg suggested I look for accommodations across the river in predominantly French-speaking Hull, which is not as clean but is a livelier place than Ottawa. Hull has bars, nightclubs, ladies of the evening, and at least one good restaurant, Chez Henri. The bars have signs reading "*Défense de Blasphème.*"

I wrote home, "I think I prefer the vermin and whores, which Legg says infest Hull, to the shabby respectability of the Capital. Who knows? I may come back speaking Canadian French! And if I bring a mistress I know that you, my dear parents, will welcome her to Hazel Hedge with your ever-open arms."

Mother had been using Colonel Henry Bankhead of Montgomery, who headed the U.S. Embassy in Ottawa, as a mailing address for me. In addition to sending orange marmalade, she sent warm clothes and even a comforter. "It isn't worth paying duty on. It's an old thing. Perhaps he can get it through customs without complications." She asked the colonel if he could suggest a good place for me to board in a pleasant household.

In an aside to me she added, "It would be far more satisfactory than eating at joints & counters & vermin—& mistresses pall when the novelty wears off. I think you should consider limiting yourself to beer and wine. Whisky ruins your palate to say nothing of what it does to your health. Also, it's a fine time to cultivate a pipe—it's such a companionable thing & you are so busy lighting it, you smoke much less. Think of the great pipe-smokers of England and Scotland."

I answered that I had found accommodations in Ottawa, "the only advantage being that it is not far from work. The landlady is decrepit, a sweet person named Mrs. Dench. There are no French mistresses. I pay $5 a week with breakfast. The room is large and reasonably shabby, but with an eastern exposure—and warm." The outside temperature was consistently below zero. I didn't stay there long before moving into a big house at Forty-two Stanley Avenue, with Jim Beveridge and Don Fraser and a couple of other filmmakers. It was only two blocks from Film Board headquarters, which was in an old converted saw mill.

Moving into Forty-two Stanley was not without its complications. We borrowed most of our furniture from another habitue of the Film Board, Jane Marsh, who was separating from her husband. It was fine furniture and everything looked nice when we gave our housewarming party, starting with three gallons of Craik punch (my mother's recipe: nine cups rye whisky, three cups Jamaica rum, six cups tea, one-half cup lemon juice, grated peel of six lemons.) The guests arrived with unquenchable thirst, and the punch bowl was drained as if it had no bottom. I went out and bought more liquor, and began using more tea and less rum and whisky.

Most of the guests left when we got down to sherry. About twenty, including the inhabitants, stayed, and we danced and played darts and sang, sitting in candlelight before the fire. After a while, we had scrambled eggs and rolls and coffee. We were all pretty scrambled by then. Everyone complimented us on the house, which we took with sour smiles because Jane Marsh had just informed us that in two weeks she would be taking back both her husband and the furnishings.

My work on films started off briskly, and I had little time to see all the people Jeanie suggested, or do the things she thought would make me more acclimated and comfortable, including moving to a better neighborhood, learning to ski and to speak French. She wrote me that two Montgomerians would be coming to Detroit to buy a car, and would drive up to Canada to see me. "Elizabeth & William Nicrosi will leave here tomorrow—you will remember that Elizabeth is Betty's mother & Richard Cromelin's sister."

When they arrived, I was deep into my first editing assignment on a travel film that was just being finished on the Banff-Jasper Highway. I didn't see them at all. All day long I would cut a sequence, Mr. Legg would criticize it, and I would do it over again. I also helped select the music and assist with the recording. I was rewarded when Legg gave me a credit line on the film.

After that I was to go on location with Irving Jacoby, a young New Yorker who had worked for Grierson in London. He was making a film on ice hockey, called *Hot Ice*. I learned a good deal from him and his cameraman about shooting. For the first time I saw a script translated into film and experienced the difficulties and excitement of production—a far cry from Minnesota.

Legg went off to New York to pick up his wife and three small children arriving from London. While he was away, I occupied myself in the lab, watching the experts make wipes and dissolves, a process which even now I only vaguely comprehend. They were also printing on a Bell and Howell continuous process printer, which is more difficult, but appears easier.

I postponed calling Colonel Bankhead until I had time to buy an overcoat, earmuffs and galoshes. The colonel had the whole third floor of the handsome American

Legation building; he needed that much space to move around in. I couldn't tell whether he was short or tall because his efforts to arise were quite unsuccessful, his measurement around the middle being a good country mile.

I warned him about the parcels coming from Jean. He asked me to Thanksgiving dinner. I can't remember whether it was our U.S. Thanksgiving or the Canadians', which is celebrated at a different time.

I had already begun to know John Grierson. At least, I was exposed to some one-way conversations he had with other people. He is a stick of dynamite, ever ready with explosions under control, emitted when he thinks they will achieve whatever he has in mind. Over lunch at the Chateau Laurier cafeteria, I overheard two small explosions, both with a purpose. He quite firmly told a Mr. Smith, who is one of three Civil Service Commissioners for Canada, "You just tell so-and-so to go easy on that," and right afterwards, "I do not like the design on the airmail stamp. Who do I see about it?" Mr. Smith, glad that the criticism was leveled at another department, readily told him. Grierson said, "Good. I will see him early next week."

Grierson had earned his spurs fighting for documentary film in England, and came to Canada in 1938 (not the first time) on the recommendation of Ross McLean, secretary to the high commissioner for Canada. He was to study the Canadian Motion Picture Bureau, which was part of the Federal Ministry of Trade and Commerce, to determine how it could be expanded to make fuller use of film in Canada.

The report came to the attention of Prime Minister Mackenzie King, who then asked Grierson with McLean to write legislation that would enable the government to develop such a film program, the objective being to "make Canada not only better known to itself but to others."

When the National Film Act was passed in 1939, Grierson was off and running. He attracted top filmmakers in England and New York, some as technical advisers and others as producers. Basil Wright was one and Raymond Spottiswoode another. He had brought Stuart Legg and Stanley Hawes with him, and had discovered Norman McClaren—the animator who learned to draw directly on film—in Scotland.

Legg told me that Grierson had debated most of the men prominent in the British Parliament before he came to Canada, and fought hard and effectively for his causes. I could see how. His words were hard, fast punches—each punch to the middle delivered with smoothness. His wit, his satire, his invective were superb.

I had the occasion to be on the receiving end of it some time later, when I showed him early footage on my first film, on Army cadets, hoping he would overlook what was missing. Perhaps it was fortunate for me as a filmmaker that I didn't get away with it.

He said, "All I saw is a lot of hands and feet, heels and knees shoving me in the face. You refused to recognize the simple action and make it clear. You tried to improve on it. You were showing off. You've wasted the government's money and precious film on a job that would have wowed a film society back in 1928, but you haven't got anything I would show to an audience now."

I didn't feel too badly because about the only person who had escaped bitter criticism around the place was Legg. Jim Beveridge was given one crack at "Canada Carries On" and removed. Don Fraser had a dressing down. Sydney Newman, an artist from Toronto, was told that he had a "B-grade picture mentality."

Newman said it was his vulgarity that persuaded Grierson that he "had the common touch." In later years when Newman himself was head of the Film Board, he said that "Grierson was insulting, and used every possible technique to invoke a response, but had the incredible faculty of bringing out the best in us, deep wells of understanding and responsibility."

He had the great ability to inspire young people, and he attracted many from all over Canada, and a few like myself from the United States. I wrote home, "What bright young people these Canadians are! Canada, like the South, is experiencing a Renaissance, & it finds its support, if not its expression, among the keen young minds here. They are idealists, not concerned with making a lot of money but interested in making good films."

A nucleus of these lived at Forty-two Stanley. All were males except a sweet, amusing and useful young woman named Margaret Ann Bjornson, whom Grierson had discovered in Winnipeg. She had no place to stay so we took her in. She was a godsend. She got up early and made breakfast for everyone, and started us off on our film assignments in good humor.

We all worked hard, and in turn played hard. When Irving Jacoby came from the United States, he said, "I didn't get a job, I joined a club." There were riotous and simple-minded pleasures with some vivid accounts of carnality, roistering and booze. But day and night, often at night, by sustained effort we delivered the product.

On weekends we skied, endlessly. I was terribly bad. That's how I met Doris Duke. We both fell into the same gully at Rockcliffe Park. We toiled out of it together. "Aren't you Mrs. James Cromwell?" I asked. "Why, yes, I am." "Your husband said in a interview that you were an excellent skier," I said doubtfully. "He would," she gasped as she slipped and slid with me up the hill. Another time it was Lady Diana Gordon-Lennox, the best woman skier on the Canadian Olympic team, who always skied wearing a monocle, but somehow saw my plight and gave me some pointers.

The person who probably taught me the most was Jenny, a girl I spent a lot of time with that first year in Canada. In the fall we had our first weekend date at a friend's cottage near Wakefield in the Laurentians.

On Sunday we went swimming in the morning. The sky was cloudless, but a cold wind was blowing and the water was icy. We took our tea in the afternoon and had it on a hillside where we watched the sun sink, casting long shadows over the smooth folds of the valley below. The last light faded the scarlet of our hilltop maple to rose, then to purple.

Fall becomes winter early in Canada, and turned into "glorious skiing weekends." I bought a good pair of boots and had them fitted to rented skis. Jenny and Ross McLean drove up with me. It had been snowing for three days, but Saturday was cold and clear and the plows had kept the highway open. There was no sleeping late Sunday morning. By ten we were off on our skis up the St. Cecile de Masham road.

I was guided to a hillside identified as "a good nursery slope," free of stumps and stones. The snow was a good eighteen inches deep but soft and fluffy and no good for sliding until we packed it, by snow-plowing down with our skies and climbing up herringbone fashion. After awhile, it was hard enough to give us a thrill sliding down, and later on it got so fast I had to brake my speed with turns. I would start off down the hill slowly and awkwardly and make perhaps two turns successfully and on the next turn go down taking a large scoop of snow with me. Then Jenny gave me some fine instruction in the art of doing a turn called "the stem christie."

Late in the afternoon, I had some "Moose Milk" (rye mixed with milk). After that when I fell, it was very pleasant to forget about weight-shifting and edging the right ski and flexing the knees, and just lie back in the damp white fluff and take in the glories of nature. The sky was a deep blue above the pines on the ridge of the hills and the sun sparkled the icicles hanging from the trees with a million reflections, and cast long purple and deep blue shadows on the fields of snow.

The weather was consistent. It was always terribly cold. At home in Alabama my family worried. Dad wrote: "We are concerned about your health." From Mother: "Will you promise me that if you get sick you'll wire me and I'll come up and nurse you? You will certainly need warm underwear. I cleaned the lumber room and went through the trunks and found a dozen sets of long winter underwear and will send them. I hope you stay inside and write in your spare time—it's the only way to become a writer."

37

No Spare Time

THERE WASN'T ANY SPARE TIME. MY NEXT ASSIGNMENT WAS TO WRITE the script for a film entitled "Timber Front," about Canada's lumber industry, its colorful past, and its contribution to the war effort. I was learning a lot about Canada and the Canadian people. Most of those I met had their origins in the British Isles, and were closely following what was happening in England.

It was brought closer to me when Grierson's sister Ruby, a sociologist and film director, was on her way to Canada to do an assignment for the Film Board. Her ship, *City of Benares*, which also carried ninety British children, was torpedoed and sunk. Ruby was not among those rescued. We all had looked forward to her coming. She was much admired for a film she had made on "Housing Problems"—as well as for standing up to her brother. *

She had literally turned the housing film over to those appearing in it, saying to the slum dwellers, "The camera is yours. The microphone is yours. Now tell the bastards what it's like to live in slums." To her brother she said, "The trouble with you is that you look at things as though they were in a goldfish bowl." Grierson answered, "Yes, I do. So what?" Ruby replied, "Well, I'm going to break your goldfish bowl."

Soon afterwards I had a chance to talk to a cameraman named J. D. Davidson about the situation in London. I asked about the air raids: "We get at least four a day and if we stopped for them, no work would get done. If you are in one of the new buildings constructed of steel and concrete, you are fairly safe except on the top floor." About shelters: "The trouble is, no shelter is really safe unless it is about 40 feet underground, and there are not enough bomb-proof shelters for everyone."

* Forsyth Hardy, *John Grierson, A Documentary Biography* (London: Faber and Faber, 1979).

Davidson said bomb strikes radically complicated traffic, often tripling commuting time. But he praised the efficiency of transportation authorities in keeping things moving. "When an above-ground subway station has been wrecked, there is a bus on the spot in the morning to take you to the next station." Davidson also paid tribute to the London fire fighters, who had to endure derisive laughter when they had nothing to do but practice their drills. "Now they have the toughest job of anybody, and many of them have been killed in action," he said.

When bombs destroyed water mains, fire fighters developed a system of pumping water from the Thames, stringing a series of portable pumps together to pump the water through two or three miles of hose. Davidson reported all this in his crisp, British, matter-of-fact voice. But he abandoned his composure when I asked about the destruction of historic buildings. He pressed out a half-smoked cigarette until it came apart in the ash tray.

"That's what makes you so bloody mad," he said, speaking low and between his teeth. "They've got a lot of the old landmarks. The law courts have been wiped out. So is St. James. St. Margaret's is not so bad. They got the dome of St. Paul's, but maybe it can be replaced. [It was, but not until 1962.] I'll tell you there's no friendly feeling left for Germany or any German in London now. There's raw hate that will live long after Hitler is dead and we are dead."

The *Montgomery Advertiser*, which I subscribed to, didn't report much about the war unless it related to something local. In May of 1940 it carried a story with a startling statement from Alabama's Governor Dixon, in which he "took it for granted that in the event of a German victory Canada will be ours." I showed it to several Canadian friends and it made them pretty sore. I wrote a long letter to the editor. In part, I said:

> The Canadians are working steadily for a British victory. They are careful to make plain to Americans their identity as loyal subjects of George and Elizabeth. At the opening of Parliament, the stately figure of the Gentleman Usher of the Black Rod raps loudly on the door of the Commons to announce that a message from His Majesty the King is to be read in the Senate chamber.
>
> They are proud to be North Americans and think there should be another name for citizens of the United States because they are Americans just as much as we are . . . Canadians let the English know they are not Tories and not Imperialists. They are people of the New World, who as Gov. Dixon pointed out, think and act

very much as we do, reading the same magazines, seeing the same movies, driving the same cars. But it does not follow that Canada wishes, or will ever wish, no matter what becomes of England, to become the 49th State in our union.

This was about the only time I did anything about Jeanie's admonition "to write in your spare time." I had been too busy learning the intricacies of scripts, cinematography, recording sound effects and editing.

In Montgomery, my parents were spending a great deal of their time looking for job opportunities that would get me back to Alabama when my Rockefeller Fellowship was over. Since there were no openings for filmmakers there, they felt that a newspaper was the next best thing. They thought the moment had arrived when they heard that a monthly newspaper, the *Southern Farmer*, with a hefty circulation, was for sale for sixty thousand dollars.

They went so far as to talk to our cousin William Baldwin, vice president of the family bank, about borrowing the money. The paper seemed to be a financially prudent investment, with 100,000 paid subscribers in Alabama and the Southwest, and provided a good income for its owner, a Mr. Stern. However, as it turned out, he had made his money by going from state to state by day coach to sell ads. He often spent his nights on the train or in railway stations. Understandably, he wanted to retire. At the same time a Mrs. Maude Brewer had gotten an option to buy, and was looking for someone to edit the paper *and* get the ads. Mother took a dim view of Mrs. Brewer. "She is not the kind of person you would care to be associated with, neither intelligent nor liberal."

She consulted Dick Hudson and Grover Hall, both executives of the *Montgomery Advertiser* and *Journal,* who said that "editorially the *Southern Farmer* is just a 'cut and paste' job. And there are questions about its circulation figures. There are piles of unclaimed newspapers returned to the post office each month."

Dad, who had been negotiating with Mr. Stern's brother-in-law, came back with the news that a Mr. Luke Lu of Nashville was going to purchase the paper outright for cash. Everyone was relieved, and it was certainly all right with me, since I didn't want to be an aggressive advertising salesman, nor to leave Canada.

In fact, I had just finished the highway film and was enthusiastically starting another project—a film that several of us wanted to make on our own. In a letter to my father I said,

I stayed in Ottawa this weekend instead of going to Montreal to see Maurice Evans in *Hamlet*. The Film Board has let me have a couple of thousand feet of 16 mm Kodachrome. I have borrowed two cameras, and weather permitting, am embarking on my first production. Don Fraser and Jim Beveridge are the other members of my team. We will work on weekends and in our spare time.

The idea of the film is to show the warm relationship among the hundreds of Ottawa people of all classes who come together on the ski slopes on Saturday and Sunday. Little French Canadians strap on barrel staves. Civil Servants board streetcars for the outskirts of Hull where the Gatineau hills begin. And the wealthy drive in their big cars, with skis racked on top, to lodges farther up in the mountains.

Housemaids, bank clerks, schoolboys and girls and cabinet ministers—all ski. Some are good enough to take the jumps, and some, like me, are thrilled by the gentle slopes, but when we put on skis we seem to get on a common footing, or unfooting as it were. Social distinctions that are assiduously preserved in town are swept aside on the slopes. It is a great leveler. We all fall down at some time.

Despite our good intentions, we did not get far with our film. First, there was bad weather whenever we had time to shoot, and even if the weather had been good, we would not have had enough time away from our regular assignments. But it was an exciting idea to have gotten to the point where we even thought we could do it.

I was buoyant in an interim report I sent to the Rockefeller Foundation, requesting that my fellowship be renewed for another six months: "I don't know how long I shall be here. There is always more to learn and I have only begun my training as a filmmaker. Here, the focus is on Canada. My ambition is to return to the South, to Alabama if possible, and to make pictures about the people and for the people who are near my heart."

I wrote to Jean:

It is a time of decision. Shall I come home with a view to returning to Montgomery, in what capacity I don't know, but determined to earn enough to maintain Hazel Hedge? Or shall I stay here as long as I can, learn film work, and be ready to go wherever I can do most good by writing and making films? Where, with no property and separated from the tender family feelings that draw me back, I could be more on my own.

My decision is not simply whether to return to the South. This I intend to do sooner or later, but with what idea shall I return? Shall I come back bound to the past or pledged to the future? My decision goes deeper than choice of work. I could never think freely in Montgomery, with all I have to lose and with all who would be hurt by it.

Jeanie reacted by writing me to forget that she had urged me to come home: "Please ignore everything I have said in those whimpering self-indulgent letters, except how much I love you. Nash and I wouldn't have you do anything except what you want to do. In a few years you'll be getting married and that's another thing. You must marry the girl you love—not to please me. I'll be too hard to please—not for me, but for you I want the best."

I wrote back, "When I said 'divorce myself from home and family' I meant not literally, but free myself from the ties of sentiment. My letter was written as cold-bloodedly as I could make it and your reply made me very proud and happy and sad."

Painting by Anne Goldthwaite of Nash with his golf clubs.

I wanted to come home for Christmas, but when I talked to Grierson he put the choice squarely before me: "Why should I assign you to a production? If you go home you will not be here if needed." Then he said that my stay in Canada should be determined by how much I was getting out of it, and if I am not progressing, I should go where I can move faster. He added that if I am dissatisfied, it is partly my fault for not finding work to do on my own.

Jean and Nash had plenty to keep them busy in Montgomery. Jean already had the houses and grounds of Hazel Hedge to attend to, the Altar Guild of the Church of the Ascension, and countless luncheons and dinners for in-town and out-of-town guests—and now she took on British War Relief. Dad stayed with golf and hunting.

He wrote me with pride about playing sixteen holes, beating both Judge Bucken and Julius Rice "in spite of my arthritis. I didn't have much of a dove shoot last week. Snipe are coming in and I shall go down Thursday and try them out. The season closes on the

31st, and quail season closes February 20th. If you can get them through customs, I'll send you some."

His favorite companions were his hunting dogs. Jean wrote to tell me about a movie they had seen called *The Biscuit Eater* about a little white boy, his colored friend, and a pointer: "The dogs were remarkable. There were pictures of the Field Trials showing them working so beautifully. Dadda punched me every minute & said, 'Old Dan, Look, that's just like Old Dan!' In another second I'd get some more hard punches only this time it was 'Old Taffy,' who was making the point and holding it. It's a lovely movie, but my arm is black and blue."

Jeanie was immersed in fund-raising for armaments for her beloved England. This in turn led to her strong support of all Roosevelt's pro-British policies. In this she became involved with a Craik cousin, Ms. Juliet Morris of Richmond, Virginia, who was described in Drew Pearson's "Merry-Go-Round" column as:

> A prim white-haired little woman who comes every day rain or shine to listen to the debates in Congress on the Neutrality Bill, which she opposes.
>
> On her blacklist is Senator Styles Bridges, the isolationist from New Hampshire. When he was to speak, she stopped the elevator before it got to the hearing room floor and told the operator to let her out—"I will not listen to that windbag!"

Jean's pro-English stance was not well received by some of her friends. She wrote that "Dr. Hubbard, for example, is violently anti-British and talks about war debts. I get so mad I can't go over there. I try to keep Britain as much before the public as I can, but a lot of people don't care."

She put so much of her energy and time into it that she became tired and ill.

> I think I have had my first attack of old age. I had never realized that I was vulnerable. Nash could age, Mama grow old, Judy break and Charlie look ill—but I, Jeanie, would never be touched by age.
>
> I could and would always fly up steps & dash into the markets, carry all the chairs out, paint a room & dig a garden bed, give a picnic for 30 people & cook the supper, cut flowers & boughs, and have people in for the evening, take a drink & do the Black Jack Davy, read all night and not tire. Well, I am just plain mortal.

38

A Trip to Nassau

JEAN WAS EXHAUSTED FROM HER BRITISH WAR RELIEF CRUSADE. February, which is a wet and cold month in Montgomery, seemed the right time to accept a long-standing invitation from Georgia Saffold Oates Gossler to visit the Gossler place, Harborside, on Hog Island in Nassau. She could get some sun there, and relax. Her main problem was her wardrobe. The Gosslers' friends were rich, and there would be social activity. "There are no spring clothes here or even in Birmingham, & none are expected for 4 weeks—so I am beside myself," she lamented. "I *won't* go in a gunny sack!" She bought material and got help from Rosa Parks, the seamstress whose defiance of Jim Crow laws led to the bus boycott in Montgomery. Together they sewed feverishly.

Jean wrote me, "I am off tomorrow for Nassau. My clothes are very pretty & I hope they are suitable. I am taking white accessories, and have a number of Jeanie hats. I got your camera from Hawkins who has never used it, & 2 color films and I know how to put them in (John Shaffer showed me). I feel just like a bride, with so many stockings & veils & all the things a lady should have & I never do—gloves & cold creams & a lovely new permanent. I am really quite grand."

According to my father, Nash, she got off "in flying colors, and looked lovely. I felt very proud of her. Mary and Louise and Nancy and Hawkins were all down to give her a send-off." She flew into Miami on Florida Airlines, with a stopover, during which she bought a bathing suit. She would find on arrival that she didn't need it quite yet: "It is very cold, 55 degrees, and blowing hard and the noise the coconut fronds make in the wind is like the wildest arctic gale."

The next morning the skies were clear, and in a long letter she described the setting: "The harbor in front of the house is filled with great yachts and sailboats, a lot of them today since the Nassau Race ended here this morning. It is still quite windy & they are bobbing about in this amazing blue water & dazzling sunshine. Behind the house is the sea, where we will swim when it is warm enough—the most beautiful beach I ever saw. We will just walk out over the lovely English lawn—but the trees are coconut, not elm, and the flowers hibiscus & bougainvillea."

Just when there would be any time for swimming seemed doubtful. Every day was so full of social events that Jean had to keep a calendar:

We sleep until 11 and then get dressed for the first activity, which may start with a sail across the harbor and a 14-mile drive along the coast to the old Beach Club, where about 100 people are lunching.

You go to the bar & order several martinis or daiquiris (I never order anything but tomato juice or sparkling water. I'm afraid I might miss something) and after a lot of milling around & talking to the fascinating & wild-looking old Baroness d'Erlanger & Prince Serbatoff & a snooty Mrs. Cartwright of Cannes—a typical Riviera American, you take a plate and go down the buffet line. You find your place at a table for 40 people and sit between people you have never seen. I sat next to a dull little self-important vice consul who takes his job more seriously and more swell-headed than George Waller ever did.

As soon as lunch is over you get in a car and rush off to the races with Lady Jane Williams Taylor, Brenda Fraser's grandmother. The Axel Wenner-Grens from Sweden are there, sitting close around their guest, Greta Garbo, to protect her from staring eyes. She is in slacks, very sallow with no make-up, and definitely not beautiful.

Then we go to the paddock & pick our horses. I take a 5 shilling bet on one. The horses are very tiny, raised here on the Islands & the jockeys are even smaller—little niggras about 12 or 14, but they ride well. It is cold and after 5 or 6 races, I leave & drive to Lady Jane's house & have tea. Later a large party comes in & drinks unending cocktails. The house is filled with autographs & photographs of Queen Mary, Lord So & So, Lady This & That.

Old Sir Frederick, with a pointed white beard & great cape, is about 77, absolutely ignored by Lady Jane. I found him charming & interesting, with a marvelous memory. He was Manager of the Bank of Montreal. He quoted me a wonderful poem about Lincoln by Edward Markham, which I must look up.

About 7 o'clock we left for the launch and in spite of the cold took a trip up the harbor & back. It was unreally beautiful, the moon, almost full, flooding the whole harbor, Venus is the little sister star so near, the yachts are lighted up. Every palm tree at Harborside has an indirect light in it and we enter something like fairy-land.

A huge wood fire is crackling at one end of the 60-foot living room and the dining room table is twinkling with candles at the other, and laden with food. Someone brings more martinis and I still decline. I haven't drunk anything but a little champagne or white wine and now and then a beer. It's funny, but I never want it. We went from there by launch to a miniature casino, very elegant with a courtyard and fountain and dimly lit dance room and splendid orchestra. I literally fell into bed.

Just up the beach from the Gosslers' is the famous Porcupine Club, with a restaurant outside serving those who are on the beach from a lovely buffet counter where you help yourself to anything you want—hot dishes, great cold rare roast beef, turkeys, lobster, hams, salads, and wonderful desserts. You can eat lunch in your bathing suit, shorts, pajamas or an old bathrobe. I go swimming every day.

On the harbor side, the Porcupine Club has an *elegant* dining room where you have to dress properly. At my first party there, I was seated at the table of the Duke of Windsor, who is Governor of Nassau. He made a speech and toasted the King. Everyone stood, all up and down the line, with champagne glasses lifted murmuring "To the King." It sounded rather thrilling as if we were drinking to Charles II or Bonny Prince Charlie.

I sat next to a charming man from Richmond, who told me an awfully funny Negro story in the course of which he said, "They were going to ex-communicate the preacher." I said, "You've been away from the South too long—niggra's don't ex-communicate their preachers—they turn 'em out of the church."

I am having a wonderful time. I wonder why I even worried about my clothes or whether I would fit in. I feel perfectly at home & my clothes look very pretty. Across the table was a woman with pigeon-blood rubies that a Maharajah would envy & I never even realized that, except for her, I was the only person there without pearls.

The other night there was a magnificent fancy "Head Dress" ball at the Jungle Club. I picked up the megaphone, covered it with silver paper, put a long white scarf over my head to look my part in the Black Jack Davy, & sang it with gestures. The 300 to 400 people there could all hear me and enjoyed it.

One afternoon we went on Vincent Astor's yacht for cocktails & had dinner that night with the Wenner-Grens on the "Southern Cross," the yacht that picked up the survivors from the Athenia. Axel Wenner-Gren is the wealthiest man in Sweden, & possibly in the world. We had dinner on a solid silver service. We couldn't tell anyone where we were going since their guest, Greta Garbo, refuses to have big parties given for her, & Marguerite didn't want to let her scores of other friends know about it.

Wenner-Gren left the next morning—flew in his own plane to Washington & then to Europe to try to negotiate peace—he knows Hitler & Goebbels both well. A marvelous man—hugely big & wonderfully handsome with the most spiritual quality in his face —placid & tranquil without a line in it—he has made every penny of his money himself. Also at dinner was Sir Harry Oakes—the gold miner who was kicked off a freight train & fell in a desert & found so much gold dust on his clothes that he decided to dig for gold there & found it. His face is lined & rugged & he looks & talks the typical self-made tycoon. The contrast was interesting. Lady Oakes is Australian & very sweet & natural & cordial.

I've told you nothing about the long-time Negro residents of Nassau. In town, there is always something amusing & picturesque to see. The other day it was a funeral, 6 blocks long with 2 bands. The dead man belonged to 4 lodges, & it was exactly like a scene from Green Pastures, in marching time with jazz. The immediate family followed in a little red-curtained carriage & relatives walking behind the hearse. I wish I could have taken pictures, but I was not supposed to carry a camera & look like a tourist.

Marion (Oatsie) is having the most marvelous time. She has her pick of all these wealthy, idle young men with yachts & boats & places here & in Palm Beach—& some delightful young foreigners too. You'd never know there was a war in Europe or people starving anywhere—but my Social Conscience has gone to sleep & I am just enjoying it all & wish you (Nicky) had been born with a gold spoon in your mouth and were with me here. You are so much more charming & amusing & better-looking & cuter & smarter & sweeter than any of the young men I've met.

I felt very well in Nassau. I never drank anything & kept my stomach safe. I swam every day & never cooked a meal or went to market or cut a flower—but I had to go to a lot of parties, 3 or 4 a day & I smoked while other people drank. Some time you and I will come back together & visit the Gosslers. Philip has gotten quite fond of me. You can bring your camera and we will take pictures together.

That was not to be. World War II intervened.

39

The War Comes Closer

*J*EAN RETURNED TO MONTGOMERY FROM NASSAU IN EARLY MARCH TO renew her British War Relief activities and to act as a sort of surrogate mother to English "flyboys" training at Maxwell Field Air Base. On weekends she entertained them at Hazel Hedge, and weekdays she worked at getting ready to feed them.

"This week I'll have a tureen of crab & shrimp gumbo, a bowl of rice, a big salad and a fowl. Next week I'm going to have a leg of lamb & string beans & quantities of young roasting ears and a large freezer of fresh pineapple sherbet. Then I'll recover from the weekend."

The aviators in training were often referred to her by friends and friends of friends. Jill sent Jud Shaplin, the boyfriend of a girlfriend of hers. He was an embryo anthropologist from Harvard, coming to make scientific measurements of the space allotted in planes to the pilot and the bomb-release, so that it could be made to fit British pilots who were smaller than their American counterparts.

Robert Frazer, secretary to Senator Lister Hill of Alabama, wrote to tell Jean that Lieutenant Wego Chiang, the son of Generalissimo Chiang Kai Shek, would be stationed at Maxwell Field, and hoped she would ask him out some time. She did, for lunch with several friends, including Grover Hall of the *Advertiser*. Afterwards she commented: "The food was good, but the company didn't mix well & I was too tired to try to blend them."

Grover wrote a letter thanking her: "You had no business having us out, because plainly you were not feeling well. Nevertheless you did it, and carried it off with accustomed grace."

John Grierson, the Scot who headed the Canadian Film Board where I was in training in Ottawa, was among those who visited Alabama. He went on a tour of one of the power dams of the Tennessee Valley authority (TVA) and was much impressed. He asked his guide, "Did your Uncle Sam, as you call your government, pay for all this?" The guide replied, "Yes sir!" Grierson commented, "In my country they would call that Socialism." "No sir," said the guide, "This ain't no socialism. You see, this here dam belongs to the people."

In Montgomery there was a lot more talk about the war. Jean was getting letters from mothers of her English "flyboys," thanking her and telling about conditions over there. One expressed her joy at having her son home again for a few days, to see his newborn son.

Nash's English grouse-shooting friend, Vyvyan Harmsworth, wrote at length from Thrumster House in Caithness, Scotland:

My dear old Alabam, I left my house you visited near London two years ago

Nash with the Griersons.

before the German gents dropped 11 eggs around it, but I haven't missed a thing. Soon after we came here they hit our village and bagged 15 kiddies plus two men having quick ones in a pub nearby.

Last week they tried again, getting a woman and 2 children, and leaving a 500 lb. bomb ticking away on our grouse moor. If it gets a grouse or two, we will have them on our table. We can use the meat, and I can't see well enough to shoot them any more.

I am one of 1,500,000 Home Guards who are elderly gents but keen as mustard, reporting alien activity. While waiting for something to happen, I exercise my mare and 6 dogs, and garden—growing food and a few flowers. My eldest son is chasing U-boats somewhere in the Atlantic. He says it's a bit cold these days, but otherwise seems to be enjoying the sport. He owes the Huns one, since his ship was sunk and he had a lucky escape.

There seems to be a great probability that our gallant ally, La Belle France, is going to join up with Hitler, and fight us. It really is not without its humorous side, though rather awkward since we have about as much as we can handle. What we need are more ships, planes and guns. This is a mechanical war and machines are going to win it, plus good stout hearts, a commodity of which we have a good supply over here. Cheerio, old smiler, and give my kindest regards to Mrs. Read, and tell her how grateful we are for her British War Relief. Yours, VYV

Dad was depressed. He wrote me: "If the Germans win over the English, it will mean an upheaval all over the world. Living conditions will become harder and we will adopt a policy of isolation and commence immediately preparing for war. I am longing for the time you will be here. Jean says that your scholarship will be over July 1. I am sorry to speak about it, but you will have to do some serious thinking. These are serious days."

Dad went to Savannah, where his brother Isaac died. He left Jeanie in bed quite ill, and found her still there when he got back. Dr. Pollard had told her she would have to stay in bed if she wanted to get back to normal. My father wrote: "For Isaac it was a happy release. For 17 years he was a sufferer and only his religious faith sustained him through it all. I never heard him complain. Your Aunt Mary died just two months before and the two wills were drawn so as to dovetail. He left me silver and jewelry handed down from our mother. He left you $7500. It will come to you in time."

Peyton Rous, the cousin who had come from Baltimore to live with the Read boys when they were growing up in Corsicana, Texas, wrote: "Isaac was my hero, and never failed to be that, not even when he fell into the ditch of the breakwater at the fish tank, and came out an obscure, green shape, so thick was the scum upon him. He was wise and kind and humorous and right—like his mother, Aunt Ellen."

For my twenty-fourth birthday, April 16, Jean sent a nostalgic gift to keep me reminded of Alabama—five old wood engravings of Montgomery, nicely framed to hang on the wall. They had been illustrations in *Harper's Magazine* around the Civil War time.

One was from the foot of Commerce Street where several Negroes and a mule are working the corn fields that I remember across the river. Another was the Confederate Senate in open session. The nicest was Jefferson Davis addressing the citizens from the balcony of the Capitol, with two little Negro boys standing on the bases of the pillars outside holding candles, and a great mob of people throwing their hats in the air. And there was one from the Big Basin on Dexter Avenue, before the fountain was put in.

My main birthday present was money Jeanie offered to advance so that I could get a car, since Uncle Isaac's bequest had not been processed. I had already turned my old car in to a Montgomery dealer, Lawrence Byers, as down payment on the new one, and had a three hundred dollar credit. I asked Jean to pick one out and deliver it to me in person, and come to Ottawa for a summer visit. Jean said that Mary Webber and another friend would come with her to help with the driving.

She said that Nash was too busy selling Mama's (Jennie Baldwin's) house on Perry Street to get away. The money from the house was to be divided between her daughters Sheila and Judy, who needed it. Nash had signed a sales agreement with people who wanted to take over the house in July, but the current renters had a lease until September.

Jeanie decided to go to Canada without him. "Besides, he hates tourist camps & likes hotels & I think camps & cooking as we go would be so much more larky."

Through the spring Jean's letters to me were about the garden and Hazel Hedge visitors.

The biggest scuppernong vine in the arbor is dead to its roots. But the grass is green & the flowers lovely & the drawing-room as cool & under-the-sea looking as ever, only prettier. It's full of white gladioli & white hydrangeas & gardenias.

Anne Goldthwaite & Elizabeth Thigpen & Miriam Arrington were here the other day. Miriam was so interesting, having just come from Austria. We are all such ardent lovers of France & England & such haters of the Totalitarian states that we had a fine time together.

Willey brought her daughter Petunia's house guest, a Miss Putnam from Boston, for lunch. Such a clam—she didn't open her mouth except to eat lots of waffles & chicken hash & fresh new peas & corn-on-the-cob, with strawberries & cream & curds for dessert. Miss Putnam believes in equality for the Negroes—you can imagine how that riles Willey.

Ethel Jane Bunting came by on her way to Sonny's June wedding in New Orleans. He is marrying this year's Queen of Carnival. Ethel Jane says, "Of course Sonny Westfeldt would marry the Queen of Carnival!"

Connie Wash wrote to ask if she and Pat could come for 10 days, and I said "Yes," although I'm giving a big buffet lunch for a wedding on the 26th. The boy is asking his young friends, including a Rockefeller. I'm the only person who knows about the "R" so far.

By the next day, everybody did.

Before Jean could leave for Canada, she had to fix up a couple of her cottages. "At Irene's I'm going to change the bright green cupboards & bookcases to a sort of salmon pink to suit her furnishings. Also, the ceiling is horribly cracked and will have to be papered."

Letters from home brought me the news. "The Pollards go to Prattville every Sunday to see Jean who is still institutionalized there . . . We received a formal invitation to the graduation of Ben's daughter, Ruby Miller, from State Normal School and will attend and send a gift . . . The cupola blew off Godpapa Baldwin's old house on Perry Street in a big storm . . . Your father asked me to enclose this receipt for your poll tax."

I got quite a few letters of advice about my impending military service. William Baldwin, who graduated from Annapolis, wanted me to get into the Naval Reserve. Marion Rushton, a reserve colonel in the Army, thought I should apply for Army Intelligence. He said he would write to his friend, a Major Johnson, who was going to be named Assistant Secretary of War, to see if there might be something in Washington for me.

Sheila wrote: "I can't believe we aren't headed for the Dark Ages. When I asked

Dos Passos what he would do, he said, 'Exactly what I did last time. Stay out of it as long as I could find anything to do that made sense and then join the ambulance corps, because I would be more miserable killing people than if I stayed out altogether.'"

Darlie said, "Well, I wouldn't like to see Hitler victorious—but after all, England and France are poor choices!"

Mother thought that with her great hero Winston Churchill in charge, the British would surely win, and she was greatly concerned about what was in store for her friends with German names in Montgomery. "I had poor old Ryker to dinner the other night. He is ill about it. The thing I dread is the hysteria of people suspecting everybody & being cruel to innocent victims like Ryker and Rolf Schmidt."

She wrote to me, waxing sentimental, "I am out on the porch watching the most gorgeous rain—it is soaking 'into the deep-delved earth' and that makes me think of the next line of the poem, 'Provencal song & sunburnt mirth' and I think of France and the 'warm South'. As if it took a line of Keats to make me think of France! As if I ever think of anything else except England—and Hitler—and there's nothing we can do—just sit by & see all that is beautiful in the World go!"

At the end of June, Dad and Jeanie came to Canada together, although they almost didn't make it. As they were about to leave they found that wartime had brought a new requirement. They had to have passports and visas to cross the border. They had them sent to Sheila's in New York and picked them up on their way through.

They thought they would have me with them on their return trip, since my Rockefeller scholarship would have ended, but even before they arrived in Ottawa, John Grierson offered me a regular job at the Canadian Film Board. I was delighted, of course, and accepted. Jean and Nash didn't talk about their disappointment. As Jean said, "It's your decision."

Father wrote me his feelings when he got home. "We did have such a happy summer together, and I shall always recall those joyous trips to the golf games. We all go hastening through life overlooking the opportunities right under our noses. For the most precious things of life, time slips by and they are gone with only the dismal regret at parting. I am beginning to feel old and unwilling to meet new conditions. I need the encouragement of youth near me. All my heart, my precious Son. Dad."

On September 14, 1940 Congress passed the Selective Service Act. Dad suggested I take out an insurance policy, possibly applying for double indemnity, and reminded me that "when you come home in December you will be compelled by law to register and then it will only be a short time before you are drafted." Jean thought I shouldn't come home for Christmas. "It is so much more important for your career that Grierson have you there to send out on location when he needs you. Therefore I won't feel a bit badly about not having you here. I don't want you to come home & register & be drafted. Stay there. A snowy Christmas will be a new experience."

That fall, Jean reached her goal of one thousand dollars for British War Relief by giving a big benefit. She wanted Gertrude Lawrence, who was in Montgomery appearing in a play with Tallulah's husband, John Emery, to come.

> I pursued her, took her orchids from the Committee, had letters printed to distribute at the theatre, got her manager to give a high school lecture about her play—and did a million other things to be sure she would be at the benefit. She didn't come. The best I could do was sell her 25 B.W.R. Christmas cards!
>
> The drawing room looked too beautiful, with fresh rugs and shining clean paint (just scrubbed) and gleaming brass & copper & a lovely light coming through the gold curtains—a simmering fire though it is still too warm for it, and the most gorgeous flowers—masses of bronze marigolds & chrysanthemums & red leaves from the curb market. We had tea with the gold tea set & daiquiris & little buttered biscuits with ham. And we've already made a start on the next $1000.

When the benefit was over, Jean turned her energy to the presidential election. Roosevelt was facing stiff opposition from the isolationists, and there was a strong "America First" sentiment. "Lend Lease" would be voted on by Congress in March.

Jean wrote me: "I am so nervous over the election that I can hardly stand it. I'm so afraid Willkie will win. I wish you could have heard FDR's speech from Hyde Park last night. I thought it was so moving." She resented the "Willkie plutocrats," and was especially vehement when Claire Booth Luce, whom she had admired as a writer, came out against Roosevelt. It was a real shock to me when Jean wrote, "She is a bitch!" I had never heard her use that word before except when alluding to a female dog.

A letter addressed to "Darling Nicholas" came from Hilda Gruenberg, who was in New York City working for Roosevelt. "If you're in Canada, as I think you are, you are missing a pretty exciting campaign. I got spit on today by a Willkie-ite, and was pretty upset, but father told me that when he was 9 years old some little boys asked him who he was for and he said Cleveland, and they gave him a black eye. So at least it's not new."

Mother wrote that Nash had cast his vote early in the neighboring town Bogue-homme, "but for some reason I had to go to the fire station on Highland Avenue. We didn't know the results until late in the evening. At 9 o'clock Loula Dunn and Mary Webber and Willey Gayle and a few others gathered in the drawing room to listen to the radio, and by 1 we were able to relax with champagne and oysters."

I came home for Christmas to find Montgomery in the midst of a week-long celebration of "the War Between the States." On the agenda were a skeet shoot, a fox hunt and the annual Blue and Gray football match.

A marching band wearing Confederate uniforms and high boots had come from Robert E. Lee High School in Texas, to lead an "America on Parade" march, during which Alabama-grown roses were thrown out of fighter planes from Maxwell Field Air Base. There was, of course, a Confederate ball with a queen.

For myself, I was busy registering for the draft. The law required "Individuals outside the continental United States on registration day to appear before a local board for registration within five days of their return to this country."

I complied.

40

Basic Training

On Friday, February 18, 1941, I became number 34021230 in the U.S. Army. This was done at Camp McPherson Reception Center, near Atlanta. Induction was leisurely, with considerable waiting around, then being marched two by two to various wooden buildings known as mess halls, barracks, and the induction center. Supper in the mess hall was better than the lunch on the L & N Railroad that took us to the camp.

The *pièce de résistance* of both meals was stew, but the army's stew offered the most resistance in the form of tough chunks of meat, and more stew could always be obtained from the cook. Breakfast at 6:30 a.m. consisted of fried eggs, grits, toast, coffee, an orange each and corn flakes and french fries.

So far all had gone smoothly, considering the fact that it was only about three months since the Draft Act passed, and 6,443 new three-person civilian draft boards were given the task of screening more than sixteen million men between the ages of twenty-one and thirty-five, to find whether they were fit for service.

The draft boards were mainly composed of veterans from World War I, who accepted almost all of the men they screened, and sent them off to Army camps for basic training. Most of the camps were ill-prepared to feed, clothe and house so many men, let alone train them. They made do. Alabama registrants numbered around 425,000, sent by nineteen draft boards.

I wrote home that "my draft board No. 2 in Montgomery provides the best bunch. We have been joined by the seediest crowd from the country. Some can't even read. One sad, undernourished man had never made a bed before. I had to do it for him."

Nobody liked McPherson Reception Center, where "they worked you like a slave and treated you like dirt." I requested a transfer to the Signal Corps Replacement Center at Fort Monmouth in New Jersey where they had photographic training, and a film unit. I was told that while my request was being considered I should stay on at McPherson after most of the boys were sent to other camps.

This had its disadvantages for those of us remaining. We inherited all their KP and guard duty. Thirteen hours in the kitchen scrubbing floors, washing pots and pans, carrying water, and dishing out chow is no fun, I can tell you.

Finally, after about a month, we were shipped off with a lot of newly processed Alabama draftees to Camp Blanding in Florida, for basic training. The colonel in charge of the trip made me "a temporary sergeant" so that I could be his assistant leader.

I was given a certificate that read

> To Whom it May Concern: Special confidence being placed in the integrity and ability of Nicholas Cabell Read, who is hereby appointed leader of a contingent of selected men from Local Board No. 2 of Montgomery County, and is charged with the enforcement of Selective Service regulations during the journey. All men in the contingent are directed to obey his lawful orders during the journey.

I shared a drawing room with the colonel, whose orders were "Lights out at 11 o'clock & see that no one leaves the train." No one did, until the train arrived at our destination near Jacksonville. Camp Blanding was a real pleasure after McPherson.

I arrived with a mild cold, which grew progressively worse, soon developing into a very sore throat. I felt as if there were a red hot poker down my throat. The doctor attached to the battalion said he didn't think it was strep, but I couldn't see how a cold would give me such a bad time. I was confined to my tent, and only got up to gargle warm salt water.

The doc mopped my throat each morning with some sort of acid. It was very disagreeable & made me spit blood. It was not exactly encouraging when one of my companions told me that one of his friends had the same trouble and "they had to cut his vocal cords clean out." This did not strike me as funny, and I got worse and soon couldn't eat anything at all. I gave the doves Dad had sent me to my Captain Faulk.

There were five others living in my tent. Only one was educated —a cartoonist from Birmingham. The other four were "po-white" mill hands. One of them, Burgamy, looked like a chimpanzee and acted like one. However he was the spokesman for the group, and philosophized, "It's not bad to have the clap. You don't have to worry about catching it."

I had taken out the maximum amount of government life insurance, ten thousand dollars, which cost me about $6.70 per month. I thought about this insurance when I had to walk the mile to the hospital with a temperature of 104. There, at Mother's suggestion, John Kohn of Montgomery came to see me. He rounded up a doctor who diagnosed my trouble as acute laryngitis. Wasn't that what George Washington died of? Anyway, I got better and could soon eat solid foods again.

I was well before I received "get well" letters from my former house mates in Canada. Jim Beveridge wrote that the pleasure of getting my letter was offset only by my bad throat, and urged me to hold on to my title of Corporal Read "since it is always the corporals who get the big jobs after the war."

Margaret Ann Bjornson, the only girl filmmaker living at Forty-two Stanley Avenue, wrote that "had you still been in our trust the pneumonia would never have got you" and that her "main grievance at the moment is the dearth of mirrors in this place. Last Sunday there were so many people working on themselves in front of the bathroom mirror that James had to stand fully dressed in the bathtub to brush his teeth."

While I was in the hospital I drew up plans for a new cottage Jean wanted to build at Hazel Hedge. She liked what I did and the contractor found it acceptable, so they proceeded to clear the way at the Pineleaf gate. All Jean's cottages had names. This was to be called, appropriately, Blanding Castle.

I began to observe, if not participate, in what was happening around me: "Weekends here are much like college dance weekends though I have only seen one woman in our domain, but I understand that last Saturday night a notorious whore swept the tents from about 2 o'clock on. On purely physical standards I should rate this hand-maiden of the dawn equal to a score of college girls."

Captain Faulk sent for me to thank me for the doves, which he had enjoyed. He also gave me some good news. He said it was certain I would be transferred to Fort Monmouth in Red Bank, New Jersey. A few days later, he had filled out six or seven pages of information for the transfer.

I wrote in a notebook I was keeping at the time, "I'll miss Captain Faulk. He is a wonderful man. He lends his men money when they need it, supplies them with whiskey, and whenever possible gives them leave."

My train north from Atlanta was a streamlined super coach called "The Southerner," which left at 7:30 p.m., and arrived in Newark, New Jersey at 1:40 the next afternoon. All seats were reserved and it cost $13.75 against a thirty-one dollar Pullman. The food in the diner was better and cheaper, and the washrooms just as nice.

There was a bar and a lounge with radio and the latest magazines. No passengers were taken on after leaving Washington, D.C., when the lights were turned dark blue and pillows provided so we could sleep.

I couldn't sleep. I kept thinking of Hazel Hedge, and how when I had some free choice in the matter, I had gone far away to Canada. I thought if I ever get home, I'll never leave again.

The first thing I did when I arrived at Fort Monmouth in mid-March was to buy a supply of notepaper that had the name and address and official seal and slogan of the Signal Corps printed at the top. It read:

Company ___ ___ Signal Training Battalion
Signal Corps Replacement Center
Fort Monmouth, Red Bank, N.J.
Pro Patria Vigilans

I filled in the blanks after "Company" with an "E" and before "Signal" with "5th," added Barracks 218, and wrote the first of many letters home. I felt I had finally arrived.

The lieutenant and sergeant major who met me at the Replacement Center seemed to know I was coming, but when I signed in for photographic training, the lieutenant hinted that it would be much better for me to choose cooking or truck driving, "since there is a shortage in those occupations." However, he obligingly sent me to Co. E for "Photography," declaring that what happened next would be up to the captain.

I lost no time in wiring Irving Jacoby at the Film Board in Canada, who was a friend of a friend of Colonel Gillette who was in charge of the film unit, and asked him to ask his friend to tip off the colonel about me. That's how I got to the captain, who had me fill out a card of information on my film training, which he said he would show to Gillette.

It took another month to get through the training given to everyone who came to the Recruitment Center. Finally, there was a notice on the bulletin board that "Nicholas Read, having successfully completed his basic training, will report to photographic group No. 2 to Lt. Stohr." I assumed that meant I was on my way to the Training Film Unit, although before I could get there I was sent for an interview with another captain, who strongly urged me to apply for radio repair work instead.

In the course of all this I moved three times to new barracks, which involved turning in my bed and bedding at each location, before moving on to the next for a re-issue. Each time I had to lug all my personal belongings from barrack to barrack.

On the way I saw a great deal of Fort Monmouth close up, and found it quite attractive. Two rows of inoffensive brick houses, one for officers and the other for non-coms, flanked a large playing field. The field used to merge with a golf course, but most of that had been sacrificed to make room for scores of wooden barracks and mess halls. The construction of these left no grass in the area, only brown sand which the wind blew into eyes, ears, nose and all corners of the barracks.

A step away was a recreation building with chromium tube chairs and tables with the latest papers and magazines and inkstands, a piano on a small stage and a juke box. There was a good library in the administration building. I was told that the Elks lodge in Red Bank put on pretty good dances for the soldiers, but was advised to avoid the dances at Long Branch sponsored by another group, which had twice as many parental chaperons as girls.

Outside, the leaves were just beginning to appear. Across the marsh from camp I could see pear trees in bloom and along the edge of the golf course, sprays of choke cherry. The marsh had ducks, and there were also red-wing black birds, blue herons, and, in a dead tree on the far bank, a huge osprey nest.

In general photography I learned something about operating a Mitchell camera, but that's about all. Living conditions weren't bad, except for the food. I encountered a soldier from another company, a tall sandy-haired Johns Hopkins graduate from Baltimore, who had come over to eat in our mess, "where the food was said to be better." How any food could be worse, I don't know. The food at Blanding was quite delicious by comparison.

It was hard to get an overnight pass without paying a substitute two dollars to take guard duty, and I was not fed up enough to go AWOL, though this was often done without repercussions. I consulted my Delta Psi address book for the names of members who might live nearby. It revealed half a dozen, most of them old gents from Yale with seats on the stock exchange, living in Red Bank or in Little Silver or Rumson.

I decided to wait another two weeks to get a Special Privilege Pass that would allow me to leave as soon as my assignments were done at five o' clock Friday. This would enable me to get in to New York City for weekends. Waiting for the pass gave me plenty of time for reading and reflecting—and writing. One afternoon I wrote out my thoughts about Roosevelt and the war, and what most of my fellow recruits felt about it:

It's an April day and I'm stretched out on the golf course, now a drill field, soaking in the sun. Up at the barracks most of Co. E is in full uniform to receive its pay, which accounts for my liberty this afternoon. Not until next month do I take my alphabetical place in line and salute for my little allowance.

Magazines came yesterday. I bought *Time* and the *New Yorker*. Things are certainly bad but I see no reason for gloom. The British knew they were taking a chance in Greece and though they may lose the whole Mediterranean they haven't lost the war until they lose the Atlantic Ocean.

It's very easy to say we are not getting the right sort of leadership and I agree that the President hasn't taken the public into his confidence, but he knows there is a very strong sentiment against our involvement in this war. You may call these people isolationists, but most of them think they are pretty good Americans.

The administration is putting tremendous pressure on them to take a different view. For all practical purposes we are in the war now, with convoys to England, except for an official declaration that might help British morale.

There is no enthusiasm among the draftees for the war. Our Captain, who went though World War I, gives us inspiring little talks about the glory of dying for one's country. They fall flat with the "heroes" of Basic Group No. 4, Co. E, 5th Battalion.

He thinks the recruiting advertisement, "Learn While You Earn" is misleading. You are not here to be taught a trade. The only trade you must learn is soldiering. You are here to serve your country, not to be served by it. The truth of this is beginning to dawn on me.

But how does our vote fit into this? As I understand it, we draftees still have that privilege . . . I have a feeling that a great many mothers' sons are on their way to war without having much to say about it. The "why" should be reviewed for the soldiers. I think that one reason for Hitler's military achievements is the enthusiasm of his troops. The Germans believe they are fighting a glorious crusade.

Our lack of understanding of what democracy means & the injustices & failures that our system has permitted & which have obstructed for many the meaning of democracy are now catching up on us & sapping our strength. In a short time we've got to make our cause seem vital.

41

The Film Unit

T WAS ALMOST A MONTH LATER THAT I GOT MY TRANSFER INTO THE Training Film Production Laboratory. There I knew I would find other filmmakers, some very well-qualified and professional, and all there because they were young enough to be drafted. I had heard that one of these was Paul Husserl, a managing editor of *Time*, who had produced a number of documentary films. Another was Jason Bernie, son of the old maestro, who had come fresh from Universal's cutting rooms, and there was Don Robinson, who had written scripts in Hollywood.

Most of the Hollywood filmmakers had money saved or were receiving some kind of retainer from their high-paying jobs. Sgt. Gil Scott, who used to get one thousand dollars a week from Fox plus eleven thousand just last year in percentages from various musical projects, was collecting fifty dollars a week in addition to his Army pay. I had to buy him a pack of cigarettes because he couldn't get a hundred dollar bill cashed.

Gil's father was vice president of MGM, and Gil was Darryl Zanuck's assistant before he got in the Army, so he is a good man to know. I wrote to ask Jeanie, "If you ever have a moment's spare time, send a box of brownies to Gilbert Scott, T.F.P.L."

The Hollywood filmmakers were quite bored with doing training films. Being in documentaries, I didn't mind so much, but resented the fact that most of our assignments had nothing whatever to do with filmmaking.

If a camera had recorded my activities today there would be pictures of me raking leaves, digging up roots, helping to assemble a house, and carrying pails of water. The film cutting—if & when it begins—promises to be just as dull but less physically demanding.

I forgot to tell you that the Film Unit also has responsibility for the carrier pigeons that live in cages alongside our barracks. They date back to World War I, and seem to have been left behind when some earlier communications unit was transferred. We inherited them, and it is our job to feed and water them, and clean their cages.

For weekends a Special Privilege Pass had come through, allowing me to get away for overnights. It took less than two hours to get to Manhattan by bus, and only three dollars for a round trip ticket. My Aunt Sheila Hibben, of the *New Yorker* magazine, offered me a home away from home in Manhattan, with good food and conversation enlivened by the presence of her daughter Jill, when she came down from Radcliffe, as well as her political friend and boss, Suzanne La Follette.

Also, I had relatives from the Read side of the family—Marion Rous with a widespread musical coterie, and her brother Peyton Rous and three college-age daughters. There was also easy access to cut-rate theater tickets that I got through the U.S.O—$3.50 for *A Watch on the Rhine*. When I saw *Major Barbara* by George Bernard Shaw, a program note from GBS said that "America is giving Britain her old destroyers & we are sending her our old plays."

There were also parties given by some of the rich and famous in New York. I went to one at Ann Morgan's, where a *Life* magazine photographer took a lot of pictures, including one of me and a girl I met there who later turned out to be a suspected spy for the Russians. My picture, along with hers, was in *Life*, much to my chagrin and embarrassment.

When Irving Jacoby came down from the Film Board, we had a great talk and a wonderful seafood dinner for $1.25 on upper Broadway—four oysters on the half shell, clam chowder, a whole broiled lobster with both claws. From Montgomery, my best friend, medical student Brannon Hubbard, met me for drinks at the St. Regis. He brought news of the death of Grover Hall Sr., the editor of the *Advertiser*, who had won a Pulitzer in the 1920s for courageously waging war on the Ku Klux Klan.

At Fort Monmouth, Sergeant Riley was puzzled and intrigued by a wire sent to me from New York—"Do you know anyone called 'Petunia?'" he inquired. I admitted I did. "Well, that's a funny name, but she wants to know if you can take her to a Princeton party." With my Special Privilege Pass, I could. "Tunie" looked lovely all weekend and certainly put the northern lassies in the shade.

I also saw something of Hilda Gruenberg, who had been on a Rockefeller Fellowship in Minnesota with me. We went to a play called *Mr. and Mrs. North*, which had its moments of excitement (I'm always thrilled by dead bodies in closets), but it paled in comparison to the movie *Citizen Kane*, which we saw afterwards—a great production in every way.

I had a heart-throb in the person of a girl named "Beppie," whom I had dated at the University of North Carolina. She wrote me a note enclosing a forget-me-not, and in New York I began to fall in love with her. Ever on the alert, Jeanie ran long distance interference from Montgomery, but this time I answered back, "You have a perfect right to comment on any girl I go with & I also have a perfect right to draw my own conclusions."

I had been notified that the $7,500 I had inherited from Uncle Isaac was now available, and decided to splurge on a new convertible, on the premise that with increased production of war vehicles, there would soon be a shortage of such cars. I found a handsome Ford with white sidewall tires for $1,086, to be available as soon as my old car could be brought up from Alabama to trade in. George Stoney, who was coming up anyway, agreed to drive it.

I asked mother to put my golf sticks and my tennis racket in the trunk when it came, since there were still seven holes on the old course at Fort Monmouth that would be pleasant in the evenings after chow. I had come to know some friends of

Nick and Jean with Nick's new convertible.

Marion Rous, the Lichtensteins, who had a magnificent place on a high bluff over the Navasink (Shrewsbury) River. They urged me and Don Robertson to come whenever we wished to use the tennis courts, and to just phone Mary, the cook, if we wanted to stay for supper.

They had three very attractive English children living with them. Mr. Lichtenstein knew their father through his stamp collection. Their father looked after the King's collection and Mr. Lichtenstein traded stamps with George V. I was at the Lichtenstein's when I heard on the radio that Axel Wenner-Gren was in Washington straight from Hitler and Goering with a peace offer, and recalled that Jeanie had met him in Nassau. Mr. Lichtenstein hates Roosevelt so I was never quite clear in my mind whether he's for England. He used to go to Germany twice a year and admired certain things Hitler had done and the German general staff and efficiency. His forebears came over here in 1848, but he keeps up with his old world relatives.

News from Montgomery was worrisome. Nash wrote that his neuritis was getting to his right hand. I replied, "I'm sorry to hear that your neuritis is into your hand. It isn't apparent from your writing. Good luck on the shoot. If you handle your gun as well as your pen you should bring home the birds."

The energetic Jean was still doing everything she had always done, including more work for British War Relief. She also made progress on the building of the new cottage I had designed. Often she went to bed not only tired, but ill. I continued to urge her not to do so much, and not to work so hard nor worry so much about the state of the world: "Take it easy, Pet. I'm pretty anxious to see you but I want to see you strong & well & not a nervous & physical wreck."

I invited my parents to come to see me, and found a small hotel not far from the Fort on the Seabright shore. "It's an old-fashioned brownstone place with verandas & straw mats & wicker furniture. Rooms are $2-$3 without meals." I got nowhere. Finally I wrote Jean, "I have a plan that should scare you. Unless you take better care of yourselves, get a cook, and rest a little each day I'm going to stop writing entirely. I am quite serious about this. If you retaliate by refusing to send money, I will live on my income of $21 a month."

In Red Bank, I was spending a lot of time at the Elks Club, where rehearsals were underway for the "Bottlenecks of 1941," an amateur musical composed and performed by those of us in the Film Unit. Among them was Robert Churchill, who along with Sy Wexler, became my life-long filmmaking friends in Hollywood. I was in the male dance chorus & helped backstage with props. The MC was Marshall

Hazeltine, who had lived in Europe most of his life and got out of Paris just ahead of the Nazis. He looked very charming and handsome in his tux.

There were eight original songs, several very amusing skits, and a documentary film on the peeling of *The 8 mm Potato*. There were girls too, several very pretty Red Bank lassies. It took a lot of rehearsing. While waiting around, we used the Elks Club bowling alleys and ping-pong and billiard tables—all for a nickel apiece.

Our theme song was "The Pigeoneers," written by Ed North, who after the war went to Hollywood to write the epic film about General Patton. In our production, the Pigeoneer song was sung by Bob Churchill and a buddy:

> We're the guys who clean the cages for the pigeons,
> And a pigeon is a very dirty bird
> We could make it more explicit if you made a private visit,
> It's difficult to find the proper word,
> That's why we sigh
> And so do I
> A pigeoneer is not a happy bird.

When the show was given in mid-June, my friends and relatives attended. Jill and Irving Jacoby came over from Manhattan. She had just graduated from Radcliffe and was getting a job at Simon and Schuster. Louise Mohr, a veteran of Jean's little theatre, arrived from Montgomery. And Stoney drove my car up from Alabama in time to get there for the performance.

The show was a success, and we were asked to bring it into New York to be recorded for NBC TV. This was at a time when there were still only about 80 receiving sets in New York. I took a half-ton, eight-wheel army truck and driver and helper to get our scenery and the sets there. We rehearsed all day until 4:30 the afternoon of the broadcast. I wondered how many TV sets would pick it up.

I had a rum collins with Leslie Gwyer in the sunken court at Rockefeller Center at about six, when the rain came down and drove everyone out except an interested spectator unmindful of the deluge. It was Mr. John D. himself, sitting at a table in rapt silence, rain dripping from his glasses.

With "Bottlenecks" out of the way, there was a let-down. I was depressed about the war, bored with my work, and seriously considered switching to Officers Candidate School. I didn't feel that what I was doing was contributing anything to the war effort, and I was deeply concerned about what was happening in Europe and Africa.

I wrote: "If Russia suffers a quick defeat, all is lost. But if she can hold out, and if we can send supplies, then England can win. Senator Byrd painted a sorry picture of our production achievements in the U.S. 'Tanks, planes & guns are trickling out instead of pouring forth in sufficient numbers.'"

Every day it seemed to me that I was just marking time. I asked for a week's furlough to go back to visit the Canadian Film Board. The furlough came through and I drove to Ottawa to see Grierson and Legg—and my girl Jenny. What a week it was. I wrote Jean about it:

> The first night we went to a party at Stanley Avenue, and stayed until I noted a moon three-fourths full in the sky and so Jenny and I left in the interest of romance. Oh Gosh, I was full of romance that night, and liquor too.
>
> The next day we took a picnic and invaded Pink's Lake through beeches & balsam, wild raspberry and juniper & blueberry bushes and told the nosy little boys in charge we were great friends of the Radmans to whom this lovely little lake belonged. We made our way to the cliffs where granite rocks curve down into green water 50 feet deep. Jenny had brought her rubber mattress, a most practical apparatus which you blow up—if you don't have high blood pressure—and use as a raft on the water or couch on land.
>
> We ferried our food and my camera across the lake to the rocks on this mattress. I pushed it carefully along swimming with the other hand, while she circled around keeping a sharp watch for submarines & enemy aircraft. Later it was our bed on the other side.

Jean must have been concerned about my relationship with Jenny, because in my next letter home I wrote that I was depressed trying to bring myself to the point of breaking off with her. "The fact is I don't really love her, and she should know this. It is unfair to string her along. She should forget me & start looking for a husband. What do you advise, Miss Chatfield?"

I must have done all right because a few weeks later I wrote again, "Don't worry about Jenny. She took it almost too well." Jean then wrote a fine letter concluding with some good advice, "Don't think that a pretty face hides a beautiful soul. When you find the right girl take her on a rainy canoe trip or something & find out." I felt rather silly having worried so much. With her it wasn't the real thing either.

Things had changed at Forty-two Stanley Avenue. It was still the social center, but the terrible news was that Margaret Ann Bjornson was leaving for Ontario to get married, and the boys were losing "the floor under their feet & the roof over their heads." Grierson, who always discouraged marriages involving his staff, berated her for "taking the easy way to achieve maturity: in bed with a man instead of working hard at a job & making herself a name." She left while I was there, amid alcohol and tears and a great crowd of sad young men kissing her good-bye at the station.

At the Film Board I found there had been changes too. Grierson was operating in the upper levels of government, working closely with MacKenzie King, of whom he said, "He's the greatest secret radical in Canada."

Grierson and Legg were full of plans to get me back to Canada, but nothing very practical. It was agreed it would be hard to get me out of the U.S. Army and into Canada. After visiting Canada, I was impressed with the low morale of troops in the United States. I decided to try to organize a program in which outstanding and independent speakers such as William Shirer, Dorothy Thompson and John Gunther would visit the camps and talk on subjects aimed at providing answers to our paramount question, "Why are we here?" with something more substantive than "because you drew a low draft number."

It would be in the "Town Meeting of the Air" format, with open discussion and bull sessions in the barracks. We insisted that only enlisted men would run the show, although officers would be invited to attend since they needed some answers, too. Our idea died aborning. Before we could do anything we had to have a signature from a general even to hold meetings, and to reach the general we would have to go through a chain of command—all officers.

We settled back to doing what we had been doing with some adjustments, waiting for something to happen. The golf clubs had arrived, but most of them mother sent turned out to be women's clubs I'd never seen before. I didn't complain but wrote "They will do. I will need 5 and 6 irons, which are missing."

There was not much time for golf, since GI discipline had come to the Film Unit—beds made just so; march to work on time; fatigue details. I continued working on Project 176, a training film on *Basic Tank Driving*, but it seemed endless. I had a long talk with Lieutenant LePore who was in charge. He told me something I already knew, that I was in the wrong place for the films I wanted to make.

I spent some time in New York City with Jean's old beau, Steve Partridge, a

reporter who had tried to help me when I first got to New York, but in the past
year had lost his job and been drinking heavily. He had written mother and she
had sent his letter on to me:

"It is not possible to tell you the ordeal I have been going through. I fight on,
hope on. I would so much like to justify your goodness to me through the years.
Sometimes I look at Mars, Saturn and Jupiter in a straight line (almost straight) and
around 11 o'clock Orion is in the Southeast. I blow you a kiss on them all and each.
I cannot see far ahead. Any day could turn darkness into light for me. Will it?"

Christmas came and went over a long weekend. I caught an airplane ride at
Mitchell Field to get to Montgomery. I only had a few days, but it gave me time to
tell Jean about the conversations in Canada, and some of the wild ideas to get me
back to the Film Board. I told her that Grierson would be coming to Montgomery
with Mrs. Grierson, on his way to New Orleans and the west coast, and that I had
invited them to stay at Hazel Hedge.

My train trip back to Fort Monmouth after Christmas was made interesting
by an encounter with a former North Carolina friend who was going to Africa to
work out details for sending American warplanes to the British for delivery on the
Libyan front. I missed the stop at Newark, but got a bus to Red Bank. I was in time
to warm over the doves I had brought for my dinner, and deliver a jar of Jeanie's
artichoke pickles to my Lieutenant, who had expressed a fondness for them.

I saw Margaret Legg and Spottiswoode in New York and heard that the Griersons
were en route to California via Montgomery. He was going to Hollywood to try
to get more U.S. distribution of Canadian films. One of Legg's films was already
playing on Broadway, but he was told that he had to tone down the commentary
because it was too hostile to Japan, intimating that Japan might attack certain U.S.
possessions, specifically Hawaii and the Philippines. This was of course before Pearl
Harbor.

In January Grierson arrived in Montgomery and stayed at Hazel Hedge, where
he and Jeanie addressed the problem of getting me from the U.S. Army to the
Canadian Film Board. J.G. asked her if she knew any Generals and when she said
"No, I only know a colonel," but added "He is good friend of the assistant secretary
of war," Grierson said, "That will do."

I had kept my hopes pinned down because I don't believe in getting them
knocked down. I was building up my body in daily workouts with Gil Scott at the
YMCA, with a view to transferring to the Air Corps if all else failed.

While waiting, I saw the last of New York I would see for awhile. I went to the Village Vanguard with Stoney, who wanted to hear Leadbelly, an old Negro well known for his prison and work songs. George told me the origin of one of the songs, "It's a Bushwah town." It seems that two white people took Leadbelly and his wife to Washington, D.C., where they had great difficulty finding a place that would serve food to both white and colored, and the white woman had exclaimed: "Washington is such a bourgeois town." Leadbelly wanted to know what that meant and made up the song "It's a Bushwah Town," with a last line, "It's the home of the brave, the land of the free, I don't want to be stepped on by no bushwahzee."

Some of my hours off were spent nearby at the ancestral estate of a general, on the south side of the North Shrewsbury. His daughter-in-law, Mariedna, told me that before he retired from the Army he used to fly to work in New York every day in a green amphibian plane and fly back to play polo. On one occasion he landed next to the polo field, and went almost literally from plane to horse.

After one delightful evening there I was asked back the next day to explain to the children (two boys aged eight and ten) about the sex or sexlessness of mules—a subject I had covered in general the night before. When I arrived, the youngsters were vainly trying to hitch Buella, a horse, to an ancient carriage, presumably to get her to a donkey for mating purposes. Buella must have had other plans for she calmly sat down in the shafts.

When the official ratings were about to come through at Monmouth, I reported home that I thought I would make staff sergeant, which would pay seventy-two dollars a month, as compared to being a corporal at sixty, but even that would be twice as much as I made as a private. However, before anything could happen to my rank, I was abruptly transferred to Canada.

This happened on January 31, 1942, by authority of an AG War Department letter, signed by the Commanding Officer of the 15th Signal Service Regiment, which transferred me to the Enlisted Reserve Corps, where I would be assigned to work with the National Film Board of Canada, starting February 11.

Sheila wrote mother, "I never saw anyone so on top of the world and wild with joy over his transfer. He was just crazy happy. Indeed he has been so this whole week." It was fortuitous that I had already planned a party and written Dad, "Do you have a hunt planned? Do you think you could send up doves for 14 people? What are the hazards of such a large shipment? Is the dry ice method too expensive?"

According to my letter home,

The party was grand, and the birds were magnificent, simply wonderful. Everyone raved about them and ate two apiece. I had suggested wild rice mixed with plain, which is the way Sheila fixes it, and we had that and orange salad with alligator pear but only lettuce instead of romaine, and green peas and hot rolls, very fine ice cream and a birthday cake. [It was the birthday of two of the guests, Jules Buckens and Nelson Schraeder.]

I bought three bottles of good American red wine I got at Sherry's—a Schoonmaker on the Pape Noir order. We used two of them and gave the extra one to the Van Tynes, where we held the party. They had retired upstairs when it was underway, and when I discovered their supper was a few sandwiches, I fixed a nice tray with birds, etc. and took it to them. They were awfully appreciative. And how they do like the chutney you sent them!

Once again let me praise the doves, Dad for getting them and you, Jean, for sending them.

42

A Beginning and an End

WHEN I GOT BACK TO CANADA EARLY IN 1942, AS A CORPORAL IN THE U.S. Army, I found that much had changed at the Canadian Film Board, as well as at Forty-two Stanley Avenue. There had been a life and death struggle between Film Commissioner Grierson of the Film Board and Frank Badgley, who headed the original Canadian Government Motion Picture Bureau in the Federal Ministry of Trade and Commerce.

Grierson argued that with Canada at war and the far greater need for information and propaganda films geared to a full realization of a good life everywhere in the world, bureaucracy should not be allowed to block the way. "We need creative freedom in place of the Civil Service red tape that binds the Bureau to a film and a half a year, as compared to the forty films that we at the Film Board made in our first year of existence." He recommended that the Bureau be placed under the Film Board, and when this did not happen, he resigned.

Too many people had been exposed to the new films—and to Grierson—to let this occur. "Why Lose a Genius?" headlined the *Winnipeg Free Press*. Even in Quebec, where French Canadians are reluctant to support programs engineered by the British government, there was appreciation for the many films he had made in the French language. Few had been done before. The prime minister supported him, and after a year's grueling fight, Parliament voted in favor of his recommendation to put the Film Board on top.

At Forty-two Stanley Avenue, after Margaret Ann Bjornson of Winnipeg left to get married, Mary Elizabeth "Bunty" Butters arrived. She had come to Ottawa from Vancouver with Roger Barlow, a cameraman working for the Board. When he went to the States to make a documentary on a Negro farm family, she took the room recently vacated by Don Fraser, who had been sent to Halifax to direct a film on the *Canadian Navy*. The "navy" was an overstatement. Actually, these were the freighters that transported armaments and other supplies to war-torn Britain.

When I came back, there was "no room at the inn" for me at Stanley Avenue, and I was invited to move into the Roxborough flat of an older friend, Maurice ("Windy") Wiseman, whom I had come to know during my earlier stay in Canada. He was the trade commissioner, a rather distinguished man who traveled in the best circles, and who had become interested in the use of documentary films to encourage trade. He had never married, due to extensive injuries he incurred in World War I, and he befriended many of us young people at the Board.

My mother had met Windy on an early trip to Canada, and was delighted that he would "take me under his wing," as it were. She felt he would contribute much to my cultural life—and be a restraint on my partying. "I wish you'd rest more, I don't mean work less, but when work is over go to bed & go to sleep, and don't drink too much." Windy didn't try to restrain me, and wrote mother that I was no bother, being there only "from some hour after midnight until after he had left in the morning."

From the moment I alighted from the train in Ottawa, I ignored Jean's advice and joined friends on the ski slopes, on the way to a long stopover at Chez Henri in Hull for hot buttered rums (the wonderful powers of this drink cannot be exaggerated), then a short stop at Windy's to change clothes for a big party at Forty-two Stanley. Everybody was there and in honor of me they served Craik punch, and we emptied the bowl several times.

Grierson was in top form, and Margaret Ann was there with her new husband, Alan Adamson, Grierson's administrative assistant. They brought seventeen-year old Gordon Weisenborn, who had just arrived from Chicago on a two-year internship at the invitation of Grierson, who knew and much admired his father, a well-known painter. Jim Wright came with Lady Diana Gordon-Lennox wearing her monocle. Weekdays she graced the office of High Commissioner Malcolm Macdonald (Ramsey's son), and in off hours taught him how to ski.

I met the new resident at Forty-two Stanley, "Bunty," whom I described in a letter home as "quite captivating. Nothing serious, but diverting. She, I might say, went for me, but I suspect she goes for anything in pants." I had taken my old girl Jenny to the party and we left before midnight, lured out by a big moon. I got back to Roxborough about 4 a.m. and Jenny roused me at ten to go to skiing. We met several of the others from Stanley Avenue on the slopes.

That afternoon I gave a spectacular skiing performance, which I described in a letter home:

> I paid $5 to take the tow up the hill. The rope gives you a terrific jerk and should you lose your balance and persist in hanging on, it will just take part of you up leaving the rest of your body along the way. I arrived at what must be the top of the world in one piece, but I wasn't sure whether I was whole when I got to the bottom. In one fall I went forward over my skis (the sign of a good skier they say) and then did a complete somersault, sliding half way down the mountain on my back with my head down hill.
>
> That evening I had only enough strength to lay on the broken-down sofa at 42 Stanley with Bunty, listening to music on the phonograph, and I began to be as taken with her as she had been with me.

Ten days later I wrote mother,

> I have been a poor correspondent due to my working hours and playing hours, which combine to leave little time for anything else.
>
> I am physically exhausted though in good health, and in love, a perennial state with me, as thou knowest. The object of my adoration is none other than the homely but utterly bewitching Miss Butters. She has touched my heart. Some might say I wear it on my sleeve and it therefore is in easy reach of many, but no matter, it is now in her possession and I have hers in return.

Jean answered, "I wasn't surprised to hear that you were in love. I'm glad it isn't Jenny again & I do hope Miss Butters is nicer. If she is really 'bewitching' that's enough—but I greatly doubt it. Don't go too far until you are sure & then go as far as you like."

My first assignment after coming back to the Film Board was to work on *Timber Front*, a film I had scripted when I first went there on my Rockefeller Fellowship. I was also to redo the shooting on *Army Cadets*, which Grierson had found so objectionable in 1940. This time he wasn't around to criticize. In fact, he was very ill. His year-long battle with the Bureau had taken its toll.

I visited him in his room. He made me pour him a small drink. He looked like death, but his voice poured out, eloquent as ever. He upbraided me for not seizing the greatest opportunity ever offered to a young man. "Stop being a lance corporal. You ought to be a general," he thundered. "I have worked a miracle up here. You have the whole United States. When the war is over, go back to the States and do the same thing. Start in the South. I will come down and help you."

He sank back into the bed holding his pounding heart. Gosh, he was terrific, but pretty sick. The doctors told him he had to stop working for awhile and take a rest. He and Margaret went to Fort Lauderdale in Florida for several months. He has indeed worked miracles in Canada. He smote the rock and made the water flow forth. I prayed that God would grant him the power to smite again.

I went west to an Army training camp at Banff in the Canadian Rockies to re-shoot the Cadet film (later called *100,000 Cadets*). I arrived at the end of April on my twenty-sixth birthday. I wrote Dad:

> The weather is perfect, so warm that we swam out of doors at the upper hot springs and sunbathed at the foot of a snow-covered mountain. I wish you could see the golf course. It isn't green yet, but even in the winter the fairways are beautifully kept. A large black bear was sunning himself plunk in the middle of one.
>
> The Army people here have been grand to me. Each day they put hundreds of men through exercises and maneuvers for us to watch. Today I fired a Bren gun and a tommy gun on the range. The Bren is a light machine gun and a lovely weapon. The officers have all risen from the ranks. They are the finest group of army men I've ever met. The boys here are learning to be real soldiers, tough, disciplined and self-reliant.

Legg liked our filmed rushes and decided to expand them into a segment for the *Canada Carries On* series. For this we had to do some extra shooting in the mountains and of the Civilian Defense Corps in Calgary. Between assignments I saw Bunty intensely, reporting to Jean that "We have a good time together. She is a fine girl and we are in love."

Almost immediately I was assigned to my next film, on the Canadian postal service, where I was to work with a new friend, Ted Scythes. We were to be under the direction of an old friend, Julian Roffman, who had come back to Canada from the New York City film lab, where I first met him when I was at Monmouth. As was usual in those days when everyone in the team shared in every stage of the work, and because we were not competitive but cooperative, the credits on the film when it finally emerged as *Canadian Mail* were "Directors/Camera: Julian Roffman, Nicholas Read & E.W. Scythes."

Much of the P.O. film was to be shot in the Canadian wilderness, where settlements were entirely dependent on planes for mail as well as other supplies during the seven months of winter. In my next letter I described our first trip out:

We started from Quebec City, and flew on to Rimouski, about 350 miles down the St. Lawrence, a town where the snow was piled 15 feet high on either side of the road and many of the cars were equipped with skis in front and rubber treads in the rear. We transferred to a plane with skis instead of wheels to get us to our final destination, Baie Comeau.

Our pilot, Bud Jones, who looked like some young airman out of "Captains of the Clouds," carried an assortment of passengers, freight & mail to a score of snow patches cleared in the forests. He squeezed his Dragon Rapide down between the rocks & pines, to unload trappers, lumberjacks, canned goods, whiskey, gasoline, sides of meat—and mail bags. Where there was no landing strip, he slid the mail bags out through a hatch in the floor of the plane to land on a cleared place in the snow.

In some places hills over 1000 feet high hemmed in the village, and air currents tossed the plane about like a cork on the waves. It's too dangerous to fly low but the bush pilots have an accurate eye and the mail sack usually lands near red flags stuck up in the snow. They have nothing but contempt for the young bombardiers target practicing a few miles down the river; "They'd never find the mail if we dropped it the way they drop their bombs."

Baie Comeau is a company town of 2000, mostly French Canadians working for a big new paper mill owned by the *Chicago Tribune*. They don't share Mr. McCormick's political views, but do point with pride to the $150,000 Catholic Church, community house with bowling alleys and squash courts, skating rink, dance floor, and movie theater—all provided by the Chicago publisher. Eight years ago there was nothing here but bushwhacker's cabins, and the mail came in by dog sled.

Today it's a town with city lights, a drug store and even a taxi service. The workers get good wages, and buy their model homes on the installment plan. Their children go to French or English schools, and are treated at a well-equipped hospital. What's the catch? Why all this paternalism? Exploitation? My hunch, based on a few conversations, is that these people would prefer the smell & filth of Quebec's narrow streets to Comeau's isolation. The plane is the only way out.

This morning I went through the blinding flakes of a big snowstorm to Easter communion at the little Anglican Church.

A handful of people sang "Hallelujah—Christ the Lord is Risen Today." Countless hangovers from last night's Paper Makers' Ball put real fervor into the confessions at both churches. All agreed that the rum punch was poison even for paper makers. The waiters had got drunk with everyone else and there were five fights. Blow the lid off on Saturday night—that's the escape.

Jean replied, reminding me that last Easter I had been at Hazel Hedge, but said she was glad I was in Quebec and not in Australia or Burma. "I thought of you all day. It's hard to say 'Christ is risen'; this Easter we might add that he died in vain. Your old English friend Tom Evans has been captured by the Japanese in Singapore, and is in a prison camp—if he's alive. Bob Hellendale is at Angel Island in San Francisco waiting to embark for Australia. Thank heavens Morris Baldwin is home on leave before shipping out—Marion Oates just might change her mind and marry him, he looks so swell in his Navy uniform."

In Montgomery, Jean continued her work with British War Relief, and home-away-from-home activities for the English flyboys at Maxwell Air Base. "Two of them are here with me on the Terrace. It is Mother's Day. Mac is reading in the hammock with a glass of iced tea in his hand. He tells me that it is the ice he misses most when he goes back to London. Kirke is writing his mother, telling her of the remarkable American phenomenon of Mother's Day."

I was back in Ottawa, working on the Army film. All the shooting was done, also the cutting, and the commentary, and I was impatient to get it out of the way. "Nuts, nuts, nuts! How did I ever get into this business. I've just discovered that the lab failed to print the edge numbers on the two thousand feet of sync sound track I have to match with the picture. Six hours extra work right now and more headaches later."

I looked forward to summer, and urged Jean and Nash to come up and visit me when the heat got too unbearable in Montgomery. Jean wrote that she didn't have time to even think at the moment—what with her war work and the house and cottages, and taking care of in-town obligations and out-of-town guests, and her new poodle, Baa. "I am crazy about her. She is a perfect lamb, so affectionate

& sweet & so comical and clownish—but I can't seem to house train her."

Sheila and Jill visited Hazel Hedge for a week, and after that there was a round of obligations for Jean. "At Mrs. Saffold's request I did the flowers for the Whiting-Tunis debut. They were really lovely, but I was too tired to go to the party. I hate big mobs like that anyway, so I stayed home and painted the kitchen cabinet."

Her next letters were about guests:

> Tom Hibben is arriving at Tuskegee to use the clay soil to make bricks for a new housing project there. I wonder if he will bring Carmella & the boy & Ernestine Evans with him. E. E. is really a member of their household now. Mr. Campbell of Tuskegee has been here to see *Casa de Vaca* [one of the rental cottages, converted by Jean from an old barn]. It is exactly the type of house he wants Tom to build, sun & air & flat on the ground where pigs & chickens & goats can't get under it. He has asked for my plans & specifications.
>
> Michael Straight, who took leave as Editor of *The New Republic* to take a pre-flight course at Maxwell Field, came for breakfast along with his friend Chaplain Chase. Afterwards, I took them to Martingale to a negro baptizing in the creek. The candidates were rather young & didn't get happy, but some sisters on the bank did. I've seen much better, but it was impressive & good. The Chaplain, who is from Boston, took it all much too much like Harriet Beecher Stowe, but Michael enjoyed it immensely, and we had a superb picnic under a magnolia tree.
>
> I had a lunch last week for Nancy Smith's sister-in-law Gert from the mountains of "Tinissee," who was much impressed with my "exotic" food—curry & Indian Pandarins & Monte Bianca in home-made meringue shells . . . and a high tea for Marion Oates who brought Sir Lindsay Hoag, in command of Napier Field at Dothan [Alabama]. He's awfully nice and raved over the house, which was a mass of flowers—pear boughs to the ceiling.

Jean did all the cooking and the flower arrangements, which were integral to each gathering. Ben Miller was her only helper most of the time. They had been working together since Ben came to Hazel Hedge when he was sixteen years old. He was there in the good times when there were plenty of servants, and went through the Depression when he was almost alone except for Joe Lee, the gardener.

By northern standards, even before the war, Negroes weren't paid much in Montgomery. Ben was getting nine dollars a week, with a room above the garage, and his meals. Joe Lee got a little more money, but only his noon meal. The defense industries up North were offering better jobs at higher pay. Joe left early in 1942 to move to Washington, D.C.

Jean wrote me: "Mr. Joe Lee has left. He's been here so long and I am so dependent on him it's like having the big elm go. Gosh how I miss him. Of course the garden will go to pieces. And now Ben Miller is behaving unpleasantly—I think it's because Joe's getting $85 and Ben is supposed to take on some of his old yard work. He does as little as he can. He cuts the front lawn & that's about all. In fact he isn't doing much inside work at all."

Her loss of Joe and her trouble with Ben was coupled with my news about Grierson resigning from the Film Board. She wrote "I am utterly devastated at the news of John Grierson. How simply awful—worse than Churchill dying. I take it much harder than 'Mr. Joe' leaving me."

When I answered her letter, I said that "A small matter that has been worrying me is Ben's salary. It is none of my business, but I can't help mentioning it. While Ben undoubtedly is not worth in actual work-value more than $9 a week, he is worth a lot more for intangible reasons. With the lure of better salaries up North, he is likely to be drawn away from you. I would hate to see this happen. If it is not too hard on you economically, I suggest you pay him a bit more."

Ben mowing the lawn.

Jean replied that she had already raised Ben's salary to twelve dollars a week.

Not that he is worth it—but everyone is losing their butler boys. Sister Bess's has gone. People who have had the same ones for 40 years. Ben has figured out how many hours of pay at 40 cents an hour he would have to work. He doesn't count the time he takes for his meals (nor his house, gas, heat, hot water and lights) but I can't get anyone else. I had a boy help rake leaves & haul manure at $2 a day. He wasn't worth 50 cents.

Ben's raise hasn't helped much. He is still sullen and disagreeable, never speaking to me—or grunting when I say good morning, insolent too, and lazy. If he's going to quit I wish he'd go on & do it, though I know I can't get along without him.

She didn't say anything more about Ben for a few weeks, and then she wrote:

I wouldn't write you about this if it hadn't turned out alright. Georgia and Philip Gossler are in Montgomery to do over "Belvoir," since the old family portraits don't fit with Philip's new art. I asked them to dinner with Dr. & Mrs. Hubbard. Ben was to come at 7:00, and he came after 8. I had crushed the ice & taken out the drinks, and of course set the table & cleaned the silver, gotten out the good china. When he got there, Callie spoke to him and he didn't even answer. She said to me, "What's happened to Ben? He isn't the same as he used to be."

For dinner we had a great aspic of chicken—with pieces of white meat, and deviled eggs and artichoke hearts. Almost half the aspic mould was left over, and I asked him to put it away, saying "Ben, I've helped your plate (I gave him the dark meat and a lettuce and tomato salad.) Put the rest up, it will last me a week." Instead, he left his plate and ate the aspic.

The next morning when he brought my tea I said I wanted to talk to him. "You aren't happy in your work. You don't care anything about me any more. Do you want to go where you can get what you all call big money?" I got no further when he picked up the tray and stormed out of the room, talking hysterically, "Alright I'll go, if you want to git rid of me."

I followed him downstairs & he was still talking & refused to listen. I said that "I wouldn't have just spent $50 on a new roof for your room if I wanted you to leave, but you aren't the same Ben any more, & you aren't interested in me." Ben said, "Then we're even and you don't care nothin about me neither." I told him I certainly did, but I'd rather he'd go than be as unpleasant as he's been for the last 2 months—that the only life I had was in this house & if it couldn't be happier I wouldn't stay myself.

He changed overnight. It was like the old days. You can't imagine what a relief & pleasure I felt. Ben said "Good mornin," and "Yes Maam" & "Sure will" in place of a sullen silence. He still doesn't give me any of his ration coupons, though I feed him two meals a day. And last Sunday, the day Gussie comes, there was no Crisco so she made biscuits using my precious butter. There was plenty of bread for toast but she said, "Ben don't like toast. He like biscuits." And when I got some liver for their breakfast Ben complained, "There ain't no fat." I said, "Here's 50 cents. You can go & buy fat but I have no ration points."

I couldn't ask the Gardeners to Sunday breakfast as I had no butter, no lard for rolls, no bacon. Butter has gone to 16 points a pound so I never expect to see a piece. I might add that Gussie won't give me any of her points either, and she eats a lot though she only comes part-time. And she has an advantage over me—pig's feet & mullet aren't rationed! However, she is leaving for Detroit and I am not sad.

In fact, this letter is really to reassure you about Ben. He is still as sweet as a lamb on a May morning. It's a blessed thing too. This is the hottest it has ever been this early in the summer. Over 100 degrees every day, 97 at 7 a.m. I hop in and out of the pool all day, dropping my clothes at the side. I just tell Ben to look the other way.

From left to right: best man Maurice "Windy" Wiseman, Nash, Jean, Jill Hibben Hellendale, Nick, and Bunty.

I wasn't sure whether it was Ben's pay or the ration points that had come between them, but urged Jean to keep the peace at any price: "You'll never be able to reform Ben, but neither will you be able to replace him. Ben is worth more than his work on the place. His very presence has a high value and I would not risk losing him."

Again I asked her to come with Dad to Canada, not only to get out of the heat, but to see me. When I wrote this I didn't think I was asking them to my wedding, but that's the way it turned out. Everything happened very suddenly, probably because there was some free time between the finish of one film and the beginning of another. My friends at Stanley Avenue made all the arrangements. Bunty and I were married July 18, 1942, at St. John's Anglican Church in Ottawa.

Mother had no time to protest. Only Grierson, who always tried to keep his staff from getting married, asked Margaret Ann to try to persuade me not to do it. She replied, "It's too late. I'm already making thin cucumber sandwiches." At the wedding, Dada was darling to Bunty. Jean said later that she put cotton in her ears to blot out the ceremony.

We had planned a honeymoon in New York, while Jean was going to visit friends in Maine. My father returned on the train to Montgomery. He had a heart attack en route, and died soon afterwards.

43

Picking Up the Pieces

Nash Read was seventy years old when he died. The funeral was at Hazel Hedge, the burial at Oakwood Cemetery. There was an editorial in *The Montgomery Advertiser*:

> Nash Read had a zest for living, and to him life meant ties with a circle of family and friends which centered at Hazel Hedge.
>
> There was so much living to be done that he never got around to the irksome task of accumulating enmities or hatreds; nor was there time for pushing or shoving his fellow-man around. There was genuine warmth in his greeting, and he knew how to give or sacrifice without the impression of doing either. That is about as sound a measure of living as has yet been devised.

Jean did what needed to be done at such times. She made all the arrangements for the service and selected a thin slab of marble for the tombstone, which would fit in with the old tombstones in the Baldwin lot. She took care of the will, with guidance from CPA Robert Troy, and the inheritance taxes "after going through piles and piles of papers to find canceled checks that would verify what I had paid for years back to build the cottages."

She moved from the big "pink room" upstairs with its many windows and a fireplace, its ceiling-high four poster bed and an antique secretary topped by a bookcase with glass doors, and a comfortable lounge chair beside a tea table, to the modest "blue room" down the hall. She felt it was large enough to take care of her personal needs. There was a "sleigh" bed and bedside marble table, a lamp for reading, a dressing table with mirrors, and a chest of drawers and an armoire for clothes—there being no closets. She also kept at hand the Martha Washington sewing table used by her mother.

The down side, according to Jean, was the bathroom. "The pipes were put together with zinc, which had tin in it & there won't be any until the war is over. It means tearing up the bathroom floor & doing it all over, but that's better than not being able to use the bathroom. I can't get the furnace chimney fixed either. It fell in a tornado before Nash died & I can't find out who has our tornado insurance—but I can't get a brick mason anyhow. I'll just have to make do with a carpenter to patch up the holes."

Soon after Nash's death and Jean's return from Canada, two more deaths "in the family" occurred. One was Morris Baldwin, listed as "missing in action" after his cruiser was torpedoed not far from Guadal Canal in the South Pacific. All the Baldwins were distraught, and his mother, Kate, was inconsolable. Jean spent some time with her, saying "She just weeps and weeps and weeps."

The other was "Aunt Sally," an old colored woman who had been coming to Hazel Hedge since before I was born. She was one hundred years old, and from the time I was a little boy she would come every week to pray with my grandmother. When she died, William Baldwin gave money and paid for the vault, and had his men make a road to the old plantation burying plot. One of our friends sent a blanket of dahlias.

When they got there for the funeral at 3:30, it had already been held, according to Mother,

by her uppity grandchildren from Detroit & Chicago who resented her being a white folks' darky. Well, she was if ever there was one, and she would have wanted us there.

God, we've got trouble. Marie Wells' cook came in the other day & said "Somebody's taken a $10 bill out of my purse," and when Marie was sympathetic, [the cook] said, "Nobody's been in this house but you." Of course it's what all white people say & she turned the tables. Marie asked her who told her to say that & she admitted it was her "club."

At Nash's funeral, Jean noted that the Baldwin lot at Oakwood was in need of attention, but it was fall before she could get to it and spring before she finished. The soil was hard and dry. She hired a yard man at two dollars a day to help with

Nick and
Aunt Sally.

the digging. "We started by taking off the old gate to the cast iron fence that surrounded the lot, and trimming dead branches off the magnolia tree & the bushes. Then we dug up the dead plants and tackled the weeds, and put in winter grass. It was hard work. I wonder when I will get it through my head that I am not a young woman?"

In the spring, Ben helped plant beds of iris & narcissus & pansies, and lots of English daisies—

> they were only a penny a plant at the Farm Market. When it rained, Ben stayed right with me, and we had some nice talks. He told me his dream about the "Boss" being back home sleeping in 4 beds—not all at one time—but moving from one to the other. Ben never knew where to find him. I, too, had the most real & vivid dream about Nash coming back. He looked exactly right, in his brown-checked worsted suit with his arms stretched out when he saw me.
>
> Nash had been so little trouble & amused himself so much that it's amazing what a terrible void there is without him. I just can't sit in Mama's room at night with his empty chair. I miss him for breakfast, & planting & raking the leaves & picking up pecans—not that he ever did much of it, but he always stood around & bossed. I never dreamed I was going to miss him so terribly, nor that he had become such warp & woof of my life.

Her friends rallied around, but most especially she appreciated the attentions of her flyboys, some of whom literally dropped in from the sky onto the tarmac when they were in the vicinity. She wrote that George and Ray had called her every day from Decatur after Nash died and soon after "George had brought his twin-engine bomber down in Montgomery on his way to Mississippi," by putting his radio out of commission and landing presumably to have it fixed—but really to see her. "He came out about 7:30. I knew the first thing he'd want was a mint julep. I had it ready."

Ray arrived unexpectedly en route to Craig Field for Advance Training, and Mcleod came all the way over from Moultrie, Georgia, the other side of Thomasville. Mac gave her "the most exquisite little gold wrist watch" when he went overseas. "I hope that Ralph gets up this weekend, the last before he leaves for England. I'll never see him again of course, & I really love Ralph."

He arrived on Saturday about six o'clock just for the night, to say goodbye, "He has been wonderfully sweet to me—and his little visits have been something to look forward to. I will miss him terribly. But with food rationing it will be harder to entertain my boys, although if they are not too hungry I can always make do with onion soup. But liquor is going up 50 cents a bottle and limited to two quarts."

On one occasion she took in a young Air Force Captain and his wife who had no place to stay before he headed out for India, under the command of Brig. Gen. Robert Oliver of Montgomery. It was "Bob" Oliver's job to muster supplies, men and equipment to maintain all the U.S. Air Forces in China, India and Burma, against the time when the big movement would start against Japan. She drove them to Maxwell Field and saw the take-off and described it in a letter to me.

> They went in one of those unbelievable transport planes—4 motors & tires bigger than the biggest truck & 2 great tanks of gas as large as those you see on freight trains. There were 2 crews and 6 civilian pilots. The instrument board was the most amazing thing—thousands of buttons and dials. It looked like a kaleidoscope.
>
> The plane was packed with men and supplies going to our Army outposts—doctors and medicines, and things for the soldiers from their families including boxer shorts, homemade cakes and candy, and a case of Scotch whisky. In four days the plane will be landing in Delhi. It was very thrilling to see that monster rise into the air and take off direct for India.

In a later letter she reported that the plane had come down in a swamp in British Guiana, but no one was hurt & they even got out all the luggage and freight. She didn't say whether the Scotch whisky made it.

Like every widow, Jean took on a lot of things that Nash used to do, such as getting new license plates for the car. "I had to stand in line for hours at the Office of Price Administration to get the new number put in my gas ration book. But after I saw how much gas it took to run that plane going to India, I don't see why they give us any gasoline at all."

She had her own problems with the Office of Price Administration when they notified her that she had charged sixty dollars a month rent although the maximum rent was fixed at fifty dollars. "We do not want to prejudge the issue, but if you are violating Maximum Rent Regulation No. 53, you are subject to civil action, including a suit for damages brought by your tenant, and also to criminal prosecution. Please contact Mr. Lamar Quailes of this office." Jean contacted Mr. Quailes, and no action was taken.

Jean wrote me that Montgomery had gone bicycle crazy, and that Gould and Mary Beech had sold their car, and wanted to buy my bicycle, which was still in the garage. She took her own car on a final out-of-town trip, before gas rationing, to Anniston, Alabama for a nostalgic visit with the Kilbys.

"Everything was the same as before. The weather was perfect, and the food delicious. Only Nash wasn't there sending Bedford back and forth to the kitchen for everything Bedford suggested. 'We didn't know if you'd like oatmeal' & Bedford would go & come back & say 'We didn't know whether you'd like batter cakes or not' and then go again.'"

In Montgomery she gave a wedding reception for "Petunia" and Chip, whose Connecticut mother had warned him, when he first came down for training at Maxwell Field, not to fall in love with any "little southern flower." The story got around and Southern manners being what they are, everyone who met his mother at the wedding, didn't call her "Petunia," but used her real name, "Mary Gayle."

A more intimate ceremony was held in October, when Jeanie opened two bottles of Pinot Noir, and with some old friends stood under Nash's portrait in the dining room and toasted him on their twenty-ninth wedding anniversary.

Up in Canada, I was busy. The pace of film production for the war effort had accelerated after the Dieppe raid on the French coast, where many Canadians were killed or captured. People had been hoping for and expecting victory. Late that night, Grierson, listening on a small, high-powered radio to a German account of victory in the battle, was convinced that it didn't sound like Nazi propaganda, and telephoned the editors of a couple of newspapers to forewarn them. He was right. Dieppe, for the Canadians, was a disaster.

The word soon got out that the Germans had manacled the captured soldiers and treated them like criminals. Within ten days Grierson produced a film to show how German prisoners were treated in Canada. The only print was made for the sole purpose of getting the pictorial footage to the Nazis. When the film was seen by the German officers, the Canadians were released from their chains.

On my return to Ottawa from my father's funeral, I found I was in great demand at the Film Board, and that my honeymoon with Bunty had to be postponed again. It was October before we got to New York City to use our reservations at the Barbizon Plaza Hotel "at $5.50 a night with a continental breakfast thrown in."

A paper carton containing coffee and a roll was indeed tossed at our door each morning, but it didn't take us long to find that the coffee wasn't hot and the rolls so hard they must have been recycled from the day before. We got our breakfast elsewhere and moved into a week of frenetic activity, starting off with a big party for Brannon Hubbard and Berry at the St. Regis, the night before their wedding at St. Thomas Episcopal Church on Fifth Avenue.

It was Bunty's first meeting with our family friends, and we were anxious that she make a good impression. She did, especially at the St. Regis reception. We both were a bit hung over the next day from the champagne, and possibly seeing the bride and groom through our own bloodshot eyes, agreed that though Berry was a pretty bride, the newlyweds looked a little tired. They went to Sea Island off the coast of Georgia. We hoped they got a rest.

In New York, Bunty and I divided our time between shows and people, with some shopping in between. Bunty bought herself a nice wool dress, and a little black feather hat and veil, and at a mill end shop on Thirty-fourth Street got forty-five dollars worth of material to take back to Canada for curtains and a sofa cover.

The plays we saw were: *Porgy and Bess*, *Angel Street*, and *By Jupiter*. The people were our relatives, the Rouses and the Hibbens, as well as all my Army friends from Fort Monmouth who had been transferred by the Signal Corps to film studios in Astoria, Queens on Long Island.

Bunty loved New York, and everyone was crazy about Bunty. She hit it off with our scientist cousin Peyton Rous, who took her to visit the Rockefeller Institute. He thought she had great capacities in the field of bacteriology, and if we lived in New York I'm sure would have gotten her a position there. We had lunch with the rest of the Rous family—his sisters, Marion the musician and Helen the artist, and Aunt Frances wearing her medals and badges and greeting us with a song.

In Astoria, where the Army had a wonderful plant with every facility Hollywood could provide, Bob Churchill was directing three all-sound training films with elaborate studio sets. This was quite a departure from the old days in the Film Unit at Fort Monmouth. We also saw Lt. Bill Bloom, who had gone to Officers Training School after New Jersey, but ended up with everyone else in Astoria. He advised me not to try the OTS route to active duty, that he had tried that route and in the end was assigned again to Fort Monmouth.

I met another old friend, Jules Bricken, for drinks in New York at Les Artistes, where the walls were covered with nude ladies by Howard Chandler Christie. I shall never see another magazine cover by him without visualizing the lady in the nude.

Jules had good news, just having got a contract to write the music for a show for Mr. Shubert. And "Mike" (Don Robertson), my tennis-playing, play-writing friend from the Film Unit, had rewritten his play and was assured it would be produced within the year.

He thought Bunty was wonderful, and said that if he had met her first, I would have had a lot of competition. I wrote mother, "Bunty has blossomed out. She has really changed a lot—for the better, and I'm more in love with her now than ever." Mother wrote that the Hubbards had come home enthusiastic, and that Dr. Hubbard and Ann especially had raved about her. "I'm as pleased as punch & smirk as if I'd made the match."

I had hoped we could stay for Jill's twenty-first birthday, the end of November, but I had to get back to Ottawa to go over the footage I had already shot for the army film, before being sent to British Columbia to finish it. It was high speed work all day and all night for the first three days, plus another week re-assembling and writing a shooting script. I had arranged to take Bunty west with me, since she is from Vancouver, and I wanted to meet her family. Jean offered to pay her way, but Windy beat her to it, buying her a round trip ticket as a wedding present.

We had a letter from Sheila reporting that the party given for Jill's birthday was a huge success.

> She was utterly, transfiguringly happy. It was a graduation and birthday all in one and she was completely drunk with joy. We had Kip and Polly, Susie [La Follette], Jill's friend Jack Goodman and a couple of others. The dinner was just about perfection, if I do say so. When we poured the Burgundy, Kip got up and made a toast to Jill.
>
> Susie asked her to respond, and she said she couldn't possibly make up anything, but could say some words she liked. She recited the whole of Marvell's "To a Coy Mistress," and said it so beautifully and movingly that I almost cried. They stayed until nearly two o'clock, which I think proved it was a good evening, and even after that Jack stayed on with Jill.

I did see Jill on a quick trip down to New York in December to take my cutting copies and title cards to the Cinefects Studio at 1600 Broadway to have the titles made and fitted in. Jill grows lovelier every year. Beside being intelligent and well-informed, she is so witty. At the Weyland Bar one night she told me the long and hilarious story of Gypsy Rose Lee's wedding. Came a pause in the tale and a sailor at the table next to ours leaned over and said, "Please go on. I can't wait to hear the end."

I saw Joe Sugarman, and my old girl from North Carolina, Ruthie Crowell, briefly. She hasn't changed much, but she and her husband, Woodie, have had a hard time. He hardly made enough to buy food as a radio announcer in Kingston, North Carolina. Later they moved to New Jersey where he made the great sum of twenty-five dollars a week. Now he is doing better at WQXR in New York, but may be drafted shortly and Ruthie doesn't want to go back to Newton with the baby. Mrs. Crowell has never recognized Woodie because he is Jewish.

I took a little time to go shopping for Bunty and got some material for our sofa. They didn't have more of the stuff Bunty wanted so I took a chance and selected an entirely different piece. She liked it, and when I got back to Ottawa, she measured and pinned it to the sofa. I scraped and varnished a dining room table she had bought at a junk shop for seventy-five dollars. And the evening before we left, we tried out a new stove by making biscuits.

We got to the train so late we found ourselves on a troop train filled with RAF boys headed for the Pacific. The proximity of those young airmen, on their way to protect our ships from Japanese kamikaze and other attacks, had a sobering effect on me. I thought about my minuscule contribution to the war effort, and how little I was doing when young men of my age were risking their very lives. I decided that I must exert the utmost effort and achieve highest efficiency to justify my work as a civilian, and as soon as possible find some way to transfer to active duty.

The war news from Africa was encouraging when we left, and by the time we got to British Columbia there was good news from the Pacific. "If only Dad were alive to enjoy these glad tidings. I can hear him now denouncing or belittling 'those damn Japs.'"

We also had good news about the prospects for our filming. I had assumed there would be transportation problems, what with having to get the crew and equipment to and from far-out locations. However, the Army was ready with a big station wagon and gas. All we needed was good weather for outside shooting, but what we got, as usual on that coast, was rain.

However, it did give me time to spend with Bunty's family, most especially her 82-year old grandfather, Dr. Richardson, and her brother Tommy, recently made Lieutenant Butters, who lived at Campbell River on Vancouver Island. They took us on a lovely drive over the Malahat pass, where the scenery is exactly like the description one reads of Norway. Unfortunately, the afternoon was not sunny, but there was a beauty about the low-hanging clouds on the mountains not to be found on a clear day.

We stopped at an inn on the way back, where after dinner in front of a big fire, at our urging Dr. Richardson began to talk about some of his experiences. He is an obstetrician and runs a hospital where he works twelve to fourteen hours every day delivering babies, and "can't remember when I got as much as 6 hours sleep a night." He had taken time off to see Tommy graduate and meet us.

He has snow-white hair and a moustache, a ruddy face and blue eyes with a twinkle. He has a large girth but a very alert figure, and a warm deep voice. He reminisced about life in the Yukon during the gold rush, and the early days when the railroad was being pushed through the mountains. He recounted experiences in World War I, where he volunteered for service at the age of fifty. He served through the worst of the fighting, and was awarded the Order of the British Empire.

He was a wilderness man, and still fished and hunted game. He had his dog Buck, a retriever, with him. Buck brought in wood for the fire, and seemed to understand every word the doctor said. I kept thinking how much he had in common with Dad, except for how he felt about the Japanese. He was bitter about the internment of West Coast Japanese at the beginning of the war, having lost his valued Japanese help, who were also his good friends.

Since then he had lived alone with Buck. I suppose dogs get along better with him than women, because he and Bunty's grandmother had not spoken to each other for many years. Bunty's mother, and brother Dennis, a fisherman, also lived at Campbell River. She was very Anglophile, and served us high tea in thin cups with sliced cucumber sandwiches.

I hadn't realized that Bunty was an accomplished equestrian until her grandfather gave her a saddle as a wedding present. She did a lot of riding and some jumping while we were there. And we used part of Jean's Christmas present money to buy both of us riding habits. Bunty stayed at the Empress Hotel in Victoria when I went with the film crew, about thirty miles down *Juan de Fuca* Strait to Outer Point Camp at Looke, to shoot the film. Our headquarters were Harbour House at Whiffen Spit, a good place despite paper thin mattresses and a scarcity of hot water.

The weather wasn't particularly good, and when we finished, we returned directly to Vancouver to board the train for Ottawa. It wasn't long before we were snaking our way through Kicking Horse Pass in the Rockies. The sun came out and the glistening white peaks were beautiful beyond description. It was good to see snow again, but I was anxious to get back to the Film Board to look at the rushes and break down and cut about seven miles of film we had shot in the west. I enjoyed working on that picture more than any job I'd done so far.

In our absence, our landlord Des Roches had raised the rent from forty dollars to fifty dollars, and wanted four dollars a month for the garage we were not using, having put our car in Margaret Ann's garage for the winter after draining out the water and taking out the battery. We took our case to the Rent Control Board.

I worked with Julian Roffman and Ted Scythes on the film. Bunty was home learning to cook. I got her the *Boston Cookbook* and was on the track of one of Sheila's that was out of print. At my urging she was also doing a lot of reading. "She's got to learn about the South," I wrote Jean. She started with *Mind of the South* by Cash, pretty heavy going. Mother said it was about the wrong kind—"people as common as pig's tracks," and sent her *Lanterns on the Levee*, by Will Percy.

Bunty was excited to learn that we had pomegranates at Hazel Hedge, and was curious to see other bushes growing there—the Cherokee rose, a Chinaberry tree and an oleander. In the evenings we read, or saw friends, made our Christmas cards, and made love. We asked Jean for instructions on how to play pinochle and Russian Bank, but I don't remember ever playing them.

Ottawa was full of war talk and opinion, and I got a lot of both from my friends at the Board. I became concerned about U.S. diplomatic policy in Africa and our somewhat shady dealings with Darlan and other fascist collaborators. Jean wrote a furious letter, adding to her condemnation of Chamberlain the Archbishop of Canterbury.

In Montgomery, Jean enrolled in a nutrition course.

I don't think it can hurt me, as it would so many young inexperienced cooks, and it's the only way I will be allowed to work at the New Canteen at the R. R. Station for traveling soldiers. I am Teacher's Pet. Can you believe that? And I'm learning a great deal. Of course, the nutritionist knows nothing about cooking as we know it, but I am mastering vitamins and am taking my own diet more seriously.

I wonder whether nutritionists care about the taste of food? I don't believe they do. Her recipe for meat loaf was the exact one I use for Baa-baa & Mrs. Black [Jean's other dog.] However, my certificate says I am qualified to cook for those boys who sometimes come through the station in the middle of the night, and I shall outdo myself. I am always available, since there is nothing to hurry home for!

We tried again to get Jean to come to Canada for Christmas, but she refused, giving as her excuse:

> Baa will be coming into heat and there is no place to leave her. I wouldn't trust Ben. Negroes all think it's denying nature & dog's pleasures not to let them breed with any Spitz or cur that comes along.
>
> Also, I think you both should see my point-of-view about going to Canada. I just can't do it yet. It's all too fresh, all the regrets, the self-recrimination. I just can't. I keep myself well in hand, and have fought so hard against any kind of nervous collapse, but I can't expose myself to that trip, to the Lord Elgin Hotel and the people who were so good to us my last trip with Nash. You must come to me when you can and when you want to. I long to see you again.

While we were in the West, she had taken a trip to Mobile with her good friend Mary Webber, the social worker who had lived at Hazel Hedge for so long, but who would be leaving permanently soon. Mary had been offered the top position in her field in the state, but turned it down, saying she'd rather not have a lot of jealous men to deal with.

Jean noted it was the last chance for a trip before rationing began. They stayed at a new hotel across the causeway and bridge from Mobile, at Point Clear, which had been known only for its oysters before the hotel was built.

The new hotel was very fancy, built in the shape of a star, so that every room had a view of the water. Jean wrote: "It is beautifully kept with a lawn running right down to the beach, where I go swimming. However, the beach is not as smooth, nor the sand as white as it is at Mary Esther's on the gulf, where we usually go from Montgomery. Still it was good to get away, but lonely coming home to an empty house."

Her letter to me was heavily censored with words and sentences cut out, possibly because it was postmarked Mobile, a port city. She urged me to avoid writing on both sides, noting that her last letter from Mac in England was so full of holes she had a hard time figuring out that his squadron had won the King's Pennant in appreciation of their great record, and that the only thing missing from their celebration was ice for his drinks.

The house wasn't empty for long. Baa came home from the vet, and a little squirrel got into the kitchen for a short stay.

Pearl Harbor brought renewed activity by the British War Relief volunteers, who gave their weekly teas for Air Force trainees at Hazel Hedge. And as usual, there was a flow of old and new friends for meals.

Saturday night was all an accident. I had asked Loula & Willey to dinner, and Chips and Tunie came by for a drink. I had discovered that what I had thought was Scuppernong wine given me by Marianna Rushton was a gallon jug of corn liquor 1935, good old aged Game Cock Rye, and it was delicious. It blew your head right off. In half an hour we were all drunk as hoot owls, and a really grand dinner of crab gumbo & barbecued lamb was rather wasted.

About Christmas, you mustn't worry about me at all. I'll have some soldiers in, and the old cousins Alma and Mildred [Maxwell] who live so close can come for breakfast. I am really far happier here in this house than I would be anywhere else. I am sending you more shelled pecans and a plum pudding, and I'm sending one to Dr. Richardson, too.

Later she reported that since she had never met Dr. Richardson and he wasn't quite sure who she was, he had written to thank "Miss Hazel Hedge."

In Montgomery there was an unusual heat wave with temperatures in the 90s. In Ottawa it was 40 below zero when we received the letter and her presents, which included Christmas decorations as well as shad roe. We put the creche she had made from a gourd on the bookcase, and the little angels on either side of the gold edged soup tureen filled with holly.

On Christmas Eve, we went to a big party and had hangovers the next day which I "treated" with eggnogs made from a Four Roses recipe from a *New Yorker* ad. We opened our gifts, and Bunty put the turkey in the stove and we both went to sleep again. The turkey rolled over and basted itself until it was ready for us to take to a party that Beveridge was giving at Stanley Avenue.

We had to stop on the way to buy the liquor, since Jim had come down with the mumps and the party was going on without him. Queues at the liquor store were a mile long and each customer was allowed only one bottle of each kind. In order to get enough I handed out ten dollar bills to strangers and if they were buying "un" I said "*Achetez pour moi deux—un de rye, un de rum*" and they met me outside with the bottles and change.

In Montgomery Jean spent most of the Christmas holidays working at the Canteen. "I went down at 6:30 this morning. I love getting up and driving down in the dark with the great silver star in the East & millions of swallows chattering in the sycamore trees. It gives me such a good start on the day, which is spent making sandwiches and soup and serving them to soldiers and airmen who have nowhere else to go. I'm very much needed, since many of our volunteers are taking care of their own families over Christmas, and here am I without a family!"

44

Trying to Get Overseas

New Year's Day, 1943, dawned bright, clear, and cold in Ottawa. The temperature for Christmas week had hovered around thirty degrees below zero. A blizzard coming in from the west would bring it much lower. In Winnipeg it was fifty-six below, and moving our way.

"We tried to ski yesterday but the wind was literally painful on the face. 'Bottleneck' got stuck in the snow, but so did all the other cars, and we all dug and pushed together. Most of the time we kept our car in the yard, with an electric element bolted on the engine block so that the oil wouldn't freeze, and at night I placed a lighted lantern under the hood to keep the battery warm. I guess it won't be long before we won't be using it at all, when strict gas rationing comes."

Mary Webber wrote from Montgomery that "two cocktails at Georgia's New Year's Eve did Jeanie in." I wrote to Jean, "I can't blame you for drinking New Year's Eve but I still urge you to 'take it easy, Pet.'"

Bunty and I hunkered down, listening to Charlie McCarthy and getting the news on the radio, reading books and making love, alternately. I was reading *The Unknown Country*, a book by a Canadian newspaper man, and the *Managerial Revolution*, a socio-political thesis I should have read long ago because of its obvious influence on Legg.

Domestic bliss notwithstanding, my New Year's resolution was to get overseas where the action was. Bunty was willing for me to go, but insisted on starting a baby before I left. I wrote Jean, "I have so far objected to a third party, but if I should go I suppose I shall have to give in to her wish. Up to now we have been very careful to prevent conception. Well, from now on, it is no holds barred. Of course we may have the prevention whether we want it or not."

At Christmas we gave two housewarmings since our apartment was not large enough to get everyone in at the same time. The early one was for the newcomers, and the later one for the "oldsters" including Grierson and Ross McLean, Stuart Legg, the Spottiswoodes, the Andersons, Diana and Jim Wright, and of course Windy.

About twenty-five of these "oldsters" came and eight stayed for a late supper. It was a good meal, and Bunty topped it off with Jean's "good and easy" dessert made with apples and pecans under a sugar crust. In pecan season, Jean sent an endless supply picked as they fell to the ground.

I had good conversations with both Legg and McLean about my desire to go abroad. I had already told Grierson about my wish to get to the war front: "I must go in search of my manhood. I can't stand being here when my friends and all the others are risking their lives." Grierson was sympathetic and said that he would work on this and have some answers for me and for Julian, who also wanted to go, in a couple of weeks.

His approach would be to make us special war correspondents for the Film Board. I knew he meant to do it, but with his new commitment as Manager of Canada's War Information Board, and his move to an office on Parliament Hill, I suspected there would be delays. My unstated reaction was: "I'll believe it when I walk up the gangplank or climb aboard."

Talking to Legg and McLean was helpful. While our overall mission would be to do one or two films on Canadian forces overseas, it would be up to Legg to pick the specific assignments, and to McLean to get through government red tape. There would be plenty of that.

After all, I was still a corporal in the U.S. Signal Corps, on loan to the Canadian Film Board, and would have to be transferred into the Canadian armed forces before I could be made a uniformed war correspondent. Going to work in "civvies" for the Film Board would be hazardous. If captured I could be shot as a spy. The other problem was that once in the Army, I might be completely detached from the Film Board and out of the reach of Grierson.

The matter of getting equipment also presented difficulties. The Film Board had been trying for several months to procure a number of the new combat cameras designed for the U.S. Signal Corps. It was like drawing deeply imbedded teeth without an anaesthetic. The Signal Corps wanted to keep them all.

I was pretty discouraged, and my impulse was to quit and return to the U.S. Army, but that would have been like going from the frying pan into the fire. I had

explored the possibility of returning as a corporal in the Signal Corps, and applying for Officer's Training School in the United States, but was advised against this
by my old colonel at Fort Monmouth, who said he had tried that route and found
himself assigned right back to the Signal Corps. It was a Catch-22 situation.

My cousin William Baldwin, himself a Navy man with friends high up the ladder, explored the possibility of getting me into the U.S. Navy, but to no avail.

However, within two weeks of seeing McLean, he said it was pretty definite
that something would be arranged to get both Julian and me over as special correspondents for the Film Board, either in uniform or in civvies, with or without
commissions. He said it would be soon, and that we would take our orders directly
from Grierson or from Basil Wright in England.

In the meantime, my work at the Board on the Canadian Army recruitment
film, referred to as *Platoon*, kept me busy. It was an unusual picture for the Film
Board, because its form was that of a Hollywood story film. It moved along leisurely

*Nick with his gun
and his camera.*

from one activity to another, involving a young officer and his platoon, with sync sound and dialogue throughout. Considering that we had non-actors, it was turning out very well, although it did not quite get across the psychological development we wanted—that is, the breakdown of prejudice on the part of the men for their officers.

As in all films, there were problems, the first being that Julian, who was working with me, was from New York and under pressure to get back. Also, since there was a shortage of space at the Film Board, we were sent to Toronto to work in a borrowed lab at Audio Pictures Inc., which had an ancient moviola that turned out mumbo jumbo. It was impossible to cut a long sound picture on that damnable machine.

After editing, more sound would be needed, including more commentary to point up the dialogue scenes, sound effects, and music. I looked forward to doing it all, since I had been in on each phase of it since the beginning. I felt it was *my* picture.

Bunty was trying to get a job with Judy Crawley, working on public health films for the Film Board. However, Grierson wouldn't let Judy hire her, because there was to be a big investigation of the Film Board by the House of Commons, and he was afraid that one of the things they would be looking into was nepotism. There were indeed quite a few "mister and misses" among us, but most were acquired when one film worker married another.

Bunty, who was a bacteriologist, finally took a job in a blood clinic. It was dull, hard work, but the hours were good and she got one hundred dollars a month, which was pretty nice.

When I got back from Toronto, Grierson said to turn *Platoon* over to someone else to finish, since I would be going to England very soon. Jean wrote to say she was enclosing a check for one last trip to Montgomery "to say goodbye." She forgot to enclose the check, and I wrote to tell her to "forget it—we are trying to live independently financially. It is very bad for us to count on money from you."

However, there seemed to be no way of stopping the avalanche of things that came from Montgomery. We received twenty pounds of rugs and a big shipment of books. Packages arrived every week—pecans, bacon, artichoke pickles and even grits. The package containing the grits was punctured en route, and the mail room at the Film Board got a bit gritty. Bunty commented that she knew how she could find her way to Hazel Hedge—just by following the trail of grits.

Jean asked whether we thought it would hurt Windy's feelings if she bought the silver fox he had brought for Bunty from the Hudson Bay Company, since Bunty was really too short for it and didn't want it, and Jean did. "If it's okay, bring it down with you."

We went to Montgomery by way of New York City where we saw Sheila, and where Bunty shopped unsuccessfully for shoes and a coat. These were hard to find in Ottawa, where so much was rationed. However, it was spring by the time we got to Alabama, and we got warm. I showed off my new moustache, and while we were there, Willey Gayle painted Bunty's portrait.

On our way back we saw the film that Bunty's old beau, Roger Barlow, had made in Alabama. It was *Henry Browne, Farmer,* about a Negro farmer who raised peanuts and corn and vegetables, and took good care of his land by fertilizing and terracing. As Canada Lee, the commentator, said, "the barn isn't much to look at and he hasn't got a tractor—just a pair of mules to pull the plow—but it's a good farm because he and his family work hard to make the land productive."

The climax of the picture was reached when Henry Browne, his wife and their small children go to see the older Browne boy who is training to be a pursuit pilot at Tuskegee. The only false note was the clothes the Brownes wore on this occasion. I'm sure they would have put on their finest clothes, but in the film they appear in everyday work clothes with the straw hats they would have worn in the fields.

When I returned to Canada, everything was "on hold." Grierson's aim to have me and Julian go over as a roving team of war correspondents under the control of the Film Board had misfired. The Army insisted on maintaining complete control of our assignments. The only good news for me was that both Legg and Spottiswoode had seen *13 Platoon*, as it was now called, and had given it high praise.

I was more than ever impatient to get abroad, and in March enrolled in after-hours Combat Cameramen's Training School, run by the National Film Board to train cameramen for the armed services. The Army had asked NFB to train twenty cameramen for active duty. I had decided that joining the Canadian Army was the fastest way to get to the front. The only one who tried to dissuade me was my mother: "This Canadian move is a mistake. After all, you are an American. If you were injured you would get no hospital attention, no insurance for Bunty, no recompense for any kind of accident." I reassured her: "I would not lose my American citizenship by joining. If I were injured I would get a pension and hospitalization. And if I were killed Bunty would get a benefit allowance." Jean apologized: "I am sorry I said a word about your plans. You know best about what you want to do. I am really quite old & bewildered by the war."

I was encouraged to keep on trying by a letter from Gould Beech, who was over-age for the draft but had resigned from a Montgomery newspaper and enlisted "to get into action," and found himself stationed in Williamsburg, Virginia, doing public relations for the armed forces. From the day he arrived he tried to get a transfer into the fighting forces, but had been told he was too old to have the physical endurance.

His letter read: "Yesterday I passed the first test. Between lunch at 12 and supper at 4:30 I walked 14 miles, counting round trips to lunch. I got off at 9:30 due to classes and night drill. I'm to be transferred to anti-aircraft guns, and I won't need your bike any longer. Shall I send it to you in Ottawa?" I said, "No, there is too much snow on the ground here."

I was glad that my latest assignment at the Board would keep me indoors most of the time. I was to do two Army training films on tanks, mostly animation. At home I was busy challenging our landlord in the rent control case, for raising the rent between the time we agreed to take the apartment and moved in.

Bunty was developing into a fine cook. She had passed the cookbook stage and was following her own instincts, in many cases with great success. She discovered fresh shrimp at Lapoint's fish market, and we had them curried. Our first sweetbreads were a triumph, and Bunty got a lactic acid culture from the experimental farm for turning milk sour to make curds.

In Montgomery, Jean was successfully carrying on her soldier and sailor canteen at the train depot. Ben Baldwin, who was going to New York on *The Crescent*, said that while he was waiting for his berth to be made up he had heard six sailors talking about how good the chow was at the canteen in the train depot—turkey, soup, cigarettes. "I thought you would like to know that the men really think it's swell."

Sheila and Jill came to Hazel Hedge to visit, and while they were there Willey Gayle painted Jill's portrait. Ann Hubbard and Claussen Ely were married in Boston, and Major Howard Morris and his new wife Winnifred were settled near his post of duty at Army Headquarters in Brownwood, Texas. Polly Read married Teddy Morton at Camp Stewart, and we all wished her well since she deserved the best. Cousin "Tea Cake" Baldwin had a nervous breakdown and was sent to Tuscaloosa. Three of Jean's flyboys—Peter, Pat and Tommy—were killed overseas.

Jean invited Marion Rous, Nash's pianist cousin, to come down from New York City to see her, and had the grand piano tuned.

I didn't really know how congenial we would be, but she has the most avid & intelligent interest in everything. I took her to the Archives to meet Marie Bankhead, and they got along famously. On the way there we pulled over to the curb to buy a newspaper from the vendor, legless Jimmy Sheffield.

He reminded her of their earlier encounter 31 years ago, when she stopped to talk with a little boy 8 years old who propelled himself with corn cobs, because he had rickets so bad he couldn't walk. But he sang a spiritual so beautifully that Marion had paid him 25 cents to teach it to her. Afterwards Susan Dyer had used the music in her symphony or suite, & many people including Heifetz played it.

It is hideously hot, but Marion doesn't mind the heat. We dip in and out of the little pool several times a day. We read aloud and talk endlessly about the family, philosophy of life and music. She played a lot of Chopin on the piano. Nash would have loved that. He had heard Chopin first from his mother when she was teaching piano where he grew up in Corsicana, Texas.

Marion explained symphonies to me when we played them on the victrola in the drawing room, and I have had all of her dresses lengthened in the back and shortened in the front. I completely re-did the dress she is to wear at the opening of her lecture series at the Carnegie Hall Art Gallery when she returns to New York. After the opening, she wrote that with a gold necklace and a red velvet turban, she was a sensation at the Carnegie Hall debut. "The general verdict was that it was stunning!" Sheila's comment was, "I'll bet!"

Georgia Saffold's music was beginning to be heard. Her anthem was sung at St. John's on Sunday. She evidently composes the harmony & then has it taken down by a musician who can write music. Recently she was made a member of the League of Composers & Conductors—as she pointed out, "like Toscanini." She spoils it by wanting so much publicity and acting as if she were a great composer. On the other hand, she works at it, and is in a way so guileless.

When she was leaving by train for the Homestead in Hot Springs, and checking her innumerable big pieces of luggage, I found her leaning across the counter explaining her musical pin to the baggage man: "You see the whole notes are the pearls, and the half notes the black pearls, and that big diamond is the clef sign . . . It goes like this, and she hummed him a little tune Ta-Ta-Ta . . ."

She was upset at not getting a compartment. I laughed & said, "What on earth do you want a compartment for—you can find lots more people to show your pin to outside in the Pullman." I pointed to the four seats opposite her filled with nice-looking soldiers, & said, "Take them one at a time. They'll keep you busy all the way to Atlanta." Georgia never seems to mind my laughing at her. I think I am the only person that ever does. Everyone else, including herself, takes her very seriously.

She wrote to me from Hot Springs, "Were it not for your send-off and basket lunch of lamb sandwiches and Coca Cola and beer, I would have reached here more dead than alive. I shared it with four starved soldiers across the way. In Atlanta I picked up my mother, Rosie, who said she had experienced almost everything in life but an upper berth, and insisted on sleeping in one. With the help of my four companions and some marines we finally got her up the ladder.

"I slept not at all and arrived at the Homestead without my curling irons. I looked terrible but had to go to a surprise birthday dinner given by Philip who was presenting me with an emerald, since it is my birthstone. What will I do with it? Green only appeals to me in ivy & foliage, not in jewels."

Finally, the big news came. Bunty was pregnant. It was conveyed in an indirect way. "Tell Ben that Bunty may acquire that thing that he admires so much." Ben beamed & said, "Ain't that sweet! I knowed they could do it. I knowed that." Everyone began to make preparations. Jean arranged to have my antique cradle reconstructed and refurbished, and sent my christening robe and other baby dresses to New Orleans to have the yellow stains removed. Mrs. Butters started knitting. Petunia wrote from Florida that she knew where she could get diapers, which were in short supply.

Bunty was having some morning sickness, and had sciatic pains in her rump and thighs. She resigned from her job at the Blood Bank. I was pleasantly relaxed about becoming a father, and still angling for a transfer overseas.

Jean had been thinking of renting the big house at Hazel Hedge, and moving into one of her cottages, but decided against it. Sheila wrote, "I do not like to advise on such a difficult matter, but am almost sure you would be much happier staying on at Hazel Hedge. You can be mighty lonely in a cottage, too, and would not have the consolation of being in the place you love. Growing old is at best a grotesque and hideous business and if there is anything that makes it less so, it is a background of beauty."

Jean remembered her mother, "Age is really a wicked thing—except in Mama. I think she grew more beautiful & more charming with age. She never fought against it (as I do.) Her clothes were so perfect & suitable, and so was her attitude. Maybe you can't grow old well without religion."

There were problems between blacks and whites in Alabama. In nearby Opelika, Sheriff Pat Evans and his deputy were charged in federal indictments with brutality towards black prisoners, and everyone took sides. Willey Gayle, who was living at Hazel Hedge, thought the sheriff was a "grand man" and sent him ten dollars. She said everyone in Macon County knew "it was a put up job." Jean didn't believe it was, and had a terrible argument with a Mrs. Denton who said she had heard that "Mrs. Read had Yankee views and was known to be a nigger lover."

When the book publishers, Doubleday-Doran, announced a $2,500 award for the best book dealing with "American Negroes," the *Montgomery Advertiser* published a long editorial urging Southern authors to compete, representing the most intelligent whites of the South "who are just as anxious to see the southern Negro achieve a higher standard of living as their pseudo-friends in the North."

This was a summer when Jean concentrated on repairing and painting the big house and the cottages at Hazel Hedge, and taking care of her garden. "The garden is all burned up with this heat and the lawn doesn't exist. It is just raked dirt. I am deep into getting ready for the house painters, with all the shrubbery and vines to cut back. They have grown up & are rotting everything and panes are falling out of the windows which often have no cords, and many roofs are leaking. And Ben has hurt his back."

Her biggest problems were little ones—fleas, ticks and bedbugs.

I've had a great disgrace. I had a little bed in one of the cottages brought into the big house and put in Mama's room so I could rent it this summer. It is box springs on a wooden frame with a feather mattress. I rented it to the sister of an Army acquaintance of mine for a couple of weeks.

It was sweet & clean, with fresh sheets full of yellow flowers & tube roses. Sunday morning the woman called me and the bed was full of bed bugs! I had never seen one in my life. I remember as a child that Mama would go through the laundry when it came in, and once she found one and fired the washerwoman, whose name was Irene.

Mr. Adair, the exterminator, is coming today to fumigate, and I think he will have to do the drawing room too as it is ankle deep in tiny, needle-point fleas. I don't allow the dogs in the house at all—because of their ticks. Their skins are like peanut candy, simply a solid sheet of ticks. They go every week for a medicated bath but we cannot get rid of those ticks.

At least the ants and rats are under control this year. Another thing—both Baa and Blackie are on a hunger strike. They refuse all dry desiccated foods & won't touch wheat bread or milk & bark and moan for "Meat—Give us Meat, Meat, Meat" I had 45 ration points saved for butter & Crisco & bacon, but they are gone.

Brannon Hubbard has had an interesting assignment. He was in charge of a large contingent of German prisoners being sent to Montana. He said they really did believe that practically all the U.S.A. had been bombed—and were amazed to see how quickly we had built it back up!

Willey has gone to Chicago to comfort her sister, Phyllis, both of whose sons have been killed overseas—and the younger one was only 19. [The younger son Buzzy was later found to be a prisoner in Germany.]

<h1 align="center">45</h1>

<h1 align="center">An Epiphany Gift</h1>

*I*N OTTAWA THERE WAS A TOUCH OF SPRING IN THE AIR, ALTHOUGH spring is really a myth in Montreal, it goes by so quickly. We knew it was en route when our last ski trip in late May wound up on dry ground in the woods, warm enough to go without sweater and jacket.

We found a little stream that had broken through the snow and we drank from it and sat on an exposed rock and smoked, and watched a yellow plane do slow loops and rolls in a blue sky. In the maples, Bunty discovered a most wonderful frozen treat. The warm sun had brought out the sap, and the cold nights semi-froze it into delicious popsicles.

Our trip down the mountain proved quite dangerous, since the sun was behind the mountain and the trail had hardened to a very fast surface. One girl fell and broke her back, and had to be carried. I was an expert at falling, if not at staying up, so came home uninjured.

With summer on its way, we arranged to get a cottage with Bob and Cathy Anderson, up the Gatineau at Farm Point, Quebec. We urged Jean to bring both dogs and come for a visit. "There are 4 bedrooms, a wide screened porch, a cozy living room and in the kitchen an enamelled gasoline pressure stove with an oven. There are also two boats and a tepee. Please come. We will need you to gather the wild strawberries."

Jean couldn't come because she had broken her little toe, "which is the shape, size and color of an eggplant! It reminds me of Dali and I keep thinking that if he had my accident maybe his pictures would have been full of great purple eggplants. They are so much more decorative and colorful than crutches, telephones & penises."

At Farm Point we planted a vegetable garden and prepared to spend a leisurely summer. I made one site visit to Toronto for a film, visiting the big John Inglis plant that makes Bren guns, machine guns and anti-tank rifles. Before the war this had been two hundred people making a few boilers and marine engines. Now there were ten thousand employees turning out modern weapons.

Most of the workers were women. They wore slacks, had their hair tied up in turbans, and the majority were quite attractive. The prettiest girls were the guides who steered you around the place or drove you from one department to another in a snappy station wagon. In their blue uniforms they would be eligible for an Atlantic City beauty contest, and like airline hostesses, their manners as well as their bodies were well-groomed.

The factory was very clean and huge glass windows admitted plenty of light. The men's washrooms had a hot water fountain in the center—the water flowing continuously into a large circular basin, where a cylinder contained soap that flowed through conveniently placed spigots. I didn't see the plant hospital, but the cafeteria passed my inspection. The food was good and reasonably priced. Everyone seemed to be taking their time. They paused for a smoke after their meal or chatted with a friend.

The workers were relaxed. If there was an assembly line, I didn't encounter it. Perhaps the tempo there was like Charlie Chaplin's *Modern Times*—but the hands that operated the great cutting and drilling machines moved methodically. A girl did not have to raise her hand and say, "Teacher" when she wanted to go to the john. She just shut off her machine and left. Each worker had a quota and got extra pay for exceeding it.

In Montgomery, Jeanie recovered from her broken toe and provided a little home theater to celebrate Loula Dunn's birthday.

She described it to me:

> I only asked Loula, Mary Webber, and Willey. We were all to be in costume, representing someone in the news and stay in character all evening.
>
> Loula came as Mrs. Roosevelt with her hair done exactly like Mrs. R.'s, a mouthful of false teeth, a corsage of orchids, and a typewritten sheet of "My Day" pinned on her front. She had lots of maps and tickets to different places. I represented my hero, the Hon. Winston Churchill, well stuffed with pillows and wearing Dada's velvet jacket & white waistcoat, and a wide black hat, smoking a cigar, carrying a cane & gloves—and with a British insignia in my lapel.

We sat right down & discussed plans for the United Nations and what to do about the "dastardly dark deeds" of John L. Lewis—(He ought to be tarred and feathered for his strikes). That was before Mary Webber and Willey arrived. Mary was Gracie Fields to provide the singing, and I had dressed Willey as Gypsy Rose Lee.

I had taken off every stitch of her clothes except for her bra and put on a transparent gold tissue slip. She charmed Mr. Churchill.

Mr. Churchill read a letter from me to the R.A.F. boys, and Mrs. Roosevelt read "My Day" of April 30, 1943. Then I went into the kitchen and out the back door and rang the bell at the front door and reappeared as Joe Stalin. I was still wearing Churchill's pants, but had rearranged the pillows around my waist, put on a black wig and fierce upturned black moustaches and a sweat shirt decorated with red ribbons and gold stars & a picture of Lenin.

Stalin took a shine to Gypsy Rose Lee, and did a few Russian dances. Then he (I) disappeared into the kitchen again, and came forth with a magnificent dinner, including a sturgeon—from Russia, of course, fresh asparagus, new peas, a salad, cold white wine, and a glorious orange jelly birthday cake and apricot and banana ice cream. We all missed Nash so, we could hardly stand it. He would have been Churchill & been so cute & so much fun.

In her letters, Jean was always solicitous about Bunty.

She is the first person to be considered now. She must have that fur-lined coat if she stays in Ottawa this winter. Marion Oates has married a very rich man, Tommy Leiter, and now has 11 fur coats. Maybe I can take one for Bunty & it would never be missed. I have had the crib done over with a blue canopy, because it was blue when Nicky slept in it, even though the doctor says that the baby will be a girl. I don't think the test he is using is scientific. If so, I'm delighted that you will call her Jennie, but I think it is going to be a boy.

Isn't the war news exciting? I agree about de Gaulle. He's touchy & stubborn & self-important but he was the one who tried to save France & I think we should recognize him at once.

Our liquor stores are closed until September. I have 3 qts. of whisky, 1 bottle of Martini cocktails, 1 bottle of Creme de Menthe & 1 bottle of Cuban Rum. Wouldn't Nash die over such a cellar! The food situation is bad. There isn't a lb. of corn meal in Montgomery County & no grits. Think of the "solid South" being without corn meal. Thank you for the photographs. Be sure to save some film for the baby. It's impossible to get here.

In Canada nothing had been decided about my going overseas, and I was concerned that the Film Board itself would not last after the war. Would Grierson come back with his bold ideas to save it? Many thought not. Would it simply wither on a political vine? In September I wrote a plan for its continuance and sent it to Julian and others for their comments. Nothing came of it.

Jean bought the coat for Bunty that she had admired. "$160 seemed a lot to spend for a coat, but even if it only lasts this one season it will be worth buying to make a pregnant girl feel queenly—I don't mean feel queenly. I felt like a queen. We all do. But I mean make her feel that she looks queenly. You must arrange to have a private nurse for her when she comes home from the hospital. She really must not get up too soon or begin to cook & wash etc. Her whole future health depends on that."

I saw Grierson at a party arranged by Margaret Ann for Basil Wright. Grierson delivered a talk in the kitchen on practical politics. He thought it was better to work toward your objective within the existing framework than "to stick your neck out in a dramatic or romantic fashion." He said that he took the overall war information job in order to fight from the top for the Film Board.

At Margaret Ann's I met a Mrs. Nina Finn, wife of the Deputy Minister of Fisheries (no cracks, please), a charming woman, tall, dark and beautiful who sang like Marion Anderson and knew hundreds of folk songs, German, French, Kentucky, Scottish, Nova Scotian. I got to know the Finns very well, largely in the course of seeing them through a terrible tragedy.

Their house caught fire and instead of getting out with the baby, the silly little French Canadian maid rushed outside to telephone Nina's sister at the Film Board, and by the time the fire department got there the house was ablaze and little Johnny was trapped upstairs. Her piano and all her music was inside too, but the apple of her eye, a child of exceptional beauty and charm, was dead.

I loaned them my car and did what I could, but nothing really could help their grief. When you talked to "Finny" he sat and looked straight ahead. After a while you could hear a sort of rattle down inside of him and you knew he was crying, but there were no tears.

We didn't talk about the future because for them the future seemed gone. But we remained very close, and a few years after the war, Nina played an important role in our lives.

That December I had to go to New York to screen a test print of my film, now called *100,000 Cadets*. This was its final review before release, and it was a tense time for me, but I wasn't nervous until I accidentally bumped into Colonel Grier, who had been helpful in the beginning, but then became too bossy, and I had broken off relations and finished it on my own. When I encountered him he said icily, "Well, I hear you are finishing your film." I said, "Yes. That's right." "A film on Army Cadets?" he asked sarcastically. "Yes." "Do you think we could see it sometime?" "When it's finished," I replied coldly.

After lunch I decided to go over and talk with him in the lounge. "You are due an explanation," I began. "Well, I figured you were getting tired of my advice and decided to finish the film without it," said the colonel. "That's about the size of it," I said. This seemed to break the ice. He said he would wait to see the finished film because it might please him very much. We parted amicably. I was glad I hadn't kept my head in the sand. It's much better to be frank.

I didn't show him the film then, because the titles were not in place. Instead I went shopping at Lord and Taylor's and bought Bunty a very cute bed-jacket with ruffles down the front. I thought it would be a nice thing for her to wear in the hospital and when she came home.

I was still trying to get into one of the armed services, and had even written to the Major in charge of the Combat Cinema Academy in Culver City, California, about the prospects of becoming a cameraman in the U.S. Air Force. But there seemed to be no way without first getting detached from the Canadians and returning to the Signal Corps, which had to be put off until Bunty had our baby.

She was very pregnant. Norman McLaren had done a charming pencil sketch of her "in her condition." We were having a pleasant social time together. At a Halloween party, where everyone was to come as what they had secretly wanted to be, I thought she should go as a Buddha, in an embroidered coat and Chinese trousers, with her tummy exposed, but she said she had never secretly wanted to be a Buddha.

We attended a party Lady Duff gave for Windy's birthday, his fiftieth. It was very fancy and the guests were announced as they came in. There were officials galore, but we were just plain Mr. and Mrs. Nicholas Read. Bunty had borrowed a sewing machine and made herself a black velveteen skirt which fitted over her pregnancy beautifully. Once she began to sew, she couldn't seem to stop, and made pinafores and even covered a mattress.

Christmas came. We had ours in Ottawa, and Jeanie hers in Montgomery. I skied on Christmas Day. All the trees were covered with snow, and a heavy frost fog hung low over the hills. But above the mist the sky was clear and as we neared the top it broke through the fog and transformed the country into a scene of unbelievable beauty. For a few minutes the Glory of the Lord shone round about me. It was a perfect day. I started back about five with little Johnny Lecke, whose face was in bandages, having been badly scratched in a tumble from a toboggan. He was carried like an African king on the shoulders of four Nightriders. The Nightriders are high school boys who volunteer for tending to the injured. I think Johnny could have skied out under his own power, but he was the first casualty of the season and the boys wanted to show they were on the job.

It wasn't such a good show, however, because they lost control of the sled right in front of the lodge where a large crowd was watching, and the sled rolled over and over down the slope with Johnny tied securely in place, quite incapable of helping himself. However, he didn't seem any the worse for wear.

At Hazel Hedge, just a few days before Christmas, Jean had rented the pink room and the nursery upstairs to two young air force couples and one little boy for a month—"perfectly charming Yale friends taking pre-flight at Maxwell. They are so happy they won't have to have Xmas in a hotel or horrid rooms, and I am so happy to have some young people & life in this house at Xmas."

They became the nucleus of a Christmas Eve party which included others from the cottages and Maxwell Field who had no place to go, eighteen in all. Jean hung garlands and put up candles, and dressed the house with smilax, and stood in line at the liquor store to get enough rum to make Craik punch. Someone had sent a smoked turkey, and someone else a small barrel of oysters, and a case of alligator pears. There were "beaten biscuits" for the ham, and oyster gumbo and crisp French buttered bread with a grand salad, and cheese and cake and coffee. Nancy Smith came with Harwell and Pryor and played the carols and everyone sang.

Ben was so happy. He kept saying, "It's like old times. This a show nuff party like us used to have." Jean said, "No, Ben. It'll never be like that without Miss Jennie & Boss & Nicky" and Ben said, "Miss Jean, they is here—right here—you couldn't be actin' so good & singing like you is if they wasn't right here with us." Jean thought that was wonderful and it made everything all right. She was happy,

Bunty and Nash at Hazel Hedge.

and everyone had a really good time.

She got to the canteen at 7:30 in the morning in icy rain and was the only person at the Hut until after 11 a.m. "I got the coffee made & began carving turkeys & making sandwiches & feeding sailors & giving out Xmas stockings & taking in donations of pies and cakes as they came in. We had five turkeys, and as soon as we used up one, I put the carcass in the soup and that went on all day. At 4:30 I went to the Pollards for a drink & lay down for an hour & came back after midnight."

The baby was due December 31. We were already planning to have the christening at Hazel Hedge in March under the elm tree, using the silver christening bowl, with Jill there to be godmother and Windy godfather. On Epiphany, January 6, Thomas Nash Read was born and was immediately dubbed "The Chief" by Sheila and Jill in a congratulatory wire. The "Thomas" came from Bunty's father, but all agreed that he would be called "Nash" after my Dad.

Jean wrote on the eighth from Montgomery that she hadn't been able to get through on the telephone because she didn't know the name of the Canadian province, and she had a hard time using her own phone for the first couple of days because so many people were phoning about the baby. When I reached her she thanked me profusely for naming him after my father. "I am so glad you named him 'Nash.' Dada would have been so proud. I can see him now with his arms out—beaming but the tears pouring down his cheeks, 'Oh Darl, isn't it wonderful.' He would have hugged & kissed everybody he met." Nancy Smith's music class was meeting in the drawing room that day and Jean made a white fruit cake and had port and sherry, and everyone drank to the new babe and hoped he'd be as fine as his granddaddy. Ben gave up all work and made the rounds of the cottages to tell the tenants.

I wrote to describe my son as "no doubt the finest baby ever born, with brown eyes and a rosy bloom on his fat cheeks and a double chin. His appetite is fine and he sleeps except when he eats and only cries when he is very hungry. He sucks faster than he can swallow which causes a pool of milk on the bed. Bunty has to wear Mae West pads. She is occupying her time in the hospital with *War and Peace*, which will hold her for the full two weeks she is there."

Bunty's letter to Jean was even more glowing. "If there is anything cuter in the world than Tom Nash, I will die if I see it. My heart turns over every time I look at him. He is SO gay and funny. I can't really describe how I feel about him because it would probably sound trite. We giggle and laugh together all day. I am famous already as the mother of that wonderful baby. Good night, my pet. I love you very much. B."

We got a letter from Darlie, implying that "young Nash would live in a better world when socialism prevailed," but nostalgically reached back to the spring of 1916 when I was born at Hazel Hedge, and all was serene with Granny and her prayers watching over us with her great love. It was a religious Christmas, made even more so by a letter from Jean's good friend, the artist Anne Goldthwaite, who had posted it just a few days before she died.

In Canada there were festivities. The Lawtons gave a champagne party to celebrate the birth. My contribution was a sleigh ride on a bright moonlit night, with sleigh bells jingling and the icy air whistling by our muffled faces. On Bunty's birthday and to welcome her home from the hospital, we asked the Griersons and a few others over. J.G. took his drink into the bedroom, dipped his finger into it and christened Thomas Nash. Grierson said, "He looks just like the old man," meaning Dada of course, for whom he had the greatest respect and love. The Griersons had no children. He looked a long time at "the Chief" and said to me: "You must be a very proud man, Nick."

Nick and Nash.

As a present on Bunty's birthday, I had bought five yards of pink linen for a suit, and borrowed an old dress form, the kind that is raised on an iron stand, and asked Norman McClaren to drape it for me. I bought some pink roses, which Norman put at the neck, tied with a wide black ribbon. A silver brooch and band of elastic held it firm at the waist. Guy Glover wrote a little verse for me:

> A rose is pink
> A rose is for love
> This pink is for Bunty
> A rose for my Dove.

I took *100,000 Cadets* to Cornwall to show it to

Colonel Grier and the school. It was a great success, and the Capital Theater in Cornwall ran it for the next three days as part of their regular program. Grierson asked me what my plans were, and was I still thinking about going into the armed forces?

I told him I had been thinking of very little else for the past year and talking to Bunty about it. He told me that he had resigned from the overall war information job in order to come back to the Film Board, and hoped we could work out something together. He picked up the phone and called the Canadian Navy for which he had just trained five cameramen, and told them he would like to have me and Julian go overseas as war correspondents on assignment from the Film Board. He hung up to say they had agreed.

Bunty and I went to Hazel Hedge for the christening, which had to be moved from under the old elm tree because of a heavy downpour. But I held a branch over the baby and we used the silver christening bowl, and sang new words written by Mildred Reynolds Saffold to the tune of the "Bonny Blue Flag"—this time written for Nash:

> We're gathered here this day of days
> Beneath an ancient tree
> To give unto the church a child
> Born on Epiphany.

We got back to Canada in time for a big "coming out" party Margaret Ann had arranged to welcome back one of the Film Board's top producers, Tom Daly. He was "coming out" of a cast in which he had been encased for several months recovering from a serious horseback accident. The guests were greeted at the top of the stairs by the cast, topped by a white horse's head snorting brimstone and fire, and split to reveal a skeleton inside decorated with film strips. It proved to be sort of a goodbye party for me and Julian, since Grierson, holding forth in the kitchen, assured us that our foreign assignment was coming through momentarily, and that we should start packing our bags.

46

On the Fighting Front—World War II

IT WAS WHEN I RECEIVED A PRINTED AND SIGNED DOCUMENT TO THE effect that "N. Read, as a Lieutenant in the Canadian Navy, was certified as a War Correspondent authorized to follow the Armed Forces of the Crown, and entitled in the event of capture to be treated as a Prisoner of War under the provisions of Article 8 of the International Convention," that I knew my departure was imminent. I was flattered when I read on: "In the event of capture Mr. Read would be the equivalent of an officer in the British Army with the rank of Captain." That looked pretty good to me, though I didn't want to be captured.

In late May of 1944, Julian and I boarded an old RAF Liberator, bound for England. As an airplane, it was too old for bombing, but useful for transporting military personnel between England and Canada. Needless to say, it was not designed for comfort, and it was mighty cold up there. We shared the quarters with a lot of RAF men. The first thing we noticed was that unlike the Canadian Armed Forces, where officers and enlisted men intermingled, class distinction was observed between officers and noncoms in the British forces. Since neither of us was in uniform, we stuck with the noncoms.

We stopped to refuel in Gander, Newfoundland, and then flew on over the patchwork quilt landscape of Northern Ireland to Scotland. Our flight ended there, and the golf began. The porter carrying my bags gave me such a vivid play-by-play description of how Lawson Little won the open championship on a local course that I rented golf clubs while at the airport, and with Julian set off in search of the nearest course.

I bought two beat-up old golf balls for a shilling apiece, and two Scottish caddies, both named "Jack" (pronounced "Jock") took us on. My Jack was very serious and it was with his encouragement that I substituted a number two iron for the putter missing from my rented collection, and shot a forty-two, which pleased the caddie—and me, greatly. Julian, who had never played golf, sang his way around the course, charming all who heard his rendition of that old Negro spiritual, "This Train am a Clean Train" in a Scottish dialect.

The war seemed a long way off that beautiful day. I wrote home:

> The feel of the sea air, the springy turf underfoot studded with daisies and blue bells, the distant blue mountains and the surrounding cottages fitted so perfectly with my preconceived notion of Scotland that I felt it must all be some lovely, crazy dream. Afterwards we had drinks in the clubrooms. Julian who didn't drink alcohol, had a lemon fizz instead of his usual ginger beer, and I made do with several "mild and bitters."
>
> The old gentlemen sitting around with their ale, smoking & playing cards and wearing their Scotch plaid caps, made it picturesque. Outside the pub, the sight of the village with its low stone houses, casement windows, chimney pots and twisting narrow lanes caused Julian to say, "No wonder the documentary boys over here get atmosphere in their films. It's a set-up for them." The only poor thing was the dinner at a government restaurant for war workers. Our meal consisted of beans and chips, and a helping of potatoes.

We went from Scotland to London by train. It gave me my first ride on a deluxe English sleeper with a small but comfortable room, hot water for shaving, and a steward who brought hot tea at 7 a.m. The nightmare began when we disembarked at Euston Station early on a drizzly Sunday morning. There was nobody to meet us and we didn't know where to go.

Our telegram had arrived at the Canadian Film Board office on Saturday when the office was closed. We finally took a cab to Canada House on Trafalgar Square, and tracked down British filmmaker J. P. Golightly, who got us a double bed at the Park Lane Hotel for the night. He left after warning us that there "might be a few bombs flying around later."

In the middle of the night the sirens went off and a bomb must have fallen nearby. At least the windows rattled and the curtains blew in. According to Julian, I roused myself enough to say, "You sleep on top of the bed and I'll go underneath," and that's the way it was. The next morning we started through accreditation. It would have helped if we had been in uniform, but we didn't have any uniforms yet.

There were numerous interviews with numerous officials and mine especially seemed to take an inordinate amount of time. How did a United States citizen, who had been a corporal in the U.S. Army, get to be a first lieutenant in the Canadian Navy, entitled to the rank of captain if captured? I kept finding shorter ways to give the answers. We didn't have much time.

When we left Canada we had been instructed to report immediately to a naval training station that would prepare us for D-Day, which was imminent. We needed to learn how to handle ourselves and our cameras aboard the very fast and small Canadian Motor Torpedo Boats (MTB's) that had already made headlines by breaking up German convoys and raiders in the Channel. At the naval training station we were to film the trial run of a new MTB and the life of the crew on a shake-down cruise around the port. It was important that we get to the naval training station as soon as possible.

In less than a week we would be doing the real thing aboard an MTB, filming the launching of torpedoes or dropping depth charges to clear the way for the landing barges carrying Allied troops to France. Our problem would be to keep ourselves upright and our cameras steady and loaded with film on the speedy small boats while they maneuvered.

This would be especially difficult when they took evasive action after launching a torpedo and veered sharply away from their targets to put distance between themselves and the explosion. It wouldn't do to be washed overboard, although that was a possibility.

We would need to be positioned on the boats so as to get closeups of the torpedo firing, as well as long shots of the barges and the troops. Since our cameras would only hold one hundred feet of film, we would have to reload quickly in rough seas, to get everything on film smoothly with few breaks. Where to put extra rolls of film for easy access was a problem to be solved. With D-Day so close upon us, I was concerned that we might not get through accreditation in time for a shake-down cruise.

Early Monday morning we began to stand in line. We met a Lt. Cdr. Alf Tate, in charge of Navy Combat cameramen, who left us with an official who was too distracted to do more than route us to the Ministry of Information, a complex organization called the MOI, which collected and made available the wartime output from all government sources of information—be it printed, broadcast or on film.

We found our way through a lot of people there and eventually got to Canadian Public Relations. The next stop was the Supreme Headquarters American Expeditionary Forces (SHAEF), which had direct responsibility for films. We were getting closer, but needed signatures from both the Army and the Navy before receiving a final okay from the High Commissioner's Committee on the Press. It reminded me of a Gilbert and Sullivan opera.

We still had to buy uniforms and find a place to stay. When we went to Gieves and Company, the traditional outfitter for the British Navy, to get our uniforms, we asked the fitter to add "patch pockets" to the jackets to hold the extra 100-foot rolls of film we would need to get at quickly. He was adamant. "Young man, Lord Wellington himself couldn't have gotten patch pockets." Then he worked out a compromise. He would make us two uniforms, one with gold braid and brass buttons and a formal officer's hat with more gold braid, and the other a khaki battle dress with a khaki beret. We looked like bellhops in the latter, but we got our "patch pockets."

Finding a place to stay proved easier. Julian ran into an old friend, a captain who was being shipped out who turned his apartment over to us. Nor was it just any apartment. It was the Albany, probably the oldest and certainly most prestigious apartment building in London, having been occupied by both Gladstone and Disraeli. Our apartment was owned by a Lady Welby, who had gone to the country for the duration.

We moved in, accompanied by another Canadian Film Board man, Ralph Foster. Being six foot three inches tall, he got the master bedroom with the big bed. We occupied a smaller room with two single cots. The drawing room was very elegant, with a marble statue, *Mystery of Life*, presiding over our nefarious activities. Sometimes we covered her inscrutable face with Ralph Foster's big hat. We stayed there between assignments for about a year, acquiring a housekeeper who prepared our meals, washed our clothes, and darned our socks.

Nick with patch-pocket jacket.

This beautiful little palace in downtown London had a garden surrounded by a high wrought iron fence, but not so high as to be un-climbable if one forgot one's keys.

Many of our evenings were spent at home with other filmmakers and journalists who dropped by. Mealtimes we hung out at a little basement cafe and bar known as *Le Petit Club Français*, which catered to Grierson's friends. A French woman named Alwyn Vaughn ran it and was always at the bar with her beautiful cat to welcome us. We talked war and filmmaking and drank double Scotches endlessly.

In Canada, Julian stayed with ginger beer and was true to his wife, the lovely Guelda. The rest of us were not so inhibited.

We used to kid him and one night played a big joke on him. He wasn't there when we were having a party. The wife of a journalist had a little too much to drink and we tucked her into his empty bed to sleep it off. Julian came home late to find there was someone in his bed. He thought it was me until he saw all that hair, and beat a quick retreat.

We didn't go to many films in London, but I did see *The Way Ahead* with David Niven & Stanley Holloway, which had the same theme as *Platoon*, a film I had made in Canada. They both focused on the relationship between an officer and his men. The English film reflected their traditional Army approach—which was not really an approach, but an "at distance." There was less saluting and more give and take in Canada, where the military was more democratic and relaxed.

The British people were something else again. I wrote home, "Here is London, so shabby-looking. There are shortages of everything, and evidence of bombs everywhere, and I have the greatest respect for all the English. After five years of war blitz, and two big Allied invasions—first by the Canadians & more recently by Americans, they have kept their good humor & their good manners. I feel like a heel complaining about the food and lack of O. J. or anything else, because these people have really done a marvelous job."

At home, Bunty was experiencing difficulties. As I had been warned long ago, Jean would be impossible to please because she would feel that no girl was good enough for me. She made it through the wedding with cotton in her ears and a grim look, but after Dada's death she seemed to welcome Bunty into the family with letters and telephone calls and numerous gifts.

After I went abroad, at Jean's urging Bunty went to Hazel Hedge with the baby

Bunty and Nash with the Della Robbia.

for the duration. This was a serious mistake. Jean and Bunty were incompatible. Jean ran a house that was beautifully decorated and groomed daily. Bunty was a good mother, but a bad housekeeper. She neither cleaned, nor kept order.

While Jean was putting fresh flowers on the tables and mantels, Bunty was putting whatever she wanted to get rid of wherever she might be. The crisis came over soiled diapers left on the drawing room mantel. For Jean, that was the end. From then on she obviously detested Bunty.

I was unaware of all this, and wrote mother to see that Bunty had a good time. "I wish she would step out and have some fun & meet some attractive 'male animal.' I certainly do not believe in these faithful vigils kept by wives. They usually are kept because the wife has no other alternative. It's up to you to fix Bunty up with a man or men." Jean did. There were plenty of flyboys available.

Before D-Day, Julian and I were separated. Grierson could not afford to waste two combat cameramen on one story. I was left with the MTBs, and Julian was sent to a small English seaport where an immense camouflage of rubber balloons resembling war equipment was taking shape on a road to the sea, to fool the Germans into thinking it was to be the place from which the Allied armies would set forth for France.

When D-Day came on June 6, I left aboard an MTB with my camera for Normandy, not knowing until the last hour where I was going. It was as much of a surprise to me as it was to the Germans. I tied myself to an upright on the boat and kept shooting. I watched in horror as I saw the fighting men from the barges literally mowed down by German artillery in concrete emplacements on the cliffs above the beach. Our own Scottish regiment from Victoria lost most of its officers and men.

My footage was edited into a film called *Fighting Sea Fleas* at the Canadian Film Board and released to the public in Canada and the United States. It was even shown in Montgomery, Alabama, where the newspaper had an article about me, and a friend made up a humorous verse about my experience:

> Nicholas saw Normandy
> Offshore from a very small boat
> On a tossing sea.
> He didn't toss his cookies though
> He said he was too scared of foe
> And far too busy holding tight
> To keep his camera upright
> And add 100 foot rolls of film
> To properly record the fight.

After the invasion, Julian went with troops through into Belgium, and was seriously wounded. I was assigned to Italy. In Rome I had something to do with the production of the very powerful film *Open City*, which was well-reviewed by all the press. Marcello Pagliero, who played the head of the underground resistance movement and who at the end of the film is tortured and killed by the Nazis, worked for me, and I met most of the people in the group that made *Citta Aperta*, and gave the director background information about them. The film was one of the great films of all time.

After Rome I went to Casino, Facsinone, and other towns where the destruction was appalling. However, the peasants were carrying on as usual. They are the solid foundation of Italy, their bare feet planted firmly in the rich volcanic soil. None of my filming was on the war itself. That was done by Army photographers.

For the Film Board, I did special events such as an Italian soldiers parade, putting up a Bailey Bridge, a bread line and a black market, students chipping Mussolini's name off the entrance to the University, and the coverage of an agricultural meeting to get the farmers to grow what was most needed in wartime.

Usually I worked alone, but for the agricultural meeting I was assigned eight Italian

Nick on the way to Normandy.

assistants, whom I directed in French. When the job of setting up the lights and connecting the cables was finished, I wanted to buy them a drink. The reply came back, "We cannot find words to express our great enthusiasm." This gem of diplomatic verbiage from a perfect dead-pan tickled me immensely, and from then on I made it my own.

For awhile in Italy I kept a diary, which was probably why I decided to go see the Forward Line of Defense (FLD), although it was not my job to film it. On December 12 I wrote:

> It is almost impossible to find "the front" in Italy, since there is no definite line drawn between the enemy & our own troops. You go down a mushy road past tanks and ammo trucks and you come to a section of infantry lying in the ditch waiting for an order to come through on the walkie-talkie.
>
> Finally they advance a few yards and somewhere out in front and down the road there's a Jerry section of infantry who seem to be waiting too. The pace is so slow and the overall strategy and planning so far removed from the little groups who do the slogging through the mud & firing, that it is impossible to get a complete picture of advances and retreats.
>
> You get a thousand small pictures like the separate frames on a roll of movie film. Only the military editors at HQ can edit them into an orderly sequence. You ask a passing soldier where a certain unit is. He is more ignorant than you. At least you have a map and from time to time "official news." The individual soldier doesn't seem particularly interested. He is more concerned with getting out of the mud and rain & finding a bottle of *vino*.
>
> WEDNESDAY DEC. 13. I drove with Col. Ralph Bush from Rome to Brigade Headquarters, which were more like what I expected: the large kitchen of a farmhouse. A major and a captain seated at a table covered with maps—both of them deeply absorbed. Several sergeants and subalterns busy at telephone and radio sets. The Intelligence officer warming his backside by an open fire where a peasant woman was stirring an iron pot over the flames. In the farmyard were all manner of vehicles including tanks, and drivers running in & out, splattering mud on the stucco walls as they set off on their noisy motorcycles with some new order.
>
> Behind is a catering school that moves right along when Division Headquarters change, and keeps training new cooks and improving old ones. We had a sample of their pastries—quite good. Not far away was a big panzer tank truck burning at

the crossroads. Our Shermans, unseen in the vineyard to our right, were sending shells whistling overhead. Peasants were hoeing in the same vineyard. They learned to avoid mines.

There are many partisans on the roads, but it is hard to tell just who are partisans & who are not. They all wear arm bands, but I don't consider them partisans unless they carry arms. They have been quite helpful to our side up here—very different from the South, where the civilians were apathetic or openly hostile.

It's amazing how the people go on about their work in the midst of war. The day before I arrived, one of the Army cameramen was shooting the establishment of a bridgehead across the Lamone River. The shells were landing all around, and some soldiers ran the gauntlet across the slippery debris to make way for a partisan helping an old woman across. She was going over into "no man's land" to act as a midwife and deliver a child.

Dec. 14. Will shoot the delivery of Christmas mail in the morning. Spent most of the afternoon looking for the Corps post office. Passed the bodies of four Canadians who had given their lives for something. It was suggested I film them, but after a close look I couldn't do it.

Dec. 15. Moved from a high-ceiling and elegant vacated doctor's apartment where everything but an oil painting and gilt frame mirror had been removed, to a poorer section of town where our rooms are ugly but more comfortable—meaning warmer. Your feet are always freezing when you come in from slogging around in the cold mud all day.

Dec. 16. Dance at the officers club. Beautiful doll brought by Maj. Tedesco. It gave me hot pants to look at her. Auburn hair, blue eyes, tilt up nose, tilt up breasts. Gin & wine and candle light & hot jazz. Open pine wood fires in all the rooms & my heart on fire for Bunty. I wanted the Italian doll when I looked at her & then I wanted Bunty & for a few minutes with my eyes closed & the music hot & sweet I had her in my arms & we were dancing very close & smoothly.

Dec. 18. This is a bad evening for writing. At 2:30 today a shell fragment killed Ralph Bush as we were hurrying down the road from the FOL. We had gotten up to 30 miles in second gear. Ralph was driving the jeep, with Bob next to him and me on the right side, when a puff of black smoke appeared on the left hand side of the road, with no sound that I can recall. I looked at Bush and there was blood around his mouth. He said, "I think you'd better take over, sir" and slumped over the wheel.

Bob cut the switch and I kept the jeep steady, but before we got the jeep stopped his head was rolling from side to side and his eyes had gone up into their sockets. We halted at Hdq. only long enough to get directions to the field hospital, which was just down the road, and we must have arrived there in less than three minutes after he was shot. But I think he was dead when we took him out of the jeep. Seeing dead soldiers was one thing. Having one die in your arms made me realize all over how lucky I was to be alive.

DEC. 19. We prepared to leave for Ravenna, which I had looked forward to, but I felt pretty rotten. It is a very historic town—the seat of power of the last of the Roman Emperors and a thriving city in the Renaissance. However, I didn't have the inclination or time to go sightseeing, though I did go into the Apollonaise to see the remarkable mosaics depicting the life of Christ—the Virgins (some 30 odd!), the Prophets, & the Emperor Justinian. All the churches have been somewhat damaged, but only the ancient St. John the Evangelist is beyond repair. When one considers how many times Ravenna has been pillaged in the past, one feels less depressed about the scars of this war.

My last assignment in Italy was most delightful and is worth telling on its own. I joined the Canadians and Australians under General "Tiny" Freyberg of New

Nick with a jeep, as on December 18.

Zealand (called "Tiny" because he was so big). They were on their way up the boot of Italy to Venice. This is the way I like to describe it:

General Freyberg and I got there ahead of the others. His objective, he said, was to take the famous Danieli Hotel, before the British or Americans arrived, and make it headquarters for the Kiwis (New Zealanders) of all ranks, and others from Canada and Australia. The best hotels in Rome and Florence had become exclusive clubs for British and American officers. Freyberg was determined to make ours democratic.

When we first saw Venice across a patch of blue water—a wonderful sight! It was the only town all the way up from Naples that hadn't been heavily bombed. Freyberg asked for his map. Then he ordered a Mustang. This was a British fighter plane with a small bomb under the port wing and another under the starboard.

He then marked the map and asked his aide to pour Martinis. They arrived and he gave me one. "We are not going to level this beautiful place," he said, and we drank to that. We crossed the lagoon in a motor boat and entered a canal near where the bombs had cleared the way and went to a landing near the Danieli.

We knew from Intelligence that the German commander and his staff were staying in the hotel. "Tiny" sent a note in to them saying "Come out and surrender. We are in control of the town." There was quite a wait. Then a note came back saying they would come out if that photographer (meaning me) would put down his camera.

"Tiny" turned to me and said "Nick, I hate to ask you to do this. I know how much this shot would mean to you, but would you mind very much putting down your camera so we can get those guys out without hurting the hotel? We are all dirty and tired. Some of us haven't had a bath for two months."

I put my camera down and stepped away from it. The Germans came out with their hands up and their arms across their faces. We moved into the hotel as they moved out, enjoying the same service, the same fine wine, the same inferior food—the acute shortage of such staples as fats, olive oil, milk, white flour and sugar would have cramped the style of any chef. But there was plenty of hot water and we had baths.

It is good to remember such a happy scene at the end of the war before I got to the death camps in Yugoslavia. I did not have time to keep a diary there, but have reconstructed what happened from my shot list, where I recorded the scenes as I shot them, to be able to identify them when the film was developed.

On May 17, 1945, ten days after VE day, I was on my way to Trieste on the border between Italy and Yugoslavia, filming hordes of refugees—starving women and children, crippled veterans, young people and old—all fleeing from the horrors of war to somewhere they hoped to be safe. By the time I got to Zagreb, the prewar population of two hundred and fifty thousand had swollen to a million.

I was headed for the death camps of Jasenovac and its subcamp for women, Stara Gradiska, not far away. Before I got there I began to see bodies by the roadside where they had been shot, others half buried in the banks of rivers, and others floating in the water.

Finally I reached Jasenovac, supervised by the Croatian Security Police with guards from the Ustase (Croatian Fascists) who murdered or deported to Auschwitz for extermination six-hundred thousand men and women. Some of the children were taken away to orphanages. Most of the prisoners were Serbs, gypsies and enemies of the state. Only about forty thousand were Jewish. I met one man who had escaped when about fifty of them rushed the guards and seventeen got through the gates. The Ustase dynamited all who remained before the Partisans arrived.

It was only a few days later that the tide turned, and I encountered around ten thousand Ustase and Nazi soldiers being herded like cattle to the prison camps. That night I listened as local inhabitants told what they would do to them. It was chilling.

I returned to Italy, and was put in a hospital. I had begun to turn yellow, and was diagnosed as having jaundice. I was there for a month before being allowed to go back to London, where I got my final wartime assignment—to do a film co-sponsored by the United Nations Relief and Rehabilitation Administration (UNRRA), on how Greece was facing up to its post-war problems.

I shot the film and returned to the Canadian Film Board to write the narration and edit the footage. The film that emerged was *Out of the Ruins*. It was handled at the U.N. by William Wells who became a close friend, and later by Ralph Foster, who headed the U.N.'s film section after the war.

There was some talk of Spiros Skouras, president of Twentieth Century Fox, taking it over to make a one or two-reel film from the footage to be shown in U.S. theaters, but nothing came of this.

Shortly, I received my honorable discharge from the U.S. military services with the rank of sergeant. And so the war ended for me.

47

Filmmaking and Red Baiting in the South

WITH THE WAR OVER, AND MY SERVICE TO THE CANADIAN FILM Board ended, like millions of other veterans, I was looking for a job. My dream was to go south and create a film production service that would fill the special needs of Southerners, just as the Canadian Film Board served all of Canada.

The opportunity presented itself almost immediately. I suspect that Grierson, who had spent some time at the headquarters of the Tennessee Valley Authority, had something to do with it, but I am not sure. In 1944 the Georgia Agricultural Extension Service had proposed to TVA that educational films be made for the "Tennessee Valley states." Two years later this began to take shape.

In 1946, word came to me in Ottawa that TVA had agreed to sponsor an interstate agency that would produce films to enlighten residents of the Tennessee Valley states as to how to use their new cheap supply of TVA electricity to improve their economics and quality of life.

In February of that year, TVA and seven of the states in the region chartered the Southern Educational Film Production Service (SEFPS) to make such films. The states were Alabama, Georgia, Kentucky, Mississippi, North Carolina, Tennessee and Virginia. Soon afterwards, South Carolina and Florida joined, making nine in all.

The aims were to produce motion pictures and film strips for tax-supported agencies, to stimulate and coordinate the production of films by public agencies, and to provide a central source of information on films, particularly those produced within the region.

I was invited to come from Ottawa to be director of production. The Rockefeller General Education Board gave a two-year grant of fifty thousand dollars to cover equipment and overhead, and the state university at Athens, Georgia, offered to provide space and fiscal services. Each film was to be funded and staffed on its own.

I took the job, which for me had the advantage of being only a few hours away from Hazel Hedge in Alabama. Bunty looked for a house in Athens, and found a three-bedroom apartment that would be available in time to accommodate us and another baby due in December.

In the meantime and thereafter we spent a great deal of time in Montgomery. This was a mistake since Jean's attitude towards Bunty was only sharpened. My presence brought the situation to a head. I was adored. She was ignored.

My professional life in Athens was strenuous. I was raising money to make films, getting and training staff, and overseeing production simultaneously. SEFPS was in demand. There was great need for educational films that could reach people en masse who were willing and anxious to learn. It was not hard to find enthusiastic young would-be documentary filmmakers back from the war, willing to work on low budgets and learn at the same time. Among those who came were George Stoney from North Carolina, who had been a photo interpreter with the Air Force in England before becoming a Rosenwald scholar in filmmaking.

Others were Bill Clifford from New York State, who had made training films for the Army; Roy Marcato from Alabama, who was a photographer for the Air Force in China during the war; and Ledford Carter, a former Georgia school teacher, who had used film to train Army recruits. In the beginning I brought down several experienced documentary filmmakers from Canada to help train my new crew. Everybody worked hard, and we finished two or three films in the first year and got others started.

Books and People described rural library services in Alabama. *Timber Growing Today*, sponsored by TVA, expanded agricultural horizons. *Florida Wealth or Waste* was concerned with the assets and liabilities of that state. In 1947, Gordon Weisenborn, who had been in training at the Canadian Film Board, came to direct *Mr. Williams Wakes Up*, which was being produced for the North Carolina Health Department.

At about the same time, the Film Board referred the chief of information at the National Cancer Institute (NCI) to SEFPS. That's how I met my future wife, Dallas. She was looking for a film producer who could produce a documentary that would do justice to a remarkable book, *Challenge: Science Against Cancer*, published by NCI. She was long on enthusiasm, but short of money and had heard that SEFPS, a non-profit organization, was known for making quality films at low cost.

My headquarters in Athens, Georgia was close to Atlanta and the Audio Visual Services of the Public Health Service at the Communicable Disease Center (CDC), so Dallas made arrangements to see us both the same day. She went to the CDC first and sat down at the desk of the head of A/V services, waiting for him to come in. He apparently arrived to pick up his telephone and answer it saying, "No, you can't loan any of our equipment to Nick Read—even if he is making a film for the North Carolina Department of Health. He's a Communist."

Dallas was well aware of the effect that the Dies Committee hearings were having in government circles. She had just had her own experience with name-calling at the National Cancer Institute. A new employee hired to organize their files did so by putting thirteen of their seventeen 3-drawer files behind the letter "C" for Cancer, leaving only three files for everything else. From then on they couldn't find anything. The new employee resisted redoing the files, so Dallas had her transferred into another job working for a scientist who needed her considerable secretarial skills.

The employee was apparently offended and angry and went to the personnel department with the story that "Dallas and her staff were a lot of Communists." She quoted one staff member as having said, "Come to the Revolution and we'll all have strawberries and cream." Happily, the personnel department identified the remark as a joke and dismissed the complaint.

This may have tempered Dallas's reaction to the accusation made so openly about me by the head of the AV Section of the Public Health Service. Despite the comment, we met a few hours later. I showed her a few of my films and gave her some prices. She left feeling she had found the right person to do *Challenge: Science Against Cancer* and returned to Bethesda to try to get funding.

Unfortunately, before she could get back to me, in August 1947, I was put in St. Mary's, the local hospital, with an excruciating headache. From there I was taken by ambulance to Emory Hospital in Atlanta where I was operated on for a congenital aneurysm of the brain. A pioneer in neurosurgery, the first chief of that department at Emory Medical School, Dr. Edgar Fincher, probably saved my life, but my prognosis as a documentary filmmaker was poor. I lost part of my sight and from then on was subject to epileptic seizures.

Four months later, when I struggled back to my job at SEFPS, there was considerable doubt that I would be able to carry on. I was quite unsteady on that January day in 1948 when I made my way back into the red brick building at the University of Georgia, which housed SEFPS.

My wound had to heal before a tantalum plate could be inserted to go over the hole in my skull. For the time being, I covered my head with a twist of gaily colored silk wrapped into a turban, but no one was fooled as to the seriousness of the situation. My health problems often made me dizzy, but the politics to come really made my head spin.

1948 was a presidential election year that greatly affected life on campus, which was awash with political meetings. There were three candidates: President Harry Truman for the Democrats, Thomas E. Dewey, the governor of New York, for the Republicans, and Henry Wallace a Democrat running as a Progressive.

Nick with his head wrapped in a turban after surgery.

Wallace as a liberal-to-left-winger threatened to split the Democratic party, attracting quite a few on the University of Georgia campus. These included two working for SEFPS, Gordon Weisenborn, a cameraman from Chicago, and Nina Finn, a musician who had come from Canada to do music and sound effects on the films.

The situation was further complicated, since the leadership of the Alabama's Democratic Party included some who were refusing to have anything to do with the election, and blocked the sending of official representatives of the state to the National Democratic Convention. These included our family friend, Colonel Marion Rushton, who became a "Dixiecrat" rather than take part.

Personally, I was for Truman, but curious about Wallace, who before being secretary of agriculture and then vice president under Roosevelt, had achieved his reputation as a scientist who developed a new variety of field corn and later became editor of the leading farm journal.

Don West, who was a member of the Georgia "Wallace for President" Committee, came to the home of the university chaplain, Dr. David Napier, to present "The Wallace Platform." I attended, listening carefully, but Weisenborn and Finn were both present and vocal. Nina Finn then hosted another Wallace meeting at her house, to which Bunty invited friends.

A few days later, I was asked to come to the office of President Caldwell of the University to discuss a serious matter. It appears that a student on campus, who attended one of the Wallace meetings, reported to his father, who was the Finance Chairman of the state legislature, that "Communists from the film group" were running the meetings.

I learned much later that Herman Talmadge, the real political boss of Georgia, had told Caldwell to "get rid of those radicals or we will cut your appropriation." President Caldwell summoned me to his office and told me to "fire the Communists, Finn and Weisenborn, or be prepared to go yourself."

I didn't answer President Caldwell until I could call a meeting of the SEFPS Board of Directors representing TVA and the nine valley states. They listened sympathetically, but agreed that in the "current climate of red baiting," such a controversy would destroy SEFPS by making it difficult if not impossible to get money to make films.

Only Mrs. Lois Rainer Green, director of Alabama's Public Library Service, voted to keep me in the job. Except for the chairman, who abstained, the rest asked for my resignation. My dream became my nightmare. Weisenborn and Finn left immediately. Others on the staff were supportive, but that was not enough to help. George Stoney was still in England on his Rosenwald scholarship. I learned many years later, when Weisenborn came to see me to apologize for what he had done to my career in Athens, that he actually had been a Communist when he worked for SEFPS.

With great sadness, Bunty and I, who by then had two children and a third on the way, packed up and left. With my loyalty in question, and a severe health problem, it was a bad time to be looking for a job. We went to New York City where there was more filmmaking and less red-baiting, and a good director could pick up assignments. I did a short film, *Planning for Good Health,* for the New York State Health Department, and other small assignments which helped pay the rent on our railroad flat and buy groceries.

Our third child, Rebecca, was born just before Christmas, 1948 in a Manhattan hospital. On New Year's Eve I wrote mother:

> Here it is almost a New Year. The children are in bed, and dishes washed and
> put away. A couple of friends will drop by. In the fridge is a bottle of champagne

to drink a health to you and your three grandchildren, especially Rebecca, or T. B. for "Tiny Baby," as she is often called.

My drinks will be limited to one glass of champagne, since I have been told not to drink at all by Dr. Vicale, the neurologist I saw at Presbyterian Hospital after my recent convulsion. While my present medications, Dilantin and Phenobarbital, will keep me pretty much under control, the effect of alcohol on the nerve centers in the brain does just the opposite. It is not felt for 72 hours, which accounts for the fact that it did not occur to me that some fairly heavy drinking I had done a few days before the convulsion had anything to do with it. I do not mind going on the wagon.

I am not sorry to see 1948 end, except that it makes us realize we are all a year older. I even hate to see the children grow up—at least Jenny who is so adorable just as she is, and I realize too, that I've lived probably over half my life and accomplished so little. I think of the home and childhood you and Dada gave me and wonder if I will ever be able to afford and create anything half so wonderful for our children.

But I have also in this troubled year just ending come to realize that I have a wonderful wife to help me in anything I undertake. I think I'm beginning to get some perspective about fatherhood and a career, and when I get another job will be able to work out a better balance. Speaking of jobs, I'm afraid I have nothing right now that brings in any immediate cash.

The New York State job will pay $400 for about 10 days work, but it takes about two months to collect money from the efficient Dewey organization in Albany. I have some work to do for the Film Board, but I'm afraid they will hold that check since they still claim I owe them money on expense accounts from Greece and Italy.

There are a couple of short term jobs in the offing, but I am hoping to get a full time job that an old friend, Bern Dryer, has found for me in Washington, D.C. I would head a film laboratory to plan, coordinate, initiate, and integrate the production of medical films for the Bureau of Medicine and Surgery of the U.S. Navy. It not only pays a good salary on a long-time basis, but would give me free medical care at the Naval Medical Hospital in nearby Bethesda.

Dr. Vicale, the neurological specialist in scar tissue and epilepsy, had told me that the scar tissue in my brain would be undergoing changes for a couple of years. He recommended that if I took the job with the Navy, I should have a periodic electro-encephalogram done by Dr. Chohn at the Naval Hospital, "to chart what's going on in your brain."

I bought a house on Elm Street in Chevy Chase, not far from the Naval Medical Hospital, and moved the family there. I wanted Dr. Chohn close at hand in case I needed him. I wrote mother that: "My head broke open again the other night. I had what the Negroes call a 'risin' and it was very sensitive and throbbed when I coughed or bent down. It feels better now and I can comb my hair without wincing." By 1949 I was working for Captain Robert V. Schultz, who was in charge of the audio visual section of the Navy's Bureau of Medicine and Surgery. His initial assignment was to produce the films *The Military Surgeon in Amphibious Assault*, *Medical Facts of V.D.*, *Mental Security for the Navy*, *Shipboard Safety*, and *The Naval Flight Surgeon*.

It was a pretty heavy schedule, and I hoped I could get the tantalum plate installed in my head before the going got too heavy. The going had already gotten too heavy for Bunty, who on her last visit to Hazel Hedge simply gave up. Jean was always critical when they were alone, and ignored her completely when guests were present.

This was observed by Bobby Arrington when he brought his little girl by to see Jenny and stayed for awhile. At the end of the conversation Bunty walked with him through the garden. She was weeping. "It's no use," Bunty said, "she has taken my husband away from me." The next morning at an early breakfast with Dallas he exploded, "I hate Jean Read." He couldn't stand the way she treated Bunty.

In a few weeks Bunty went to Martha's Vineyard in Massachusetts, for the summer, taking the children. When she returned to Chevy Chase she said she had met another man in the Vineyard, Alfred Duhrssen, and was going to marry him. He did not want the children, nor was I willing to give them up. Bunty wanted to keep them desperately, but saw no way out. She said later, "I was too weak to fight."

It didn't take long to get a divorce in Montgomery. All one had to do was present evidence of infidelity. This Bunty agreed to provide, and the divorce was granted in May of 1950. I got custody of all three children, Nash, age six, Jenny, age four and Rebecca, age two.

48

New Directions

THE CHILDREN WERE SENT TO MONTGOMERY, ALABAMA, TO STAY WITH my mother at Hazel Hedge. I carved out a little apartment for myself at the back of the house on Elm Street, rented out the remainder, and continued to work for the Navy's Bureau of Medicine and Surgery, with plans to transfer to the U.S. Public Health Service to head a new film program there.

Shortly thereafter, NCI's book, *Challenge: Science Against Cancer*, won the prestigious and highly publicized Mary Lasker Award, and the idea for a film came to life again. By then I was in the Public Health Service and was in a position to promote the project so I became reconnected with Dallas at NCI to discuss the possibilities.

The American Association of Medical Colleges (AAMC) was initiating a film program under the leadership of Dr. David Ruhe, who had been responsible for setting up my current film program in the Public Health Service. Dr. Ruhe and the officials at AAMC agreed the AAMC would be a suitable sponsor for the film.

I worked with them on this project until I had to take leave to go into the Naval Medical Hospital for my own operation. It was time to insert the tantalum plate under the skin in my head to protect the "soft place" left by my original brain surgery. To be close by, mother came to Washington to stay with a friend in Georgetown, and spent most of every day with me at the hospital. Dallas helped out by driving Jean to and from the hospital.

One evening when Dallas was taking Jean home, my mother told her that "the surgeon had found evidence of glioma, cancer of the brain, which was the reason Bunty had left him." This was a surprise to Dallas, since there had been no mention of cancer prior to this.

Dallas had been working at NCI long enough to know a lot about cancer and felt she didn't have the whole story.

She re-read an NCI publication on glioma, and went to the Naval Medical Hospital to talk to the neurosurgeon there who had put in the tantalum plate. He handed her the same publication she had consulted at NCI. She told him she had already read it, but needed to know whether my medical record from Emory Hospital in Atlanta had said anything about cancer. He told her he didn't need to get my medical record because he had been a resident of Dr. Fincher's and had personally observed the first operation.

Dallas finally got through to Dr. Fincher in Atlanta who said he had my medical record in front of him, since it had just been requested that morning by a neurosurgeon at Naval Medical Hospital in Bethesda. There was no sign of cancer.

Before leaving the National Cancer Institute for her new job in New York City, a grant request for the film, *Challenge: Science Against Cancer* came in from the Association of American Medical Colleges, signed by Dr. David Ruhe, who would be the project director if the request were approved by NCI's Advisory Council.

At the Advisory Council meeting, Dr. Shields Warren, an influential member, spoke persuasively about the need for such a broad informational film about cancer, and moved that the grant request from AAMC be approved. It was with Dr. Ruhe's help that co-sponsorship of the film by Canada's cancer authorities was arranged, which then made it eligible for production by the National Film Board of Canada, which would give us a high quality film at a low cost.

Challenge: Science Against Cancer was premiered a year and a half later on a snowy night in New York City before an eminent audience of scientists and government officials from both countries. That same night Dallas and I celebrated our engagement. It seemed fitting since we first met years earlier discussing the possibilities of producing this very film.

The engagement had its ups and downs. My mother was not enthusiastic about my getting married to anyone, much less to someone from an unknown family in California. She often made her feelings known. Each time I came back from visits to my children, who were with her in Montgomery, I had been given a reason why our wedding should be postponed. I well remember the evening when Dallas broke our engagement and told me "to go back and tie a silver cord to your mother."

It was patched together again when my father's side of the family invited Dallas to dinner. Peyton Rous, an eminent scientist and future Nobel prize winner, had known her as a science writer for a long time, and said that he would spread the word about her admirable qualities. The word was spread even further by Dallas's professor at Columbia University's graduate school of journalism, Douglas Southall Freeman, the editor of the *Richmond News Leader*, and author of the Pulitzer Prize winning biography of Robert E. Lee. Excerpts from his letter of congratulations, praising Dallas, found their way into the social column of the Montgomery newspaper. What better way to announce an engagement in the South!

The wedding took place in the garden of the Elm Street house at the side of the pool on a very hot June 21, 1951. The ceremony was performed by the Reverend Russell Stroup, a Presbyterian minister (Episcopalian ministers could not marry divorced persons). Dr. Pen Schenker, a filmmaker from Munich, stood up for me, and journalists Lura Jackson and Judy Graves were there for Dallas.

Dallas's mother came from California for the wedding. Jean stayed in Alabama with the children, and sent her good friends, the Marion Rushtons, to represent her among the hundred guests at the wedding. These included some last minute "add-ons," such as the contractor who was still getting the house ready and came out to cut the wedding cake. "I should know how" he explained, "I've cut three of my own." After that, we all went swimming.

For the honeymoon, I chose the Cloisters on Sea Island in Georgia, where Bo and Berry had gone on their honeymoon. The hotel clerk at the Cloisters noted that we were the seventeenth honeymoon couple to arrive that day and made reservations for us at the formal dinner dance that evening. My white linen suit was hastily retrieved from the suitcase where it had been packed after the wedding. Once dressed, we joined the other honeymooners, who were all in their twenties, for an evening of chatting about weddings and honeymoons. We were much older, thirty-seven and thirty-five, and felt somewhat out of place, so we decided to skip further social activities organized by the Cloisters.

Dallas spent her time on the beach catching up with motherhood. For Rebecca, or "Beka,"

Dallas and Nick's wedding.

she read *Your Child from One To Three,* and for Jenny and Nash, Arnold Gesell's *The Child from Five to Ten.* She decided there should be a new Public Affairs Pamphlet on *Stepmothers Can Be Nice.* I outlined a film script for the Public Health Service on community health resources.

Before we left, the Cloisters captured us for a group picture of the fifty-three couples there at the time, and mailed the photograph to everyone with an invitation to come back for reunions.

Dallas flew back to Maryland and I drove on to Alabama to pick up my little girls, their belongings, and Lily Belle Jones, the nurse. She had been caring for them at Hazel Hedge, and would accompany them to Elm Street for a transition period. It was decided it would be best to have Nash, who didn't really want to leave Hazel Hedge, come later when school was about to start, so that he would be fully occupied as soon as he arrived.

Dallas's introduction to the South did not really begin until she drove with the family to Montgomery to spend the Christmas holidays. She was surprised that Hazel Hedge was "not an antebellum pillared mansion, but a pleasant big country house set in the midst of a beautiful garden. It was filled with antiques and family portraits and flowers."

She was invited to have a conducted tour of the house and meet Jean's old cousin William Baldwin who came every Sunday for dinner. They hit if off in a conversation devoted to the high cost of funerals. William, the vice president of the family bank, was known to be something of a skinflint, and they established an collegial relationship and saw each other regularly after that.

William, who was in the Navy reserve, had decided to use the burial provided for officers still on partial duty. Dallas said that giving one's body to a medical school eliminated all costs—and helped someone get through medical school.

William lived a long time, but never changed his funeral plans. He said he was influenced by a cost-cutting arrangement that went astray made by his mother, Sister Bess. She had held that a Baldwin was above being embalmed and didn't need a mortician. She died in bed and was to be carried downstairs and laid out in the parlor, but got stiff and her body had a hard time making it around a tight turn in the narrow old stairs. I never heard the end of that story.

The conducted tour through the house was done by Ben Miller, who had been with Jean for more than thirty years. He knew her and the house very well. Theirs was the kind of relationship that was later portrayed in the film, *Driving Miss Daisy.*

Ben with Lambo.

On Jean's eightieth birthday the guests sang:

> Let's drink a toast to Ben
> For Ben's the best of colored men
> Hurrah, Hurrah, we'll drink a toast indeed
> To Ben the Boss of Hazel Hedge
> And old Miss Jeanie Read.

Coming from California, where the textbooks were limited to reporting that the North had won the Civil War and freed the slaves, Dallas had been under the general impression that the Civil War had settled things. The relationship between Ben and Jean fit right in. However, she soon found that it had not changed the attitudes of many Southerners.

At a year-end Christmas dinner given by my boyhood friend, Billy Hudson, for the white employees of the newspaper he published, the greeting from the head table included "nigger" jokes—overheard by the black waiters coming and going through the room. It was as if they were not there. It didn't help much when I took Dallas to the annual ball of the Mystic Order of Rebels, where all the rebels were sworn to silence until midnight.

She felt ostracized. Even though she had plenty of dance partners, not one of them spoke to her. She thought it was because she was a Northerner. Any such treatment was especially noticeable in contrast with Southern manners in general—which were exquisite. Compliments flowed like honey, one of which repeated again and again was to the effect that "Dallas is such a good mother."

She exploded to me, "I don't even know how to be a mother, let alone a good one. If anyone says it again I think I shall scream!" She didn't. She just said "Well, I'm trying." To prove her point, she edited a family publication, *Elm Street Clarion*, a six by nine inch newsletter printed with pictures, reviewing what had happened to the family in our first year, and thereafter for eleven years. It kept everyone, including Jean and Bunty, well-informed.

Issue No. 1, dated Jan. 1, 1952, but mailed January 15, explained that "Due to circumstances beyond the Editor's control, aged 3, 5 and 7, this is behind schedule, and there's no indication that the situation will improve with the years." Issue

No. 2 in 1953, included an announcement that the Public Affairs Committee had published the pamphlet *Stepmothers Can Be Nice*. Nos. 5-6 appeared at Easter with a headline, "Merry Christmas, Happy New Year" with a footnote: "It's never too late for this warm, old-fashioned greeting."

The big event for all the Christmases was Jeanie's Christmas Eve party, in a setting of garlands and flowers, lit by dozens of candles and a fine fire burning in the stone fireplace behind an elegant brass fender. Everybody who was anybody, and a considerable number of nobodies, were invited by Jean because they would have nowhere else to go. At that first one, where all the guests wanted to meet Dallas as my new wife, she was nervous.

She took a stand near Ben, who presided over the punch bowl with its powerful mixture of rye whisky, Jamaican rum, tea and lemon juice. He knew everyone and they warmed to his presence. Dallas could greet them when they stopped by for "Craik punch." She had one glass which made her feel so much more relaxed that she asked Ben for another. He said firmly, "No'me. You is on show."

At that moment she was standing by the pin-striped Sir George Waller, who had just said, "You can always tell someone's background by whether they say 'to-mah-to' or 'to-may-to.'" She only had time to decide that a "to-mah-to" would never pass her lips, when Waller passed out. Ben caught him before he hit the floor and rolled him to one side of the rug. "Did he have another?" Dallas asked. "Yeahem" said Ben, "two."

Dallas met everybody, starting with Shearon Elebash, who had moved into Hazel Hedge after I left and became the special friend of young Nash when he lived

Shearon Elebash

with his grandmother. At the Christmas Eve party it would be Shearon's special skill to coax music for carols from the old Steinway, clogged as the strings were with the droppings from flower arrangements put on top by Jeanie.

Among the many guests, the most spectacular entrance was made by "Rosie" Saffold, who swept in from the *pôrte cochére* wearing a red velvet cloak with a white ermine collar, above which her white hair was piled high under a black lace mantilla with a pink camellia on top.

Ben saw to it that nobody (except George Waller) consumed too much punch, and the traditional good time included a performance of "The Black Jack Davy," in which Jean and I

Jean and Ben around the Craik punch bowl.

played the roles of a faithless wife and a dashing high-wayman. Dallas sang the last lines: "And the moral of this tale they say / Is just a little bit shady."

The next day Dallas got up early to keep a date she had made with Milo Howard, then head of the Alabama Department of Archives and History, to learn a little more about Alabama by taking a guided tour through the Archives.

Before Dallas could get out of the house, an old friend of Jean's, Elizabeth Thigpen, arrived carrying a brace of doves "for Nickie's breakfast." She was wearing a lavender suit, and the doves were tied together with a lavender ribbon. At breakfast Jean was like a mother bird feeding her young—offering succulent bites to me as I sat at her side. Later Dallas asked me, "How did you ever learn to chew?"

Milo walked Dallas through corridors at the Archives, which were hung with old paintings of elegantly dressed gentlemen who presumably had played a role in the growth of the state. Some he identified by name and position, but he didn't have to give her the name of a life-sized plaster figure of a rider on a horse, prominently displayed. It was the Alabama country singer, Hank Williams. She learned from Milo how Sir George Waller she had met the evening before had acquired his title. He had worked for the State Department, serving as U.S. *Chargé d'Affaires* in Luxembourg, a small country between France and Germany, before World War I. He stayed on when the Germans invaded and as he described it, "met the Hun and smelt his carrion breath!" In thanks he was named an Honorary Citizen by the Duchess of Luxembourg.

This, according to Waller, was the equivalent of knighthood, entitling him and his descendants to use "Sir" before their names. My mother wrote a ceremony for the rector of St. John's Church in Montgomery, in which Sir George passed the title on to one of his nephews: "When Jean stood up we all stood up, and when she kneeled, we all kneeled. He had a sword that he laid on his nephew's back at the end of the ritual. It went smoothly."

Milo told her a lot about his predecessor who headed the Archives for many years, Marie Bankhead Owen, the sister of two senators and the aunt of Tallulah.

She had inherited the job from her husband, an historian, and came to be known as a "tiger woman," who made her own rules and enforced them. By tradition, only white people visited the Archives, and when the black historian, John Hope Franklin, from the North came, she welcomed him, but asked him to please turn around "because I've never seen a black man all around before." She then put him at a desk surrounded by high files, "where he could take notes in private."

She worked at the job full time, collecting many of the oil portraits of prominent citizens mounted on the walls. One day on the way to work she had an accident and was taken to the hospital with a split tongue and a broken kneecap. She motioned for a pencil and paper and wrote, "To Hell with the knee-cap, Doctor, but a Bankhead without a tongue is no good to Alabama."

We both felt it was time to go home again—to get back to 4303 Elm Street in Chevy Chase, Maryland where there were problems awaiting us. The stream at the bottom of the hill had washed out of its banks and the bridge across it had fallen in. The street in front, across from the school, had so much traffic that the children were endangered and there was no place to park in front of our house The big threat was from a state and county plan to lay a ninety-inch water pipeline through everybody's backyard gardens.

That's when the Elm Street, Oakridge, and Lynn Civic Association (EOL) was organized. I was its first president and had the backing of the homeowners in the area. We went to public meetings, spoke at government hearings, signed petitions and wrote numerous letters.

EOL became known as a big fighter. We fought for stream embankments and for street stop signs. We even found another route for the ninety-inch pipeline that threatened our back yards.

We got a park that kept our neighborhood from being invaded by high rise commercial buildings that were encroaching from Wisconsin Avenue in Bethesda. We were invited to send a representative to participate officially in the affairs of Chevy Chase Section Four, which marked the boundaries of our area in the county.

At 4303 Elm Street, the house was becoming a home. It was ideally located and equipped to keep children busy and overseen in its own back yard. Perched on the edge of a deep slope, it had a huge elm tree for climbing and a pool for swimming, and at the bottom, a spring-fed stream, Coguelin Run, provided a place to wade and look for salamanders and polliwogs. A bridge across led to an embankment that went up to a B & O right-of-way where a once-a-week freight train made its ponderous way to Georgetown in D.C., on which adventurous little boys could hitch a ride for the three blocks to Bethesda.

From our house above, we could keep track of what was going on in the big back yard, whether it was the swimming pool gate left open, or mischief of some sort. A left-open swimming pool gate was considered a danger and "I didn't do it" was no excuse.

One day Dallas thought she saw smoke across the stream where Jenny and Beka, five and three, were playing with the little boy who lived next door, a seven-year-old named Poncho. She called the girls and watched them as they made their way slowly up the hill to the house.

"Were you playing with fire?" she asked. "No," they replied.

"Well, what were you doing?" asked Dallas. The girls shyly responded, "Taking our pants off." When she asked, "Why? Were you too hot?" the girls answered "No. Poncho asked us to."

Dallas sat them down on a kitchen stool and said firmly, "Now this is important." They leaned forward to listen. "Don't ever take your pants off just because some boy asks you to. Never!" They nodded in solemn agreement.

49

Combunist the Lion and Other Animals

M Y TRANSFER TO THE PUBLIC HEALTH SERVICE DID NOT GO smoothly. I arrived at a time when the red-baiting Senator Joe McCarthy was focusing on "the hundreds if not thousands of Communists in the government." President Truman initiated Executive Order 9835, establishing the Federal Employees Loyalty Program, under which each agency was to appoint its own examiner to question suspect employees.

I knew that my trouble with the University of Georgia would come to light, as would my family connections with admitted Communists Darlie and Jane Speed, and with Paxton Hibben, who though not a Communist, had been honored by the Soviets at a major gathering held at the Kremlin. I sought legal advice and got Joseph L. Rauh Jr., an outstanding liberal lawyer and prominent Democrat who had successfully represented persons in Washington unfairly accused of being Communists. My mother sent as associate counsel her old friend, Col. Marion Rushton.

Colonel Rushton identified himself as a "State's Rights Democrat," but was described in a Montgomery newspaper as "a card-carrying, dues-paying unreconstructed Dixiecrat, as much an enemy of the National Democratic Committee as Henry Wallace, Tom Dewey, Earl Browder or Norman Thomas."

As it turned out, both counsels did a good job for me. The examiner from the agency was James E. Brown, and testimony was heard by three members of the Loyalty Board of the Fourth Civil Service Region. Joe Rauh presented a carefully researched and thorough brief, but during the lunch break, it was Colonel Rushton who made friends with James Brown. He found they had a common interest in hunting birds. "Why don't you come down in the fall when the ducks are running?" he asked. "I have a nice little place outside Montgomery where the shooting is good. Be glad to have you."

When the hearing was over, and the examiner had conferred with the representatives of the Loyalty Board, Mr. Brown announced, "It is obvious that Mr. Read is not and never has been a Communist so we can save time by making the decision orally right now, without any formal report."

Joe Rauh was quick to insist that a transcript of the proceedings would be needed with the verdict: "That Nicholas Cabell Read was rated eligible on loyalty for Federal employment." This turned out to be very important, since the red scare lasted a long time. I was able to use the transcript with the verdict on several occasions to clear the way to jobs I wanted to do.

However, it didn't save our popcorn bedspread, which was laid to waste by the "lion friend" of a couple of fellow-travelers, named Jenny and Beka, aged six and four, who climbed under the spread when the bed was unoccupied. This led to the destruction of many popcorn balls, presumably by an evil lion named "Combunist." At least that's what the girls said. The bedspread had been crocheted by Dallas's mother as a wedding gift, but as Senator Joe McCarthy made plain, Communists could destroy anything. The girls explained that Combunistic lions love crocheted popcorn.

As in all families, the mornings were hectic in the our Elm Street house, with its three bedrooms and one bath, and everybody trying to use the bathroom at the same time. I got there first with a medley of songs under the shower, ranging from popular hits to Negro spirituals, and several were tossed in for the express purpose of getting the children up and on their way:

> Good mornin boss, good mornin men,
> What time of day does work begin?
> That all depends on who you are
> And who's the man you're workin' for.

I also sang some old Army songs, substituting Jenny or Beka's name and leaving out the bad words. Dallas protested, "What will the girls think when they grow up and hear the real words?" I explained, "There will be other real words by then and they won't understand the old ones."

It was during this time that the swimming pool project began. In the late spring when the children were finishing their first year at Chevy Chase Elementary School, that neighborhood children asked the little girls, "When do you open the pool?"

We suddenly realized why home-owned swimming pools had been called "an attractive nuisance." Who would be there to watch the children when Dallas and I and Kathleen Williams, who lived next door and owned half the pool, were at work? The pool had been put in years before by former owners who installed it across the property lines.

After consulting with Mrs. Williams, a neighborhood meeting was called to solve the problem and it was decided that if each family chipped in $10, it would pay for a lifeguard for the summer. We soon got one in the person of "Sonny" Crawford, an Eagle Scout in the eighth grade who had all his swimming badges.

He was idolized by the little girls, and had no trouble keeping the boys from rough-housing by suggesting that they "need not come tomorrow" if they misbehaved.

Between eleven in the morning and five in the afternoon more than one hundred children, divided by age and sex into groups of twenty or so, swam in the pool each weekday during June, July, and August. And when flash floods in the stream just behind the pool threatened to undercut it, fathers of the swimmers came on a weekend with shovels and saws and cement and shored it up with railroad ties supplied by the B & O.

The project continued for seven years. There were no injuries that couldn't be covered by a Band-Aid. When one little boy came to say goodbye because "we are moving to Chicago, where we will have our own pool," he was asked, "And will you share it with your neighbors as we do here?" He answered, "Well, I don't know. We own ours."

In the meantime, Nash got a job delivering the *Times Herald*, which in our neighborhood had few subscribers, since most people took the *Washington Post* in the morning. It meant pedaling many blocks to deliver very few papers. Forewarned, he promised to go to bed early and wake up by his own alarm at six. That didn't happen. When the alarm went off it took parental pressure: "But you have made a commitment, Nash. They are depending on you."

On the third day he leaned out his upstairs window and shouted to the driver in the street who was bringing his papers, "You're ten minutes late. I have a man on my route who likes to get his paper by seven. Divide my bundle, leaving half of my papers here and the rest in front of the Pilot's Association on East-West Highway." From then on he was on his own.

He had already become Assistant Den Chief, Bear Class of the Cub Scouts of America, and was emerging as something of a class leader. One night after dinner one of his pals who was running for class president rang the doorbell to confer. Our family had just engaged in a lively debate over who could stand on his or her head the longest and were competing on pillows on the floor of the living room. The door opened to disarray as we fell to the floor at the sound of the bell. Nash explained, "We were just standing on our heads," a perfectly reasonable explanation.

It was at about this time that Bobby Jackson, my good friend Lura's oldest son, came to live with us for a year. We pulled the ladder stairs down from the attic and converted it into sleeping quarters for the two boys. Nash stayed up there after Bobby moved away. He liked being out of everybody's reach, and being out of sight kept him from having to make his bed.

He had begun to take his dog Topper, a brown cocker spaniel, with him when he delivered his newspapers. This was our first pet. The next year at Easter grandmother sent a Belgian hare who came to be known as "Oliver" from our telephone number, OLiver 4-6594 on his collar. Then I, who was making a film in Nicaragua, brought "Mono," a little squirrel monkey from there for Beka, who rode him around town on the handlebars of her bicycle. It was the beginning of what became known as the Read zoo.

Mono escaped occasionally and climbed into trees. At one time the rope on his collar got caught in a branch and the firemen were called with extension ladders to get him down. All the neighbors gathered round for the spectacle, shouting "Get him, Tarzan!"

A long-nosed coatimundi from Mexico, equipped with sharp teeth that destroy rattle snakes in its native habitat, learned to like martinis and adopted me. Jenny acquired a beagle with a high-pitched yelp and named her Decibel. She distinguished herself by winning top prize at dog obedience school, but never learned to come when called. This caused problems on a cross-country camping trip when she didn't come when called from various national forests visited on the way. The camping trip had a direction and a deadline—to get all of us to Los Angeles in time for me to teach a summer class in filmmaking at the University of Southern California (USC).

Saving time was important, and not wasting it equally so. The girls tried to learn to pee like Nash, standing up. (It would have been so much faster than going behind a bush.)

An Easter duck named Dandelion (having turned from yellow to white) went on the same trip on the top of the camping trailer, in a pink box with a screen door labeled "Just Dandy." At one point we were passed by a honking driver, who shouted across the intervening space "Dandy's door is open." She caused no trouble as long as we stopped whenever we came to water. We did stop—seemingly at every stream and lake, literally swimming across the United States.

We all got pretty hot and parched crossing the Mohave Desert during the heat of the day, but in order to get to our California destination on the Pacific Coast by dusk, we had to keep up the pace. There we were to meet friends who had arranged to let us stay at their beach house while they went to the mountains for their own vacation. It's no wonder that upon arrival Dandy waddled into their garden pool for a dip, and ended up eating their goldfish.

When we knew I would be going to the University of Southern California, which is located in one of the hottest parts of Los Angeles, Dallas, who was born in Los Angeles and went to college there, wrote friends asking if anyone had a beach house in commuting distance of USC. Our best answer came from Narcissa Vanderlip, whose family had owned a big old house and a great deal of land at Portuguese Bend near Palos Verdes, since the early 1900s.

By 195,7 it was a gated estate with beautiful gardens, two hundred peacocks, a private beach, and a membership in the beach club. There was a bedroom and bath for each of us, three kitchens and a thirty-foot long monks' dining table for meals, a huge fireplace where a Mexican gardener named *Jesús* laid wood for a fire, and a stone porch where the peacocks came for pound cake. We borrowed a second car, a 1945 Hudson that a friend's son had used for hauling stones, but was adequate for errands and for taking the family swimming when I was at USC with ours.

The weather-beaten Hudson was an anomaly going through the gated entrance to Narcissa Drive, but it got us where we were going as long as we remembered to park it headed downhill, since that was the only way it would start. All went well until the middle of August, when at one shifting, the gear stick twisted off entirely. The timing was right for our return, and the rest of us, including Dandy, drove home by way of grandmother's in Alabama where, little did we know, we would be picking up another pet.

We were at Bobby Arrington's farm, outside of Montgomery, and he showed us a mother pig suckling her young. When Jenny squealed with delight, he asked, "Would you like one?" Jenny said, "Yes, if it could be a girl." Bobby extracted a piglet—how did he know it would be a female? It was. He also explained that his Alabama pigs had an extra rib.

He put it in a box in the back of our station wagon, and we drove on to our next stop, Belvoir, the handsome residence of Mildred "Rosie" Saffold. We had made a date for Beka and a young musician who had spent the summer with us to practice on the two well-tuned pianos at Belvoir. When we got there, we were somewhat delayed by the sight of an owl with a splint on its leg tethered to the stump of a tree in the middle of the front lawn. Inside the house was another distraction, an enormous gold harp next to a life-sized oil painting of Mrs. Saffold's beautiful daughter, Georgia, playing it.

The two girls made their way to the pianos, and Jenny and Dallas went upstairs to greet Mrs. Saffold, who was reclining in a great brass bed. She was wearing a black nightgown with a little black lace veil, and a pink camellia in her hair.

Jenny was polite but quite obviously anxious to get away. She explained that she needed to tend to her baby pig in the car, and would like to draw the owl. Mrs. Saffold, brought up on a farm, said to go get the pig and bring it to her and she would take care of it. It was only a few minutes before the pink unwashed piglet was sliding down beside Rosie between the silk sheets.

Dallas went in to see the once beautiful Georgia, who had come home very ill to Belvoir. She no longer resembled the young woman playing the harp, but looked terrible with hair half-colored, surrounded by medications—Vick's salve, cough syrup, nose drops, etc. She died only a few weeks later.

Georgia had always sent the children generous checks at Christmas, which we put aside to be spent after Santa's toys had lost their luster and other things were wanted for spring. We always said that they were from Georgia, as indeed they were, and the girls remembered her with great fondness. When we told them she had died, they got down on their knees and prayed for her, and Jenny asked, "Do you think the owl has gotten her to heaven yet?" That was one we couldn't answer.

Jenny named our Alabama pig Wilbren, a feminine version of the pig Wilbur in *Charlotte's Web* by E. B. White. She found a new home near the garbage cans under the back steps at Elm Street and thrived in her environment. She grew so big she needed a St. Bernard dog harness for her romps down the back hill with Jenny, who exercised her daily. "I don't see why Grandmother calls some people 'common as pig tracks,'" questioned Jenny.

One day in June, Dallas, who can't smell very well under the best of circumstances, came home from work to say, "This place smells like a pig pen." She became aware of the need to do something about it, since with no air conditioning, our next door neighbors kitchen windows less than a dozen feet away, were always open. She felt that the pig must go.

Jenny said she had already had an offer from one of the garbage men who said he would take care of the pig, but she had some doubts about what "take care of" meant. When she wrote an agreement to the effect that the pig would be used for breeding purposes only, he was no longer interested.

She went to the local Farm Women's Cooperative Market where she let it be known that she would give her Alabama pig "with its extra rib" to any farmer's wife who would agree to use her for breeding purposes only. The following Saturday a contract was signed and the farm truck came to Elm Street to take Wilbren away. It was a sad parting.

The story didn't end there. This pig didn't like other pigs and had to be kept in a separate pen. Not only would she not breed, but it meant extra work for the farmer who already had a heart condition. When the doctor told him he must get rid of his pigs, she was hauled away to the slaughterhouse with the rest. We heard about it from the farmer's wife, who asked us not to tell Jenny that she had to break her contract. She felt really bad.

50

Making Films

T HE WORK THAT I MOST WANTED TO DO WAS TO PRODUCE AND DIRECT documentaries. My job in charge of films at the Public Health Service gave me no time to do this. I wanted to encourage the development of films serving public health. This meant finding what was available or underway, and what was needed. It meant matching the needs for health films with potential government and other sponsors who would pay to have them made. It was essentially a desk job, telephoning and writing letters and arranging meetings—but without any filmmaking in it for me.

I formed a new company, Potomac Film Producers, with two filmmakers I knew well. One was Dr. Norman "Pen" Schenker, an eminent producer of medical films in Munich and Zurich before the war, with whom I had worked in the Navy Bureau of Medicine and Surgery. The other was an old friend and fellow southerner, George Stoney, who had been trained as a sociologist at the University of North Carolina, and was a writer before getting into filmmaking with me at the Southern Education Film Production Service.

"Pen," a physician, wanted to make films to be shown to doctors and scientists, well-funded by pharmaceutical companies. George was interested in doing educational films on low budgets that would solve problems for ordinary people. The two had nothing in common but high standards of filmmaking. It wasn't enough. Dr. Schenker returned to Switzerland, and George Stoney went to New York University where he taught films and television and eventually headed that department.

Potomac Film Producers was reduced to one. I went on working from the offices of Potomac on Connecticut Avenue. I did assignments for television such as a feature on the author Isak Dinesen when she came from Denmark on a lecture tour, and another on Castro from footage shot in Cuba. I also organized the Washington Film Council—and along the way sought sponsors to do documentary films.

Dallas organized a non-profit group of women writers like herself who had recently moved to Washington with their husbands and children, but who wanted to go back to work, at least part-time. As PR Associates, twelve of them leased space in the headquarters of the prestigious American Council on Education. The headquarters was located on Massachusetts Avenue, near Connecticut Avenue, in a handsome building that had been converted from luxurious family flats, each with its own servants' quarters. They rented former servants' quarters converted into six small offices, each with one desk shared by two part-timers on different days.

Their first and long-time client was the American Society of Clinical Pathologists, which contracted with them to create a National Committee for Careers in Medical Technology (NCCMT). Their purpose was to recruit science-oriented students to work in pathology labs performing tests for the diagnosis and treatment of patients.

In 1953, NCCMT started a national recruitment drive by printing literature and making a film, *In a Medical Laboratory*, to explain what happens in a well-run hospital lab, and who makes it happen. It was produced by Bob Churchill, one of my friends from wartime, now back in Hollywood. It was a good film.

NCCMT successfully distributed the film *In a Medical Laboratory* and recruitment literature through national science teacher and guidance counselor associations. They offered a career leading to employment in the midst of the depression, requiring only a couple of years of college science, and some on-the-job training. Moreover, these were jobs for women who were usually overlooked by employers seeking young scientists. High school girls who had done well in science were a prime target, and the campaign was a great success.

However, as the word spread, a black cloud appeared on the horizon. Numerous commercial "schools" of medical technology sprang up across the country, offering to provide certified training in short courses for a fee. Salesmen went to school guidance counselors and arranged visits to talk to parents about the schools. Dallas suggested to our daughter, Beka, that she sign up for such a home visit.

The salesman arrived when everybody was home at six p.m., and brought his own machine with a videotape. It started with a picture of George Washington University Hospital in the District of Columbia as the place where the training would take place. This was not true. In fact, George Washington University Hospital, as was the case in all other accredited hospital laboratories, could not employ commercial school graduates as "medical technologists." They hadn't learned enough to run the tests on patients for whom results could have serious consequences—incorrect diagnosis could lead to death. They could only get jobs as laboratory assistants, working under qualified medical technologists, and were mostly used to wash up and keep the glassware sterilized. The diplomas they received from such schools "certifying them as qualified medical technologists" were literally not worth the paper they were printed on.

It was only when Dallas procured two such commercial school diplomas, certifying that our dog was a qualified medical technologist, and took the dog and his certificates to a U.S. Senate oversight hearing, that the public was alerted to the situation. A picture of the dog, Strayborne, with his diplomas in the Senate Hearing Room, was on the front page of the *Washington Post* the next day.

Soon afterwards an article describing the deficiencies of such commercial schools, as exemplified by one in Michigan, appeared in a professional journal, *Modern Hospital*. Reprints were distributed widely to hospital administrators and their personnel directors by pathologists and the NCCMT.

After that, the commercial school named in the article sued the professional journal as well as pathology organizations in states where the article and its reprints had the effect of reducing enrollment in commercial schools. The total sought from the state pathology organizations was $2.5 million, from the NCCMT $750,000, and from Dallas, $250,000 for perpetrating a "malicious tort" and for trying to put commercial schools out of business.

It took two years for the pathologists to win the suit, thereby making it illegal for any commercial school to claim to train medical technologists. They could only claim to train medical technicians or laboratory assistants.

While all this was happening, I finished one documentary and had contracts for several others, and could afford to joke that Dallas was not a "malicious tort," but a "delicious tart."

My first contract took me to Nicaragua, where I was to make a film for the World Bank on the economic potential of that country under the leadership of its dictator, Anastasio Somoza. It got off to an awkward start when David Fulton, who was representing the Bank, fell into a saltwater pond, which at that very time was being viewed as an economic asset for its salt by Somoza himself. Things didn't improve when the Nicaraguan worker selected for the principal role in the documentary film was identified as an enemy of the Somoza family who had burned down another economic asset, the Department of Agriculture, in protest against Somoza's policies.

It was a bad beginning, but after that first foreign film, I was out of Washington as much as I was in. I went to Greece, Africa, Bolivia and Spain for sponsors ranging from the Methodist Church Television & Film Commission to the United Nations International Children's Emergency Fund (UNICEF). In 1954, UNICEF sent me to Greece to do a sequence on malaria and then to French Equatorial Africa to direct another on leprosy.

A pleasant diversion there was a safari by Land Rover arranged by my French hosts, who took along their own chef. A typical safari menu by Pierre included *pâté*, onion soup, *poulet en vin*, chilled wine, and *crèpes suzette*. I wrote home to mother, "It was the kind of a safari you would have enjoyed."

In addition to the usual herds of wild animals, I saw close-up a leopard that liked to wrestle and a hippopotamus that drank beer. The latter caused much embarrassment to Jenny, who in the third grade's "show and tell" said that her Daddy was having lunch in Africa on the banks of a river when a hippopotamus below him in the water opened its enormous mouth and her Daddy had poured down a beer. "The hippo smacked its lips and went away." Jenny was sent to the corner by the teacher who said that in "Show and Tell" she was supposed to tell the truth.

When I left Africa, I was given a "going-away" party at which I sang American Negro spirituals and demonstrated jitterbugging. For one who had never jitterbugged, I did very well. There was, however, no "going-away." Instead I received a cable from UNICEF asking me to stay another week to do a short film for children on the eradication of malaria by spraying DDT on the inside of the thatched huts of the natives to kill mosquitoes.

I took my two cameras and rolls of film and made my way to the village of Bogo where UNICEF personnel were working on the mosquitoes. I was given an assistant who knew nothing about filmmaking, but was introduced to the chief of the village, the Lamidou of Bogo, who was to provide whatever I needed. He did.

The Lamidou was mounted on a fine horse, wearing flowing colorful robes and a small orange embroidered pillbox of a hat. He was six feet of handsome African chief with twenty-six wives and five thousand subjects, and he spoke French. The story line for the film was simple. It introduced children sick with malaria, and a native witch doctor who used magic to cure them. The witch doctor stole the DDT when he realized it might put him out of business. As a climax, the Lamidou sent in horsemen to capture the witch doctor and retrieve the DDT.

To get a long shot of the horsemen as they approached, I had my UNICEF assistant stand at one end of a field with a camera and press a button as they came into view. I moved around with the other camera getting close-ups. The Lamidou arrived with five hundred horsemen wearing the red, purple and gold uniforms of his cavalry. As I commented later, "There I was in this Cecile B. DeMille situation with a hand-held camera and black and white film!"

The witch doctor was captured and the DDT saved, and the celebration afterwards was real, with native dancing and music. As a farewell present, the Lamidou gave me my choice of a fifty-pound jar of honey or one of his many wives. I thanked him, explaining that either would be too difficult to transport, and asked instead for the orange pillbox hat for Dallas. "I thought you would like it better than if I brought home a native wife."

The film, which was called *Big Day in Bogo*, would have pleased any child, but it had two problems. The narrator provided by the U.N. turned out to be from an enemy tribe with a different dialect. And even before that could be solved, the World Health Organization banned the use of DDT wherever it might come in contact with humans. The film was never shown, except to the Washington Film Council, which awarded me a Lifetime Membership for being the only one among them who had written, cast, shot, and produced a film in one week entirely on my own.

While I was away, my mother had celebrated her eightieth birthday by going to Greece on a Swann tour, where she set a pace for the other tourists by visiting every island, climbing the hill to the Acropolis with alacrity, and winning the first prize on shipboard for the best performance in costume. She was welcomed home by a birthday party at which poems by all the guests were recited and printed in a booklet. To the tune of "My Darling Clementine," Nancy Smith sang hers:

> In a city by the river, on an early August morn
> A star fell on Alabama, and a CHARACTER was born
> Oh, Miss Jeanie, when at first you
> Took your star upon your knee
> Did you kind of have an inkling
> What a Comet she would be?

My next film, sponsored by the Methodist Church Television and Film Commission, was to show the work being done by a Methodist mission in Bolivia. On the way to the Washington National Airport, I discovered I had forgotten to bring the lens covers for my camera.

Always resourceful, Dallas said, "Stop at a drug store and I'll get something." When she told the clerk she wanted condoms he asked, "How many? There are six in a box." I used three on the cameras and brought the rest home in the box. It was put out of the little girls reach to keep them from being used as swimming caps for Barbie dolls. When Dallas finally threw the box away, our son Nash, who emptied the trash, retrieved it and told on her—"Mother threw away Daddy's lens covers."

Cameras and lenses intact, I arrived in La Paz, Bolivia, ready for action. I even had time to buy a duty free bottle of whisky to take along for an occasional nightcap. The twelve thousand foot altitude of La Paz made me dizzy so I sat down to await the missionary coming to meet me. When I got up to greet the Methodist minister, the whiskey fell off my lap and crashed to the floor. "That's too bad," the minister said, looking pleased.

I scripted and shot *Mission in Bolivia* and spent some time exploring the surrounding country. For the most part it consisted of a broad plain, the Alto Plano, a thousand feet above La Paz in the Andes. Its inhabitants were Aymara Indians who lived as they had for centuries, in small villages around a very large inland lake, Titicaca. They herded sheep and did a little farming. The Spaniards came there looking for gold, but instead found the potato, of much more value to humanity.

The Alto Plano was made to order for a documentary film, and I made one for my own and other children. It focused on a ten-year old boy named Isaak and his family, who lived in a thatched roof cottage of adobe bricks made by the men of the village from dirt, straw, and a little water—hardened in the sun.

Isaak herded sheep, and his father tilled the soil with a hand plow and planted potatoes and a little corn and barley. A donkey provided transportation. The cooking was done in a large earthenware pot over an open fire, with an oven buried in the soil nearby for baking bread. The women spun the yarn for their clothes. The men and boys wore colorful Chulu knitted hats with Indian designs and long sidepieces. The women wore brown derbies.

The film, called *Bolivian Boy*, won a Gold Seal for excellence at the 1960 Film Festival in New York City. But that was not all that I brought home to my children.

In La Paz I came to know Ken Wasson, who ran the photographic center, and his French wife Ann, who had received the Order of the Andes for her work on behalf of handicapped children.

She was a woman who reached out to anyone in need; she rescued a young girl, Giselle Eckhardt, who needed to be rescued from a bad family situation. Ann arranged to have her live with us in Maryland, while studying piano in Washington.

When grandmother Jean heard that Giselle was coming to live with us, she said, "But a gazelle is a leaping animal, where will they keep it?" Giselle, the girl, moved into the room with the piano and a yellow parakeet who learned to say his name "*Limón*," as well as "*¿Como estás?*" ("How are you?") in Spanish. She got her music degree and met her future husband, David Whitwell, at the Catholic University.

At Elm Street, Giselle taught Spanish to Jenny and Beka, as well as to the pet parakeet, and set the stage for what mother referred to as "the South American girl project." One at a time for almost twenty years they came from South and Central America to live at Elm Street, go to school, learn English and speak Spanish.

PR Associates, as part of their medical technology recruitment program, offered a special prize of a summer job in Washington in the research laboratories of the Armed Forces Institute of Pathology (AFIP). This brought a young man who came to live in Nash's attic room. He was Jeff Hill, an 18-year old high school graduate from Ohio who had the best National Science Fair project related to pathology. He was kept on at the AFIP for four summers and years later wrote about the experience:

> L.N.D or "Life Before Nick and Dallas." I met Jenny, Nash, Beka, Carolina, Kitty, and Ninfa from Antioch, Canada, Bolivia, Greece, Peru and Maria Elena from Mexico—THE WORLD. I had come from a meat and potatoes family, and I got to know fish, rice, and wine—all new. That summer intellectual sagacity began. Each and every tenet of my life was questioned.
>
> For me, no group of people, no body of knowledge, no exposure has been more important. I had been brought up to "fight the good fight" my entire life, but had never been part of a family that had "fought" it. Then, God, I wanted to change the world, maybe I thought I could. We were all so young. Anything seemed possible.

Jeff was away when the biggest challenge arrived. She was a fourteen year old Quechua Indian girl named Teodocia, sent by Ann Wasson's International Union for Handicapped Children in Bolivia. She had lost her arms when she was run over by a street car as a little girl and her childhood was spent begging on the streets of La Paz with her mother. Ann picked her up off the street and took her to the plane. She was very dirty and had sores on her legs when she arrived at Elm Street.

Everyone tried to think of what they could do to make her feel welcome. Maria Elena from Mexico came up with the most practical approach, "I will give her a bath," and when Teodocia agreed enthusiastically, Elena put her through twice. Jenny gave her clothes, and Dallas took her to friends at the Armed Forces Institute of Pathology (AFIP) to diagnose the sores. They were caused by a fungus seldom seen in this country, and the AFIP was soon visited by pathologists and their residents from all the nearby hospitals and the National Institutes of Health, to observe the sores. Teodocia loved the attention and enchanted her visitors by showing them how she could eat, write, and draw with her feet.

She became something of a celebrity and was taken on a guided tour of the White House. She had her picture in the newspaper with Mary Switzer, head of the Office of Vocational Rehabilitation, which fitted her with artificial arms—but she preferred to use her feet.

My next filmmaking assignment was from the U.S. Department of Agriculture, to adapt an American-made film on growing wheat for use in Spain. It was to be paid for in Spanish pesetas. To spend the pesetas, I arranged passage on a Spanish vapor (steamship) to take the family to Spain. At the last minute, we substituted Giselle for Nash, who had a girlfriend and didn't want to come.

When we boarded the SS *Guadalupe* in New York, a friend who came to see us off gave Dallas a handsome green leather book embossed in gold, "A Travel Diary." In an inspired moment she gave it to Beka, who was eleven, to write about the trip, with Jenny doing illustrations. Beka wrote regularly and continuously until, as she said, "I can't do any more because my nose is getting in the way of my eyes."

On the SS *Guadalupe* the girls studied Spanish for an hour each day, and practiced on the passengers, almost all of whom spoke nothing but Spanish. We read aloud from a guidebook called *A Stranger in Spain*, and at night Dallas and I re-read *Don Quixote*.

We also made the acquaintance of some young people who spoke English, Ann Canogar from California and her husband Rafael, a well-known painter in Madrid. There was also Hugo Hamilton, who followed custom by keeping the English last name of his mother when she married the generalissimo who helped the king of

Spain escape from the palace when Franco took over.

> We had a stellar attraction in Giselle:
> Green of eye and black of hair
> This indeed was maiden fair
> Dimples in her snow white skin
> Rosebuds dwelling there within

The poem was written to celebrate her twentieth birthday, which Beka described in the Travel Diary: "At the captain's party there was a hat and a horn for each person. We all put on our party hats, but some men didn't so Gila [Giselle] went around the dining room putting their hats on. As soon as the captain and all the officers saw her doing this, they took off their own hats, so she had to go around the officers' table and put party hats on them too."

On July 30 at our first stop in Spain, *La Coruña*, there was a *fiesta* in process to celebrate economic progress. The big change taking place in *La Coruña* was the introduction of butane for cooking. Beka described the *fiesta* in the diary:

> First came smoky motorcycles, then people wearing huge heads, Spanish danc-
> ers, floats pulled by oxen, Spanish *señoritas*, and knights with spears. We followed
> them to the Plaza Mariapita which was surrounded by a high wall. Inside we saw
> a huge baker as high as the wall, made of *papier mâché*. He was set afire by a string
> of fireworks to show that bakers wouldn't be needed as much now that the town
> had butane.
>
> We had to run to make the boat, which was leaving for the next town, Gijón.
> There the conductor of the tram taking us into town insisted on showing us the
> sights because he said we were true Quixotescas, interested in everything.

We visited more towns as we followed the coast all the way to Bilbao near the border of France. By the time we got there a plan was made to leave Jenny and Beka in Madrid for several months when we left for the States, to practice the language.

In Bilbao we used pesetas to buy a Peugeot automobile, so that we could see more of Spain. Before we left, the family gave me a party for getting them there with my *pesetas*, and toasted me:

He is our knight of great renown
wearing a tantalum plate for a crown.
His barber's bowl is built right in
Hidden by hair and a flap of skin.
Instead of attacking giants and Moors
He tilts his lances at guided tours.
Dallas, Giselle, Rebecca and Jenny,
All he imagines to be his infantes,
And the Peugeot of course is his Rocinante.
And to him we offer a special toast
He's the Don Quixote we love the most.

The girls stayed in Madrid when we left for home in September. Jenny was in the same student rooming house where Ann Canogar had lived when she first came from California. She took her meals with the landlady, Carmencita, in her apartment where she operated a beauty parlor on the first floor. At mealtimes she pushed aside the bottles of hair preparation to make room for generous portions of such Spanish dishes as eels and tripe cooked in olive oil.

Beka lived in a more elegant part of the city with the Hamiltons, who used less olive oil and served such delicacies as "squid in their own ink." Both girls enjoyed the afternoon treats of bread and chocolate, a Spanish experience.

Jenny's was a sedentary life. She walked a few blocks to the Canogars where she took her baths, as well as art lessons from Ann, and was exposed to the abstract painting of Rafael. She learned to visit art galleries on her own, and was particularly influenced by the elongated figures of El Greco. Beka took lessons in *flamenco*, immersed herself in practice sessions, and became quite good. The girls saw little of each other in Madrid.

Jenny grew in shape, gaining at least ten pounds by the time she got home. She explained, "I did what you said. I ate everything put before me—to not hurt anybody's feelings, but I couldn't eat the inside of a pig's mouth. It had bristles in it!"

In Chevy Chase, they enrolled in the seventh and eighth grades three months late with no questions asked. It was assumed they would catch up, which they did. They spoke Spanish fluently. Jenny had a portfolio of drawings, and Beka could *flamenco* professionally.

However, these accomplishments did not put them at ease with their new classmates, two thirds of whom had come from different elementary schools to the junior high school—a difficult transition at best. They ate lunch at home, which separated them from their classmates at a time they would have gotten to know them.

Jenny, who had always been somewhat shy, spent her free time learning to sculpt animals. Her home away from home was the Washington Zoo. Beka, a leader in elementary school where she achieved astonishing results from bubble gum and could do one-handed cartwheels ad infinitum, found that such accomplishments availed her little in junior high.

Boys made the difference. By the time she came back to enter the seventh grade, the social cliques had been formed and she was not asked to the big "coming out" Bar Mitzvah parties honoring Jewish boys emerging into young manhood. Her own Jewish friend, the son of a psychiatrist, did not have a Bar Mitzvah.

Beka began to study and do homework with the same intensity she had shown when writing the diary of the Spanish trip, and became a good student. Her home away from home was the public library. Her friends were nerds.

At home, 4303 Elm had acquired another potential "member of the family." Dr. Ron Baecker, a computer wizard from NIH, took over space in the basement and moved in his sophisticated equipment which included a teletype printer and modem that allowed his computer to talk to other computers. Ron and his equipment were there for six years. When not with his computer, he divided his time between demonstrating for various causes, falling in and out of love, and doing whatever needed to be done to make things go more smoothly. It was a big order.

51

Howard University

M Y PROFESSIONAL LIFE TOOK A DIFFERENT TURN. IN REVIEWING documentaries for the Public Health Service, it disturbed me to discover that whether they were made in the North or the West (few were made in the South), none had Negroes either as directors or even in technical support. The grips/electricians, sound crews, even the "gofers" whose job was to "go for" whatever the bosses needed, were all white.

The reasons were not hard to find. Black electricians and sound technicians were not admitted to American Federation of Labor trade unions and therefore couldn't be hired for the technical jobs. Such jobs were where many white directors got their start, although most became involved in filmmaking when as youngsters they produced films on the 8 mm equipment their families had at home. Few black families had such equipment and courses in filmmaking were not being taught in schools.

My ambition was to get more blacks into filmmaking. I could do nothing about the American Federation of Labor, but felt that a filmmaking course aimed at black college students would be something I could do.

The opportunity presented itself when Howard University announced that it would be setting up its own TV station on campus to broadcast over FM Channel 32. There would be no problem finding programs to fill the broadcasting hours, but there was a basic one when it came to assembling the kind of backup staff a TV station requires, such as technicians, cameramen and film editors.

I telephoned Lister Hill, a fellow Alabaman, who as chairman of education in the U.S. Senate was the conduit for Howard's federal funding, and asked whether any provision was being made to train students in the techniques needed for television. Senator Hill called the president of Howard, and I was invited to come and develop a film and video program.

I took the job, although no money was provided for equipment or staff. I brought my own cameras and borrowed from filmmaking friends. They were all members of the Washington Film and Video Council, of which I was a founder and long time president. Its members included all the professionals in the Washington area, and they volunteered not only to loan equipment but to give lectures. I had acquired a great staff for free.

But there was a problem. Listed among the new courses being offered, "Filmmaking" sounded too much like fun and attracted a considerable number of students who signed up for the class thinking it would be a snap course. Gradually that changed as the students became aware of what was involved. It wasn't very long before there were enough good ones to produce a documentary film, *Where All Can Learn*, on campus. These students were committed. They wanted to become filmmakers.

I went on to train numerous black students at Howard. My classes were successful and well-attended. So many students came to my home studio on Elm Street to attend night and weekend sessions with visiting filmmakers, that the house came to be known in the neighborhood as the Chevy Chase Branch of Howard University.

The sixties were a time of rebellion in colleges, and Howard students were no exception. Four letter words had come into common use, and Dallas was "educated" too. On one occasion when she was serving punch and cookies to the students, she asked one of them his name and he answered, "Well, you've met me three times, but I guess we all look alike."

She used the common four letter language to answer him, "Don't give me that shit." He replied, "I'm sorry ma'am." She said, "Well, I'm sorry too, and I have a little rhyme to say to you:

> Shall I admit my disgrace?
> Shall I admit my true fame?
> I can seldom remember a face
> And never a name . . .

Later the young man told his classmates, "The professor's wife is sure with it."

I was featured with a picture in the Howard University yearbook, *The Bison*, describing me as "an outstanding professor who had been instrumental in starting the new School of Communications to serve the university and the black community of Washington."

This brought me and the projected new School of Communications to the attention of the president of Howard, one of whose objectives was to replace white professors with black ones. It also brought the new school to the attention of Tony Brown, a prominent black television commentator. It ended up with Tony Brown being appointed director of the new School of Communications and I was asked to leave at the end of the next school year.

During the summer I was approached by Puerto Rico to explore the possibility of heading the production of films for that country. I was invited down for two weeks to look over the situation, and was intrigued by the Puerto Ricans. They came in all colors—from light tan to black and some with blue eyes and freckles—but in no behavioral way did they resemble the blacks back home.

In Puerto Rico they acted equal. No one appeared to feel "lesser" than the whites, or to be obsequious, or have a chip on the shoulder. They said "Buenos dias" and initiated conversations, and in many other ways demonstrated equality. They were secure.

I asked, why? It was explained that while Puerto Rico did not have many slaves, it was one of the last Caribbean countries to abolish slavery between 1870 and 1890. This did not have the same effect on the integration of blacks into mainstream society as it did in the United States because the major population of Puerto Rico was of mixed blood. There had been widespread inter-marriage of the Spanish, the indigenous Indians, and the blacks that resulted in a racially heterogeneous society. There was little or no continuing denigration of blacks by whites, and no lynchings as occurred long after slavery was abolished in the United States.

The job offer was not very good. I found that I would be replacing filmmakers I had known who worked in the famous photographic unit of the U.S. Farm Security Administration before it was dissolved. I went to Puerto Rico with high hopes, but heard it was impossible to make good films under the adult educators in charge of the project, who re-wrote all the filmscripts in committee meetings. They obliterated any story line on which a director could build a film by adding everything the educators suggested. The filmmakers felt their hands were tied, and quit.

I did not take the job. Instead, I took Dallas to the nearby Virgin Islands for our last weekend in the Caribbean. We swam and snorkeled, looking for varicolored fish in the clear green-blue water and in the evening danced to the steel drums. Dallas took along her "happy dress," a light green and white striped silk taffeta, tight at the waist and full-skirted to twirl.

Then I returned to Howard University for my final year. I loved my work at Howard, and was devastated at being dropped in my seventh year when I would have attained permanent status as professor. I hated leaving my students and they were equally unhappy about losing me. I knew it would be a difficult year with Tony Brown already aboard.

The stress triggered a resurgence of the epilepsy that was the aftermath of my long ago brain operation, and I began to have "petit mal" seizures in class. They got progressively worse so I had to withdraw from teaching and resign from my job. I decided to take a long vacation, so we headed off for the Virgin Islands.

The damage was already done. On the plane I had a series of bad convulsions, and was met in St. Croix by an ambulance to take me to the hospital. For a long time I was out of my head, hearing songs that were not being sung, and dogs barking under my bed when there were no dogs there.

To a limited extent I recovered my mental and physical health, and returned to Washington, but not to Howard. I made a few films under the frayed umbrella of Potomac Films, but was still having seizures, so one of my old students, Joe Fiorelli, came in as manager. We did several films together, such as a pregnancy film, *Nine Months to Get Ready*, coordinated with Public Affairs Pamphlets, but I could no longer make films on my own.

For a more ambitious film on juvenile delinquency, *Headed for Trouble*, funded by the National Institute for Mental Health, I brought in another director, Willard van Dyke. The film was shot at the nearby Prince Georges County Police Department, where my 18-year-old son, Nash, was cast as "Butch," a boy "headed for trouble." He had been acting since he played the role of Huckleberry Finn for the local Adventure Theatre in the eighth grade, and made a most convincing juvenile delinquent.

It was the last major film done by Potomac Films.

52

Going Home Again

WHEN I GAVE UP FILMMAKING AND RETURNED TO ALABAMA, I found that everything, including my mother's situation, had changed.

Montgomery was a different place after the city-wide boycott of buses by the Negroes protesting Rosa Parks's arrest for refusing to give up her seat to a white man.

Mother had been seriously ill and in the hospital, but she was feeling better and in good spirits. Her old companion, Elizabeth Thigpen, had seen to that. She organized Jean's friends into shifts, with one or two assigned to her hospital room each visiting hour. They had brought flowers and fresh figs from the Curb Market—and gossip—but kept out bad news and visitors who were not close friends.

By the time I arrived, she was ready to leave the hospital and it wasn't long before she was back doing things as usual. "I've been terribly busy finishing up the house and garden before Christmas and running a white elephant sale for a carpet fund. And on the 18th and 19th I must do yards and yards of cedar garlands to decorate."

All this required transportation, but she preferred driving her own car. "Darling Judge Loe lets me drive in the daytime, and it's written on my driver's license. Even then I make mistakes, but Ben is the only one who knows about them and he is very sweet. The other day I swerved under the low branch of a tree coming into the yard and put a dent in the top of the car. All he said was 'Well, Miz Jean, I see you got another little tap.'"

In a letter written after a small accident Jean wrote: "It's made me rather nervous about driving. I really do drive terribly. I forget what I'm doing and more often look at Venus and Jupiter embracing in the sunset sky than at the road. I just pray every day I won't run over somebody."

Ben was always cheerful, but he could do nothing to erase the pain Jean felt when she saw what was happening to the big elm tree. It had presided over her own wedding reception, my christening, and in time would bear witness to a solemn ceremony for the burial of her black poodle Lambo, the faithful companion of her declining years. She had composed his last rites, to be read by her as Lambo was lowered into a grave dug by Ben, to join the dogs that had gone before.

The elm tree had turned yellow by the time the Davy tree man came to look at it. He inoculated it but said that it had the Dutch elm disease and couldn't be saved. "Don't cut it," Jean said. "The Big Elm and I are going down together." When the tree died she let it stay where it was, all propped up with the limbs chained to the trunk. Eventually it became just a bunch of dead limbs leaning on one another.

So many things in the big yard were broken or gone. A pecan tree at the side of the house had been split by lightning and had smashed the masonry brick wall with a "Pan" fountain copied from one Jean had seen in Italy. The garden wall, along with twenty-six loads of fertilizer and rich top soil, had been given to mother at her request by my father on their first wedding anniversary "instead of a diamond bracelet." What she had wanted was a garden where she could plant roses and other

The big elm at Hazel Hedge, shortly before it was cut down.

flowers needing better earth than the hard clay that surrounded Hazel Hedge. That's what she got, and with her helping hands, the garden had grown splendidly.

But time had taken its toll. The wrought iron gate between the house and garden was smashed and bushes and plants were missing. Gone were the grape arbor and a pergola. The large circular fountain was dry, and where was the sundial? It was a sunny day when I returned and looked for it in vain.

Many lovely reminders were still there, like the cement bench with the inscription "I know a lovely garden, a calm retreat. It is not entered by feet of flesh, but by feat of love." And nearby a row of plantation bells turned upside down and planted with bushes to mark a path. Untouched was the old well with Jean's copy of a Della Robbia. In fact, there were enough of the old treasures for me to think about doing a movie about Hazel Hedge—reminiscing back to it's days of glory. Eventually I did make a movie, but the pain of seeing Hazel Hedge in such decline made ending the movie emotionally difficult. I had to have someone else finish it. It represented the end of an era, perhaps even the finite ending of my childhood world.

Outside Hazel Hedge there were plenty of changes in the city, but they were more sociological than physical. What had happened to the people of Montgomery to make such a difference? I had been abroad making films for much of this time and had a lot of catching up to do.

It had started with the bus boycott in December 1955, when Rosa Parks, a black seamstress coming home from her department store job, refused to get up and give her seat to a white man and move to the back of the city bus, as was mandated by law. She was tired, she told the bus driver and the two policemen who came to take her off the bus.

What she didn't tell them was that she had long been active in the local civil rights movement, and was tired of being pushed around. Tired of the disrespect and bad treatment given her people just because of the color of their skins. The white bus drivers in particular often called passengers names such as "nigger" and "black ape." They made them walk around to the back of the bus to get in after paying their fares up front, and sometimes drove off and left them standing there.

Mrs. Parks had been arrested for "disorderly conduct," not for violating the segregation laws. Anybody who knew this quiet well-behaved woman would know that she could not conduct herself in a disorderly fashion. She must have used the one telephone call she was allowed to make from the jail to contact E. D. Nixon, the head of the National Association for the Advancement of Colored People (NAACP), the civic organization to which she belonged.

Nixon was known best as the leader of the Brotherhood of Sleeping Car Porters and the police department didn't connect him with Rosa Parks. So he telephoned Clifford Durr, a sympathetic white lawyer, and asked for help. They met at the jail, posted bond for Mrs. Parks, and took her home. Within the next few weeks she became the central figure in events that explained "what had happened to the people of Montgomery to make such a difference."

A small group of black women, the Women's Political Council, organized by two dynamic ladies, Dr. Mary Fair Burks, Chairman of the English Department at Alabama State College, and her colleague Jo Ann Robinson, an English professor, announced a one-day bus boycott to protest Rosa Parks' arrest. The response, mostly by women who rode the bus going to and coming from work, was impressive.

The buses were half-empty in the morning and half-empty when they went back that night. The one-day boycott was so successful that the Women's Political Council initiated a long-range effort to organize a Montgomery Improvement Association that would expand and continue a bus boycott for as long as it would take to desegregate the buses.

Thirty thousand fliers were mimeographed and distributed calling on "Every Negro to stay off the buses to protest the arrest of Rosa Parks and the segregated bus system. Don't ride the buses to work, to town, to school. If you work, take a cab, or walk."

Five days afterwards, the buses in Montgomery were empty. For the next fourteen months (381 days) the Negro people stayed off the buses. For the first time, the entire black population defied authority by joining the boycott.

Events and leadership emerged to keep the boycott going. A young black lawyer named Fred Gray returned to his native Alabama after graduation from Western Reserve Law School in Cleveland. He had made the decision that as a lawyer he would "wage war on segregation." When he passed the Alabama bar examination, he went to the Improvement Association and to Rosa Parks looking for clients, and became the lawyer for both.

As he said later, "it launched my legal career . . . my days of having little to do in my fledgling law practice were over." He knew he would be very busy, and bought his first car, a new tan 1954 stick shift Ford, to keep up with his appointments.

The mood was electric. It was an adrenalin-filled time. The Reverend Martin Luther King was the minister at the old Dexter Avenue Baptist Church located downtown, just a block from the state capital. He was asked by the Improvement Association to be the spokesman for the bus boycott.

He agreed and subsequently was introduced to the strikers at a mass meeting near the Holt Street Baptist Church. Set for seven o'clock on a workday evening, it was historic, being the first time that blacks in Montgomery had come together to protest anything. Everybody was there, including some whites. By six o'clock there was no parking space within three blocks of the church and standing room only inside. Several thousand spilled out of the church and onto the street.

The high point of the meeting was the speech by Dr. King. His sermons had always been of a religious nature. This was the first time he had spoken on civil rights. His voice rose when he cried "And you know, my friends, people get tired of being trampled over with the iron feet of oppression." According to an observer, it was that sentence that ignited the crowd, and within the space of a second, scattered cries of approval had exploded into applause and cheers that went on for half an hour.

In this eloquent address, Reverend King, their newly elected spokesman, gave a huge boost to the movement that persuaded the black population of Montgomery to stay off the buses until they could return as riders "who could choose their seats and stay in them." From then on, events moved steadily to reinforce the bus boycott. Opposition from the city government hardened the strikers resolve. They organized a transportation system, using black-owned taxicabs taking multiple riders. This was supplemented by employers getting their black employees to work, most of them housewives picking up gardeners and household help.

The practice had been for multiple riders in cabs to pay ten cents each, the same as city bus fares. When the city announced new fares more than four times as much, strikers who couldn't get a ride walked. The 1990 movie, *The Long Walk Home*, starring Whoopie Goldberg as a maid who walked during the boycott, has more recently brought this story to the whole country. The book was written in 1987 by a local Montgomerian, John Cork.

With no solution in sight, there was an upsurge of ad-

Reverend Martin Luther King, Jr.

miration for the strikers from Eleanor Roosevelt and other national figures, which resulted in much needed donations to the strike fund.

A legal solution emerged in February 1954 when their attorney, Fred Gray, filed a lawsuit challenging the constitutionality of segregated bus seating. This got their case into the federal courts, which had responsibility for cases challenging the Constitution. It was assigned to a panel of three federal judges, and by June two of these, Judges Frank M. Johnson Jr. and Richard Rives, had reached a decision in favor of the boycott. This sent the case directly to the Supreme Court.

Six months later on December 21, the U.S. Supreme Court decided that segregated bus seating was unconstitutional. Most of the townspeople were outraged. Ex-mayor "Tacky" Gayle was an effective rabble-rouser and it didn't take long for the rabble to be roused.

Singled out for special attention were the two federal judges, Johnson and Rives, who were on the three-judge panel that made the initial decision on the constitutionality of the Alabama law.

Both judges received threats against their lives and families, over the telephone and through the mail. Many who disagreed with their decision favoring the boycott attacked them wherever they found an audience who would listen, or read what they had to say. This included meetings of clubs and classes, messages from the pulpits of churches and synagogues, as well as statements to the press.

The Johnsons soon got an unlisted number, and the city police or federal marshals were posted to guard their home, a practice that continued for fifteen years. Johnson employed, as chauffeur, an armed bodyguard who accompanied him wherever he went. But the harassment didn't stop Judge Johnson from making judicial decisions to remedy inhumane conditions suffered by blacks in mental hospitals and prisons, wherever he encountered them, for as long as he was a judge.

He was particularly resented in Montgomery, "the first capital of the Confederacy," because he came from the "Free County of Winston" in the northwest hill country of the state, which had sided with the Union in the war. He became the "almost recipient" of a bomb intended for him, but misdelivered to his mother's house by mistake. Luckily nobody was home.

Judge Rives was in a vulnerable position. He had been working with his lawyer son to turn over his legal business. Tragically, Frank Rives Jr. was killed in an automobile accident. The judge's sorrow at this personal loss coincided with the public attacks on the decision of the three-judge panel. He suffered acutely. He was a deeply religious man, and was barred from his Presbyterian Church "because it would cause tension." Additionally, someone smeared red paint on the tombstone of his son. He was dropped from social activities that he had enjoyed, and was given the cold shoulder by old friends.

Two days before Christmas, shotgun blasts were fired into the Dexter Avenue parsonage and on Christmas Eve, a cross was burned before the house of a sympathizer in the residential section of town. During Christmas week, buses were fired on by snipers, and on January 10, four churches and two homes were bombed in the black community. On January 27, two more bombs went off in the black part of town.

A stick of dynamite was thrown into the house of Martin Luther King, which shattered windows and did other damage, but didn't harm his wife and baby who were the only members of the family at home. When King returned, he came out on the porch to calm the hundreds of angry blacks who had assembled with guns, bottles and rocks to retaliate. He persuaded them that a non-violent protest was the only way to go.

It is to be noted that the owners of the newspaper the *Montgomery Advertiser* did not fire either Editor Ray Jenkins or City Editor Joe Azbel for their fair handling of the news about the boycott. However, there were consequences over which they had no control. Juliette Morgan, a librarian whose letters to the editor were published, comparing the ideas of Martin Luther King to those of Mahatma Ghandi, was dismissed from her job, and later committed suicide.

Aubrey Williams, who had headed Roosevelt's National Youth Administration in Washington, had bought the newspaper *The Southern Farmer* and had come back to Montgomery to publish it, but was soon put out of business. Also affected were those who were branded "nigger lovers," like Cliff Durr, who was put out of business when he lost most of his paying white clients after he helped Rosa Parks stay out of jail. Another victim was Thomas Thrasher, the rector of the Church of the Ascension, who was removed by the vestry when it became known that he felt segregation was incompatible with church beliefs.

This had numerous ramifications. Jean Read, a pillar of the Ascension, and great admirer of Reverend Thrasher, withdrew from all church activities. No longer was she active in the Altar Guild, heading committees, arranging flowers for Sunday services, or taking Ben Miller along to polish the brass.

Besides, Ben refused to go now. He was outspoken when Reverend Thrasher came to say goodbye, "I wouldn't go to that Church again unless somethin' happened to you, Miz Jean, and then I'd follow you up the aisle a hollerin'." Tom Thrasher added, "And I would be there hollerin' too."

The Episcopal Church transferred Reverend Thrasher to Chapel Hill in North Carolina, where my son Nash was a student spending much of his time in jail for trying to desegregate lunch counters. From Chapel Hill, Tom Thrasher wrote Jean trying to dissuade her from turning against the Church of the Ascension and the minister who had replaced him. He didn't succeed. She just didn't go to church.

I had missed the attacks on the freedom riders and other such happenings in those years when Montgomery was a center of civic strife, but I was there when Autherine Lucy enrolled at the University of Alabama, breaking the state's color line in education.

Mother was putting out seeds for the birds at a table in the garden, when a black bird arrived. She said, as the bird flew in, "And in the name of Autherine Lucy, you are welcome!"

Nash and Jean.

53

St. Peter Called

JEAN HAD A STROKE AND HER DOCTOR, JANE DAY, WAS ABOUT TO PUT her in a nursing home "where she would get good care," but I intervened. I had found two practical nurses, Sarah Hammock and Georgia May Jackson, who would divide the time and be with her night and day. And Ben would be in charge when I was away.

Before this plan could go into effect, Dallas received a letter from Dr. Day telling her that "as the practical member of the family, you must see that Nick puts her in a nursing home where she will get proper care. For despite what President Johnson, Martin Luther King, and Stokely Carmichael might say, you can't leave her in a house with only Negroes in charge. As her doctor I couldn't take the responsibility for that."

We were in a quandary. Without the doctor, who would take care of Jean? I telephoned my good friend Dr. Brannon Hubbard, who had formerly worked closely with Dr. Day in Montgomery, but was now Chief of Surgery at Maryland Hospital and professor emeritus at the University Hospital in Baltimore. He said "Not to worry, I won't let that happen."

Subsequently, we received a copy of his letter to Dr. Day telling her that "as Jean's godson, I promised Jean that she would never go to a nursing home, and I will take full medical responsibility for the arrangements Nick has made at Hazel Hedge."

Jean didn't go to a nursing home, but moved downstairs into the comfortable little room between the kitchen and the front door, which had been occupied by her mother Jennie for so many years. It was close to those taking care of her, and had a coal burning fireplace and a window looking out on the garden. And Jean's last poodle, Miss Brown, was there too—always at her side.

Georgia May and Sarah Hammock did a fine job. Ben kept things running smoothly with his new duties, as well as shopping, fixing breakfast, and greeting everyone who came to the door with his cordial, "Lordy, looka who's heah!" All the family came to see her. Beka and Nash each spent a week or two, and Jenny's destination when she returned from her year abroad studying sculpture in Italy was Hazel Hedge. She stayed a month.

Jean kept a small television set in her room for Sarah Hammock, the night nurse, but refused to look at television herself, even when a guest reached out to turn it on—as when the astronauts were landing on the moon. "Jean, this is just as important as Columbus discovering America. You've got to see it. Where would we be if he hadn't sailed to the new world?" Jean answered, "In Genoa."

The evening of April 24, 1972 she told Sarah Hammock that "St. Peter has struck me off his list. He called me three times and I didn't go. Now he has said, 'When you are ready Jean, you call me.'" She must have called him loud and clear, because when I came the next afternoon, she squeezed my hand, told me "Goodbye" and slipped away. It marked the end of an era.

When I went to the funeral parlor to arrange for a "plain pine casket" as Jean had wanted, I was told that it would have to be ordered, "they just stamp them out of metal now." It was not a big funeral. Jean was in her nineties, and most of her old friends were dead. She had been quite progressive in her opinions about race issues and had treated her Negro help with dignity. This became evident at her funeral, where mourners, both black and white, came out to pay their respects as a shared experience with the "Deep Family."

Jean was buried in the family plot beside her husband under the magnolia tree at Oakwood cemetery on a brilliant sunny day that spring. Elizabeth Thigpen, at the wheel of her Cadillac, drove Ben and the servants to the funeral. Sarah Hammock, Georgia May Jackson, and Ura May, a day worker,

Ben

were dressed in their best and wore fine hats. Miss Elizabeth was a George Wallace supporter, and the license plates on her Cadillac read, "The Governor's Staff."

Dallas and I and the three grown children, Nash, Jenny and Rebecca were there, as was Jean's niece Jill Hibben, who had spent so many of her years growing up at Hazel Hedge. That night we all sat down for a family dinner around Jean's great oak table, with Ben serving as he always had.

Afterwards, Ben said the words that inspired the title of this book, "All De Deep Family Be Here." Everyone understood that he was included, but he didn't sit down to join us. It just wasn't done. Some things were too deeply ingrained.

Afterword

Elizabeth Thigpen had arranged to have a new tombstone cut with both Jean's and Nash's names on it, bbut it wasn't delivered until long after the ceremony. It read:

W. Nash Read
March 25, 1892—July 23, 1942
E'en as he trod his way to God
So walked he from his birth,
In simpleness and gentleness
In honor and clean mirth.

Jean Craik Read
August 30, 1881—April 25, 1972
Age cannot wither her
nor custom stale
her infinite variety.

It wasn't until much later that Ben, visiting the grave site, found that Nash's original tombstone was still there. He brought it home where it was kept in the storage space under the house until it was stolen, no doubt, by someone who needed a tombstone. It was a theft that was never solved.

To evaluate and protect the house full of paintings and valuable antiques upstairs, I called on Jean's good friend, antique dealer Eugenia Tuttle. She came with her helper Luzelle Davis, a huge black man who loaded and drove trucks for Swanner's trucking firm weekdays and helped Eugenia with estate sales on Saturdays.

As Luzelle's full-time employer, Mr. Swanner was aware of the arrangement and felt responsible for Luzelle. He was standing outside his warehouse office one day and observed the truck Luzelle was driving had not been latched properly and a safe rolled out the back and down an embankment and smashed into a big new car. All Swanner said was "uhh huh."

I was concerned that it might have been a truck carrying Hazel Hedge things and called Mr. Swanner to find out what had happened. He reassured me. It was a safe on his truck carrying other things that fell off and hit a Chrysler Imperial and badly damaged it, but there were no repercussions. He said it wasn't Luzelle's fault, and later he bought Luzelle a car in appreciation for many years of service.

At Hazel Hedge where I was consulting with Eugenia Tuttle on the handling of the things in the house, I happened to compliment her on the pretty suit she was wearing. She said,"Luzelle made it for me to wear to his church for a special event." I answered her facetiously, "Pretty soon you are going to tell me that Luzelle does your hair." She replied quite seriously, "And who do you think does my hair?"

Eugenia was a segregationist through and through, but the person who visited her every week in the nursing home where she died was Luzelle.

These were the good stories, and there were many bad ones. But as the saying goes, "It was not all black and white."

Within a year after Jean's death, Ben passed. I went to his funeral and offered this eulogy: "He was a special kind of man. He had great empathy with people and at the same time stuck to his principles. The radiance of his personality lightened many lives. He was a true Brother to his fellow man—to white and black alike. Now he has gone to claim a greater reward in God's Kingdom." I think I can hear St. Peter saying, as Ben did so often to arriving guests, "Lordy, looka who's heah!"

Index